AQA Geography

Exclusively endorsed by AQA

A2

John Smith

Roger Knill

Nelson Thornes

This edition printed in 2009 by:
Nelson Thornes Ltd
Delta Place
27 Bath Road
CHELTENHAM
GL53 7TH
United Kingdom

09 10 11 12 13 / 10 9 8 7 6 5 4 3 2

A catalogue record for this book is available from the British Library

ISBN 978 0 7487 8259 8

Cover photograph/illustration: Still pictures
Page make-up by eMC Design Ltd

Printed and bound in Croatia by Zrinski

Contents

AQA introduction

Nelson Thornes has worked in partnership with AQA to ensure this book and the accompanying online resources offer you the best support for your A2 course.

All resources have been approved by senior AQA examiners so you can feel assured that they closely match the specification for this subject and provide you with everything you need to prepare successfully for your exams.

These print and online resources together **unlock blended learning**; this means that the links between the activities in the book and the activities online blend together to maximise your understanding of a topic and help you achieve your potential.

These online resources are available on **kerboodle!** which can be accessed via the internet at **www.kerboodle.com/live**, anytime, anywhere. If your school or college subscribes to this service you will be provided with your own personal login details. Once logged in, access your course and locate the required activity.

For more information and help visit **www.kerboodle.com**

Icons in this book indicate where there is material online related to that topic. The following icons are used:

💡 *Learning activity*

These resources include a variety of interactive and non-interactive activities to support your learning.

☑ *Progress tracking*

These resources include a variety of tests that you can use to check your knowledge on particular topics (Test yourself) and a range of resources that enable you to analyse and understand examination questions (On your marks …).

🛈 *Research support*

These resources include WebQuests, in which you are assigned a task and provided with a range of web links to use as source material for research.

When you see an icon, go to Nelson Thornes learning space at www.nelsonthornes.com/aqagce, enter your access details and select your course. The materials are arranged in the same order as the topics in the book, so you can easily find the resources you need.

How to use this book

This book covers the specification for your course and is arranged in a sequence approved by AQA.

The book content is divided into 8 chapters matched to the 8 topics within the AQA Geography A2 specification: The first 6 chapters cover Unit 3; Plate tectonics and associated hazards, Weather and climate and associated hazards, Ecosystems: Change and Challenge; World cities, Development and globalisation and Contemporary conflicts and challenges. The final chapters cover Unit 4; 4A: Geography Fieldwork Investigation and 4B: Geographical Issue Evaluation.

The features in this book include:

Learning objectives

At the beginning of each chapter and at relevant parts of the topic content you will find a list of learning objectives that contain targets linked to the requirements of the specification.

Key terms

Terms that you will need to be able to define and understand.

Links

This highlights any key areas where topics are related to one another, as well as any useful further resources to investigate on the internet.

Case study

Relevant case studies of the themes and issues specified in A2 Geography.

Activity

Activities to help you develop the skills required in the study of A2 Geography.

Did you know?

Facts and points of interest relating to the text which highlight the relevance of the topic.

Skills

Descriptions of geographical skills needed for that area of the topic.

AQA Examiner's tip

Hints from AQA examiners to help you with your study and to prepare for your exam.

Chapter Summary

A bulleted list at the end of each chapter summarising the content in an easy-to-follow way.

AQA Examination-style questions

Questions in the style that you can expect in your exam. A2 Unit 3 questions are listed in a separate section at the end of the book.

Web links in the book

As Nelson Thornes is not responsible for third party content online, there may be some changes to this material that are beyond our control. In order for us to ensure that the links referred to in the book are as up to date and stable as possible, the websites provided are usually homepages with supporting instructions on how to reach the relevant pages if necessary.

Please let us know at kerboodle@nelsonthornes.com if you find a link that doesn't work and we will do our best to correct this at reprint, or to list an alternative site.

Studying A2 Geography

Building on your AS result

Welcome to the A2 Geography course. Most of you have probably taken your AS examinations and got reasonably good grades. To you, well done!

Some of you might still be hoping to improve on your AS results. To you, good luck!

However, neither group should feel that you are leaving behind your AS work. The course has been carefully planned so that the work in the second year develops from what was done in the first year and takes up some of the themes from that work and builds upon them.

Don't worry though. That does not mean that you are going to be studying rivers and river processes *again*, or studying the structure of cities *again*. The A2 course builds on the ideas that you developed in your study at AS and uses those ideas to look at new places and issues in greater depth. In this book the key ideas of geography are applied to a study of issues that concern people at a variety of scales from the local to the global.

In the introduction we wrote that:

Our emphasis on place, people, interactions and decision-making geography leads naturally to an interest in and concern for our environment at all scales ranging from local to global.

Then we went on to conclude the introduction by writing:

… if you continue to A2 you will develop your skills and understanding … (and) be in a position to make well-considered judgements on a range of issues and to make suggestions as to how those issues might be better managed.'

So now you should really start to think of your Geography course as a detailed study of real issues from real places. You, and your teachers, need to make your studies as real, as up-to-date and as dynamic as possible. You should start trying to prepare yourself for your involvement in the issue evaluation and decision making that you will be involved with in your working lives, in your studies, as citizens and in your private lives from here on.

Developing synopticity

One of the most important differences between studying for AS and for A2 is the emphasis that is placed on preparing for **synoptic** assessment at A2.

[This] involves assessment of candidates 'ability to draw on their understanding of the connections between different aspects of the subject represented in the specification and to demonstrate their ability to "think like geographers."' (Specification Section 4.5, page 19)

In other words, you must try to see how the different parts of the specification are linked together.

The field of knowledge and understanding that is called 'Geography' is huge and complex. Up to this point in your study of the subject it has been split up into manageable sections, so that you could understand parts of Geography. Now, however, it becomes very important that you try to see how the different parts that you have studied fit together. You need to understand that:

- Physical and human geography are linked and influence each other.

- Many aspects of human geography are inter-connected, and many aspects of physical geography are also inter-linked.

- Many issues can be considered at a variety of different scales, and that the scales are linked.

- Ideas learnt in one place, or about one topic, can often be applied to other similar places and other similar topics …

- … and so on.

Then, when answering questions in your examinations, you need to show how this understanding of synopticity can be applied to your geography in a practical way.

Responding to stretch and challenge

It is essential that all A2 examinations 'provide greater stretch and challenge for all candidates'. (*Specification Section 4.5, page 19*)

This means that there will be more occasions than at AS Level where exam candidates are asked to produce extended writing, to plan answers without the help of detailed structures provided in the questions, to answer more open-ended questions and to respond to more testing command words.

The commands that will become more important at A2 will include:

- **discuss** Put both (or several) sides of the case in a balanced way.

- **assess** Weigh up the strengths and weaknesses of a particular point of view or course of action.

- **evaluate** Like the above, but this command pushes you more towards making a decision or reaching a conclusion. In an 'evaluate' answer it is often useful to set clear criteria against which you are going to make your evaluation. In some cases it might be necessary to evaluate something from a particular point of view. Sometimes you may be asked to evaluate the strength or reliability of evidence. You may even be asked to evaluate the usefulness of a source that you are presented with in the exam.

■ **justify** This is often used in a decision making question. You have to explain why you have made a particular decision or made a choice. You have to give the reasons for your decision or choice. Those decisions must be made on the basis of clear evidence, which must form part of your justification.

You need to get used to working in this way throughout the year, so that you are ready for the examination. You will also need to become familiar with planning and writing more extended pieces of prose than you did at AS Level. In the AS exam you did not write anything that was worth more than 15 marks for a single part of a question; at A2 there will be several places where you have to write more than this, and without having any framework provided to help with your planning. Practice that too, throughout your A2 course.

A warning about stretch and challenge

QCA, the organisation that monitors the exam system, introduced the 'stretch and challenge agenda' because some people and organisations had suggested that A Level exams were becoming easier. It is not necessary to discuss the reasons for that here but it is important to stress that the stretch and challenge agenda was aimed particularly at candidates who might be aiming for a top grade, say B and above.

All candidates have to sit the same exam papers though, so you will need to think carefully about how you prepare for the longer answers and those with the more difficult command words. After careful discussion with your teachers you need to decide what grade you are realistically aiming for.

If you are aiming for a B or higher you must respond to the agenda in a very positive way. You must aim high. You should plan to write detailed answers to the more challenging questions in depth and with flair. One way to prepare for this is by tackling some of the more detailed references that are provided in the book. This will allow you to show a real depth of understanding in your answers.

Another way is by reading cross-references to topics that you have not chosen for the exam. This will allow you to build up your synoptic understanding of the subject so that you can write with greater flair.

However, *if you are hoping for a grade C but not realistically expecting anything higher* you should be prepared to concentrate on developing a basic understanding and knowledge of topics that you are studying. Take care that you develop these basics first. Also make sure that you practice planning and writing clear answers to the more challenging questions on the paper and do not try to be too ambitious at first. Clarity will be essential if you are to gain your best possible grade.

Who knows? Maybe you will, through clearly planned work at the basics, you might surprise your teachers and develop the understanding that enables you to move on to the more complex ideas later … but grasp the basics first; and remember, the book provides you with many avenues for further development if that is the way you feel that you can go.

A vital last word

The people who wrote the specification wanted to provide students with as much choice as possible. In the exam you will have the following choices:

In Paper 3:

■ You will answer three questions, from three different sections.

■ One of these will be on a physical topic (Chapters 1–3 in the book).

■ One will be on a human topic (Chapters 4–6 in the book).

■ The third will be on either physical or human, allowing you to specialise.

■ You must answer a structured question on a physical topic and a structured question on a human topic.

■ Your essay question must not be from one of the sections from which you have chosen a structured question …

■ … but the essay questions are worth more than the structured questions, so perhaps you should choose your essay question first as it is vital that you do this well.

In Paper 4:

■ You will answer **either** 4A – Geography Fieldwork Investigation **or** 4B Geography Issue Evaluation.

■ Both these papers will test some practical skills, but in different ways.

■ Both will test your knowledge of fieldwork skills and procedures, but this will form a bigger part of Paper 4A.

■ Following on from these last two points it is important to be aware that there are parts of Chapter 7 in this book that are relevant for people preparing for Paper 4B and that there are parts of Chapter 8 that are relevant for those preparing for Paper 4A.

1 Plate tectonics and associated hazards

Plate movement

As geographers, we know that all life is fundamentally dependent upon the interaction of our planet and its atmosphere. What might surprise you is how recent most of our knowledge of how the planet works is. Systematic study of the Earth began little more than 300 years ago, and no significant understanding of its structure and evolution was achieved until the past century. We may now say confidently that the Earth itself is estimated to be 4.6 billion years old, and the oldest known rocks are 3.8 billion years old – the basaltic rocks shown in the photo of Iceland are less than 1 million years old. Fossils – the remains of once living organisms – are only relatively abundant in the geological record from around 600 million years onwards, and the earliest human remains are dated at less than 2 million years old.

Iceland did not exist 20 million years ago. On a planet 4.6 billion years old these basaltic rocks are less than 1 million years in age. The rift valley shown in Fig. 1.1 marks where the North American and Eurasian crustal plates meet, and the active volcanoes and frequent earthquakes are evidence of the tectonic movement that drags these plates apart at around 2cm/year.

Our understanding of the interior of the Earth and the forces that drive changes in the surface geography have developed rapidly and are still evolving.

Fig 1.1 *A rift valley in Iceland where North America and Eurasian crustal plates meet*

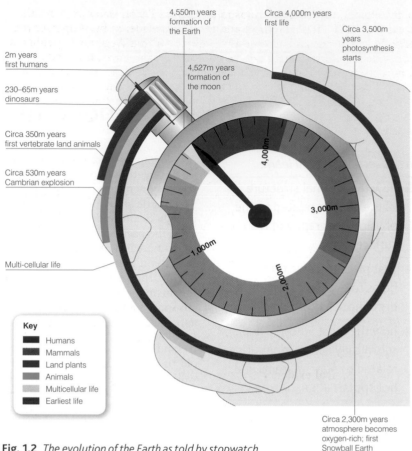

Fig. 1.2 *The evolution of the Earth as told by stopwatch*

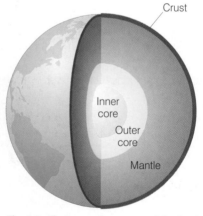

Fig. 1.3 *The internal structure of the Earth*

Earth structure

As shown in Fig. 1.3, the internal structure of the Earth can be divided into three main layers.

- The **core** is approximately the size of Mars and is the densest part of the planet, being made of rocks rich in iron and nickel. A semi-molten outer core contains a solid inner core with a temperature of over 6,000 °C.

- Surrounding the core is the **mantle**, which is largely composed of silicate rocks rich in iron and magnesium. Apart from the more rigid upper mantle, most of the mantle (asthenosphere) is semi-molten, with temperatures near the core reaching 5,000 °C. These high temperatures generate convection currents.

- The thinnest layer is the **crust**, which has the coolest, least dense rocks. These rocks are rich in silicon, oxygen, aluminium, potassium and sodium. There are two types of crust: oceanic crust, mainly basaltic in nature and around 6–10 km thick, and continental crust, which is composed of a wide variety of igneous, metamorphic and sedimentary rocks. Continental crust can be as much as 70 km thick beneath the world's major mountain ranges. The crust is separated from the mantle by the Mohorovijic (Moho) discontinuity. Together, the crust and the rigid upper mantle are collectively known as the **lithosphere**.

Plate tectonics theory

Long before plate tectonics theory developed in the late 1960s, people had noticed how continents either side of the Atlantic Ocean seemed almost to fit together; the English philosopher Francis Bacon was aware of this as early as 1620. Topographical and geological evidence built up over the following centuries and allowed the geologist Alfred Wegener to publish a theory in 1912 suggesting that the continents were once all joined together in an ancient supercontinent he called Pangaea. Wegener proposed that at some time the land masses had drifted apart until they occupied their current positions on the globe. His theory collated the different pieces of evidence that seemed to support the idea that the continents were once joined.

This evidence includes:

■ **Continental fit** – some continents (such as the western seaboard of Africa and the eastern seaboard of South America) seem to fit together if placed beside each other. This is particularly true if the continental shelves are taken into account as the true edges of the land masses.

■ **Geological evidence** – rocks of the same age and type and displaying the same formations are found in south-east Brazil and South Africa; the trends of the mountains in the eastern USA and north-west Europe are similar when they are placed in their old positions. Similar glacial deposits are found in Antarctica, South America and India, now many thousands of kilometres apart; and striations showing the same orientation when the continents are reunited, are found in Brazil and West Africa.

■ **Climatological evidence** – places as far apart as Antarctica, North America, Svarlbard and the UK all contain coal deposits of similar age that were formed in tropical conditions. They are no longer in tropical climate zones and must have drifted apart since the Carboniferous period.

■ **Biological evidence** – similar fossil formations are found on either side of the Atlantic. For example, the same reptile, called Mesosaurus, is found only in South American and southern African sediments of Permian age (around 280 million years ago). Plant remains from the humid swamps that later formed coal deposits have been found in India and Antarctica. Marsupials are found only in Australia because it drifted away from the main supercontinent before the predators that wiped them out elsewhere had migrated there.

Evidence from palaeomagnetism

Although Wegener had convincing evidence for continental drift, sceptics were quick to point out that there was no explanation of the mechanism by which continents could move over an obviously solid earth. It was not until the second half of the 20th century that three major discoveries began to suggest how this might be possible. In 1948 a survey of the floor of the Atlantic Ocean revealed a continuous ridge running largely north to south. It proved to be around 1,000 km wide, reaching heights of 2.5 km, and was composed of volcanic rocks. Similar submarine mountain ranges were later found in the Pacific Ocean extending for over 5,000 km.

(a) Pangaea: The supercontinent of 200 million years ago

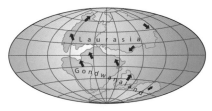

(b) Sub-oceanic forces send the land masses wandering

(c) Tomorrow's world – 50 million years hence

Direction of plate movement

Fig. 1.4 *Wegener's theory: the supercontinent of Pangaea*

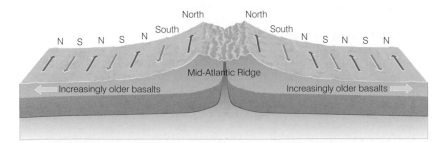

Fig. 1.5 *Evidence for sea floor spreading: sea floor striping/magnetic reversal*

Magnetic surveys of the ocean floors during the 1950s also showed surprisingly regular patterns of palaeomagnetic striping about the ridges. When lavas erupt on the ocean floor, magnetic domains within iron-rich minerals in the lava are aligned with the magnetic field of the Earth. This is fixed as the lavas cool, and unless the rocks undergo a major disturbance, they continue to record the Earth's polarity at the time of their cooling. However, as the Earth's polarity reverses on average around every 400,000 years, bands or stripes of normal and reverse polarity rocks are mirrored on either side of the mid-ocean ridges. This suggests that new rocks are being added equally on either side.

Evidence of sea floor spreading was supported by establishing the age of the ocean floor. Surveys recorded very young ages for places on or near the ridges (such as Iceland, less than 1 million years) and much older ages for ocean floor rocks nearer the continental masses (200 million years). Older crust is continuously being pushed aside by new crust. This raised a new issue: there is no evidence for the planet growing in size as ocean crust accumulates; therefore, ocean crust must be consumed elsewhere. This realisation led to the discovery of huge trenches where large areas of ocean floor were being subducted, such as around the fringes of the Pacific Ocean. **Subduction** provided the mechanism for sea floor spreading and the drifting of the continents. While the denser oceanic crust is created in some areas and destroyed in others, the less dense, more buoyant continental crust is not consumed. This explains why continental crust is geologically more complex and contains much older rocks: land masses are being moved around by the movements of the ocean crust being modified by the addition of newer rocks, and folded and faulted by collision and subduction.

Central to the theory of plate tectonics is the idea that the higher temperatures at the Earth's core, and heat released by radioactive decay of elements within the mantle, help to create **convection currents**. These zones of hotter, more liquid magma are thought to exhibit a continuous circulatory motion in the asthenosphere that causes the crustal plates to move. They pull crust apart at spreading ridges and rift zones, and pull slabs of oceanic crust back down into the mantle at subduction zones.

Key terms

Subduction: occurs when two tectonic plates move towards one another and one plate slides underneath the other, moving down into the mantle. This usually involves oceanic crust sliding beneath continental crust.

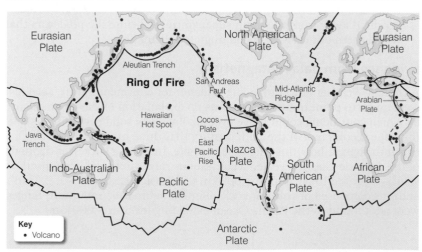

Fig. 1.6 *Plate map of the Earth, also showing volcanoes*

The Earth is often shown as being divided into seven major plates. The true picture is much more complex, with over 50 plates moving at different rates and in different directions. All plates are in motion (an average of 5–10 cm/year), but some move faster than others (up to 18 cm/year).

Did you know?

The chemistry of the ocean floor volcanics is remarkably similar all over the world. The fact that the same kind of silica-poor basalt erupts at every ocean floor-spreading ridge suggests that basalt is created by the same process everywhere. This adds more weight to the idea that convection currents in the upper mantle bring hot magma towards the surface from a common source.

■ Plate margins

Landforms associated with constructive margins

Where convection currents rise and then diverge, they can create high temperatures that cause updoming of the crust and tensional forces that pull it apart. In areas of continental crust this can produce rift valley systems, and continued rifting can lead to the creation of new areas of oceanic floor. In the oceans this rifting creates mid-oceanic ridges and basaltic lavas and dykes fill in the spaces left by the plates pulling apart.

Oceanic ridges

Oceanic ridges form the longest continuous uplifted feature on the surface of the Earth, having a total combined length of over 60,000 km. Where two plates pull apart there is a weaker zone in the crust and an increase in heat near the surface. The hotter, expanded crust forms a ridge. The central part of the ridge may feature a central valley where a section of crust has subsided into the magma below. The split in the crust provides a lower pressure zone where the more liquid lavas can erupt to form submarine volcanoes. If these eruptions persist, volcanoes may develop until they reach the surface; islands can be formed in this way. Iceland, a volcanic island on a spreading ridge of the Mid-Atlantic Ridge, is the largest example. More recently, in 1963, eruptions created the island of Surtsey to the south of Iceland.

As crust is pushed away from the heat source at the mid-ocean ridge, it cools, contracts and sinks towards the deeper regions, where it becomes covered in fine sediments. Occasionally fragments of ocean floor (ophiolites) are left at the surface during subduction, and the layers of pillow basalts and later deep ocean sediments are left exposed. A famous example of this, the Troodos ophiolite suite, can be seen today in Cyprus.

Activity

1 Construct a concept map to show the relationships between the following forms of evidence for continental drift:

■ geology

■ biology

■ climate

■ continental fit

■ sea floor spreading.

2 Write each term in a circle on a large piece of paper and use curved lines to connect the circles. On each line try to write at least one way in which the different pieces of evidence could be connected.

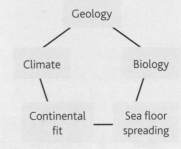

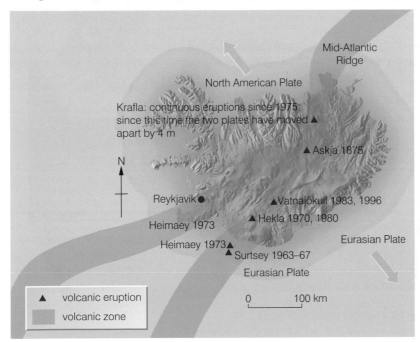

Fig. 1.7 *Location of Iceland on the Mid-Atlantic Ridge*

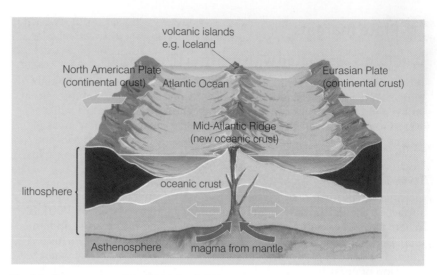

Fig. 1.8 *Cross-section of the Mid-Atlantic Ridge*

Mid-ocean ridges are irregular, curving around the planet (see Fig. 1.7). If new ocean crust was created equally on both sides, it would appear to create the possibility of overlapping new crust on concave sections and divergence on convex sections. The fact that there are no mountains of ocean floor or sudden gaps in the crust is explained by the fact that the seemingly continuous spreading ridges are frequently bisected by **transform (slip) faults** which allow the crust created at the ridges to move outwards at different rates. Seismicity associated with such movements on and around the ridges is characterised by shallow-focus earthquakes.

Rift valleys

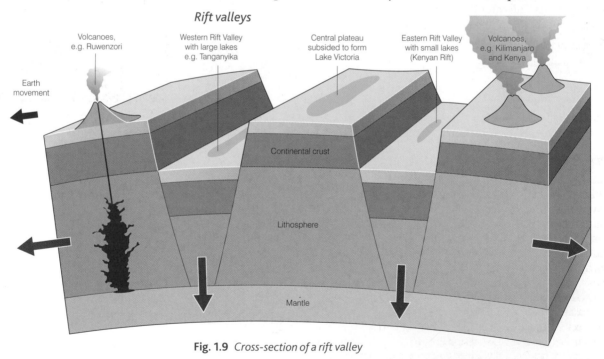

Fig. 1.9 *Cross-section of a rift valley*

Where spreading occurs beneath a major land mass, the heating and subsequent updoming of the crust leads to fracturing and rifting. As the sides of the rift move apart, central sections drop down to form **rift valleys**. The Great East African Rift Valley indicates where the crust has begun to pull apart, and active volcanoes such as Mount Kilimanjaro and Mount Kenya are surface evidence of the igneous activity beneath. At 4,000 km long, up to 50 km wide and 600 m in depth, this feature might widen still further, allowing the sea to inundate it. To the north, two rifts have widened into the Red Sea and the Gulf of Arabia, respectively. Here, the rifting has continued and new ocean floor is forming between Africa on the south-western side and Arabia on the north-eastern side. Other examples of past rift zones include the steep-sided valley of the River Rhine between Germany and France where the river runs in a down-faulted rift valley. Although there are ancient volcanics nearby to show how active this region once was, it is no longer subject to rifting.

Landforms associated with destructive plate margins

Destructive plate margins are found where plates converge. There are three types of convergent margin:

- oceanic plate meeting continental plate
- oceanic plate meeting oceanic plate
- continental plate meeting continental plate.

Activity

3 Describe the sequence of events that would start with rifting of a land mass and culminate in the creation of a new ocean.

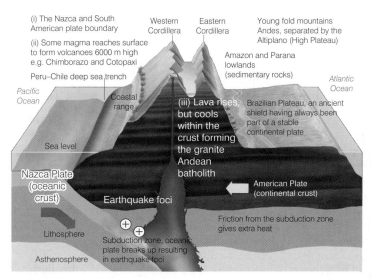

Fig. 1.10 *Cross-section of a destructive plate margin*

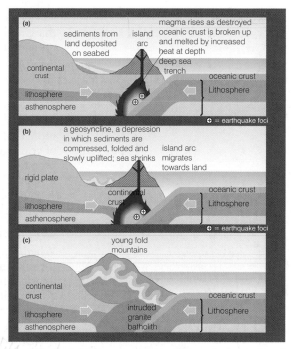

Fig. 1.11 *A subduction sequence leading to the formation of young fold mountains*

Oceanic/continental plate convergence

Because oceanic crust is denser than continental crust, when plates collide the oceanic crust is subducted, or taken down, into the upper mantle. Subduction creates several features characteristic of destructive margins. As the oceanic crust descends, friction with the overlying continental crust builds up and causes major earthquakes. Destructive margins are some of the most seismically active zones in the world, with shallow- to deep-focus earthquakes charting the descent of subducted crust into the mantle. Rocks scraped off the descending plate and folding of the continental crust help to create young fold mountain chains on the leading edge of continental masses, such as the Andes along the west coast of South America. Deep ocean trenches are found along the seaward edge of destructive margins. They mark where one plate begins to descend beneath another and can reach great depths: the Peru–Chile trench is more than 8 km deep.

The friction created by the descending slab of ocean floor also generates enormous heat, leading to partial melting of the crust. Magmas derived from the melting of old ocean floor basalts are less dense than the mantle; they try to rise up through fissures and by burning (stoping) their way through overlying rock until they reach the surface. Where volcanoes erupt on land they help to create young fold mountains such as the Andes. Because the magmas from which the volcanic lavas originate have incorporated elements of older crust and continental rocks as they rose, they are more silica rich, more intermediate or acidic in type. These magmas are more viscous and flow less easily, leaving intrusives such as batholiths within the mountain masses and generating extrusives such as andesitic lavas to erupt through volcanoes. Such 'stickier' lavas frequently block off their own vents until erupting violently to form conical-shaped volcanoes of alternating layers of ash and lava i.e. composite corner. Vulcanicity is a key feature of subduction zones; around 80 per cent of all active volcanoes are found above subduction zones.

Oceanic plate/oceanic plate convergence

Where two pieces of oceanic crust on different plates collide, one is subducted beneath the other. The crust that is subducted may be marginally the denser of the two plates or is the one which is moving more quickly. The processes that accompany subduction are much the same as in the case of the ocean/continental plate collision outlined above, but where the volcanics usually erupt on crust covered by oceans they form islands. These form characteristically curving lines of new volcanic land known as island arcs (e.g. Aleutian Islands) with deep ocean trenches (e.g. the Marianas Trench in the Pacific, which is more than 10 km deep). Such island chains may develop over millions of years to become major landmasses (Japan, Indonesia). Subduction produces frequent shallow- to deep-focus earthquakes, some of which are immensely powerful: in Indonesia, where the Australian Plate is being subducted beneath the Eurasian Plate, there was an earthquake in 2004 measuring 9 on the Richter scale.

Continental plate/continental plate convergence

Where subduction of oceanic crust draws two continental masses together, a collision margin may develop. As continents have similar density and thus buoyancy, they will not be subducted. Instead, they collide with each other. Volcanics associated with earlier subduction and sediments scraped off the vanishing ocean floor are mixed up and compressed to form young fold mountain chains with deep roots in the lithosphere. The subcontinent of India is an example: it was propelled by sea floor spreading of the Indo-Australian Plate in a north-easterly direction until it collided with the Eurasian Plate some 40 million years ago. This collision formed the Himalayan mountain chain, home of the highest mountain on earth, Mount Everest (8,848 m). The Himalayas are constantly changing, because these highly folded and faulted regions do not become seismically quiet after first impact. At this extreme altitude weathering and erosion reduce mountain height, but **isostatic lift** in some areas, produced by continuing plate motion, means that some scientists believe Everest is increasing in height by up to 2.5 cm per year. The whole region experiences high levels of seismicity, causing devastating earthquakes in Gujurat (India) in 2001, Afghanistan in 2002, Pakistan in 2005 and Sichuan in China in 2008, for example.

> The summit of Mount Everest contains fossils that were once laid down in ocean sediments but have since become elevated by fold mountain building and exposed by subsequent erosion.
>
> *earthquake.usgs.gov/eqcenterl*

Key terms

Isostatic lift: uplift of a land mass resulting from tectonic processes.

Activities

4 Make a simple cross-section diagram of a destructive plate margin involving ocean crust and continental crust, and annotate it to explain how the following features were formed:

- ocean trench
- zone of partial melting
- young fold mountains
- volcanoes
- subduction zone.

5 In which ways might the diagram look different if you had drawn an ocean crust/ ocean crust destructive margin?

Conservative margins

These margins are sometimes referred to as passive or slip margins and occur where two plates meet and the direction of plate motion is either parallel or nearly parallel. Two examples of this are the San Andreas fault in California and the Alpine fault in New Zealand. No crust is destroyed or created, although these are areas of frequent seismic activity as the build-up of friction as plates pass each other is released by earthquakes (as in San Francisco in 1989). They are not associated with active vulcanism.

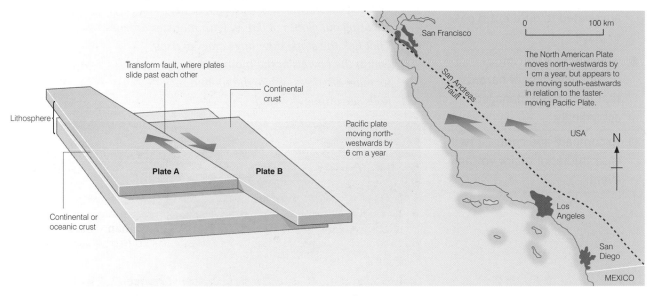

Fig. 1.12 *Cross-section of a conservative plate margin exemplified by the San Andreas Fault*

Hot spots

Maps of volcano distribution indicate that although most active volcanoes are associated with divergent and convergent plate margins, others do not conform to that pattern. For example, the Hawaiian Islands, which are entirely of volcanic origin, were formed in the middle of the Pacific Ocean more than 3,200 km from the nearest plate boundary. Some geologists believe these long-lived and seemingly stationary **hot spots** are the result of plumes of magma originating deep within the mantle. Others suggest they are created from far less depth and, in fact, are moving slowly.

As basaltic shield volcanoes erupt through the drifting oceanic crust, they may build up from the ocean floor to form an island over time. However, they become part of the plate and are gradually moved away from the heat source. Some islands will become eroded by waves and form flat-topped sea mounts called **guyots**. Newer volcanoes erupt over the hot spot and a new island is formed. This sequence can form a chain of islands if the plate is moving quickly in one direction over the hot spot (the Hawaiian chain) or a cluster if the plate is rotating more slowly around a hot spot (the Cape Verde or Canary Islands). In the case of Hawaii (see Fig. 1.13), the main island is currently closest to the hot spot and is most volcanically active. Older, less active or volcanically extinct islands extend to the north-west of the main island, having been moved away from the hot spot as the Pacific Plate moves in that direction at approximately 10 cm/year. A new island will form to the south-east of Hawaii when the Loihi submarine volcano builds up to sea level.

Fig. 1.13 *The Hawaiian volcanic chain and hot spot*

Vulcanicity

In this section you will learn:

- how variations in the type and frequency of volcanic activity are related to different types of plate

- why different volcanoes present a variety of hazards that need to be managed accordingly

- to compare and contrast two case studies of major volcanic events.

Did you know?

The effects of changes in pressure near a fissure in the Earth's crust can be exemplified by similar changes in state between liquid and gas in a fizzy drinks bottle. Even after being shaken, few gas bubbles are visible when the bottle is left to stand, but once the top is unscrewed and the pressure released there is a rush of more mobile foam (gas and liquid) to the lower-pressure zone outside of the bottle. In the same way, magma and lava are the more mobile, near-surface versions of the semi-molten rocks found at greater depths.

Key terms

Extrusive rock: igneous rock formed by the crystallisation of magma above the surface of the Earth.

Intrusive rock: igneous rock formed by the crystallisation of magma below the surface of the Earth.

This is how the Roman poet Virgil described an eruption on Mount Etna in the *Aeneid*.

> *Now to the realm of light it lifts a cloud*
> *Of pitch-black, whirling smoke, and fiery dust,*
> *Shooting out globes of flame, with monster tongues*
> *That lick the stars; now huge crags of itself,*
> *Out of the bowels of the mountain torn,*
> *Its maw disgorges, while the molten rock*
> *Rolls screaming skyward …*

Fig. 1.14 *Satellite image of Mount Etna erupting*

Volcanoes are openings in the Earth's crust through which lava, ash and gases erupt. This is the surface manifestation of the presence of magma within the Earth's crust. Molten rock beneath the surface is referred to as magma, but once it is ejected at the surface it is called lava.

The differences between these materials can be explained in part by their location. At depth the enormous pressure exerted upon hot rocks in the mantle keeps them in a semi-solid state. Fissures and fractures in the crust create low-pressure areas that allow some material beneath the crust to become molten and rise. If these molten rocks reach the surface they are said to be **extrusive** (e.g. the Borrowdale volcanics in the English Lake District), but if they are injected into the crust they are said to be **intrusive** (e.g. Shap granite, also found in the Lake District). Both are termed igneous in origin, but the latter can only be seen at the surface after subsequent erosion.

■ Extrusive landforms

Volcanic landforms vary considerably, reflecting the nature of the material erupted, the nature of the eruption and the time that has elapsed since the last activity.

- ■ **Basaltic (basic) lavas** originate largely from the upward movement of mantle material. They are most common along spreading ridges but are also found at hot spots and within more developed rift systems.

- ■ **Andesitic (intermediate) lavas** are typical of destructive plate margins where crust is being destroyed.

- ■ **Rhyolitic (acid) lavas** are most often found at destructive and collision margins.

Pyroclastic material comprises a wide range of volcanic fragments from finer-grained ash and lapilli to larger volcanic bombs. They are characteristic of more gaseous phases of eruption, where the build-up of gas beneath blocked volcanic vents creates a violent explosion, shredding the magma into finer particles. An extreme form of this, found with thick rhyolitic lavas are the rapidly moving *nuées ardentes*, glowing gas clouds of incandescent shards (seen at Mont Pelée, Martinique, in 1904). The melded fragments form a rock known as ignimbrite, ancient examples of which can be found in Wales and the Lake District. Whereas lavas may travel a few kilometres, ash can be spread widely via the upper atmosphere or mix with rain or meltwater to form highly mobile mudflows (lahars).

Volcano classification

Volcanoes are commonly classified by their shape and type of eruption.

Shape

- ■ **Fissure eruptions** – occur where an elongated crack in the crust allows lava to spill out over a large area. Typically these are found around spreading ridges where tension pulls the crust apart – for example, the eruption at Heimaey, Iceland, in 1973. When the Eurasian and North American Plates pulled apart, existing topography was drowned in a vast lake of basaltic lava. Fragments of these rocks can be seen in the columnar basalts of the Giant's Causeway in Northern Ireland and Fingal's Cave on the Isle of Staffa, Scotland. The Deccan Plateau in north-west India is composed of 29 major lava flows with 700,000 km³ of basalt.

Fig. 1.15 *Volcano types*

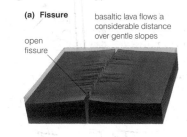

(a) Fissure

open fissure

basaltic lava flows a considerable distance over gentle slopes

Rock type: basaltic	—	Location: rifts/early constructive margins	—	Eruptions: gentle, persistent

- ■ **Shield volcanoes** – are made of basaltic rock and form gently sloping cones from layers of less viscous lava. The largest volcano in the world, Mauna Loa in Hawaii, stands 4,170 m above sea level with a volume of 40,000 km³. In reality it is much bigger, as the entire structure extends 10,099 m from the ocean floor, making it taller than Mount Everest.

(b) Basic or shield

gently sloping sides built up by numerous basaltic lava flows

Rock type: basaltic	—	Location: hot spots and where oceanic crust meets oceanic crust	—	Eruptions: gentle, predictable

(c) Composite

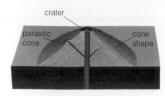

crater

parasitic cone

cone shape

(d) Acid or dome

spine forms if lava solidifies in vent and is pushed upwards

steep, convex sides due to viscous lava soon cooling

(e) Caldera

layers of fine ash and larger cinders

mainly acidic lavas possibly some ash

more recent new cone

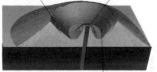

crater fills with water to form a lake or, if below sea level, a lagoon

■ **Composite volcanoes** – the most common type found on land. They are created by layers of ash from initial explosive phases of eruptions and subsequent layers of lava from the main eruption phases. Typical examples of these classically shaped volcanoes are Mounts Etna and Vesuvius in Italy and Popocatepetl in Mexico.

Rock type: andesitic	Location: destructive margins	Eruptions: explosive, unpredictable

■ **Acid or dome volcanoes** – these are steep-sided volcanoes formed from very viscous lava. As the lava cannot travel far, it builds up convex cone-shaped volcanoes. Lava may solidify in the vent and be revealed later by erosion, as at Puy de Domes in France.

Rock type: rhyolitic	Location: continental crust	Eruptions: explosive, unpredictable

■ **Calderas** – form when gases that have built up beneath a blocked volcanic vent result in a catastrophic eruption that destroys (at least) the volcano summit, leaving an enormous crater where later eruptions may form smaller cones. In the case of Crater Lake in the US, the caldera has filled with water, while in the case of Krakatoa in Indonesia and Thera/Santorini in Greece, the sea has inundated the broken remnants of the volcano.

Rock type: andesitic	Location: destructive margins	Eruptions: very explosive, unpredictable

Minor extrusive features

■ **Geysers and hot springs** – even in areas where vulcanism does not produce active volcanoes, water heated at depth in the crust by magma chambers can periodically escape as steam and hot water. A geyser (from *Geysir* meaning 'to gush' in Icelandic) is an intermittent, turbulent discharge of superheated water ejected and accompanied by a vapour phase. Where hot water on its way upwards mixes with muds near the surface, a bubbling, boiling mud volcano may form. In some places hot springs have become tourist attractions: in Pamukkale (Turkey), dissolved salts from the hot water are laid down in spectacular calcium carbonate deposits, though the area is not volcanically active.

■ **Fumaroles** are areas where superheated water turns to steam as it condenses on the surface. These features are typical of areas such as Solfatara in Italy, where the escape of steam and water mixed with sulphur-rich gases gives rise to the collective name for these features of **solfatara**.

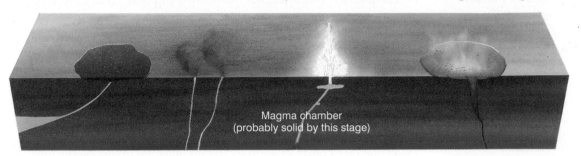

(a) **Boiling mud:** hot water mixes with mud and surface deposits

(b) **Solfatara:** created when gases, mainly sulphurous, escape onto the surface

(c) **Geyser:** water in the lower crust is heated by rocks and turns into steam; pressure increases and the steam and water explode onto the surface

(d) **Fumaroles:** superheated water turns to steam as its pressure drops when it emerges from the ground

Magma chamber (probably solid by this stage)

Fig. 1.16 *Minor volcanic extrusive features*

Intrusive features

With all volcanic regions, the majority of magma never reaches the surface but cools to form coarser-grained igneous rocks beneath the ground. These rocks may contribute to surface geomorphology through uplift, erosion and exposure at the surface. Batholiths form when large masses of magma cool very slowly, producing coarse-grained rocks. Examples are the granites that lie under Shap and Skiddaw in the Lake District. Where magma has been squeezed between existing strata it may form a sill (concordant to the existing strata) or a dyke (discordant). The Whin Sill, which stretches from near Dufton in North Yorkshire to Holy Island in Northumberland, is a hard layer of dolerite that creates distinctive landscapes. The erosion of surrounding rocks can leave dykes exposed as low ridges, as at Kildonan on the Isle of Arran in Scotland.

Fig. 1.17 *The Whin Sill, Northumberland*

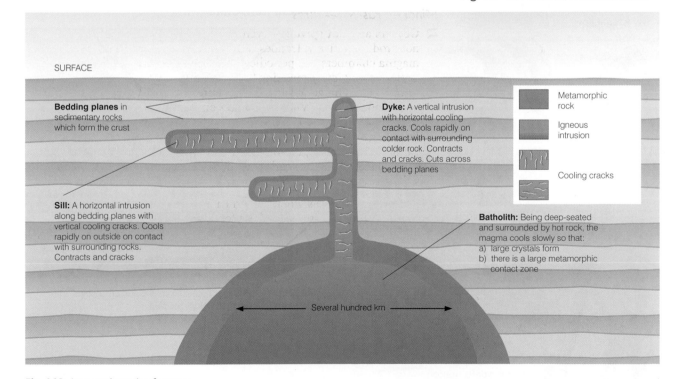

SURFACE

Bedding planes in sedimentary rocks which form the crust

Dyke: A vertical intrusion with horizontal cooling cracks. Cools rapidly on contact with surrounding colder rock. Contracts and cracks. Cuts across bedding planes

Metamorphic rock

Igneous intrusion

Cooling cracks

Sill: A horizontal intrusion along bedding planes with vertical cooling cracks. Cools rapidly on outside on contact with surrounding rocks. Contracts and cracks

Batholith: Being deep-seated and surrounded by hot rock, the magma cools slowly so that:
a) large crystals form
b) there is a large metamorphic contact zone

← Several hundred km →

Fig. 1.18 *Igneous intrusive features*

Links

For a report on volcanic activity which is updated weekly, visit: www. volcano.si.edu/reports/usgs/

Activities

1. Explain how magma type and volcano form may be linked.

2. How are the eruption style and morphology of volcanoes related?

3. Suggest reasons for the dominance of certain volcano types in different tectonic settings.

Links

The United States Geological Survey (USGS) has a worldwide map of volcano activity status which summarises potential hazards for the aviation industry at: volcano.wr.usgs.gov

Links

The FEMA website can be found at: www.fema.gov

Volcanic frequency

Estimates for the number of active volcanoes in the world vary according to how 'activity' is defined, but the figure commonly given is around 550.

- **Active** volcanoes have erupted in living memory.
- **Dormant** volcanoes have erupted within historical record.
- **Extinct** volcanoes will not erupt again.

Volcano hazard management

While eruptions cannot be prevented, they can often be predicted, and protection offered to the local population.

Prediction often involves accurate hazard mapping (mapping the previous lava and pyroclastic flows by studying geology), analysing seismic shockwave patterns, sampling gas and lava emissions and remote sensing of changes in topography, heat and gas emissions by satellite.

Seismic shock waves alerted vulcanologists to the likely eruption of Popocatepetl, Mexico in 2000, and the volcano did in fact erupt within 48 hours after the local population was evacuated. However, not all volcanoes are as predictable.

Protection involves reducing the risk of damage by preparing for an eruption. Warnings such as those issued in the US by the USGS are supported by instructions from FEMA (the Federal Emergency Management Agency) on how to react before, during and after an eruption. In the longer term, hazard mapping and land-use planning may be used to avoid development in areas at risk.

Case study

Chaitén, Chile

Fig. 1.20 *An electrical storm and ash cloud over the erupting Chaitén volcano, Chile*

Remote sensing

Geophysical

Seismicity

Hydrology

Gas

Ground deformation

Fig. 1.19 *Volcano prediction methods composite diagram, USGS*

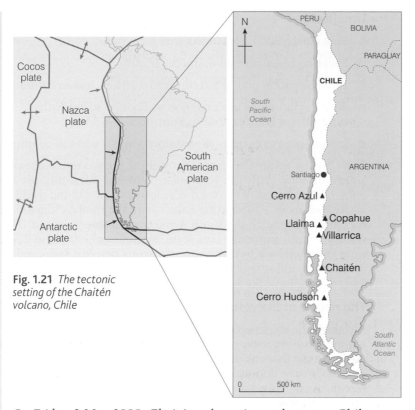

Fig. 1.21 *The tectonic setting of the Chaitén volcano, Chile*

On Friday, 2 May 2008, Chaitén volcano in south-eastern Chile erupted for the first time in around 9,400 years. The initial eruption produced a plume of volcanic ash and steam that rose nearly 17 km high. Winds carried the plume east, over the Andes mountains, into Argentina and over the Atlantic. The town of Chaitén (pop.: *c.*4,200), situated 10 km south-west of the volcano, was blanketed with ash. About 4,000 people who lived there were evacuated by boat, along with another 1,000 residents from the nearby town of Futaleufu. Smaller settlements to the south-east such as Chubut and Rio Negro also received heavy ashfalls. The ash plume was so thick in some parts of neighbouring Argentina that flights were diverted and airports, highways and schools were forced to close.

Fig. 1.22 *Damage caused by the volcanic eruption to the town of Chaitén*

Timeline

- First earthquakes felt late 30/4/08 local time.
- Eruption began around midnight 1/5/08.
- Initial eruption puts ash column to $c.18$ km, 6 hours' duration.
- Nearly continuous ash emission as high as 30 km with intermittent large explosions continued 2–8 May.
- Lava dome extrusion with sustained vapour and ash column.

The Chaitén volcano is one of many along the western seaboard of South America. With 122 volcanoes, including 40 historically active ones, Chile has one of the longest volcanic chains in the world. It is situated above a subduction zone where the Pacific Ocean Plate is consumed beneath the South American continental crust. The volcano, which featured a lava dome within a caldera about 2.5 km wide and 4 km long, is composed of viscous rhyolitic lavas and pyroclastics and is typical of the magmas rising through the young fold mountains of the Andes.

The nature of the volcanic hazard

Although the actual eruption was not accurately monitored, the nature of the eruption gave serious cause for concern. The rhyolitic nature of the lava and ash in this area meant that any eruption was likely to be dominated by pyroclastics, and aside from some reports of lava this was the case. By late May the lava eruptions had generated a new dome of around $540,000$ m^2 in area, containing a staggering 55 million m^3 of new material. The height of the ash column varied but it seems to have been estimated at 20–30 km at its peak. The subsequent collapse of the column brought a vast amount of ash to the ground. The fall of ash coated and asphyxiated some animals as well as blocking roads. The eruption also triggered thunderstorms, and a passing polar storm meant that heavy rains combined with ash to block rivers and led to flooding.

The impact of the event

On arrival, the USGS monitoring team reported that the widespread ashfall had significantly affected the local communities. Lahars (mudflows) generated by the intense rainfall mixing with the ash had cut communications in some areas and made access difficult. Elsewhere, ashfalls up to 15 cm deep had blocked rivers and contaminated groundwater supplies. By 14 May the Chilean Oficina Nacional de Emergencia announced that around 90 per cent of the town of Chaitén was flooded due to increased flows of the Río Blanco or Río Chaitén.

While casualties were low, with just one death (attributed to stress related to the eruption and evacuation), some farm animals were killed by the suffocating ash. Local hospitals treated people for breathing difficulties. Between 80 and 90 per cent of the town was reported damaged, with 20–30 per cent completely destroyed. Extensive damage to airport and marine facilities further hampered rescue operations.

Aircraft encounters:

- Three encounters between commercial aircraft flying into ash clouds from Chaitén in early May 2008.
- Damage to aircraft appears to have been minimal.

Airport closures:

■ Regional airports were occasionally closed by ash from the eruption.

■ The airport at Chaitén is closed indefinitely.

■ Chile closures: Chaitén, Osorno, Puerto Montt.

■ Argentina closures: Bariloche, Esquel, Comodoro Rivadavia.

Flight cancellations:

■ Domestic: several hundred domestic flights in Argentina and Chile.

■ International: several dozen international flights from Santiago, Chile and Buenos Aires, Argentina cancelled.

Management of the hazard and responses to the event

Prior to 2008, Chaitén was classified as a low-threat volcano. While geological records indicated that it had a history of explosive eruptions, dome building and pyroclastic flows associated with dome collapse, the length of time it had lain dormant meant it was not actively monitored. The remote location of Chaitén and the relatively low population density meant that the management of the volcano was not a high priority. Altogether Chile has only 20 volcanoes with completed geological studies, seven of which have completed hazard assessments, and seven more that are monitored to some degree. There is only one volcano observatory in Chile, and until the USGS team arrived on 16 May 2008, there was no real-time monitoring of the eruption.

The immediate response to a rapidly evolving threat focused on the need to evacuate more than 4,000 people from the town of Chaitén, 10 km from the volcano, after the initial eruption. By 3 May the Chilean Navy had helped to evacuate some 3,900 people, and forcible evacuation orders were issued to encourage those who did not wish to leave. Emergency measures included the following:

■ Residents were told not to drink the water, because the reservoirs in the area were covered in a layer of ash.

■ Chilean officials distributed fresh water and protective masks.

■ The Chilean government ordered a 50-km exclusion zone around the town.

■ The government issued a monthly disaster stipend of the equivalent of between $1,200 and $2,200 per month per family.

■ Financial aid to small businesses was granted and a 90-day freeze on payment of existing loans to the state bank Banco Estado to aid businesses in trouble because of the eruption.

A key development was the involvement of the Volcano Disaster Assistance Program (VDAP) to aid monitoring and prediction of subsequent eruptions. Real-time seismic monitoring began on 17 May and assisted with interpretation and forecasts. As a **Volcanic Explosivity Index (VEI)** 5 category eruption (>1 km³ magma, ash to a height of 20 km), the monitoring of Chaitén was seen as important to help the Chilean government and to help model explosive rhyolitic eruptions in the future. The volcano continued to experience more minor eruptions, featuring gas and ash plumes, for the rest of 2008, highlighting the difficulties agencies face in dealing with the aftermath of one volcanic event.

Key terms

Volcanic Explosivity Index (VEI): relative measure of the explosiveness of volcanic eruptions. The scale goes from 0 (minimum) to 8 (maximum).

Activity

4 Down the middle of a sheet of A4 paper, create a timeline of events associated with the Chaitén eruption using the information above.

■ Any events to do with the physical, volcanic processes should be summarised on the left-hand side and any events involving the effects on/ actions of people should be written down the right-hand side.

■ Use light colour shading to classify specific events as:

a Red – a hazard caused by the eruption of lava and pyroclastics.

b Blue – a secondary effect such as blocked streams.

c Orange – a commercial impact on industry of any kind.

d Green – any measure taken to reduce risk or the damage caused.

Explain why it was difficult for the Chilean government to reduce the impact of the eruption by prediction or precaution.

Mount Etna, Sicily

Fig. 1.23 *Mount Etna erupting, Sicily*

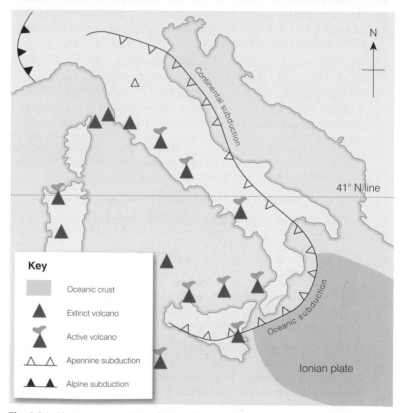

Key

	Oceanic crust
▲	Extinct volcano
⩚	Active volcano
△ △	Apennine subduction
▲ ▲	Alpine subduction

Fig. 1.24 *The tectonic setting of Mount Etna, Sicily*

Case study

Mount Etna, Europe's highest (3,310 m) and most active volcano, has a volcanic history stretching back over 5,000 years. It supports rich agricultural land, and it is estimated that nearly 25 per cent of Sicily's population live on its slopes. Due to its activity and nearby population, Mount Etna has been classified as a **Decade Volcano** by the United Nations (UN). It displays dramatic volcanic scenery created by several caldera collapses and changing eruptive centres. There have been at least 60 flank eruptions and many summit eruptions since AD 1600, and around half of these have occurred since the beginning of the 20th century; since 2001 Mount Etna has seen an eruption every year. Unlike Chaitén, it is a well-monitored and actively managed volcano.

Etna lies in a setting that is structurally highly complex and not yet fully understood. Its vulcanism stems from the subduction of the African Plate beneath the Eurasian Plate; deformation of the plates associated with subduction allows magma to rise to the surface through weaknesses in the crust.

Nature of the volcanic hazard

Although Etna has been known for a long time to be an active volcano, it still presents a significant natural hazard. The fertile volcanic soils support agriculture, with vineyards and orchards spread across the lower slopes of the mountain and the broad Plain of Catania. The volcano displays a wide range of eruptions, from the relatively minor to the major explosive variety. Mount Etna is a composite stratovolcano that typically erupts basaltic lava, which has a low viscosity and is consequently able to travel significant distances. Aside from the main vent, fissures open up, releasing lava flows from a variety of locations, and 'hornitos' (small parasitic cones) spatter lava from the side of the cone.

Other potential hazards

1 **Seismic activity connecting with eruptive activity** – potentially serious damage caused to building and public infrastructure around the volcano.

2 **Gas plume emission, volcanic dust and ashfalls** – high-magnitude explosive events at summit craters can lead to the formation of eruptive columns of ash, the fallout from which presents significant problems to settlements and agriculture, and risks for road and air traffic.

3 **Flank collapse before or following** – one of the most hazardous processes that can occur at a volcano is a collapse of one of its flanks, leading to a huge avalanche of volcanic debris, as once occurred at the Valle del Bove.

4 **Phreatic eruptions** – these are steam-driven explosions that occur when water beneath the ground or on the surface is heated by magma or lava, generating an explosion of steam, water, ash blocks and lava bombs.

In 1669 extensive lava flows from Etna engulfed the village of Nicolosi, and in 1928 a large lava flow destroyed the town of Mascali in just two days. While new fissures and cones meant that lava could flow in different directions, in 1992 lava headed directly toward the village of Zafferana in a very efficient lava tube system over 7 km away, without essentially losing heat and fluidity. More recently, in 2002–3, the biggest eruptions for many years threw up a huge column of ash that deposited material as far away as Libya, 600 km to

Skills

1 Web searching is made more efficient if you are precise about the area of information you need before you begin.

2 As you work through this section you can get additional information and virtual tours at: www.swisseduc.ch

Key terms

Decade Volcano: a volcano identified as deserving particular study because of a history of destructive eruptions near to populated areas.

the south across the Mediterranean Sea. Seismic activity associated with these eruptions caused the eastern flanks of the volcano to slip by up to 2 m, causing structural damage to many houses. Following intense eruptions in late 2006, in the early part of 2007 several major episodes of lava fountaining began, with ash emissions and explosions on the eastern side. In May 2008 a flurry of earthquakes accompanied the opening of new fissures and the eruption of lava flows that travelled some 6 km down the Valle del Bove, stopping just short of the village of Milo.

The impact of the event

It is estimated that only 77 confirmed deaths can be attributed to eruptions on Mount Etna, and in recent years there have been few fatalities. The majority of those were caused when visitors strayed into hazardous areas, such as the nine tourists who were killed in September 1979 near Bocca Nuova by a phratic explosion, or the two tourists killed in April 1987 at the south-east crater by a similar event. In the last 20 years all deaths on Etna have been from lightning strikes and accidents.

Fig. 1.25 *A house engulfed during the 2002 Mount Etna eruptions*

The eruptions of 2002 are, perhaps, more typical of the impact of vulcanism on Etna. The eruption completely destroyed the tourist station at Piano Provenzana and part of the tourist station around the Rifugio Sapienza on the south side of the volcano. It took the lava two weeks to reach the tourist centre of Rifugio Sapienza. On 29 July 2002, the airport of Sicily's second city, Catania, was forced to close while the runways were cleared of ash. The winter tourist industry was affected as visitors stayed away because of safety concerns. On 4 September 2007 a violent eruption from the south-east crater saw lava spewing up to 400 m into the air, where strong winds sent ash and smoke into the towns below. Catania-Fontanarossa Airport shut down operations during the night as a safety precaution.

Management of the hazard and responses to the event

Etna has a long history of people living nearby and consequently much experience of managing eruptions. In most instances local people have rebuilt their own properties from salvaged materials or relocated elsewhere, and government intervention has been rare. A significant early intervention did occur during the eruptions of 1991–93 when Zafferana was threatened by a lava flow. Initial attempts at stalling the lava flow proved unsuccessful when lava surmounted the hastily constructed earth barriers on the approach to the town. To disrupt and redirect the flow, explosives were detonated near the source of the lava flow, to break up a very efficient lava tube system that had been guiding the lava for some 7 km downslope. The main explosion on 23 May 1992 destroyed the lava tube and forced the lava into a new artificial channel which took the lava away from Zafferana. During the 2002 eruptions, dams of soil and volcanic rock were put up to protect the tourist base at Rifugio Sapienza and helped to divert the flow. The Italian Army's heavy earth-moving equipment was brought in to block and divert lava flows. None of the towns on Etna's slopes were damaged, but there were losses in agriculture and tourism. The Italian government pledged immediate financial assistance of more than $8m (£5.6m) and tax breaks for villagers.

Monitoring

The Catania Section of the Istituto Nazionale di Geofisica e Vulcanologia (INGV) has monitored the volcano for 20 years with a permanent network of remote sensors (seismic, geodetic, magnetic, gravimetric and videos) connected in real time, by radio and/or mobile phone, to the acquisition centre in Catania.

Data continuously recorded by permanent stations are also integrated with discrete observations, surveys and laboratory analysis to evaluate in real time the activity level of the volcano and issue warnings.

Geochemical monitoring programmes test gas/fluid emissions to help predict new eruptions and warn of dangerous gas emissions. In recent years gas emissions from both the summit craters and the flanks of Mount Etna have also been monitored using remote-sensing techniques and on-site monitoring devices. The SO_2 plume flux from the summit craters has routinely been measured by correlation spectrometry from a ground vehicle and, occasionally, from a helicopter. The SO_2 flux data help observers estimate the volume of single magma batches that migrate upwards into the volcanic system.

Links

For the activities, you might like to use a GIS site such as maps.live.com or earth.google.com (these use 3-D landscaping facilities to better understand the nature of the terrain) or multimap.com to explore the area more thoroughly.

Activities

5 Write a report comparing and contrasting the Chaitén and Etna eruptions.

- Support your arguments with data from additional sources such as economic and development profiles for each country.
- You may wish to complete a timeline for Etna to help your comparison.
- Conclude by making suggestions for how, if necessary, future eruptions in either country might be managed more effectively.

6 Study the photographs in Figs 1.14 and 1.23 and diagrams of the Mount Etna region. Try to identify as much evidence as you can that suggests that:

a Mount Etna is an active volcano with a long history of eruptions.

b The area is well populated and features industry (including farming).

c The volcano is a tourist attraction.

Make a simple sketch plan of the area shown in the map. Annotate the plan with your evidence for tourist activity and reasons why you think it is subject to erosion.

Suggest why it is that settlement and tourism can coexist with an active volcano in close proximity.

Seismicity

In this section you will learn:

- the causes and main characteristics of earthquakes

- why earthquakes present a variety of hazards that need to be managed accordingly

- to compare and contrast two case studies of major earthquake events.

Links

For a map showing the locations of recent earthquakes, see: neic.usgs.gov

Earthquakes

Earthquakes occur almost continuously over the surface of the Earth, with an estimated 18 earthquakes of magnitude (M) 7.0 or larger every year. Many are so small in magnitude and/or distant that they are not normally of any concern. Large earthquakes near centres of population are some of the deadliest of natural hazards, killing hundreds of thousands of people.

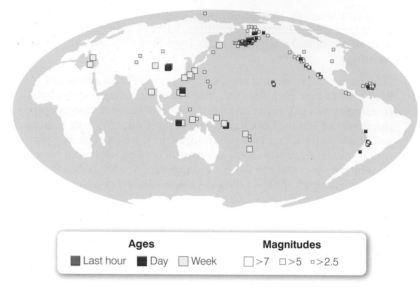

Ages		Magnitudes	
■ Last hour ■ Day □ Week		□ >7 □ >5 □ >2.5	

Fig. 1.26 *Earthquakes occur all the time. This map shows events above magnitude 2.5 on the Richter scale for one week in August 2008*

Earthquakes occur when a build-up of pressure within the Earth's crust is suddenly released and the ground shakes violently. The point within the crust where the pressure release occurs is known as the **focus**. This can be found at a range of depths:

- shallow focus: 0–70 km deep

- intermediate focus: 70–300 km deep

- deep focus: 300–700 km deep.

The seismic shock waves have their highest level of energy at the focus; energy decreases as the waves spread outwards. The place on the Earth's surface immediately above the focus is called the **epicentre**. It receives the highest amount of energy and so is the most potentially hazardous location.

Seismic waves travel out from the focus. There are three main types:

- **P-waves** (primary) are the fastest and shake the Earth backwards and forwards. These travel the fastest and move through solids and liquids.

- **S-waves** (secondary) are slower and move with a sideways motion, shaking the Earth at right angles to the direction of travel. They cannot move through liquids but do much more damage than P-waves.

■ **Surface waves** – these travel much nearer to the surface and more slowly than P- or S-waves but are more destructive than either. They include L-waves (long waves), which cause the ground to move sideways, and Raleigh waves, which make it move up and down.

Earthquake: Off W Coast of Northern Sumatra, 9.0 MW
Location: Latitude 3.3° N, Longitude 95.8° E
Time: 2004/12/26 00:58:50 GMT

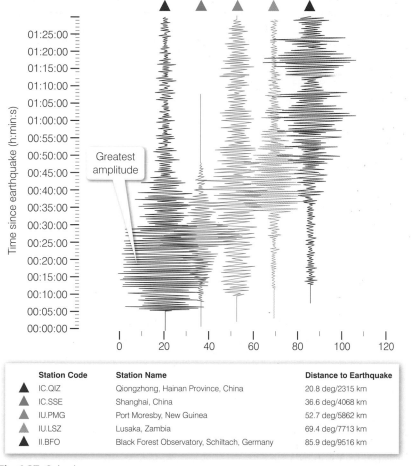

	Station Code	Station Name	Distance to Earthquake
▲	IC.QIZ	Qiongzhong, Hainan Province, China	20.8 deg/2315 km
▲	IC.SSE	Shanghai, China	36.6 deg/4068 km
▲	IU.PMG	Port Moresby, New Guinea	52.7 deg/5862 km
▲	IU.LSZ	Lusaka, Zambia	69.4 deg/7713 km
▲	II.BFO	Black Forest Observatory, Schiltach, Germany	85.9 deg/9516 km

Fig. 1.27 *Seismic waves*

Magnitude and frequency

The **magnitude** of an earthquake is the amount of energy released by the event and is usually measured on the **Richter scale**. This is a logarithmic scale, with each unit representing a 10-fold increase in strength and a 30-fold increase in energy released. Thus, an earthquake measuring 7.6 on the Richter scale (as in Pakistan in 2005) has an amplitude of seismic waves 10 times greater than one measuring 6.6 (as in Iran in 2003). The intensity of an earthquake is measured on the 12-point Mercalli scale which reflects the effects of the event.

The **frequency** of earthquake events varies greatly between seismically active regions (such as the Sunda Trench off the south-west coast of Indonesia) and seismic zones within the shield areas of ancient crust (e.g. Greenland). Seismometers are instruments that measure and record the shock waves created by earthquakes. They locate and measure the size of shock waves and are used in establishing patterns of seismic activity that may help to predict future earthquakes.

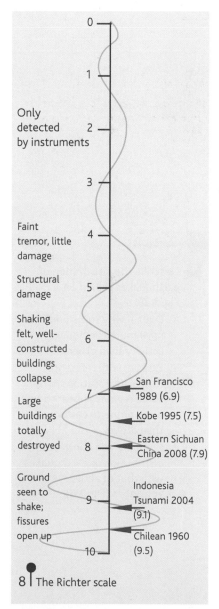

Fig. 1.28 *The Richter scale of earthquake magnitude*

Aftershocks are earthquakes that follow on from the main event and may last for months afterwards. They are generated by the Earth settling back after the disruption of the first displacement. Some aftershocks are significant events in their own right and hamper rescue and rebuilding programmes: the 9.3-magnitude Indonesian earthquake of 2004 (see pp29–33) was followed by a series of aftershocks, one of which was 6.1 in magnitude.

Location	Date	Magnitude
Chile	22 May 1960	9.5
Prince William Sound, Alaska	28 March 1964	9.2
Off west coast of Northern Sumatra	26 December 2004	9.1
Kamchatka	4 November 1952	9.0
Off the coast of Ecuador	31 January 1906	8.8
Rat Islands, Alaska	4 February 1965	8.7
Northern Sumatra, Indonesia	28 March 2005	8.6
Assam, Tibet	15 August 1950	8.6
Andreanof Islands, Alaska	9 March 1957	8.6
Southern Sumatra, Indonesia	12 September 2007	8.5

Table. 1.1 *The 10 biggest earthquakes of all time*

Effects of earthquakes

The effects of earthquakes include a wide range of geomorphological effects from ground shaking to landslides, avalanches and tsunamis. The severity of the effects depends on a range of factors such as the magnitude of the earthquake, the distance from the epicentre and the nature of the underlying geology. Secondary effects include:

■ **Tsunamis** – enormous sea waves generated by disturbances on the sea floor. They are most often triggered by earthquakes and submarine landslides. The most devastating recent example occurred in December 2004 in Indonesia (see Case study later in this section).

■ **Liquefaction** – this is where violent disruption of the ground causes it to become liquid-like when strongly shaken. Such extreme shaking causes increased pore water pressure which reduces the effective stress, and therefore reduces the shear strength of the soil so it fails more easily. Liquefaction can sometimes cause the movement of groundwater. Even though the surface may appear dry, excess water will sometimes come to the surface through cracks, bringing liquefied soil with it, creating 'soil volcanoes'. The liquefied soil may flow and the ground may crack and move, causing damage to surface structures and underground utilities. Buildings can 'sink' as a result of liquefaction. In some cities, such as San Francisco, where development has occurred on reclaimed land in the Bay area, the ground is far more likely to fail due to liquefaction. It is estimated that US$100,000 million worth of damage was caused by this secondary effect of the 1989 earthquake.

Activity

1 Describe the distribution of earthquakes shown on Fig. 1.29.
   a Explain why some areas have more earthquake activity than others.
   b Explain, with reference to specific locations, why some regions appear to be more prone to earthquake than others.
   c Compare and contrast the distribution of earthquakes with that of active volcanoes (Fig. 1.6).

■ **Landslides and avalanches** – where slope failure occurs as a result of ground shaking.

■ **Human impact** – this covers a wide range of effects and depends upon population density and distance from the epicentre. Strong shaking of the ground can cause buildings, roads and bridges to collapse, and disruption to gas, electricity and water supplies. Some human impacts occur immediately around the time of the earthquake event and are termed primary effects. Others develop later, often as a consequence of the primary events, and include fires from ruptured gas mains, scarce or contaminated water supplies and loss of trade from the cessation of industry. These secondary or longer-term effects vary enormously in severity and frequently depend upon the ability of the region to recover, which is in turn linked to economic strength.

Distribution

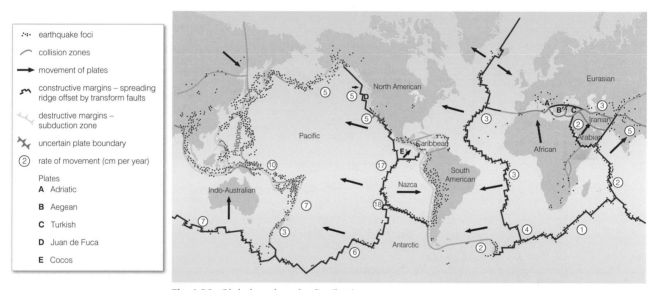

Fig. 1.29 *Global earthquake distribution*

Fig. 1.29 shows that earthquakes are not evenly distributed over the planet but tend to occur in broad, uneven belts. This is because the vast majority of earthquakes are related to plate motion and are, therefore, found around plate boundaries. The most powerful are related to destructive plate motion where the descent of oceanic crust creates frequent shallow- to deep-focus earthquakes. Earthquakes at constructive margins are often submarine and usually distant from human habitation, presenting a relatively minor hazard. At conservative margins, where plates slip past each other, a series of fault lines marks where the crust has failed catastrophically. The San Andreas fault, for instance, is not a single feature but a broad shatter zone of interrelated faults. In addition to this, earthquakes occur in regions that do not appear to be near active plate margins. The earthquakes in China and central Asia occur along extensive lines of weakness related to the collision of India with the Eurasian Plate over 50 million years ago.

Did you know?

The UK experiences many minor earthquakes every year. Old fault lines along areas of relative weakness that have existed for millions of years are regularly reactivated by crustal stress originating elsewhere. The 5.2 magnitude earthquake that hit Market Rasen in Lincolnshire in February 2008 probably resulted from jostling of an enormous block of rock known as the Midlands Microcraton with the softer rocks on either side of it. Pressures generated by the Mid-Atlantic Ridge pushing the Eurasian Plate eastwards were most likely responsible for the build-up and eventual release of pressure.

Earthquake management

Prediction

There is currently no reliable way to accurately predict when an earthquake will occur, though earth scientists are able to indicate where quakes are likely to be found. Methods used to try to detect an imminent earthquake include:

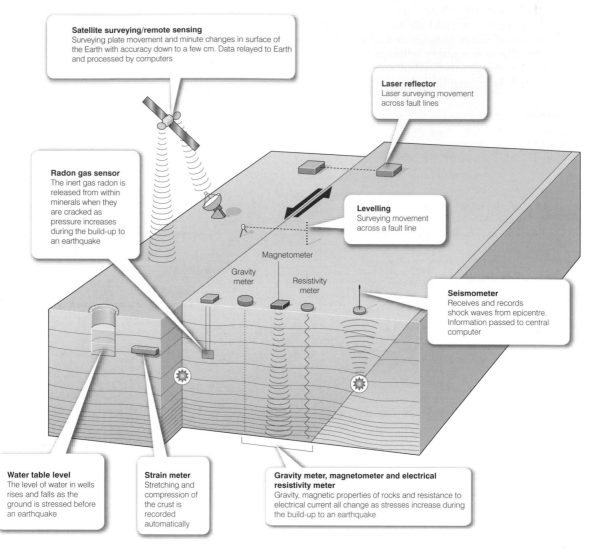

Satellite surveying/remote sensing
Surveying plate movement and minute changes in surface of the Earth with accuracy down to a few cm. Data relayed to Earth and processed by computers

Laser reflector
Laser surveying movement across fault lines

Radon gas sensor
The inert gas radon is released from within minerals when they are cracked as pressure increases during the build-up to an earthquake

Levelling
Surveying movement across a fault line

Magnetometer

Gravity meter

Resistivity meter

Seismometer
Receives and records shock waves from epicentre. Information passed to central computer

Water table level
The level of water in wells rises and falls as the ground is stressed before an earthquake

Strain meter
Stretching and compression of the crust is recorded automatically

Gravity meter, magnetometer and electrical resistivity meter
Gravity, magnetic properties of rocks and resistance to electrical current all change as stresses increase during the build-up to an earthquake

Fig. 1.30 *Earthquake prediction techniques*

■ **Seismic records** – studying patterns of earthquakes and using these to predict the next event. Seismic shock waves are recorded on a seismometer or seismograph. When the Earth shakes, the entire unit shakes with it, except for the mass on the spring which has inertia, and remains in the same place. As the seismograph shakes under the mass, the device records the relative motion between itself and the rest of the instrument, thus recording the ground motion (see Fig. 1.30). In fact, these mechanisms are no longer manual, but instead work by measuring electronic changes produced by the motion of the ground with respect to the mass.

■ **Radon gas emissions** – radon is an inert gas that is released from rocks such as granite at a faster rate when they are fractured by deformation.

- **Ground water** – deformation of the ground can cause water levels to rise (compression) or fall (tension) independently of atmospheric conditions.

- **Remote sensing** – there is some evidence that electromagnetic disturbances in the atmosphere directly above areas about to have an earthquake can be detected.

- **Low-frequency electromagnetic activity** – the Detection of Electro-Magnetic Emissions Transmitted from Earthquake Regions satellite has made observations that show strong correlations between certain types of low-frequency electromagnetic activity and the seismically most active zones on the Earth. A sudden change in the ionospheric electron density and temperature was recorded a week before a 7.1 magnitude earthquake occurred in southern Japan in September 2004.

Even in areas that are very closely monitored using a variety of methods, predictions of earthquakes are not wholly reliable. For example, in the 1980s along the San Andreas fault in California, studies of patterns of earlier events and monitoring of crustal stress led to predictions of an earthquake at the segment of the fault near Parkfield between 1988 and 1992. The predicted earthquake actually happened in 2004. There had seemed to be a more accurate prediction in 1989 when 'foreshocks' were identified and a warning was issued five days before the Loma Prieta or 'World Series' (7.1 magnitude) earthquake occurred. However, this does not mean that all earthquakes follow the same pattern.

In Haicheng, China, in 1975, observations of changes in land elevation, ground water levels and peculiar animal behaviour led to an evacuation warning the day before a 7.3 magnitude earthquake struck. An increase in foreshock activity triggered the evacuation warning that saved many lives. However, there was no warning of the 1976 Tangshan earthquake, magnitude 7.6, which caused around 250,000 fatalities; or the 2008 earthquake of 7.9 magnitude that killed around 69,000 people in eastern Sichuan, China.

Protection

Because earthquakes cannot be prevented, most countries that are prone to them have a range of ways of reducing the potential damage. Typical of these is the approach taken by the Japanese authorities, who focus on three main areas of protection:

1 making buildings/cities more earthquake-resistant

2 raising public awareness about disaster prevention via an education programme

3 improving earthquake prediction.

Better evacuation routes and sites to receive evacuees make cities better able to withstand an earthquake. To reduce the risk of fire after an earthquake, the Japanese government encourages the building of fire-resistant buildings, and has acquired advanced firefighting facilities. In addition, all new buildings must meet strict earthquake-resistance standards. In June 2007 new laws came into effect whereby new properties must now be double-checked to ensure they meet safety regulations even after gaining approval from ministry-licensed auditors. This created financial problems for Japanese construction firms, but was deemed necessary after well-publicised recent cases of falsification of earthquake safety data on dozens of hotels and apartment blocks.

Areas of specified observation have been designated for areas prone to earthquakes, such as Kobe, and/or of special national significance, such as Tokyo, where the Tokai observation area provides a dense network of monitoring equipment offering constant real-time evaluation of

Did you know?

It is important to point out that, although the designs listed in Fig. 1.31 have both strengths and weaknesses, new building design is evolving all the time. For example, the Torre Mayor building in Mexico uses 98 seismic dampeners, specifically incorporated to absorb and dissipate earthquake energy. See more at www.torremayor.com.mx

earthquake risk. In these densely populated areas, a variety of building strategies are used: single-storey buildings are more resistant to ground shaking but also reduce population density, thereby lessening the chance of a high fatality rate. Other buildings are provided with a soft storey at the base, often used as a car park, which is designed to collapse, allowing the upper storeys to be lowered to the ground with a cushioning effect provided by the crumpled remains of the ground level structure.

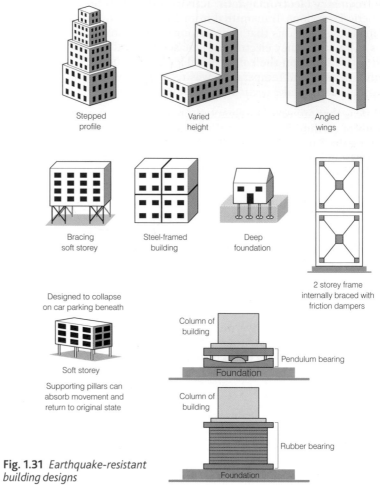

Fig. 1.31 *Earthquake-resistant building designs*

In Tokyo, like many other earthquake-prone cities, citizens are advised to keep some supplies such as water, food and blankets as well as a first-aid kit and emergency tools. A police information sheet ensures people know what to do at each stage of an emergency.

To reduce the risk of fire, 'smart meters' are installed in some countries. These are fed seismic data to allow them to shut down gas supplies automatically in the event of an earthquake.

Land-use planning attempts to identify the areas of a city most at risk and seeks to locate vulnerable land uses such as schools and hospitals away from high-risk areas.

Insurance dedicated to earthquake damage is available but, even in rich countries such as Japan, few people are willing to pay for such specific cover. Only 7 per cent of the population of Kobe, which was badly affected by an earthquake in 1995, had any such insurance. In some ways this reflects a worldwide fatalistic attitude to earthquake risk. Most people do not think anything will happen to them, and the lifestyle or economic attractions that drew them to live in high-risk zones often prove to be greater than the fear of what an earthquake might do. In addition, elected governments are reluctant to take the long-term view and spend the vast sums needed to improve earthquake precautions when the electorate seems to put more value on other services or tax relief. Similarly, many governments pass strict planning laws regarding construction in high-risk areas, but these prove difficult to enforce, especially in poorer countries. In the Turkish earthquake of 1999, many of the buildings that collapsed were shown not to be built to the required safety levels.

Case study

Indonesian tsunami: December 2004

The Great Sumatra-Andaman earthquake of 26 December 2004, which registered 9.1 magnitude, was the third biggest recorded since 1900. It triggered the tsunami responsible for the greatest loss of life in a tectonic event since reliable records began. While large earthquakes are not uncommon, major tsunamis are rare; and the unusual combination of events that led to casualties as far away as South Africa made many people re-evaluate the nature of tectonic hazards.

The nature of the seismic hazard

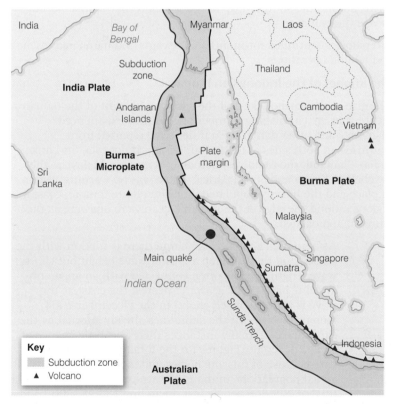

Fig. 1.32 *A tectonic map showing the Indonesian subduction zone*

The Sunda Trench off the south-west coast of Indonesia marks where the Australia Plate (part of the larger Indo-Australian Plate) is subducted under the Burma Plate (part of the larger Eurasian Plate). A 15–20 m slip occurred along 1,600 km of faultline in two phases over a period of around three to four minutes. This might sound relatively small, but it was the longest rupture ever recorded in an earthquake. The epicentre was approximately 160 km offshore in the Indian Ocean, just north of Simeulue island off the western

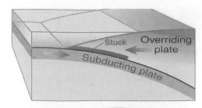

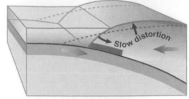

Earthquake starts tsunami

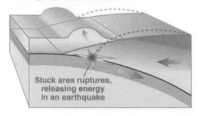

Stuck area ruptures, releasing energy in an earthquake

Fig. 1.33 *Cross-section showing how the Indonesian earthquake of December 2004 was caused*

Did you know?

Tilly Smith, a 10-year-old British tourist on a beach in Thailand at the time of the tsunami, had studied tsunamis in geography at school and recognised the warning signs: the receding ocean and frothing of the water. She alerted her parents and together they warned others on the beach, which was evacuated as people headed to higher land and safety.

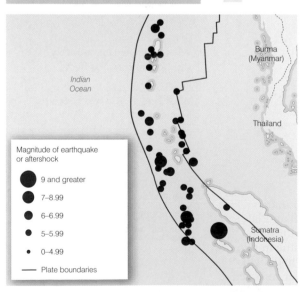

Magnitude of earthquake or aftershock

● 9 and greater

● 7–8.99

● 6–6.99

● 5–5.99

• 0–4.99

— Plate boundaries

Indian Ocean

Burma (Myanmar)

Thailand

Sumatra (Indonesia)

Fig. 1.34 *A map of the main earthquake and aftershocks experienced after the December 2004 Indonesian earthquake*

coast of northern Sumatra, and the focus was 30 km below sea level. The sea floor overlying the thrust fault would have been uplifted by several metres as a result of the earthquake, displacing several billion tonnes of seawater. This generated waves close to the Sumatran shore of over 20 m in height which were able to penetrate some 800 m inland. Waves behave very differently in deep water than in shallow water. In deep ocean water, tsunami waves form at a lower height but travel at great speed (500–1,000 km/hr). In shallow water near coastlines, a tsunami slows down to only tens of kilometres an hour but forms large destructive waves: when waves reached Banda Aceh they had reached 24 m in height, and were reported to have risen to 30 m in some areas when confined by topography.

The trend of the faultline was north/north-west to south/south-east, therefore the tsunami waves travelled mainly in a westerly (towards the Indian Ocean) and easterly direction. Places such as Bangladesh, bordering the Bay of Bengal, were close in distance but avoided major damage because the waves moved more weakly towards the north. In contrast, some distant places such as South Africa, 8,500 km away, experienced a freak high tide of 1.5 m above normal as long as 16 hours after the earthquake. Kerala on the west coast of India was seemingly protected by land, but refraction of the wave forms around the southern tip of India meant that Kerala did not escape the tsunami.

Aftershocks continued for months afterwards and hampered rescue and rebuild operations.

The impact of the Indonesian tsunami

The size of the earthquake and the speed and height of the tsunami meant that an astonishing number of countries experienced casualties and other damage. Fatalities were reported from countries on both sides of the Indian Ocean: Indonesia, Sri Lanka, India, Thailand, the Maldives, Somalia, Myanmar, Malaysia, the Seychelles, Kenya and South Africa. There was no warning system in place and the heavily populated, but often quite remote, coastal regions around the edge of the Indian Ocean were unaware as the tsunami approached.

As tsunamis approach the shore there is friction with the seabed and they develop a greater wave height but shorter wave length. This is often connected with an apparent drawing back of the seawater nearest the coast as the wave is about to reach shore. In the December 2004 tsunami, waves hit the shorelines already affected by the earthquake; in many instances there was little chance of escape or rescue. Figures for the total casualty list still vary because of missing bodies and incomplete records of actual populations in many countries, but the UN listed a total of 229,866 people lost, including 186,983 dead and 42,883 missing. These statistics conceal other tragic facts, such as that relief agencies such as Oxfam reported that as many as one-third of the dead were children who drowned, and that in some coastal areas, four times more women than men were killed as they waited on the beach for returning fishermen or stayed to protect children. The international impact of the event was highlighted by the loss of up to 9,000 foreign tourists in what was the peak holiday travel season. Many were from northern Europe, with Sweden alone reporting over 540 fatalities.

Activity

3 Study the map shown below.

  a Describe the pattern of fatalities caused by the tsunami.

  b Explain how some countries suffered greater losses than others.

  c Suggest how the spread of casualties might have influenced the worldwide public response to the disaster.

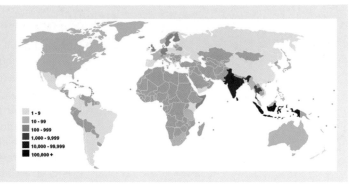

1 - 9
10 - 99
100 - 999
1,000 - 9,999
10,000 - 99,999
100,000 +

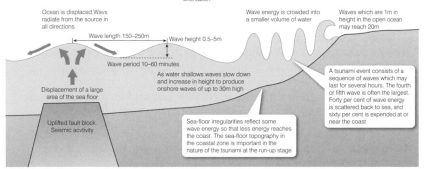

1 Generation of a tsunami in deep ocean (tsunamigenesis)
Tsunami are difficult to detect by ships due to small waveheight and long wavelength

2 Tsunami run-up
Nature of the waves will depend upon:
• cause of the wave, e.g. eruption or earthquake
• distance travelled from source, as energy is lost as they travel
• water depth over route affects energy loss through friction
• offshore topography and coastline orientation

3 Landfall
Depth and destruction will depend upon land uses, population density and any warning given, as well as the physical geography or relief of coastal areas

Ocean is displaced. Wavs radiate from the source in all directions

Wave length 150–250m

Wave height 0.5–5m

Wave period 10–60 minutes

Displacement of a large area of the sea floor

Uplifted fault block. Seismic acvtivity

As water shallows waves slow down and increase in height to produce onshore waves of up to 30m high

Sea-floor irregularities reflect some wave energy so that less energy reaches the coast. The sea-floor topography in the coastal zone is important in the nature of the tsunami at the run-up stage

Wave energy is crowded into a smaller volume of water

Waves which are 1m in height in the open ocean may reach 20m

A tsunami event consists of a sequence of waves which may last for several hours. The fourth or fifth wave is often the largest. Forty per cent of wave energy is scattered back to sea, and sixty per cent is expended at or near the coast

Fig. 1.35 *The steepening of a tsunami as it approaches the coast*

Impact of the Indonesian tsunami

Table 1.2 *Human cost of the Indonesian tsunami*

Country where deaths occurred	Confirmed deaths	Estimated deaths	Injured	Missing	Displaced
Indonesia	130,736	167,736	—	37,063	>500,000
Sri Lanka	35,322	21,411	—	—	516,150
India	12,405	18,045	—	5,640	647,599
Thailand	5,395	8,212	8,457	2,817	7,000
Somalia	78	289	—	—	5,000
Burma (Myanmar)	61	400–600	45	200	3,200
Maldives	82	108	—	26	>15,000
Malaysia	68	75	299	6	—
Tanzania	10	13	—	—	—
Seychelles	3	3	57	—	200
Bangladesh	2	2	—	—	—
South Africa	2	2	—	—	—
Yemen	2	2	—	—	—
Kenya	1	1	2	—	—
Madagascar	—	—	—	—	>1,000
Total	≈184,167	≈230,210	≈125,000	≈45,752	≈1.69 million

Activity

4 The data in Table 1.2 repesent one account of the impact of the Indonesian earthquake of 2004.

a Why are some figures still estimates years after the event?

b Suggest reasons why some categories of information are missing in some countries.

c These figures do not exactly correlate with UN figures issued soon after the event. Why is it often necessary to look at more than one source of information when investigating geographical events on the internet?

Hint: bias (fair or slanted?), date (old or recent?), authority (amateur or professional?), provenance (reliable?).

The impact on coastal fishing communities was particularly devastating, with high losses of income earners as well as boats and fishing gear. In Sri Lanka, fishing is a major economic activity that had, in recent years, begun to generate substantial foreign exchange earnings from export. After the tsunami, more than 60 per cent of the fishing fleet and industrial infrastructure in Sri Lanka's coastal regions was destroyed.

Contamination of drinking water supplies and farm fields by salt water was a significant problem in many coastal regions.

The altered depth of the seabed and disturbance to navigational buoys and even old shipwrecks made shipping in the Malacca Straits more hazardous.

Tourism was badly hit as tourists chose to avoid the area for fear of repetition of the earthquake and/or tsunami hazard. This key source of foreign currency earnings is crucial to the economic well-being of the region, but despite assurances that most tourist infrastructure was undamaged, many stayed away and income fell.

There was an enormous environmental impact with severe damage to ecosystems such as mangroves, coral reefs, forests and coastal wetlands.

Management of the hazard and responses to the event

While tsunami warning systems were in place for the Pacific, the Indian Ocean had no such system, which in part reflects the economic status of the countries that border that ocean. There was no warning of the event, and although it is unlikely that any warning system could have saved people living very close to the epicentre, there is evidence that it could have warned those living further away.

The main response was to attempt to deal with the aftermath of the event. However, the sheer scale of the event, the changed topography, broken communication links and the need to cooperate across national borders, presented significant problems.

The main concern of humanitarian and government agencies was to provide sanitation facilities and fresh drinking water to contain the spread of diseases such as cholera, diphtheria, dysentery, typhoid and hepatitis A and B. The fear of disease from the vast number of bodies led to rapid burial or burning in some instances. This drastic policy may have contributed to the relatively low incidence of disease overall. The World Food Programme provided food aid to more than 1.3 million people affected by the tsunami.

 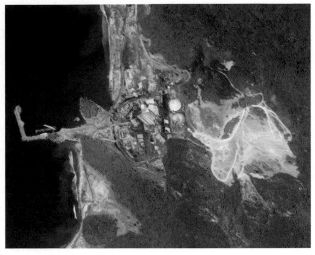

Fig. 1.36 *Before and after the Indian Ocean tsunami*

Worldwide, US$7 billion in aid was promised for damaged regions, mainly from richer countries such as the US ($0.95 billion) and countries more closely connected to the region (Australia, $0.82 billion).

The problems in delivering promised financial help to the stricken nations meant that by March 2005 the Asian Development Bank reported that over US$4 billion in aid promised by governments had not been delivered, with Sri Lanka reporting that it had received no foreign government aid.

Worldwide publicity coupled with the magnitude of the disaster meant that charities were given considerable donations from the public. For example, the British public gave £330 million, a sum greater than that donated by the British government.

Indian Ocean Tsunami Warning System

A significant outcome of the 2004 tsunami was the beginning of greater international cooperation to find a way to help predict similar events in the region. Delegates at a UN conference held in January 2005 in Kobe, Japan, agreed the development of an Indian Ocean Tsunami Warning System. This will provide warning of approaching tsunamis to inhabitants of nations bordering the Indian Ocean, and is intended to lead to an eventual International Early Warning Programme. The warning system comprises 25 seismographic stations relaying information to 26 national tsunami information centres along with three deep-ocean sensors. The system was scheduled to become active in late June 2006, with UNESCO playing a leading role in coordinating international cooperation and funding.

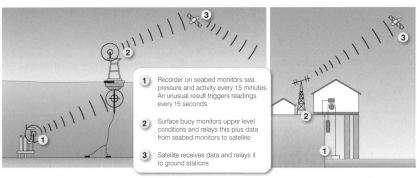

1. Recorder on seabed monitors sea pressure and activity every 15 minutes. An unusual result triggers readings every 15 seconds.
2. Surface buoy monitors upper level conditions and relays this plus data from seabed monitors to satellite
3. Satellite receives data and relays it to ground stations

Fig. 1.37 *The Indian Ocean early warning telemetry system*

Indonesia suffered another, smaller tsunami on 18 July 2006. Around 530 people are now known to have died when a 2 m-high wave hit a 200 km stretch of Java's southern coast after an undersea earthquake. The warning system was not ready in time to predict this event.

Fig. 1.38 *The tectonic setting for the Sichuan earthquake, China 2008*

Case study

Sichuan, China: May 2008

On 12 May 2008, an earthquake of magnitude 7.9 struck 90 km west/north-west of Chengdu, Sichuan, in south-eastern China. This earthquake was China's worst since 1976, when 242,000 people were killed in Tangshan. Sichuan is a predominantly rural area, but although the five main cities of the province were little affected, the death toll rose to nearly 70,000 by June 2008.

The nature of the seismic hazard

The cause of the earthquake was related to stresses resulting from crustal material slowly moving from the high Tibetan Plateau and converging with the strong crust underlying the Sichuan Basin and south-eastern China. Tectonic convergence is related to the northward movement of the India Plate against the Eurasian Plate (velocity *c.* 50 mm/year). The convergence of the two plates is responsible for the Asian highlands and the motion of crustal material to the east away from the uplifted Tibetan Plateau.

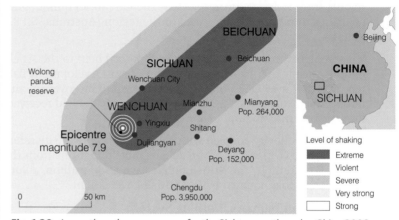

Fig. 1.39 *An earthquake energy map for the Sichuan earthquake, China 2008*

Activity

5 On a copy of the earthquake energy map, analyse the image shown in Fig. 1.39 and answer the questions relating to the source:

a What does this source tell me?

b What can I infer from this source?

c What does this source not tell me about this issue?

d What extra questions do I need the answers to?

Try to answer the questions raised as you work through this case study.

The intense shaking of the ground was devastating in the area near the epicentre. Near Qingchuan, some 1.5 km of surface faulting was observed. Surface cracks and fractures occurred on three mountains in the area, and subsidence and street cracks were observed within the city.

Aftershocks

As of 17 June 2008, more than 12,600 aftershocks have been recorded, including an aftershock on 25 May measuring 5.4 in magnitude in Qingchuan county which killed another eight people, injured 927 and destroyed 400,000 homes.

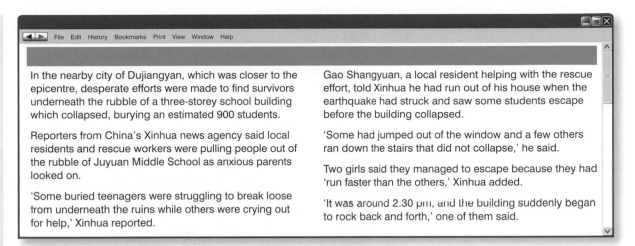

In the nearby city of Dujiangyan, which was closer to the epicentre, desperate efforts were made to find survivors underneath the rubble of a three-storey school building which collapsed, burying an estimated 900 students.

Reporters from China's Xinhua news agency said local residents and rescue workers were pulling people out of the rubble of Juyuan Middle School as anxious parents looked on.

'Some buried teenagers were struggling to break loose from underneath the ruins while others were crying out for help,' Xinhua reported.

Gao Shangyuan, a local resident helping with the rescue effort, told Xinhua he had run out of his house when the earthquake had struck and saw some students escape before the building collapsed.

'Some had jumped out of the window and a few others ran down the stairs that did not collapse,' he said.

Two girls said they managed to escape because they had 'run faster than the others,' Xinhua added.

'It was around 2.30 pm, and the building suddenly began to rock back and forth,' one of them said.

news.bbc.co.uk/1/hi/world/asia-pacific/7396650.stm

The impact of the event

The earthquake was one of the deadliest to strike China in recent years and its effects were felt as far away as Taiwan, Thailand, Vietnam and Bangladesh. Although the area has a long history of tectonic activity, it seems it was not prepared for an event of this magnitude.

- Some 69,185 people were killed, with another 18,467 missing and presumed dead. The number of people reported injured was estimated at 374,171 in the Chengdu-Lixian-Guangyuan area.

- Over 45.5 million people in 10 provinces and regions were affected, with around 15 million people evacuated from their homes. More than 5 million buildings collapsed and 21 million buildings were damaged in Sichuan, leaving over 5 million people homeless. The towns of Beichuan, Dujiangyan, Wuolong and Yingxiu were almost completely destroyed.

- The total estimated economic loss was US$86 billion.

- Landslides and rockfalls damaged or destroyed roads and railways in the Beichuan-Wenchuan area. Coupled with the mountainous terrain, this made it very difficult for rescuers to gain access to the region. At least 700 people were buried by a landslide at Qingchuan, and a train was buried by a landslide near Longnan, Gansu province.

- Landslides also dammed several rivers. This, combined with heavy rainfall, created 34 barrier lakes which potentially threatened about 700,000 people downstream.

- Fracturing of 2,473 dams meant that as the rescue operations wore on, more time had to be devoted to containing the threat of a dam burst.

- Eight schools were toppled in Dujiangyan, killing and trapping school students.

Activity

6 Read through the information above and decide whether the events represent short- or long-term effects of the Sichuan earthquake.

a Draw a Venn diagram to help you classify the short- and long-term effects.

b Why are some events difficult to categorise?

Fig. 1.40 *A bank building in Beichuan after the earthquake*

Table 1.3 *One disaster relief agency's version of the extent of the damage and the state of the relief operations*

Population	Damages
46,200,000 affected	21,000,000 buildings damaged
15,000,000 evacuated	5,000,000 buildings collapsed
10,000,000 living below the poverty line (est.)	8,426 water plants damaged (6,033 repaired)
5,000,000 homeless	7,000 schools destroyed
374,159 injured	53,294 km of roads destroyed
69,172 dead	(52,152 km restored)
17,420 missing	
2,000 orphans	
Relief	**Economy US$**
1,500,000 temporary homes mandated to be built	86,000,000,000 Estimated total economic cost
40,500 under construction	3,370,000,000 China's Disaster Relief Fund
171,600 built	8,000,000 CERF grant
14,100,00 garments	8 years to rebuild
4,820,000 quilts	29,000,000,000 to 43,000,000,000 (est.) required for local economy to recover
2,460,000 tonnes of coal	
1,430,000 tents	
1,150,000 tonnes of fuel oil	

Management of the hazard and responses to the event

The earthquake was not predicted, although the area is prone to earthquakes. Sichuan is a region that has been largely neglected and untouched by China's economic rise. China did not create an adequate seismic design code until after the devastating Tangshan earthquake in 1976, and even then it was difficult to enforce building regulations in outlying areas. Prior to this, most buildings were not built to withstand earthquakes, and these were the most likely to collapse.

The Chinese government responded immediately to the Sichuan earthquake and sent in 80,000 troops to coordinate the rescue efforts. The mountainous terrain and size of the devastated area meant that some soldiers were parachuted into the remotest areas, and essential supplies were dropped from aircraft.

As secondary threats emerged from the growing barrier dams, soldiers used explosives to divert water from Lake Tangjiashan into the quake-damaged town of Beichuan.

It was apparent early on that the scale of the problem was too great for one country to deal with, and that there was a very short time span to protect those at further risk. In response to urgent appeals for aid, by the end of June 2008 the Chinese government had allocated 95 billion yuan (c.US$13.6 billion) to the relief fund, while domestic and foreign donations had yielded over 55 billion yuan in money and materials.

Fig. 1.41 *Dams in the Sichuan area before and after emergency operations to reduce the impact of the earthquake*

Activities

7 To what extent do non-government organisations (NGOs) such as charities play a role in managing disaster relief? What are some of the potential advantages and disadvantages of reliance upon donations from charities?

Use the weblinks given in the Links box to start your investigation based on the Sichuan earthquake.

8 Discuss the following statement using any information from these case studies or your wider reading: 'The ability of any nation to overcome the plate tectonic hazards it faces in the future will depend more upon its wealth than its physical geography.'

Links

Use the following weblinks to research the role of charities in mangaging disaster relief:

www.redcross.org.cn

www.oxfam.org

ocha.unog.ch

In this chapter you will have learnt:

- the Earth has an internal structure divided into the core, mantle and crust

- the crust is divided into mobile plates that are made up of continental and oceanic crust

- plates are moved by convection currents in the upper mantle, which causes them to pull apart (constructive margins), collide (destructive margins and collision margins) or slip past each other (conservative margins)

- the crustal movements at these margins are closely related to volcanic and seismic activity

- hot spots occur even in mid-plate locations above mantle plumes and generate volcanoes

- volcanoes are formed from molten lava and pyroclastics derived from magma chambers in the crust

- volcano shape and style of eruption are related to the composition of the lava

- the types of magma generated in different tectonic settings help to explain the differing nature of volcanoes

- volcanoes are classified as active, dormant or extinct and many have a long history of eruptions

- the management of volcanic hazards is often related to the eruptive nature of the volcano, its proximity to people, as well as the economic wealth and technological expertise of the country it is in

- earthquakes occur due to a sudden release of stress (pressure/tension) in the Earth's crust

- earthquakes are closely related to plate margins but may be found in areas distant from the margins where crustal weaknesses occur

- the magnitude of an earthquake relates to the amount of energy released at the focus; the intensity reflects the effect this energy has on the Earth

- tsunamis are generated by submarine earthquakes in shallow-water environments relatively near the coast

- the impact of seismic hazards is often related to the magnitude and frequency of earthquake(s) experienced in any region

- the management of seismic hazards depends on the economic wealth and technological expertise of the country they occur in and, increasingly, on international cooperation.

Weather and climate and associated hazards

Major climate controls

The nature of the climatic region we inhabit largely determines the key decisions in our lives. It affects what we do and when we do it, the food we eat, the clothes we wear, how we travel, the sports we play and how we spend our leisure time. People in the UK frequently discuss the changeable and seemingly unpredictable **weather** in a manner that bemuses people from other countries in different climatic zones.

Fig. 2.1 *Muir Glacier in 1941 and 2004. Of Alaska's large glaciers 99 per cent are retreating, but a handful, surprisingly, are advancing. Is this evidence for global warming or a natural fluctuation in a glacial cycle?*

AQA Examiner's tip

You must analyse every photograph or diagram in an exam question thoroughly. Make sure you can differentiate between what is definite ('there is an ice-filled valley in A but this is replaced by water in B') and what is speculative ('this is evidence of glacial retreat and may be linked to global warming'). Every photo is deliberately chosen as a stimulus; it is meant to make you think and start to see connections.

Activity

1 Study the two photographs above and decide:
  a what you can definitely see in the photographs
  b what you can infer
  c what you cannot tell
  d what questions you would need to ask before commenting on the link between the photographic evidence of glacial retreat and the possible influence of global warming.

Two thousand scientists, in a hundred countries, engaged in the most elaborate, well-organized scientific collaboration in the history of humankind, have produced long-since a consensus that we will face a string of terrible catastrophes unless we act to prepare ourselves and deal with the underlying causes of global warming.

Al Gore, speech at National Sierra Club Convention, 9 September 2005

Key terms

Weather: the state of the atmosphere at a given time and place.

Climate: the average weather conditions of a place or an area over a period of 30 years or more.

Public awareness of the **climate** and, more particularly, the increasing conviction that accelerated climatic change presents the key challenge to our planet, has helped to make the topic increasingly newsworthy. Understanding of how the atmosphere works has developed significantly over the last 50 years as computer modelling has helped predict weather patterns and suggest future climatic trends. In reality, the complex nature of the interactions between the atmosphere and the planet make long-term prediction difficult.

Weather can be simply defined as the state of the atmosphere on a local level and over a short timescale. It is largely concerned with factors such as the temperature, the amount of sunshine or cloud and the level of rainfall and humidity. Climate refers to average atmospheric conditions over a much longer time frame and over a wider area; it is often defined as the average weather conditions over a 30-year period. As well as the characteristics associated with daily weather reports (including temperature, pressure, wind, humidity and precipitation), it is also concerned with calculating daily, monthly and yearly averages that help to build up global patterns.

■ The structure of the atmosphere

The **atmosphere** is a mixture of gases, with some liquids and solids, held close to the Earth by gravity. While the atmosphere can be said to extend to 1,000 km from the Earth, most of it, in terms of mass, is concentrated in the lowest 16 km, with 50 per cent of it being found below 6 km. The composition of the atmosphere is relatively constant in the lower 10–15 km where most water vapour is held, but across this zone it can vary spatially and over time, causing fluctuations in temperature, pressure and **humidity**. While the main components are nitrogen (78 per cent) and oxygen (21 per cent), the remaining gases are also very important as changes in carbon dioxide and methane are closely linked to global warming and reduction of the ozone layer has been linked to increases in harmful ultraviolet radiation reaching the surface.

Key terms

Atmosphere: the mixture of gases, predominantly nitrogen, oxygen, argon, carbon dioxide and water vapour, that surrounds the Earth.

Humidity: a measure of the amount of moisture in the air. Absolute humidity tells us how much moisture is in the air (g/m³). Relative humidity expresses this amount as a percentage of the maximum that air of a certain temperature could hold.

Table 2.1 *The composition of the atmosphere*

Gas	Percentage by volume	Importance for weather and climate	Other functions/source
Permanent gases: nitrogen	78.09	Mainly passive	Needed for plant growth
oxygen	20.95	Mainly passive	Produced by photosynthesis; reduced by deforestation
Variable gases: water vapour	0.20–4.0	Sources of cloud formation and precipitation, reflects/absorbs incoming radiation keeps global temperatures constant; provides majority of natural 'greenhouse effect'	Essential for life on earth can be stored as ice/snow
carbon dioxide	0.03	Absorbs long-wave radiation from earth and so contributes to 'greenhouse effect'. Its increase due to human activity is a major cause of global warming	Used by plants for photosynthesis; increased by burning fossil fuels and by deforestation
ozone	0.00006	Absorbs incoming ultraviolet radiation	Reduced/destroyed by chlorofluorocarbons (CFCs)
Inert gases: argon	0.93		
helium, neon, krypton	trace		
Non-gaseous: dust	trace	Absorbs/reflects incoming radiation forms condensation nuclei necessary for cloud formation	Volcanic dust, meteoric dust, soil erosion by wind
Pollutants: sulphur dioxide, nitrogen oxide, methane	trace	Affects radiation; causes acid rain (not methane)	Mostly from industry, power stations and car exhausts

While atmospheric pressure decreases rapidly with increasing altitude, changes in temperature are more complex and enable the atmosphere to be conveniently subdivided into four main layers.

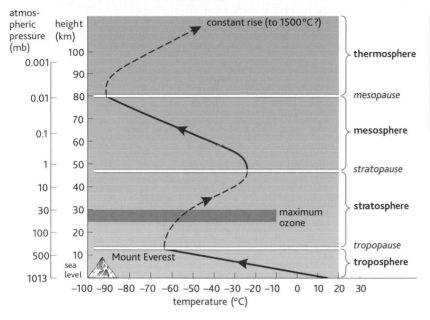

Fig. 2.2 *The structure of the atmosphere*

Troposphere – this zone lies closest to the Earth and is the zone where most weather processes take place. It exhibits the highest temperatures as solar radiation warms the Earth's surface which, in turn, warms the air directly above it by conduction, convection and radiation. However, this effect decreases rapidly with distance away from the surface and air temperature drops by 6.4 °C with every 1,000 m gained in height. Wind speeds also increase with increasing altitude as frictional drag with the surface plays a diminishing role. This is the most unstable layer and contains most water vapour and particulate matter. The end of the troposphere is marked by the **tropopause**, an isothermal layer where temperature remains constant as altitude increases. It marks the upper limit of the zone of weather and climate.

Stratosphere – this zone is characterised by a steady increase in temperature (temperature inversion) as a result of absorption of solar radiation by the ozone layer (*c*.25–30 km). The ozone layer absorbs much incoming ultraviolet (UV) radiation that would be harmful to humans otherwise. The atmosphere is noticeably thinner in this zone as pressure decreases with height and there is a lack of vapour and dust. Wind speeds increase with height towards the **stratopause**, another isothermal layer.

Mesosphere – temperature declines rapidly to *c*.–90 °C in this zone as there is no water vapour or dust to absorb radiation. It is characterised by very strong winds, approaching 3,000 km/hr, and culminates in another isothermal layer called the **mesopause**.

Thermosphere – this is so named because of the increase in temperature resulting from the absorption of UV radiation by atomic oxygen found at this altitude.

■ The atmospheric heat budget

By far the greatest amount of energy coming into the atmosphere is from insolation i.e. incoming short-wave solar radiation. Some energy derives

Key terms

Troposphere: one of the four thermal layers of the atmosphere, extending from the surface to a maximum of 16 km.

Activity

2 a Make a large copy of the structure of the atmosphere diagram shown in Fig. 2.2 (you can only draw – no writing).

b For each of the four sections of the atmosphere choose three key facts or figures to annotate your diagram.

c Give your partner a 'guided tour' of your diagram, explaining why your chosen facts are important in understanding the atmosphere. Your partner's task is to try to add at least one more thing that would have made your tour more complete.

d Repeat this sequence but exchange roles. How would you improve their version?

from the Earth (e.g. volcanic sources) and energy released from large urban areas. The amount of energy received from the sun is determined by:

■ **The solar constant** – varies slightly and affects longer-term climate rather than short-term weather variations.

■ **The distance from the sun** – the eccentric orbit of the Earth around the sun can cause up to a 6 per cent variation in the solar constant.

■ **The altitude of the sun in the sky** – the equator receives more energy as solar radiation strikes the Earth head-on, whereas at 60°N or 60°S it approaches at a more oblique angle, giving twice the area to heat up and more atmosphere to pass through.

■ **The length of day and night** – the 23.5° tilt of the Earth means that regions near the poles (north of 66.5°N or south of 66.5°S) receive no insolation at certain times of the year.

Not all radiation that approaches the planet actually reaches the surface. Absorption of incoming radiation by ozone, water vapour, carbon dioxide, ice particles and dust reduces the amount reaching the Earth, as does reflection from clouds (up to 90 per cent reaches the surface with thick cloud cover). Some radiation is also reflected back from the surface itself, for example from snowfields (up to 80 per cent is absorbed). The ratio between the amount of incoming and reflected radiation is called the **albedo**, with the figure for the Earth being around 4 per cent. If we add the amount of incoming radiation absorbed by gases, reflected by water and clouds, scattered in the atmosphere and reflected by the surface, then only around 24 per cent directly reaches the surface, with another 21 per cent arriving from diffuse radiation. This short-wave radiation is converted to heat energy and warms the surface of the Earth which, in turn, radiates long-wave (infrared radiation) back into the atmosphere. While incoming short-wave radiation penetrates the atmosphere relatively easily, long-wave radiation is largely trapped. Although some 6 per cent is lost to space, water vapour, carbon dioxide and other greenhouse gases absorb 94 per cent of this terrestrial radiation, retaining heat in the atmosphere (the greenhouse effect).

Key terms

Albedo: the reflectivity of the Earth's surface.

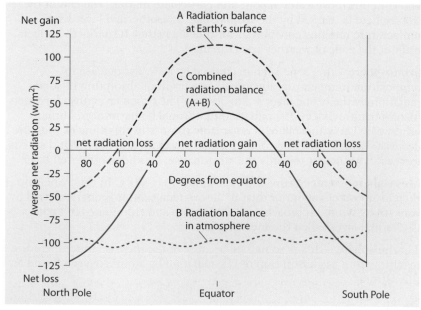

Fig. 2.3 *The heat budget*

The Earth is not heating up or cooling down as there is a balance between incoming insolation and outgoing terrestrial radiation. However, there are significant spatial differences within the atmosphere. This is because although energy is lost through radiation throughout the atmosphere, the net gain in radiation is not experienced in the polar regions where there is a net deficit between incoming and outgoing radiation (negative heat balance). In contrast, at lower latitudes (the areas between 40°N and 35°S) there is a net surplus of radiation (positive heat balance). This imbalance is rectified by major heat transfers:

■ **Horizontal heat transfers** – around 80 per cent of the heat transferred away from the tropics is carried by winds including the **jet stream**, **hurricanes** and depressions. The remaining 20 per cent is transferred by the movement of warmer ocean currents polewards.

■ **Vertical heat transfers** – energy is transferred from the warmer surface of the Earth vertically by radiation, conduction and convection. Latent heat (the additional energy required to change the state of a substance) also helps to transfer energy. For example, additional energy is required to change water (e.g. the ocean) into vapour, which may then rise until it condenses as water droplets much higher in the atmosphere (e.g. as cloud). **Precipitation** (vapour back into water) will release energy and warm the upper atmosphere. This vertical motion not only transfers heat from areas of positive heat budget (such as the equatorial surface) by cooling as the air masses rise, but is linked with the horizontal movements at higher altitude which help to transfer warm air towards the poles.

Factors affecting insolation and the heating of the atmosphere

The radiation balance can also be altered by regional differences in the proportions of land and sea (e.g. by reflecting radiation to different degrees), by altitude, wind direction and even by aspect on a local scale. Diurnal variations between day and night, as well as seasonal differences, can also produce imbalances over time.

Long-term effects

Altitude of land – insolation heats the surface of the land which warms the air above it by conduction and convection. As higher land is further away from the main heat source, the main mass of land heated by insolation, it is relatively cooler. Furthermore, the density of air decreases with height, adding to the cooling effect as particles are further apart. The average rate at which air temperature drops with increasing altitude is 6.4 °C per 1,000 m (the **environmental lapse rate**). If temperature increases with height there is said to be a **temperature inversion**.

Altitude of the sun – at higher latitudes the heat energy from the sun has to pass through more atmosphere which increases loss to absorption and scattering. Near the equator it passes through less atmosphere and so heats the land more.

Proportion of land and sea – land and sea react differently to insolation. While land heats up more quickly, the relatively lower density of the sea means that it heats more slowly and its transparent nature means that heat penetrates to a greater depth (up to 10 m). Water has a greater specific heat capacity than land which means it requires twice as much energy to raise 1 kg of water by 1 °C than it does for land. Consequently, in the summer land heats up more rapidly but the oceans will retain their heat for longer, acting as thermal reservoirs that cool less rapidly in winter. As a result, coastal regions have a smaller temperature range than inland areas.

Prevailing winds – as the temperature of an **air mass** is determined by the area over which it originated and the surfaces over which it has passed, winds blowing in from the sea tend to be cooler in summer and warmer in winter than winds that have travelled over land.

Key terms

Jet stream: an intense thermal wind in the upper troposphere.

Hurricane: a tropical cyclonic storm having winds that exceed 120 km/hr.

Precipitation: the conversion and transfer of moisture in the atmosphere to the land and sea. It includes all forms of rain, snow, frost, hail and dew.

Environmental lapse rate (ELR): the normal decline of temperature with altitude, usually about 6.4 °C per 1,000 m.

Air mass: a large body of air with relatively similar temperature and humidity characteristics.

Ocean currents – surface ocean currents are caused by the influence of prevailing winds blowing across the sea. Warmer ocean currents migrate polewards, away from the equator, and colder currents replace them by moving towards the equator in a circulatory motion known as a gyre. Put simply, these currents move clockwise in the northern hemisphere and anticlockwise in the southern hemisphere, and warm or cool the air temperatures in coastal areas. The effect of the rotation of the Earth is to cause water in the oceans to move westwards. This general 'piling up' of water towards the west is counteracted by return flows such as the narrow, fast-moving Gulf Stream. The north-eastwards movement of these warmer waters is a key factor in raising the air temperatures that help to deliver the mild winters and cool summers of the British Isles. Elsewhere, cooler currents such as the Labrador Current off the northeast coast of North America can reduce summer temperatures if winds blow cooler air on shore.

The ocean conveyor belt – the transfer of cold water at depth from the polar regions to the equator is like a conveyor belt. As water cools at the poles the formation of ice leaves the remaining water saltier and denser. The denser water starts to sink through the water column. It sweeps the Antarctic continent at a depth of around 4 km and then into the major ocean basins. These motions are reciprocated by the movement of the less salty and, therefore, less dense surface currents which move north towards the North Atlantic from the Indian and Pacific Oceans, see Fig. 2.4. These warmer waters have a significant effect on the temperature of the North Atlantic as they give up about one-third of the energy they had previously stored from the sun.

The North Atlantic is warmer than the North Pacific, which gives rise to higher rates of evaporation and higher salinity. The sinking of the saltier, denser water in the North Atlantic drives the conveyor belt and, over time, the cold current feeds into the Pacific where it mixes with the warmer, less dense water found there, reducing the overall density level of the water.

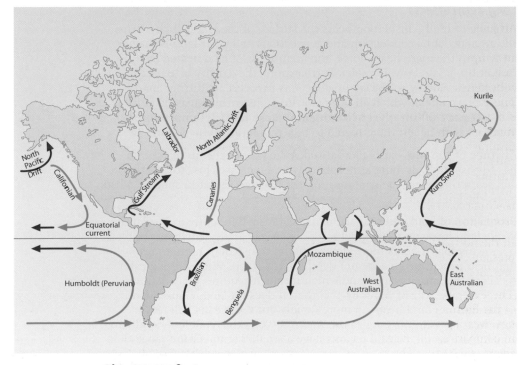

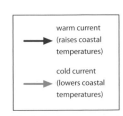

warm current
(raises coastal temperatures)

cold current
(lowers coastal temperatures)

Fig. 2.4 *Ocean currents related to winds*

Short-term factors

Seasonal changes – insolation is distributed equally in each hemisphere at the spring (around 21 March) and autumn (around 22 September) equinoxes, i.e. when the sun is overhead at the equator. In the summer (around 21 June) and winter (around 22 December) solstices, when the sun is directly overhead at the tropics, maximum insolation is experienced in the northern hemisphere and the southern hemisphere, respectively.

Diurnal range – the length of day and night varies in all locations away from the equator. At the poles, there is no insolation during winter months when the regions are tilted away from the sun, and there are up to 24 hours of daylight in the summer when they are tilted towards the sun.

Local

Aspect – slopes alter the angle at which the sun strikes the Earth. South-facing slopes in the northern hemisphere receive more of the available insolation than north-facing slopes which might remain in shadow for far longer. This has a significant impact on agriculture, e.g. south-facing slopes have enough sun to grow crops and a longer growing season than north-facing ones that receive less sunshine and have fewer frost-free days.

Cloud cover – clouds may reflect, absorb and scatter incoming radiation but can also act as an 'insulating blanket', keeping heat in the lower atmosphere. Therefore, when there are clear days temperatures rise more rapidly as more insolation reaches the surface, but when there are clear nights they fall quickly as terrestrial radiation reduces the surface temperature. Conversely, when it is cloudy temperatures do not rise as high or fall as low.

Urbanisation – urban surfaces tend to absorb more heat than natural surfaces during the day and radiate more at night, creating urban heat island effects.

The general atmospheric circulation

Horizontal air movement is known as wind, though, as we have seen, air can move vertically as well. Winds are caused by differences in air pressure, with air moving from areas of higher pressure to areas of lower pressure. Variations in air pressure occur because of changes in temperature and altitude. Air pressure decreases with increasing height from the surface of the Earth. When air temperature increases it becomes warmer, less dense and will rise, creating an area of low pressure beneath. The reverse is also true; as air cools it becomes denser, sinks and creates an area of higher pressure. Air pressure is shown on maps by isobars, lines joining places of equal air pressure. As pressure diminishes with height, readings taken at any altitude above sea level must be normalised (reduced) to sea-level values to remove the effect of altitude. Where pressure changes rapidly across an area there is said to be a strong **pressure gradient** and isobars will be shown close together. This is similar to the way that contours are drawn close together to represent a steep slope on a map.

In the northern hemisphere, winds blow anticlockwise **into** a low-pressure zone and clockwise outwards, **away from** a centre of high pressure, as a result of the effects of the **Coriolis force** and friction.

The Coriolis force is the deflection of winds because of the rotation of the Earth. The whole surface of the Earth rotates every 24 hours; however, a point near the pole traces a very small circle and moves slowly in comparison to one at the equator which travels over 40,000 km at a speed of 470 m/s. The result is that winds are deflected to the right in the northern hemisphere and to the left in the southern hemisphere with the amount of deflection increasing towards the pole. In the mid-latitudes and in the mid-troposphere the pressure gradient and the Coriolis force are in balance and winds do not move from high to low pressure so much as between them, parallel to the isobars. This is called the **geostrophic wind**. At lower altitudes, friction induced by contact with the surface of the Earth reduces the effect of the Coriolis force. This frictional force is less pronounced over the smoother surface of the oceans. At higher altitudes, frictional forces are reduced and the effect of the pressure gradient dominates, with winds travelling from high to low pressure across the isobars.

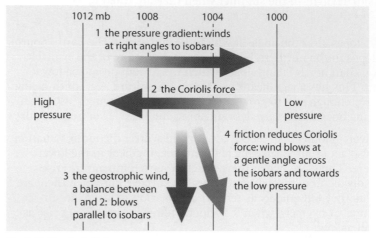

Fig. 2.5 *The Coriolis force*

Key terms

Inter-tropical convergence zone (ITCZ): a result of the heating of part of the Earth's surface, caused by the concentrated insolation from the overhead sun. This leads to heating of the air lying on that surface. The heated air becomes less dense and rises. This draws in cooler air that flows across the surface to replace the rising air. Air streams are drawn in from both north and south of the equator and they meet in the area from which the air is rising.

Anticyclone: a high-pressure system.

Activity

4 a Describe the causes of the ITCZ and the weather associated with it.

   b Why does the location of the ITCZ change with the seasons?

Differences between the amounts of solar radiation received at the equator and polar regions would seem to indicate a simple movement of air towards the poles from the warm tropical regions. However, the rotation of the Earth complicates this as we have already seen, and as early as 1735 George Hadley developed a model to explain atmospheric circulation in the tropics. Today we refer to Hadley cells on either side of the equator to describe the intense insolation which causes warm air to rise by convection. The low pressure created drags the trade winds in towards the equator where they are forced to rise. The zone where they meet is called the **inter-tropical convergence zone (ITCZ)**, a kind of meteorological equator which shifts north and south during the year. In reality it is not a continuous belt of cloud and rain, and some prefer the term inter-tropical discontinuity (ITD). The hot air rising in the ITCZ becomes cooler with altitude, and condensation leads to dense cumulonimbus cloud formation and heavy rainfall. At high altitude the air cools to the point that the density differences that caused it to rise initially are reduced and it moves polewards. In the northern hemisphere the air circulates as upper westerly winds as it is deflected by the Coriolis force. At around 30°N and 30°S the cooler air starts to sink back towards the surface. As it descends it helps to create higher pressure beneath, and because it warms at the same time, it is capable of holding more moisture. These areas of higher pressure and clear skies are called subtropical **anticyclones**. At ground level some of the air returns towards the equator as trade winds, which are also deflected by Coriolis force, to the right in the northern hemisphere and to the left in the southern hemisphere. The winds at the ITCZ are very light and the area is known as the doldrums.

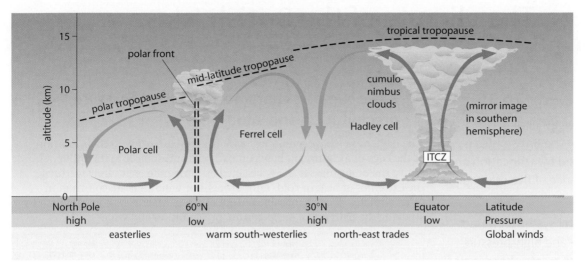

Fig. 2.6 *Tri-cellular model of atmospheric circulation in the northern hemisphere. The cross-section shows the location of the ITCZ and the circulation within the tropopause*

The remaining air travels towards the poles, forming the south-westerlies in the northern hemisphere. These winds pick up moisture when they cross the ocean and are responsible for bringing a lot of wet weather. When these winds meet the colder air of the Arctic at the polar **front** they rise up to form the boundary between the Ferrel cells and Polar cells, the latter extending to the poles. This area of warmer, unstable air is closely associated with mid-latitude depressions and heavy rainfall.

The position of the ITCZ changes according to the seasons. The sun is located directly above the Tropic of Cancer on 21 June, which pulls the ITCZ north of the equator, whereas on 21 December it is over the Tropic of Capricorn and the ITCZ moves into the southern hemisphere.

Key terms

Front: a boundary between a warm air mass and a cold air mass, resulting in frontal rainfall.

The climate of the British Isles

In this section you will learn:

- how the weather and climate of the British Isles is determined by its location and the influence of five major air masses

- how frontal systems interact with low- and high-pressure systems to create changeable weather patterns

- to compare and contrast the causes and effects of storm events.

Activity

1 Fig. 2.7 shows the temperatures (winter and summer), rainfall and wind-speed maps for the British Isles.

   a Describe the pattern of temperature variation over the British Isles for:
   summer (July)
   winter (January).

   b Suggest reasons for the variations in temperature across the maps and over time.

   c Describe the pattern of rainfall and wind-speed variation over the British Isles with reference to:
   latitude
   longitude
   altitude
   distance from the coast.

Basic climatic characteristics: temperature, precipitation and wind

The British Isles have a uniquely variable climate owing to their location at the edge of a continent, between two seas and subject to the influences of five major air masses. It is classified as temperate as it rarely features the extremes of heat or cold, rain, drought or wind that are common in other climates. The changeable nature of the climate is best exemplified by studying the patterns of temperature, precipitation and wind.

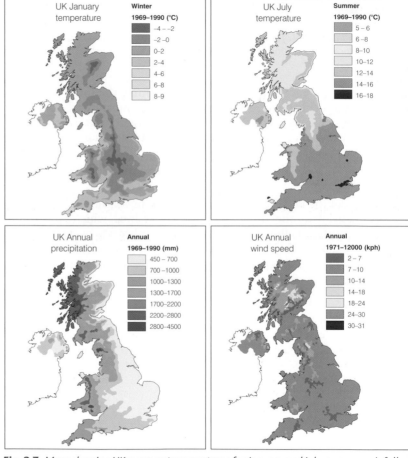

Fig. 2.7 *Maps showing UK average temperatures for January and July, average rainfall and average wind speed*

Temperature

The maps showing temperature variations over the British Isles (Fig. 2.7) for January and July show the influences of the key factors in determining the temperature. The temperatures in July are seen to reach a peak in southern regions and generally decrease towards the north. This is largely explained by the reduction in the amount of insolation at higher latitudes. There is also a tendency for places further from the sea to experience higher summer temperatures, on average, as the cooler temperatures of the seas have less influence inland. In larger land masses this is referred to as continentality, but it is evident even in a relatively small country like the UK.

In addition, the altitude of some areas means they are cooler, as temperatures drop by around 6.4 °C for every 1,000 m gained in height. The Southern Uplands of Scotland are seen to be cooler than the more northerly central valley area between Glasgow and Edinburgh. The effects of prevailing winds and ocean currents are evident in the higher winter temperatures seen in the land bordering the Irish Sea, as warmer air associated with the North Atlantic Drift brings warmer Gulf Stream waters to the western areas of the British Isles. The impact of these warmer waters and winds is seen more clearly during the winter and Fig. 2.7 clearly shows that the north-to-south rise in the temperature gradient is heavily skewed towards the south-west, with Anglesey in North Wales being considerably warmer than the Wash in East Anglia.

Precipitation

Fig. 2.7 shows that the west and north of the British Isles show greatest precipitation. The south and, in particular, the east of the country, receive less. The key factors affecting this pattern are the direction of the prevailing winds and altitude. Relief or orographic rainfall occurs when moist air that has been travelling over the sea is forced to rise over upland areas. As it rises and cools, the air reaches dew point (the point where air becomes saturated), condensation occurs and this may lead to rainfall. In areas such as Keswick in the Lake District, rainfall averages around 1,500 mm/year, whereas at Tynemouth at a similar latitude on the east coast only 660 mm of rain falls. This is due to the rain shadow effect, as air that has lost a lot of moisture over the hills (e.g. of the Lake District and Pennines) will sink back down, warm up and, as warmer air can hold more moisture, is less likely to generate rainfall.

Britain is particularly affected by frontal rainfall. This occurs when warmer air is pushed up over a wedge of colder air where two air masses meet in a frontal system. This commonly occurs where cooler polar air undercuts warmer tropical air. As the warmer air is forced to rise it cools, the water vapour condenses and forms cloud and rain over a wide area. This is especially the case in winter months when successive low-pressure systems, or depressions, approach the western shores of Britain.

Some rainfall is due to extreme localised heating of the ground, especially during the summer months. This convectional rainfall occurs when the air above the ground is warmed, becomes less dense than the surrounding air, and rises. When it reaches dew point, condensation occurs and clouds develop, but very strong heating produces highly unstable air which continues to rise, creating cumulonimbus clouds. Within these tower masses of vapour, large water droplets can form which, when they are big enough to overcome the updraughts of rising air, will generate sudden, intense rainfall, especially in the south and east of Britain.

Wind

The map in Fig. 2.8 shows average wind speed over the UK and the inset shows average wind direction. The most common direction from which the wind blows in England is the south-west, but this is variable from day to day and winds from other directions are quite frequent, with long spells of easterly or north-easterly winds not unusual in winter. The strongest winds are found in the west and north of the country as these areas face the prevailing south-westerly winds. There is also a clear link with altitude and many upland areas experience very high wind speeds as the air has fewer obstructions to its progress. In general, wind speed increases with height, with the strongest winds being observed over the summits of hills and mountains, e.g. places such as Great Dun Fell in Cumbria (857 m) can average over 114 days of gale a year. A gale is defined as wind speed of over 63 km/hr for a duration of at least 10 minutes.

Air masses affecting the British Isles

The unique situation of the UK at the edge of continental Europe and affected by five major air masses helps to explain the complex weather experienced in this region. Air masses are largely uniform bodies of air that have remained over an area for a period of several days and have assumed the temperature and humidity characteristics of these places. These are known as source regions and include the high-pressure belts of the subtropics such as the Azores and the Sahara, and can be classified by their **latitude**, e.g. polar (*P*) or tropical (*T*) and the **surface** they develop over, e.g. maritime (*m*) or continental (*c*). Latitude determines temperature and surface affects humidity/moisture.

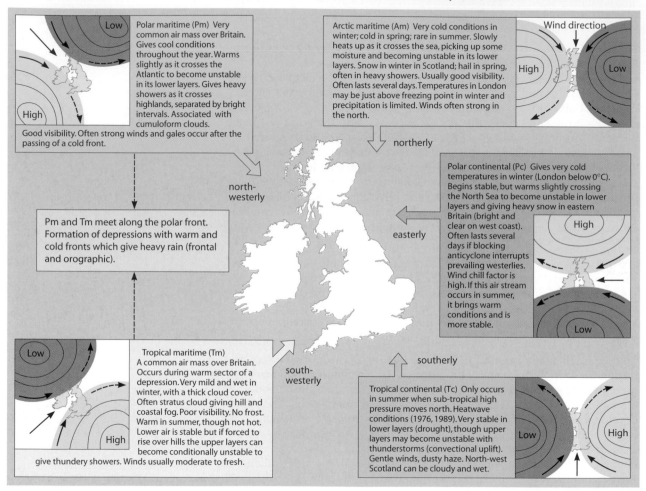

Fig. 2.8 *The five major air-masses affecting the British Isles*

The nature of the five major air masses that affect the British Isles is determined by the temperature and humidity characteristics of their source regions and the area they travel over to reach these islands. Polar air moving south warms on its journey and tropical air from the Azores will cool. These conditions depend upon variable conditions in the source regions, routes, surfaces, seasons and the vertical profile of the air mass.

Fronts develop where two or more air masses meet. Because they have different densities and temperatures, they do not necessarily immediately mix. Where less dense warm air is forced to override denser, colder air, a warm front will develop. If colder air is forced to cut under a warmer air mass, a cold front will occur. Both types of front result in air rising, cooling and condensing to form cloud and precipitation. These fronts extend for hundreds of kilometres and have a gentle gradient, e.g. the polar front occurs where the tropical maritime (*Tm*) air meets polar maritime (*Pm*) air out over the Atlantic Ocean. The mixture of warm, moist *Tm* air by cooler *Pm* air produces mid-latitude depressions that regularly deliver cloud and rain to the west of Britain.

■ Depressions: origin, nature and associated weather changes

Depressions affecting the British Isles predominantly begin in the North Atlantic where *Tm* air from the south and *Pm* air from the north meet. The warmer, less dense air rises and is removed by strong upper atmosphere winds (jet stream). This rising, twisting vortex of air produces a wave form at sea level in the polar front which becomes more exaggerated as the wave form develops, eventually becoming a depression. The **embryonic** depression usually moves in a north-easterly direction guided by the polar jet stream. As the low-pressure zone develops in a **mature depression**, the cold front advances more rapidly and more warm air is forced to rise. The resultant decrease in pressure creates a more pronounced pressure gradient and winds blow in towards the centre with increasing strength. The effect of the Coriolis force means that these anticlockwise-travelling winds come from the south-west. The warm rising air cools at altitude until dew point is reached and condensation produces cloud. As uplift continues, cloud thickens and precipitation is initiated along the warm front.

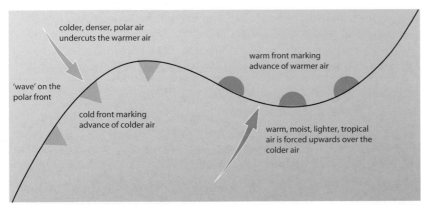

Fig. 2.9 *The life-cycle of a depression*

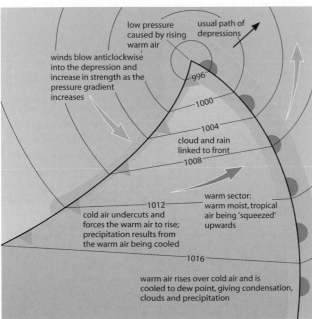

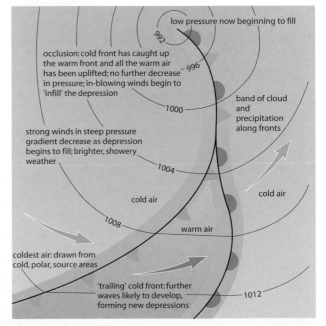

Instability: unstable atmospheric conditions leading to rising air frequently associated with cloud formation and precipitation.

Stability: balanced pressure conditions; air is unable to rise above a low level, associated with dry conditions and little cloud cover.

As the warm front passes, there is a rise in temperature within the warm sector. This warmer air, which is not being forced to rise as rapidly as the air at the warm front, produces less cloud and precipitation is less likely. Some clear skies may develop before the more rapidly advancing cold front undercuts the warm sector and forces warm air to rise. The steeper gradient of this front often creates thicker cloud and more intense precipitation than at the warm front as **instability** forms towering cumulonimbus clouds.

In time the more rapidly travelling cold front catches up with the warm front and undercuts it to raise the warm sector air above the surface. This **occlusion front** occurs first in the centre of the low and extends outwards. As the colder air begins to infill the depression there is less uplift of air. Reduction in condensation means there is eventually less cloud and precipitation. Winds weaken in strength as the pressure gradient is reduced and, in time, the low-pressure zone is eradicated.

Activity

2 Study the synoptic chart in Fig. 2.10.

a Describe the weather at places A and B shown on the map.

b Explain why they experienced different weather despite being less than 200 km apart.

c Describe and explain the weather that place A is likely to experience as the mature depression passes over the British Isles from west to east over approximately 12 hours. Refer to:

  i changes in wind speed and direction, cloud cover and precipitation

  ii how these changes are related to the sectors of the depression.

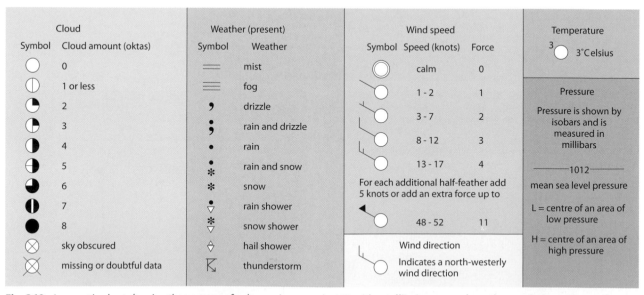

Fig. 2.10 *A synoptic chart showing the passage of a depression over the UK, with satellite images and weather symbols*

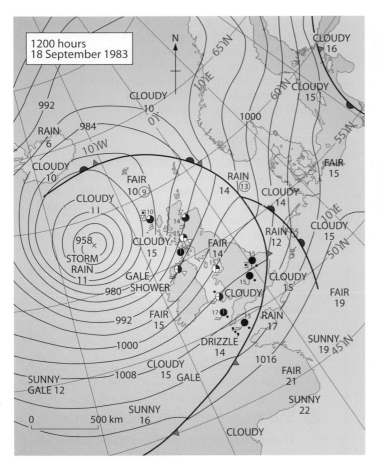

■ Anticyclones: origin, nature and associated weather conditions in winter and summer

As depressions represent the passage of low-pressure air, so anticyclones are characterised by high pressure. The air that descends from the upper atmosphere is cooler, drier and denser than the air at ground level. As it descends it warms and can easily hold on to the moisture it has retained, leading to limited condensation and reduced precipitation. This stable air can cover several thousand kilometres and presents a gentle pressure gradient, with weak winds blowing clockwise out from the centre of the high-pressure area. The passage of anticyclones tends to be much slower than is the case with depressions. The weather associated with days or even weeks of settled weather depends upon the season.

Summer anticyclones

These are characterised by clear skies which allow for the maximum amount of insolation, producing temperatures of over 25 °C during the daytime. Significant radiation loss by night can lead to short-lived temperature inversion and the formation of dew and mist which are usually clear quickly during the morning. The differences in the rate of warming of the sea and land can produce land and sea breezes, while onshore winds, especially along the east coast of Britain, can create **advection fog** (locally known as sea fret or haar). This occurs when relatively warm air moves across a cooler surface such as the North Sea. Major anticyclones over Britain and north-west Europe can deflect low-

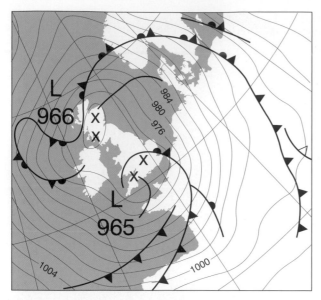

Fig. 2.11 *A high-pressure zone affecting the British Isles*

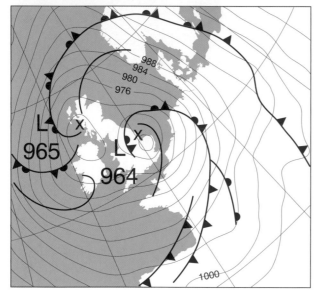

Fig. 2.12 *A low-pressure zone affecting the British Isles*

pressure areas to the north, reducing the likelihood of cooler, wetter air in summer. If this persists it might create the conditions for a heatwave, particularly if the air has originated from a tropical continental (*Tc*) region such as North Africa. Sustained, intense heating when the air has quite high humidity can give rise to localised uplift and thunderstorms.

Winter anticyclones

When the sun is low in the sky during the winter months and less insolation is available to warm the British Isles, the clear skies of a high-pressure zone mean that the moderate gain of warmth during the day (< 5 °C) can be more than offset by rapid loss of heat at night (< 0 °C). Surface cooling frequently gives rise to **radiation fog** and frost which may persist because of the weak sunshine during the day. When dry, cold *Pc* air from central Asia and Europe moves west across the North Sea it can bring heavy snowfall to eastern regions. Where blocking anticyclonic cells exist for days over Europe, the deflection of warmer depressions away from Britain can bring dry, freezing conditions. These can produce a low, sharp temperature inversion leading to persistent cloud, sometimes known as anticyclonic gloom.

■ Storm events: their occurrence, their impact and the responses to them

While the British Isles have a relatively moderate climate, extreme weather events do occur and the 1987 storm that devastated large areas of southern England was, perhaps, the most significant storm event since 'The Great Storm' of 1703. The storm of 1987 is also memorable for the way that it evaded normal weather prediction services as it became unexpectedly severe during the night of 16 October. The depression resulted from the mixing of very warm *Tc* air from North Africa and colder air from the North Atlantic and, in part, originated during the aftermath of Hurricane Floyd along the east coast of the US. It was tracked across the Bay of Biscay but on the evening of 15 October it suddenly began to intensify and veered northwards towards the mouth of the English Channel. The deepening of the depression to 958 mb was believed to be the result of a very strong jet stream and warming over the Bay of Biscay which, together, probably released latent heat energy, warming the air even more relative to its surroundings and reducing pressure even further. The centre of the low pressure tracked over Britain for six hours during the night, with extreme wind speeds being experienced along the south coast. For example, winds of 115 km/hr gusting to 141 km/hr were recorded at Dover.

The effect of the storm was lessened by the fact that fewer people were about at night, but the severity of the storm meant that:

- 16 people died

- many houses suffered damage to roofs and walls

- over 15m trees were uprooted

- a ferry was blown ashore

- communications were broken, with trees falling on railway tracks and roads, as well as damaging power lines leading to power blackouts.

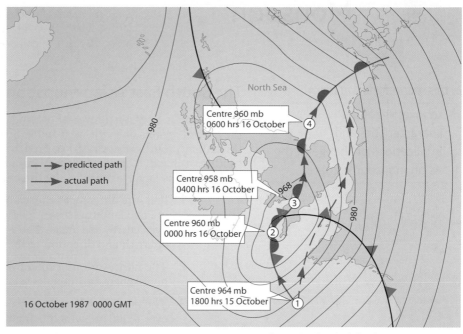

Fig. 2.13 *The track for the storm of 1987*

Prediction

The storm of 1987 gained an almost mythical status as the storm that proved the weather forecasters wrong. In reality this 'once in a hundred years' event was very difficult to predict because of the speed of the drop in pressure. An evening weather forecast by the Met Office correctly described the current state of the depression and its likely path. The veering of the storm to a more northerly track was noticed too late to allow for effective warning. Most people were asleep and would have been unaware of additional warnings had they been available.

Responses

- The clear-up took considerable time with emergency crews being drafted in from northern regions where damage had been more slight.

- Losses from the storm totalled £1.4 billion in the UK alone, where around 70 per cent of the damage occurred. One in six households in south-eastern England submitted insurance claims.

- A Met Office enquiry recommended that observational coverage of the atmosphere over the ocean to the south and west of the UK was improved by increasing the quality and quantity of observations along with refinements made to the computer models used in forecasting.

- A significant clean-up of fallen trees was criticised by ecologists for removing damaged broad leaf trees that would have recovered with time.

Activity

3 Fig. 2.13 shows the track for the storm of 1987. Using the information from this graph:

  a Draw a simple line graph to show how air pressure (y-axis) changed over 15 and 16 October 1987.

  b Annotate the graph to explain the variations in the pressure recorded.

  c Suggest why:

    i prediction was not likely to adequately prepare the public in the south-east of Britain

    ii a more typical storm track over north-west Scotland would be potentially less damaging.

Monsoon

In this section you will learn:

■ to investigate the characteristics and implications of change to the Asian monsoon climate.

The South East Asian monsoon

A monsoon is a seasonal reversal of wind direction which is found along the coastal regions of south-west India, Sri Lanka, Bangladesh, Burma (Myanmar), south-western Africa, French Guiana and north-east and south-east Brazil. The South East Asian monsoon is the most significant of these and is largely controlled by three factors:

1 Pressure differences caused by extreme heating and cooling of large land masses in relation to the smaller heat changes over nearby sea areas. These differences determine the strength and direction of the associated winds.

2 The northward movement of the ITCZ during the northern hemisphere summer.

3 The mountain barrier of the Himalayas (with many peaks over 8,000 m), which is high enough to influence the general atmospheric circulation in the region.

The summer or south-west monsoon

During the summer, the shift of the overhead sun towards the Tropic of Cancer pulls the ITCZ northwards with it. The intense heating of the region of northern India, Pakistan and central Asia produces a large area of low pressure. The monsoon climate tends to have its highest temperature just before the rainy period. Once the rainy period starts, clouds block incoming solar radiation to reduce monthly temperatures. As this warm air rises it draws in warm, moist equatorial maritime and tropical maritime air from the Indian Ocean to the south. As this air crosses the geographical equator it is diverted to the north-east as a result of the Coriolis force.

As it approaches the Western Ghats of India, and later the southern slopes of the Himalayas, it delivers substantial amounts of precipitation, e.g. Cherrapunji has 13,000 mm of rain in four months. Rainfall comes from the orographic and convectional uplift of moist air as it approaches the Himalayas. At the same time, the release of latent heat on condensation creates more instability and triggers more uplift. The full extent of the summer monsoon is best illustrated by the average arrival dates in different parts of the region. While in Sri Lanka in the south the monsoon usually arrives by 10 May, it will not generally appear as far north as Pakistan until 5 July.

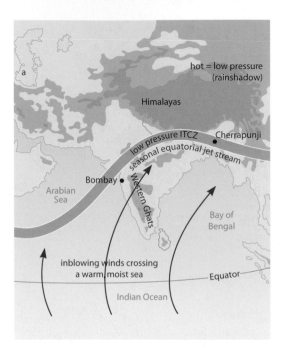

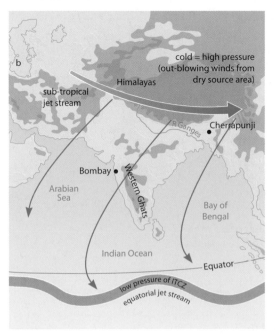

Fig. 2.14 *Summer and winter monsoons over India*

The winter or north-east monsoon

During the winter, as the overhead sun moves southwards, the ITCZ and equatorial jet stream move to a position just south of the equator. The low pressure over central Asia is replaced by a large area of high pressure as the region cools dramatically. Subsidence from the Siberian High suppresses uplift. The air masses that dominate this period are dry (*Tc, Pc*) as their source area is semi-desert, and they become drier still on crossing it. As the air mass sinks towards the Ganges plain it warms further, making precipitation less likely. Bombay receives less than 100 mm of rain during these eight months, as opposed to 2,000 mm during the four months of the summer monsoon. It usually takes around 11 weeks, from 1 September to 15 November, for the winter monsoon to travel from the north to the south of India.

The average figures for monsoon intensity and arrival times hide a wide variation. In 1987 north-west India suffered a failure of the wet monsoon while Bangladesh experienced high rainfall and subsequent flooding. More recent evidence suggests that the central Asian monsoon might well be intensifying, probably as a result of global warming.

Tropical revolving storms

Tropical revolving storms are slow-moving systems of extreme low pressure. They are known as hurricanes, tropical **cyclones** and typhoons according to their location.

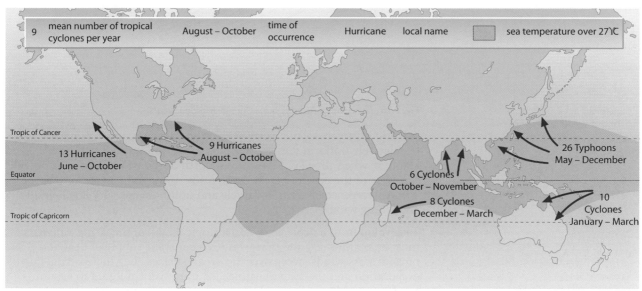

Fig. 2.15 *The global location of tropical storms*

The common factors in the genesis and development of tropical revolving storms include:

- Very warm tropical oceans (sea temperatures > 26 °C), where the ocean has been warmed to a depth of at least 50 m. This is necessary to ensure sustained heating over a wide area which, in turn, provides a heat source to create a large mass of warm, unstable air.

- They occur most commonly in autumn as this is when sea temperatures are at their highest, temperatures having built up over the summer.

- They are found within the trade wind belt as this is where the surface winds warm as they blow towards the equator.

■ They are usually located between latitudes 5–20° north or south of the equator.

■ They travel westwards on unpredictable courses.

■ On landfall they move towards the nearest poles and are another way in which surplus energy is transferred away from the tropics, along with vertical displacement through the atmosphere.

■ Away from their ocean heat source they rapidly lose power and eventually become storms before they are classified as depressions.

Hurricanes

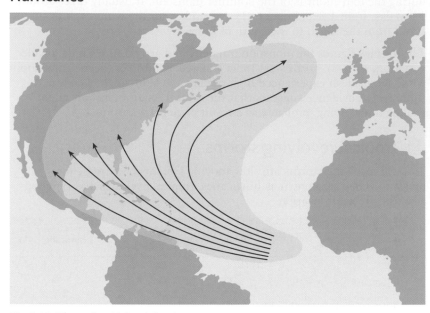

Fig. 2.16 *The paths of Atlantic hurricanes over recent years*

Atlantic hurricanes can be over 600 km in diameter and are characterised by relatively uniform temperatures, pressure and humidity. By late summer, when the ITCZ has moved north of the equator, heating of wide expanses of the ocean to great depth leads to warming of the air above. The convergence of air at low levels and uplift creates very low pressure and strong winds.

To develop from a depression into a tropical storm, the rising air currents must be maintained and that requires a constant supply of heat and moisture. As winds sweep over the ocean surface they increase the rate of evaporation and the latent heat needed to transform liquid to vapour is transferred to the rising air. Later, as the moist air rises it will condense to form cloud and heavy rainfall, releasing latent heat and further driving the storm. Once the storm has developed to a mature stage, a central eye develops with a diameter of 30–50 km. This is an area of subsiding air, with light winds, clear skies and anomalous high temperatures. The descending air increases instability by warming and serves to increase the intensity of the storm. Wind speeds of 160–300 km/hr are not uncommon, with larger hurricanes creating widespread damage and significant threat to life. Associated with the high winds are storm surges which are broad waves of water pushed ahead of the storm and exacerbated by the rise in sea level allowed by the intense low pressure beneath the hurricane. Intense rainfall leading to run-off on land feeds swollen rivers which may have their outlet to the sea impeded by the inundation of seawater driven by storm surges into estuaries and other low-lying land.

Once hurricanes reach land they rapidly decline in terms of energy. This is because the storm loses its source of heat and moisture over land and increased friction slows it down. If it carries on moving away from the tropics over the sea, the increasingly cooler waters beneath restrict the amount of energy available and ultimately reduce the pressure differences. The average lifespan of a tropical cyclone is 7–14 days.

Category	Wind speed km/hr	Storm surge (m)
5	(≥250)	(>5.5)
4	(210–249)	(4.0–5.5)
3	(178–209)	(2.7–3.7)
2	(154–177)	(1.8–2.4)
1	(119–153)	(1.2–1.5)
Additional classifications		
Tropical storm	(63–117)	(0–0.9)
Tropical depression	(0–62)	(0)

Fig. 2.17 *The Saffir-Simpson hurricane scale*

Case study

Hurricane Katrina: August 2005

During late August 2005 Hurricane Katrina made landfall around New Orleans, Louisiana, US. The cost of the damage it caused was estimated at over US$80 billion and around 1,830 deaths were related to the hurricane and subsequent flooding. The embryonic storm formed over the Bahamas on 23 August. It strengthened and by the early morning of the 24th it was given tropical storm status and named Katrina. It moved westwards and just before it made its first landfall over Florida on the morning of the 25th, it reached hurricane strength. Although the storm weakened over land as a result of the removal of the ocean heat source, it intensified to hurricane force once over the warm waters of the Gulf of Mexico, rapidly growing from a Category 3 to a Category 5 hurricane on the Saffir-Simson Hurricane scale. The very warm waters of the Loop Current, an offshoot of the Gulf Stream, helped to reduce pressure and raise wind speeds further. By the 27th, the storm had reached Category 3 intensity, and it reached Category 5 status on the morning of the 28th, reaching its peak strength at 1.00pm. With maximum sustained winds of 280 km/hr and a minimum central pressure of 902 mb it became the fourth most intense Atlantic hurricane of all time. Later on in the same hurricane season it was surpassed by Hurricanes Rita and Wilma, but its track over one of the most densely populated parts of the Gulf coast of the US made it the most damaging.

Although Katrina had reduced in intensity when it made landfall near Buras, Louisiana on 29 August it was still a powerful Category 3 hurricane. Moving northwards it made its final landfall on the Louisiana/Mississippi border, still as a Category 3 hurricane. The rapid weakening of Katrina during the last 18 hours or so leading

Activities

1 As you read through the case study on Hurricane Katrina try to note down the 20 key facts or events that you believe were most responsible for the level of damage caused.

2 Using a timeline, place these events in chronological order with the mainly physical factors above the line and the mainly human factors below the timeline. Where events occur over several days use an open or closed bracket to encompass the time involved.

3 Mark on the diagram:
   a when the storm created most damage
   b any of the agencies that tried to deal with the impact of the storm
   c the time when you feel that the management was most lacking.

Key terms

Eyewall: tropical storms will typically have an eye approximately 30–65 km across, usually situated in the geometric centre of the storm. With some storms, particularly when wind speeds exceed 185 km/ph, the diameter of the eye narrows to less than 20km and a cycle of eyewall replacement may begin. Outer rain bands intensify into a ring of thunderstorms to become an outer eyewall, which steadily rob the original eyewall and eventually leave a larger, more stable eye. The temporary weakening of the storm during eyewall replacement is followed by a gradual strengthening once replacement is complete.

Table 2.2 *Death toll for Hurricane Katrina by state*

Alabama	2
Florida	14
Georgia	2
Kentucky	1
Louisiana	1,577
Mississippi	238
Ohio	2
Total	1,836
Missing	705

up to the first Gulf landfall appears to have been primarily due to internal structural changes, specifically the deterioration of the inner **eyewall** without the complete formation of a new outer eyewall. As the hurricane moved inland over southern and central Mississippi it rapidly lost intensity, to become a Category 1 later on the 29th as the heat source of the warm ocean was removed, and became a tropical depression by the 30th.

Impact

On 28 August the mayor of New Orleans ordered a general evacuation of the city as Katrina approached with a storm surge predicted to add up to 8 m to the level of the sea. The anticipated impact was exacerbated by the low-lying level of land along the Gulf coast of the US and, in particular, in New Orleans, parts of which lie below sea level.

Along the coast, winds of up to 217 km/hr helped to create storm surges of 3–8.2 m above normal levels. Rainfall of 200–250 mm fell on much of the eastern part of the Louisiana state while peaks of up to 380 mm were recorded.

The most dramatic impact of the storm surge on the low-lying coast of west and central Mississippi was to inundate it to between 10–20 km inland, particularly along bays and rivers where the water could gain easiest access. The combination of a large storm surge, torrential rain and the already swollen state of the Mississippi river meant that the already artificially enhanced levees of the river broke in over 50 places, flooding roughly 80 per cent of the greater New Orleans area. Breaches in the floodwalls defending the city were later estimated to be responsible for up to 70 per cent of the flooding. The damage to life and property meant that the estimated final cost rose to 1,836 deaths and over US$81 billion, making it the most costly hurricane ever to hit the US and the deadliest in terms of loss of life since 1928.

Claims for disaster relief suggested that the damage area extended to some 233,000 km², approaching the area of the UK.

- Over 3 million people had no electricity.

- Thirty oil platforms were damaged in the Gulf and nine oil refineries were closed, reducing production by up to 25 per cent.

- Around 5,300 km² of forest lands were destroyed in Mississippi, a loss of US$5 billion for the forestry industry.

- The estimated total economic impact in Louisiana and Mississippi could exceed US$150 billion.

Over 1 million people left the damaged region, with places as far away as Chicago receiving an additional 6,000 people. By January 2006, although some 200,000 people had returned to New Orleans, it was still less than half its pre-Katrina population.

Many homeowners in the damaged areas have found that the high cost of damage to the region has resulted in revised insurance premiums becoming unaffordable or insurance cover unavailable.

Environmental impacts

- Many areas suffered devastating coastal erosion, e.g. Dauphin Island was breached by the storm and much of the sand was transported across the barrier island into the Mississippi Sound. This had the effect of shifting the island landwards

- The US Geological Survey has estimated that 560 km² of land in the Chandeleur Islands became submerged by the impact of Hurricanes Katrina and, later that autumn, Rita.

- Breeding grounds for marine mammals, migrating birds, turtles and fish were lost as about 20 per cent of the marshlands were inundated by seawater.

- During the clean-up, flood waters from New Orleans polluted with raw sewage, heavy metals, pesticides and nearly 25m litres of oil were pumped into Lake Pontchartrain.

Management

The National Response Plan indicates that initial response to a disaster is a local government responsibility until its resources are exhausted, then appeal may be made to county, state and then federal level. It appears that many of the problems that arose developed from inadequate planning and communications systems.

- FEMA made some preparations that ranged from delivering supplies to providing refrigerated trucks to deal with the anticipated dead.

- Volunteers assisted people emerging from New Orleans as the storm made landfall, and continued for more than six months after the storm.

- Of the 60,000 people stranded in New Orleans, the Coast Guard rescued more than 33,500.

- Approximately 58,000 National Guard personnel were activated to deal with the storm's aftermath, with troops coming from all 50 states.

- The Secretary of the Department of Homeland Security took over the federal, state and local operations officially on 30 August 2005, and in September Congress authorised a total of US$62.3 billion in aid. The president and former presidents combined to appeal for contributions for victims.

- Although FEMA aimed to provide housing to more than 700,000 people, only one-fifth of the trailers requested in Orleans Parish have been supplied, resulting in an enormous housing shortage in the city of New Orleans. FEMA has also paid for the temporary hotel costs of 12,000 individuals and families, but by July 2006 there were still about 100,000 people living in 37,745 FEMA-provided trailers.

- By one month after the storm, evacuees had been registered in all 50 states. Most evacuees had stayed within 400 km of their homes, but as many as 60,000 households moved over 1,200 km away.

- International aid was significant, with over 70 countries pledging monetary donations or other assistance, e.g. Kuwait donated US$500m. A host of charities led by the American Red Cross raised over US$4.25 billion from voluntary contributions.

Within days of the start of the event, public criticism regarding the government's role in preparing for, and responding to, the hurricane grew. Media images of stranded families and reports of deaths from thirst, exhaustion, as well as looting fuelled the criticism. Many believed that poorer, black people living as they did on the lower-lying land had been most affected by the flooding that followed the bursting of the levees. Their perceived lower status was seen by some as a contributory factor influencing the slow response of a white-dominated government.

Activity

4 As you read through the case study on Cyclone Nargis repeat the timeline exercise you carried out for Hurricane Katrina.

Case study

Cyclone Nargis, Burma (Myanmar): May 2008

Cyclone Nargis hit Burma (Myanmar) on 2 May 2008 along the low-lying southern coastline of the Irrawady Delta. It devastated Irrawady, Yagon and Bago and also affected Mon and Kayin divisions/states. In its wake Nargis left a death toll of over 130,000 and damages estimated at US$4 billion.

In late April 2008, an area of low pressure developed in the Bay of Bengal about 1,150 km east-south-east of Chennai, India. The Indian Meteorological Department (IMD) and the Joint Typhoon Warning Centre (JTWC) began to track its progress:

■ **27.04.2008** The IMD classified the system as a deepening depression, while the JTWC classified it as Tropical Cyclone 01B. It tracked slowly north-north-west to a position 550 km east of Chennai.

■ **28.04.2008** The IMD upgraded the status of the system to cyclonic storm. Cyclonic Storm Nargis was located about 550 km east of Chennai. The storm built during the day and was reclassified as a severe cyclonic storm with a discernible concentric eye feature.

■ **29.04.2008** Nargis became a very severe cyclonic storm with winds of 160 km/hr and appeared to be heading for a landfall in Bangladesh or south-eastern India, but as the subsidence of drier air weakened and disorganised the storm it veered north-eastwards, and later on the 29th, it strengthened yet again.

■ **01.05.2008** The cyclone headed east and rapidly intensified as the presence of an upper level trough helped to further reduce pressure.

■ **02.05.2008** As it approached Burma, Nargis became a Category 4 storm exhibiting peak winds of 215 km/hr. Later on the same day Nargis made landfall at peak strength on the south-east coast of Burma in the Irrawaddy Division. As it passed over Burma it gradually weakened and turned to the north-east, close to Yangon, still producing winds of up to 130 km/hr.

■ **03.05.2008** The IMD issued a last warning on the storm and it quickly weakened as it approached the Burma–Thailand border.

Impact

The impact of the cyclone was immense, affecting several countries, with Burma the worst hit. It is now recognised as Burma's worst ever natural disaster and the worst Asian cyclone since 1991. The storm surge met with little resistance as it tracked eastwards over the low-lying Irrawaddy Delta, much of which is only just above sea level. With a total population of about 3.5 million people and a population density of 100/km^2, the Irrawaddy Delta is one of the most densely populated parts of the country. Most of the casualties were killed by a 3.5m wall of water that was accompanied by 190 km/hr winds.

Burma

■ An estimated 1.5 million people were affected, with early figures indicating at least 138,000 people reported dead or missing. The scale of the devastation and the difficulty of collecting accurate information in such conditions means that most of the missing are now presumed to be fatalities.

■ Damage to the economy of at least US$4 billion was reported.

■ About 450,000 homes were destroyed and around 350,000 were damaged.

■ Approximately 600,000 hectares of agricultural land were damaged and 60 per cent of farming implements were lost.

■ Roughly 75 per cent of hospitals and clinics in the area were destroyed or badly damaged.

■ Diarrhoea, dysentery and skin infections afflicted some survivors crammed into monasteries, schools and other buildings after arriving in towns already under pressure before the cyclone.

■ Bogale is one of the southernmost towns in the Irrawaddy Delta. Initial reports said that 95 per cent of houses in the low-lying town had been washed away and that about 10,000 people had been killed by the huge sea surge.

■ Labutta, a small town in the south-west of the delta region, was devastated, with early estimates of about 50 per cent of houses being destroyed.

Sri Lanka

Among other countries affected by this storm, Sri Lanka experienced heavy rainfall which led to widespread flooding and landsliding. Ratnapura and Kegalle were the most affected regions, and as many as 3,000 families may have been displaced, with up to 35,000 people affected in all, though with relatively few fatalities.

Management

The aftermath of the storm was characterised by a lack of information and an apparent state of confusion for most of the aid

and rescue organisations. Since 1962 the country has been ruled by a military junta with a poor human rights record and limited contact with many countries in the outside world. An apparent refusal to accept the scale of the problem and a reluctance to accept outside help or even allow aid teams into the country appeared to exacerbate the situation.

Aid agencies reported being impeded by official obstruction as well as the physical difficulties of moving around in a devastated area where roads were flooded or washed away. Increasingly, private supplies of food and aid were being sent into the devastated areas and left with highly respected buddhist monks to distribute rather than the mistrusted government agencies. As pledges of foreign aid began to build up owing to restricted access, Burma's ruling generals were increasingly criticised and the Association of South East Asian Nations (ASEAN) intervened to help facilitate exchanges between Burma's ruling junta and international donors.

ASEAN Secretary General Surin Pitsuwan reported that the UN, ASEAN and the Burmese government needed at least US$1 billion to deal with 'a tragedy of immense proportions'. This was to cover the most urgent needs (food, agriculture and housing) for the next three years.

Donor countries pledged nearly US$50m in aid at a joint UN and ASEAN donor conference in Yangon on 25 May. However, the junta refused to allow ships from France and the US to enter Burmese ports as they were perceived to be critical of the regime.

In July 2008, the UN appealed for more than US$300m in additional aid to cope with the effects of the cyclone which had destroyed 42 per cent of Burma's food stocks.

Activity

5 Compare the timelines for Hurricane Katrina and Cyclone Nargis. Choose one of the statements below to discuss in an extended piece of writing.

    a 'The impact of tropical storms Katrina and Nargis was beyond the scope of governments to manage effectively.'

    b 'The differing levels of damage between Hurricane Katrina and Cyclone Nargis reflect the relative economic power of the two countries.'

Climate on a local scale – urban climates

In this section you will learn:

- how the growth of cities has affected the nature of the atmosphere and how these changes impact upon everyday life.

While we may consider climatic regions, by definition, to be large areas characterised by similar climatic conditions that persist over time, in reality they are not entirely homogeneous or constant. The term microclimate involves the study of climate on a much smaller scale. It might focus on the differences between the conditions existing deep in a valley as opposed to a nearby hillside, or on a large urban area in contrast to its rural hinterland.

Microclimates and, in particular, temperatures in urban areas may differ from surrounding countryside for several key reasons:

1 Buildings tend to absorb more heat than natural surfaces and can store heat.

2 They create additional particulate matter in the form of dust and other condensation nucleii which, in turn, affects the amount of sunlight that reaches the city.

3 They affect the amount of moisture in the air.

4 Tall buildings, in particular, affect the way air moves across the city, so wind velocity is reduced.

Temperatures: the urban heat island effect

The artificial materials used in buildings and roads, such as concrete, brick and tarmac, have a higher thermal capacity than natural surfaces, enabling them to store heat during the day and release it slowly at night when the air around is cooling as a result of radiation loss. While such stored heat is the main contributor to urban–rural temperature differences, further heating of the air is provided by central heating, traffic fumes, factories, power stations and even people themselves.

Temperature differences between urban and rural areas can vary from 0.6 °C (day) to 3–4 °C (night). The latter variation is helped by reduced radiation loss from cities because of additional cloud and dust cover. Differences in summer can be up to 5 °C and even in winter the city can be up to 2 °C warmer. Over a year London is about 1.3 °C warmer than surrounding rural areas. This is called the **urban heat island effect** and is most noticeable when wind speeds are low as they tend to reduce temperature differences by dispersing the build-up of warm air or cloud cover. Reduction in the amount of sunlight received is determined by the amount of cloud cover and the season. In winter, when a weak, low sun struggles to warm the atmosphere in the UK, cloud and dust can absorb up to 50 per cent of available insolation.

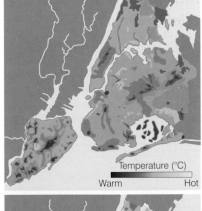

Temperature (°C)
Warm   Hot

Vegetation
Dense   Sparse

Fig. 2.18 *New York heat island*

Activity

1 Compare the temperature and vegetation maps for New York, US in Fig. 2.18.
  a Describe and suggest reasons for temperature variation across the city, e.g. from the centre to the edge.
  b Suggest how and why temperature might vary according to vegetation distribution.

■ Precipitation: frequency and intensity, fogs, thunderstorms, and their relationship to urban form and processes

Because the air is usually warmer in cities it can hold more moisture and relative humidity levels are up to 6 per cent lower. In addition there is less vegetation which, in conjunction with the lack of exposed bodies of water means **evapotranspiration** is reduced. In terms of cloud cover, cities appear to experience more frequent and thicker cloud cover than surrounding rural areas, mainly as a result of convection currents above urban areas and the higher concentration of cloud-forming nucleii in the air. The higher levels of cloud cover help to explain why precipitation is, on average, around 5–15 per cent greater in terms of the mean annual totals in large urban areas. In addition, and partly as a result of the urban heat island effect, monthly rainfall is about 28 per cent higher 30–60 km downwind of cities, when compared with upwind precipitation.

Added to this effect is the up to 400 per cent greater incidence of hailstorms, as strong heating, particularly in summer, gives rise to very strong convection, and a 25 per cent greater chance of thunderstorms. If precipitation falls as snow, it tends to lie on the ground for less time as the higher temperatures lead to more rapid snow melt than in the countryside.

Fogs and mists tend to be thicker and persist for longer over cities, particularly when anticyclonic conditions mean winds are too weak to blow them away. This is largely because the greater concentration of condensation nucleii encourages condensation and enables mist/fog to form more easily.

■ Air quality: particulate pollution, photochemical smog and pollution-reduction policies

The quality of air in urban areas is invariably poorer than in the surrounding countryside. Cities may experience up to seven times more dust particles in their local atmospheres than rural areas. The dominant factor influencing this is the burning of fossil fuels, particularly from vehicular and industrial sources. The gaseous and solid impurities resulting from these fossil fuels mean that, in comparison with rural areas, urban areas might have as much as:

- ■ 200 times more sulphur dioxide (SO_2)
- ■ 10 times more nitrogen dioxide (NO_2)
- ■ 10 times more hydrocarbons
- ■ twice as much CO_2.

These human-made pollutants tend to increase cloud cover and precipitation and cause photochemical smog, all of which give higher temperatures and reduce sunlight. In particular, SO_2 and NO_2 are major contributors to the acid rain problem.

Pollutants can be classified as either primary or secondary. Usually, primary pollutants are substances directly emitted from a process, such as the carbon monoxide gas from a vehicle exhaust or sulphur dioxide from factories. Secondary pollutants form in the air when primary pollutants react or interact, e.g. ground-level ozone – one of the many secondary pollutants that make up photochemical smog. Some pollutants can be both primary and secondary.

Key terms

Evapotranspiration: the combined losses of moisture through evaporation and transpiration.

The structure of the urban climatic dome

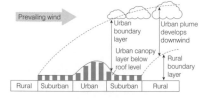

The morphology of the urban heat island

DT_{u-r} is the urban heat island intensity, i.e. the temperature difference between the peak and the rural air

Airflow modified by a single building

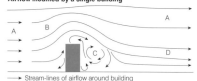

→ Stream-lines of airflow around building

Fig. 2.19 *Effects of the urban climate zone*

Major primary pollutants produced by human activity include:

■ **Sulphur oxides (SO$_x$),** especially SO$_2$, are emitted from the burning of coal and oil.

■ **Nitrogen oxides (NO$_x$),** especially NO$_2$, are emitted from high-temperature combustion. They can be seen as the brown haze dome above or plume downwind of cities.

■ **Carbon monoxide (CO)** is a colourless, odourless, non-irritating but very poisonous gas. It is a product of incomplete combustion of fuel such as natural gas, coal or wood. Vehicular exhaust is a major source of carbon monoxide.

■ **Carbon dioxide (CO$_2$)** is a greenhouse gas emitted from combustion.

■ **Volatile organic compounds (VOCs),** such as hydrocarbon fuel vapours and solvents.

■ **Particulate matter (PM)** is measured as smoke and dust. PM$_{10}$ is the fraction of suspended particles $10\,\mu$m (micrometres) in diameter and smaller that will enter the nasal cavity. Ultra-fine particles at or below PM$_{2.5}$ are smaller than $2.5\,\mu$m and will enter the bronchial tubes and lungs causing respiratory problems.

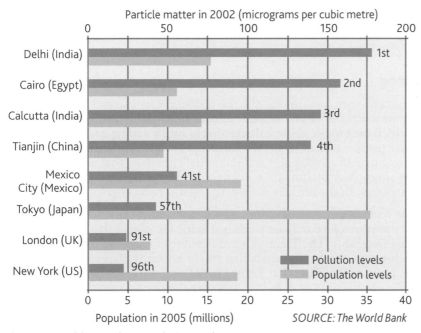

Fig. 2.20 *World particulate population graph*

■ Activity

2 Study Table 2.3 overleaf (actual and estimated growth of the top 15 largest cities in the world) with Fig. 2.20 (world particulate pollution graph).

Comment on the distribution of the world's most polluted cities and the likely effects of urban growth in the near future upon pollution issues in these cities.

Table 2.3 *World cities with populations over 5 million (1980–2015). Populations shown in millions*

City	Country	1980	2005	2015
Tokyo	Japan	28.5	35.2	35.5
Bombay	India	8.7	18.2	21.9
Mexico City	Mexico	13.0	19.4	21.6
São Paulo	Brazil	12.1	18.3	20.5
New York	US	15.6	18.7	19.9
Delhi	India	5.6	15.0	18.6
Shanghai	China	7.6	14.5	17.2
Calcutta	India	9.0	14.3	17.0
Dhaka	Bangladesh		12.4	16.8
Jakarta	Indonesia	6.0	13.2	16.8
Lagos	Nigeria		10.9	16.1
Karachi	Pakistan	5.0	11.6	15.2
Buenos Aires	Argentina	9.4	12.6	13.4
Cairo	Egypt	7.3	11.1	13.1
Los Angeles	US	9.5	12.3	13.1

Smog

Smog is a term used to describe the mixture of smoke and fog. This occurs when smoke and sulphur dioxide from coal burning either mix with existing fog or cause a thickening of fog by adding additional condensation nucleii to already saturated air. Today smog is more likely to originate from vehicular and industrial emissions that are acted on in the atmosphere by sunlight to form secondary pollutants. These can also combine with the primary emissions to form photochemical smog.

The London Smog of 1952 formed when an anticyclone settled over southern England and remained static for around five days in early December. The Thames basin is prone to radiation fogs as it is sheltered from westerly winds that might normally disperse them. The temperature inversion that formed over London trapped polluted air and a combination of dense fog and sooty black coal smoke produced a dense, persistent smog. The fog was so dense that residents of London could not see in front of them. The extreme reduction in visibility was accompanied by an increase in criminal activity as well as transportation delays and a virtual shutdown of the city. During the four-day period of the fog 12,000 people are believed to have been killed as a result of respiratory problems.

Photochemical smog

This forms when sunlight hits various pollutants in the air and forms a mix of chemicals that can be very dangerous. A photochemical smog is the chemical reaction of sunlight, nitrous oxides (NO_x) and volatile organic compounds (VOCs) in the atmosphere, which produces airborne particulate matter and ground-level ozone.

As these compounds are seen as the by-products of urban industrial society, photochemical smog is considered by many to be a problem of modern industrialisation. It is present in all modern cities, but it is more common in cities with sunny, warm, dry climates, e.g. Los Angeles, US.

Pollution-reduction policies

In the UK air quality targets set by the Department for Environment, Food and Rural Affairs (Defra) are largely the responsibility of local government and mainly targeted at air quality in cities. A network of air quality monitoring centres records and publishes the levels of the key air pollutants.

Localised peak values are often cited, but average values are also important to human health. The UK National Air Quality Information Archive offers almost real-time monitoring of 'current maximum' air pollution measurements for many UK towns and cities. This source offers a wide range of constantly updated data, including:

- ◼ hourly mean ozone ($\mu g/m^3$)
- ◼ hourly mean nitrogen dioxide ($\mu g/m^3$)
- ◼ maximum 15-minute mean sulphur dioxide ($\mu g/m^3$)
- ◼ 8-hour mean carbon monoxide (mg/m^3)
- ◼ 24-hour mean PM_{10} ($\mu g/m^3$).

Defra acknowledges that air pollution has a significant effect on health and has produced a simple banding index system to create a daily warning system made public via media such as the BBC Weather Service to indicate air pollution levels.

UK air quality indicators for sustainable development

The indicators for air quality and health provide two measures of how air quality has changed over time and include trends in annual levels of ozone (O_3) and particulate matter (PM_{10}). These are the two types of air pollution believed to have the most significant impacts on public health through long-term exposure.

Urban background particulate matter levels have shown an overall decreasing trend since 1993, the first year for which data were available, as have roadside particulate levels.

While rural ozone levels have shown no clear long-term trend, urban background ozone levels have shown an overall increasing long-term trend since 1993, mainly due to the reduction in urban emissions of nitrogen oxides, which destroy ozone close to their emission source.

Fig. 2.21 *Temperature inversion in Los Angeles, US, traps pollution to create a classic smog*

◼ The effects of urban structures and layout in wind speed direction and frequency

Wind speed is reduced in cities by as much as 30 per cent because there is increased frictional drag as the wind is obstructed by buildings. Conversely, very tall buildings can channel wind in between narrow spaces creating a canyon effect where, locally, wind speeds are higher. This effect, combined with turbulence, can prove hazardous to people at street level.

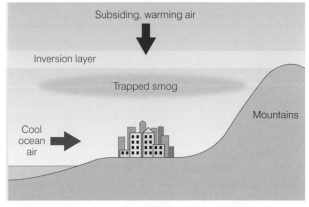

Fig. 2.22 *(a) The change in wind turbulence with increasing height above city; (b) Modification to airflow generated by a urban structures*

Global climate change

In this section you will learn:

- that enhanced global warming is considered to be the major environmental threat to life on the planet

- how people and governments act locally, nationally and internationally to mitigate against the effects of climate change.

> Over the last few decades there's been much more evidence for the human influence on climate ... We've reached the point where it's only by including human activity that we can explain what's happening.
>
> *Dr Geoff Jenkins, UK Met Office's Hadley Centre for Climate Prediction and Research*

Climatic change

Fossil records of earth temperatures indicate that global temperatures have always varied. The Earth has swung between relatively cooler phases which have generated ice ages (glacial periods) and warmer periods when ice has retreated (interglacial). In between these phases there has tended to be an irregular transition between the two states, with shorter-term peaks and troughs masking gradual longer-term increases or decreases in temperature. In recent years detailed analyses of these natural fluctuations have suggested that an accelerated warming (over and above what could be expected naturally) is taking place. This has been termed 'global warming'.

Global warming is the observed increase in the average temperature of the Earth's atmosphere and oceans in recent decades. The Earth's average near-surface atmospheric temperature rose by $0.6 \pm 0.2\,°C$ during the 20th century. The majority of scientists believe that most of the warming observed over the last 50 years is attributable to human activities.

Climatic change over the last 20,000 years

The geological record provides significant evidence for climate change over the last 3 billion years. The recent geological record of Britain, for example, indicates the existence of identifiable climate change over the last 20,000 years since the end of the last ice age. The evidence for these recent changes is largely based upon:

- **Glacial and postglacial deposits** reflecting the work of ice and meltwater over the landscape, e.g. the varved lake deposits of Lake Pickering in North Yorkshire.

- **Fossil landscapes** such as the glacial valleys of the Lake District or the granite tors of Dartmoor could not be produced under current climatic conditions.

- **Changes in sea level** as water was released from melting ice caps has led to the drowning of valleys in some areas, e.g. Cornish rias, and removal of the ice caps has led to isostatic uplift in other areas, e.g. the raised beaches of Arran, Scotland.

- **Shifts in vegetation belts** as postglacial warming allowed for the migration of species into areas where they would once have perished. This is supported by pollen analysis showing which plants were dominant at a given time. Where pollen grains are preserved, e.g. in an oxygen-free peat bog, their location and relative abundance can be taken as representative of the vegetation dominant at any given time. Changes in pollen concentrations at increasing depth through peat deposits can help to reconstruct previous characteristic vegetation and climate.

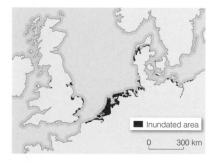

Inundated area

0   300 km

Fig. 2.23 *Map showing potential worst-case scenario for sea level rise if global warming creates a 2.5 metre rise*

Links

To remind yourself about varves, rias and isostatic uplift, see Chapter 5 of *AQA AS Geography*.

- **Tree-ring dating** (dendrochronology) is based upon the usual addition of one tree ring for each year of the life of a tree. For example, warm and wet years may produce a thicker ring whereas colder, drier years produce thinner rings. The patterns of growth over many years are used to produce tree-ring timescales which can give surprisingly accurate age-specific climate information stretching back up to 10,000 years.

- **Sea-floor analysis** of microfossils such as radiolaria and foraminifera found in cores drilled from deep sea oozes provide a rich source of climatic information. Isotopes of oxygen and carbon provide complex information about climatic change. For example, the ratio of O-18 and O-16 isotopes in calcareous oozes is a good indicator of the presence or absence of glacial phases. O-16 is lighter and more easily evaporated from oceans and deposited in glacial ice on land or in ice sheets, whereas O-18 is heavier and more of it remains behind, raising the O-18 ratios in the oceans. In warmer phases, more O-16 is released and ice records reflect these changes. These changing ratios plotted through time are represented as isotope curves and indicate variations in the volume of ice at any given time, which, in itself, reflects colder and warmer periods.

- **Ice core analysis** provides a record dating back over 10,000 years from sites in Antarctica and Greenland. In colder periods less CO_2 is trapped in the ice on formation and the reverse is true in warmer periods.

- **Radiocarbon dating** using the isotope of carbon, C-14, is perhaps the most accurate technique employed where preserved organic matter is available. Carbon is taken in by plants during the carbon cycle and as C-14 decays radioactively at a known rate, its abundance can be compared with C-12, which does not decay. The ratios of these isotopes can help to determine the age of plant remains up to 50,000 years.

- **Coleoptera beetles** have many species which today, tend to inhabit specific climatic regions. Analysis of the previous distribution from fluvial, lacustrine and terrestrial sediments can help to indicate the location of earlier climatic belts.

- In more recent history, a variety of information has been used to date climatic fluctuations, including records of vines growing successfully in southern England between AD 1000 and 1300 and 'frost fairs' held on the frozen River Thames in Tudor times. Since the 1870s daily weather reports have been kept and records from parish registers give additional information.

Recent global warming

Since the onset of the 1980s there appears to have been a considerable warming of our climate, with the 1990s being the hottest decade of the last century. This, together with the apparent increase in variations from the norm for Britain's expected weather, appears to add evidence supporting the concept of global warming.

Global warming can be defined as an accelerated warming of the atmosphere in recent years. Most scientists now relate this accelerated warming to the presence of additional 'greenhouse' gases trapping extra energy within the atmospheric system. It is evident in the observed increase in the average temperature of the Earth's atmosphere and oceans in recent decades.

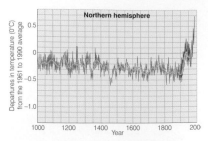

Fig. 2.24 *The hockey stick graph of temperature variation for the last 100 years*

The hockey stick debate

Much discussion concerning whether the current trend in rising global temperatures is unprecedented or within the range expected from natural variations is based on differing interpretations of temperature change recorded over the last 200 years. The 'hockey stick' shaped graph showing sustained temperatures for around 1,000 years and then a sharp increase since around 1800 is seen by many as definitive proof of the human influence on climate. However, others have suggested that the data and methodologies used to produce this type of figure are questionable, as widespread, accurate temperature records are only available for the past 150 years. Much of the temperature record is recreated from a range of 'proxy' sources such as tree rings, historical records, ice cores, lake sediments and corals. However, this is only one in a number of lines of evidence for human-induced climate change. The key conclusion that the build-up of greenhouse gases in the atmosphere will lead to several degrees of warming rests on a broad range of evidence.

■ Global warming: possible causes

The increased amounts of carbon dioxide (CO_2) and other greenhouse gases are the primary causes of the human-induced component of warming. They are released by the burning of fossil fuels, land clearing and agriculture, and lead to an increase in the greenhouse effect. However, greenhouse gases are necessary for our survival on earth. They help to trap some of the solar radiation that would otherwise be irradiated back out to space. Without them our planet would be as much as 30°C colder. We have an atmospheric composition that has evolved over millions of years and even slight changes in the atmosphere can have enormous impacts in terms of which species can survive and which cannot. Over the last 100 years the atmospheric concentration of CO_2 has increased by about 15 per cent and continues to increase by around 0.4 per cent per year. While it is generally accepted that atmospheric warming will continue, there is not as much concensus as to the extent, speed or likely regularity of that rise. However, a doubling of atmospheric CO_2 levels would increase global temperatures by 2–3°C, with the effect being more marked at higher latitudes.

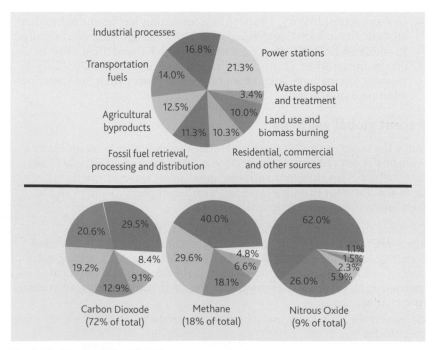

Fig. 2.25 *Concentration of GHGs*

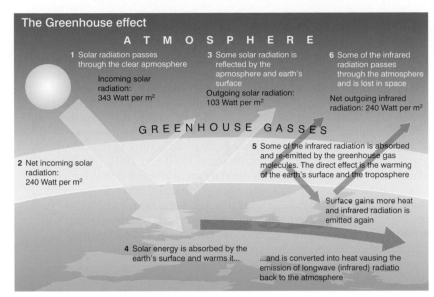

Fig. 2.26 *The enhanced greenhouse diagram*

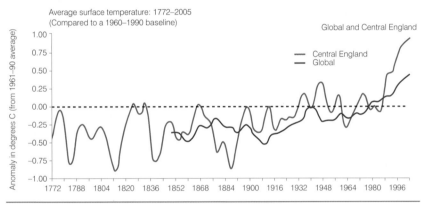

Source: Met office, Hadley Centre for Climate Prediction and research

Fig. 2.27 *Global temperature graph*

Global warming: possible effects

■ It is very likely that human activities are causing global warming.

– It is probable that temperature rise by the end of the century will be between 1.8 °C and 4 °C.

– It is possible that temperature rise by the end of the century could range between 1.1 °C and 6.4 °C.

– Sea levels are likely to rise by 28–43 cm.

– Arctic summer sea ice is likely to disappear in the second half of century.

– It is very likely that parts of the world will see an increase in the number of heatwaves.

– Climate change is likely to lead to increased intensity of tropical storms.

IPCC Fourth Assessment Report on Climate Change, published in February 2007

This brief summary of the Intergovernmental Panel on Climate Change (IPCC) report presents a stark vision of the likely effects of enhanced global warming on the planet. Current and predicted changes are outlined over the following pages.

Activity

1 Create a brief report summarising the evidence for global warming for a reader who is not convinced that the effects are anything more than natural variation.

Key
☐ Sea ice extent
— Median ice edge

Fig. 2.28 *The extent of ice melt at the North Pole, 1980–2007*

Ice caps

Global warming is responsible for a remarkable and frightening shrinkage of the ice caps. This not only means that more water is being released into the oceans, but without the cooling effect of the ice the oceans are getting warmer. Both of these factors mean that the oceans are expanding. The most obvious effect of this is sea level rise. The Arctic has lost 1.7 million km² of ice since 1980, shrinking to 6.1 million km² in 2005, leading some scientists to predict that the Arctic sea ice could disappear by 2050, or even as early as 2013 according to the most alarming forecasts. Significantly, between 1980 and 2001, 30 major glaciers across the world had thinned by an average of 6 m. Much of the land around the ice caps that has been permafrost is starting to partially thaw. For example, in Siberia land that has been frozen for 45,000 years is now thawing, releasing a lot of methane which hydrates into the atmosphere. Methane is a greenhouse gas which will add to the atmospheric mix and generate further warming.

Rising sea levels

The melting of ice and the thermal expansion of seawater as more energy is absorbed are likely to have a significant and increasing effect on sea level. According to the IPCC global average, sea level rose at an average rate of 1.8 mm per year from 1961 to 2003. The rate was faster from 1993 to 2003 (about 3.1 mm per year) but the total 20th-century rise is estimated to be 0.17 m. The Stern Report indicates potential sea-level rises of 28–43 cm by 2080, although other authorities say that at the extreme end of these calculations the complete melting of the polar ice could increase sea levels by 4–6 m. The rise of sea level, particularly when coupled with higher tides and stormier weather, will pose real threats to low-lying communities in places such as the Netherlands and Bangladesh, as well as many smaller islands in the Indian and Pacific Oceans. Even in the UK rising sea levels will threaten significant areas of lower-lying coastal areas and estuaries. In many areas of East Anglia and the Thames Estuary the gradual sinking of the south-eastern part of Britain, coupled with gentle coastal gradients, means that minor rises in sea level pose significant threats of flooding.

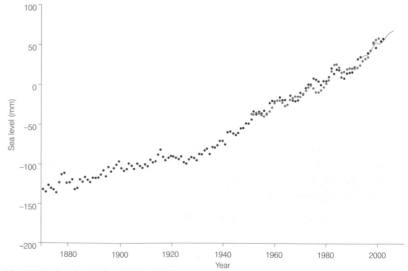

Fig. 2.29 *Sea-level rise, 1980–2007*

■ Climatic change

Many places experience warmer temperatures overall, though it might not be easy to predict the patterns and rates of change. The total temperature increase from 1850–99 to 2001–5 is 0.76°C, but the rate of change seems to be accelerating. Of the 12 years from 1995 to 2006, 11 rank among the 12 warmest years in the records since 1850 and the global surface temperature warming trend over the last 50 years averages out at 0.13°C per decade–nearly twice that for the last 100 years.

The predicted global changes for average temperatures will encompass widely varying regional responses. It is likely that land areas will warm much faster than the oceans, particularly those land areas in northern, high latitudes, and this will be most pronounced in the cold season. Additionally, it is very likely that heatwaves and other hot extremes will increase.

The impacts of climate change are difficult to predict, but Table 2.4 indicates the likely development of perceived trends in climate based on the climatic data reviewed by the Stern report.

Table 2.4 *Predicted trends of global climate change*

Phenomenon and direction of trend	Likelihood that the trend occurred in late 20th century (typically post-1960)	Likelihood of a human contribution to the observed trend	Likelihood of future trends based on projections for 21st century
Warmer and fewer cold days and nights over most land areas	*Very likely*	*Likely*	*Virtually certain*
Warmer and more frequent hot days and nights over most land areas	*Very likely*	*Likely (nights)*	*Virtually certain*
Warm spells/heatwaves. Frequency increases over most land areas	*Likely*	*More likely than not*	*Very likely*
Heavy precipitation events. Frequency (or proportion of total rainfall from heavy falls) increases over most areas	*Likely*	*More likely than not*	*Very likely*
Area affected by drought increases	*Likely in many regions since 1970s*	*More likely than not*	*Likely*
Intense tropical cyclone activity increases	*Likely in some regions since 1970s*	*More likely than not*	*Likely*
Increased incidence of extreme high sea level	*Likely*	*More likely than not*	*Likely*

Food shortage and disease

Africa, the Middle East and India are expected to experience significant reductions in cereal yields mainly as a result of reduced rainfall in these areas. China and central Asia are likely to see an increased risk of malaria, with an additional 290 million people potentially exposed to the disease by the 2080s.

Severe water shortages

Reduced rainfall and the salination of groundwater in coastal zones as sea levels rise will reduce the amount of water available for drinking and irrigation, putting millions more lives at risk. An additional 3 billion people could suffer increased water stress by 2080, with North Africa, the Middle East and India likely to be the worst affected.

Extreme weather events

It is difficult to be absolutely certain about the perceived relationship of extreme weather events and global warming. To prove cause-and-effect relationships requires long-term correlation of weather and climate-change data. However, many climatologists believe that evidence to back this link is now accumulating. In 2003, a study by the World Meteorological Organization blamed global warming for the record number of extreme weather events such as tornadoes. In 2006 Greg Holland, of the National Center for Atmospheric Research in Boulder, Colorado, US, claimed that the apparent increase in hurricane frequency and magnitude was a direct result of climate change, and that the wind and warmer water conditions that fuel storms that form in the Caribbean are increasingly due to greenhouse gases. Increases in extreme storm events related to global warming appear to be clearer in storms with winds above 50 m/s according to a recent survey (2008) reflecting on 25 years of satellite data of major storms in the Atlantic and Indian Oceans.

■ Monsoon climate and climate change

More than half the world's population are believed to depend on the annual Asian monsoon to bring much-needed water for agriculture and basic human needs. Variations in the monsoon rainfall have significant effects on the lives of billions of people. In 1994, the UN's IPCC warned that global warming could intensify and increase the variability of the monsoon. Although initially Indian climate data did not appear to support this conclusion, more recent rigorous analysis has revealed that monsoon rains are getting heavier.

Global warming is apparently intensifying the monsoon in central India in much the same way as it is believed to be boosting the power and number of storms and other extreme weather events across the world. Analysis of heavy monsoon rains in central India between 1981 and 2000 reveals that they were more intense and frequent than in the 1950s and 1960s. Their frequency has increased by 10 per cent since the early 1950s, with the frequency of severe rains doubling over the same period.

While the increase in rainfall might bring some benefits to people who rely heavily on the seasonal downpours to support their agriculture, there are also some extreme environmental and economic impacts. Heavy rains can be perilous, causing landslides and flash floods. Surging floodwaters in the 2002 monsoon killed more than 800 people in Bangladesh, India and Nepal, displacing millions of others. If the trend continues, it is predicted that increased flooding will lead to crop damage, with drastic effects on agriculture and food security.

Scientists from Liverpool University predict that by the end of the century India will experience a 3–5 °C temperature increase and a 20 per cent rise in all summer monsoon rainfall. However, they also point out that other areas of India will be affected by drought as climate patterns change, and suggest that changes to the water cycle, particularly in regions strongly influenced by water-based ecosystems, could also cause an increase in waterborne diseases such as cholera and hepatitis, as well as malaria.

The impact of the Asian monsoon increasing in strength could well have knock-on effects elsewhere. Australian scientists believe that severe drought conditions will increasingly encroach into the southern parts of Australia and the west of Indonesia as moisture is drawn away from more southern regions to feed the Asian monsoon. The spread of these droughts to areas of the countries that are currently little affected could

Links

For more information on global warming, go to:
www.climatehotmap.org

Activity

2 Create a concept map to show how the impacts of global warming might be linked.

be most damaging during the summer months when agriculture is most vulnerable. Possible secondary effects might include food shortages and wildfires.

Possible effects on the British Isles

Changes in weather and climate in Britain have tended to focus on speculation about a new, more Mediterranean climate. In reality the effects are likely to be more varied as Britain's climate is greatly affected by its location on the edge of Europe and, in particular, by the influence of the North Atlantic Drift.

In Britain the annual average temperatures look set to rise by 2–3.5 °C by the 2080s, with the south and east of the UK most likely to see the largest rise in temperature, in contrast to the north and west which will see the least. Most of the warming will be in the summer and autumn, where temperatures in the south-east could rise by as much as 5 °C, or 4 °C on average.

Precipitation in winter could increase by 10–35 per cent in all areas of the country. The summer will see less precipitation than we see now and will therefore be much drier, with a possible reduction of 35–50 per cent in precipitation. The largest changes are predicted for the southern and eastern parts of England; the smallest changes are forecast to be in north-west Scotland.

Less snow might fall throughout the UK, with a possible decline of 60 per cent in parts of Scotland and up to 90 per cent elsewhere.

There is increasing evidence to back up these changes in weather in the UK and across the world:

- four out of five of the warmest years ever recorded were in the 1990s
- the 1990s was the warmest decade of the last millennium, with 1998 being the warmest year globally since records began in 1861
- 2006 was the warmest year on record in the UK
- January–June 2002 was the warmest start to a year in the northern hemisphere
- the total number of cold days (where the average temperature was under 0 °C) has fallen from between 15 and 20 per year prior to the 20th century to around 10 per year in recent years
- 1995 saw the most hot days in 225 years of daily measurements – 26 days above 20 °C.

Higher temperatures could:

- reduce water levels in soil, leading to greater soil moisture deficits in summer–this might affect the types of crops and trees that can survive
- lead to the loss of several native species, especially if combined with less rainfall; warmer climate would allow plants to grow further north and at higher altitudes
- lead to a longer growing season, e.g. more grass for dairy and beef cattle, but cereals could be hit by drier summers
- mean even milder winters which, in turn, could lead to an increase in the number of pests
- benefit tourism if there are longer, warmer, drier summers
- reduce snow cover in winter, with insufficient snow for skiing in Scotland.

Wetter winters could:

■ benefit water supplies

■ mean more losses due to more storms and flooding.

Rise in sea level and increase in the frequency and magnitude of gales and storm surges could:

■ result in more flooding, especially around estuaries

■ have a major impact on housing, industry, farming, energy, transport and wildlife.

■ Responses to global warming

Findings of the Stern report

■ There is still time to avoid the worst impacts of climate change, if we take strong action now.

  – Climate change could have very serious impacts on growth and development.

  – The costs of stabilising the climate are significant but manageable; delay would be dangerous and much more costly.

  – Action on climate change is required across all countries, and it need not cap the aspirations for growth of rich or poor countries.

  – A range of options exists to cut emissions; strong, deliberate policy action is required to motivate their take-up.

  – Climate change demands an international response, based on a shared understanding of long-term goals and agreement on frameworks for action.

  – Key elements of future international frameworks should include:

    • emissions trading

    • technology cooperation

    • action to reduce deforestation.

Adaptation: Stern Review on the Economics of Climate Change, 30 October 2006
© Cabinet Office/HM Treasury

■ Links

The full Stern report can be found at:
www.sternreview.org.uk

International responses

The global nature of enhanced climate change has led to a gradual realisation that countries cannot act individually if they are to be successful in reducing damaging emissions and avoiding the worst likely impacts. Increasingly governments have agreed to cooperate to try to derive common policies and commit to unified actions. In reality these intentions have been difficult to realise.

The Kyoto agreement

Britain is signed up to the Kyoto Protocol. Under the UN Framework Convention on Climate Change (UNFCCC), emission limits were agreed with participating countries and they undertook to ensure they would reach these reductions in greenhouse gases.

The resulting Kyoto Protocol, adopted in December 1997, agreed emission limits for industrialised countries for a 'first commitment period' of 2008–12 from a base year of 1990.

■ Russia agreed to the treaty in November 2004, clearing the way for the treaty to become legally binding on 16 February 2005 – meeting the criteria that more than 55 Parties to the Convention had ratified the Protocol, including countries responsible for at least 55 per cent of industrialised countries' carbon dioxide (CO_2) emissions in 1990 (at the start of 2006 a total of 162 countries had ratified).

■ The US and Australia have signed the Kyoto Protocol, however they have not ratified the treaty and remain outside the legal requirements of the Protocol.

■ In 2003 the UK government pledged to reduce CO_2 emissions by 20 per cent, on 1990 levels, by 2010. Currently, not only is the UK not on course to meet this target, but greenhouse gas emissions are on an upwards trend, driven by an increase from the energy sector. The government responded to this trend with the DTI Energy Challenge announced in 2006, which sets a revised target to cut CO_2 levels to 60 per cent of the 1990 level by 2050.

■ In 2008, the UK government pledged to reduce CO_2 emissions to 80 per cent of the 1990 level by 2050.

■ The Kyoto Treaty expires in 2012, and international talks began in May 2007 on a future treaty to succeed the current one.

■ China might have passed the US in total annual greenhouse gas emissions and Chinese Premier Wen Jiabao has called on the nation to redouble its efforts to tackle pollution and global warming.

Carbon credits

These are part of a scheme that allocates permissible amounts of carbon usage to countries according to their apparent need (given their size, level of industrialisation, etc.). They are used in national and international emissions trading schemes that have been implemented to mitigate global warming. The aim is to cap total annual emissions and let the free market assign a monetary value to any shortfall through trading. Credits can be exchanged between businesses or bought and sold in international markets in a way that is meant to balance the costs and benefits of CO_2 emissions. For example, if an organisation unable to use its quota sells excess credits to a richer country or organisation that requires more to avoid exceeding its own limit then it can be argued that they both benefit.

Credits are also used to finance carbon reduction schemes between trading partners. Many companies sell carbon credits to commercial and individual customers who are interested in lowering their overall carbon footprint by 'carbon offsetting'. By purchasing credits from an investment fund or a carbon development company, companies concerned that they might exceed their own credit limit can, in theory, counteract this by buying additional credit.

Action in the UK

The EU emission trading system

Emissions trading allows the government to regulate the total amount of emissions produced by setting the overall cap for the scheme, but gives companies the flexibility of determining how and where the emissions reductions will be achieved. Participating companies are allocated allowances but can emit in excess of their allocation of allowances by purchasing allowances from the market. Conversely, a company that emits less than its allocation of allowances can sell its surplus allowances. The environmental outcome is not affected because the amount of allowances allocated is fixed. The EU climate change programme attempts to address the need to reduce CO_2 by means of an emissions trading scheme known as the EU Greenhouse Gas Emissions Trading Scheme. Members can either make these savings within their own country, or they can buy these emissions reductions from other countries.

Key areas for action

The UK produces energy from a variety of sources. With over 80 per cent of our energy coming from fossil fuels we generate enormous amounts of CO_2 – a problem that could be dealt with in three main ways:

■ reducing CO_2 emissions from power stations before it is released into the atmosphere

■ using sources of energy that generate less CO_2 such as nuclear or 'alternative' energy sources (including solar, wind, wave, etc.)

■ reducing our demand for energy by using less in our industry, transport and homes.

Table 2.5 *Greenhouse gas reduction target (1990–2008/12) under the Kyoto Protocol*

Switzerland, Central and East European states, the EU (inc. UK)	–8%
US	–7%
Japan, Canada, Hungary, Japan	–6%
Russian Federation and Ukraine	0%
Norway	+1%
Australia	+8%
Iceland	+10%

Links

To find out more about the impacts of climate change, go to:
earth.google.co.uk/outreach

Energy production

By 2004, total electricity production in the UK stood at 382.7 TWh (up 23.7 per cent compared to 309.4 TWh in 1990), generated from the following sources:

■ gas – 39.93% (0.05% in 1990)

■ coal – 33.08% (67.22% in 1990)

■ nuclear – 19.26% (18.97% in 1990)

■ renewables – 3.55% (0% in 1990)

■ hydroelectric – 1.10% (2.55% in 1990)

■ imports – 1.96% (3.85% in 1990)

■ oil – 1.12% (6.82% in 1990).

Most of the UK's electricity comes from thermal power stations burning gas, coal or oil. A modern nuclear power station emits around 16 tonnes of carbon dioxide per megawatt hour compared with 356 tonnes for gas and 891 tonnes for coal-fired stations. Nuclear power stations may be cleaner in terms of greenhouse gas emissions but they cost a great deal to build and the need to deal with their radioactive waste means they are more expensive once decommissioning costs are included in the overall costings. However, some countries, such as France, generate up to 75 per cent of their energy by nuclear means and the British government is likely to replace its current older nuclear power stations as they reach the end of their life.

The energy industry is under increasing pressure to reduce emissions of greenhouse gases. CO_2 emissions in the UK were over 500 million tonnes in 2005. Some of these reductions will be achieved by carbon capture and storage (CCS), where CO_2 emissions from thermal power stations and petroleum processing plants are stored underground; this approach is gaining growing attention among power and oil producers. One possibility could be to store CO_2 under the North Sea. Disused oilfields have the capacity to store up to 10 years' worth of the UK's total annual carbon emissions and old gas fields could offer 30 years' capacity. Salt-rich layers of rock beneath the sea floor (saline aquifers) can trap CO_2 pumped down into them. At the moment dumping CO_2 in the North Sea is prohibited, but the UK government is pursuing amendments to the relevant laws so CCS projects can be approved.

Renewable energy sources

The government is committed to putting in place mechanisms that mean 10 per cent of our energy will come from renewable sources (including solar, wind, wave, tidal and geothermal power) by 2010 (3 per cent in 2009).

- Wind power is clean, sustainable and inexpensive, but many people dislike seeing the turbines on open land and regard them as a form of environmental damage.

- Geothermal power (heat from the ground) is largely untapped. The heat energy stored in the uppermost 10 km of the Earth's crust is equivalent to 50,000 times the total energy stored in all the world's oil and gas.

- The temperature a few metres below ground in the UK is around 12 °C. Ground-source heat pumps are now available to pump this heat from below ground to warm individual homes.

- Chicken, pig and human excrement are all currently being used to generate electricity. The first UK generator using animal dung began in 2002.

- Biodiesel to run vehicle engines with far lower CO_2 emissions can be made from most vegetable oils, including soya bean oil and the oil from oilseed rape (canola). Some companies manufacture it from used oil from restaurant fryers and it can be mixed with ordinary diesel. Recent reports indicate, however, that the switch to biofuel crops has affected world food supply and pushed up prices.

Local Responses

- In the UK many citizens can access funding to reduce the amount of energy used in their homes by improving insulation.

- Recycling schemes now encourage re-use of most household waste including cans, plastics and bottles.

- Since agriculture is responsible for about a fifth of the world's greenhouse emissions; emissions can be reduced by buying locally produced food.

- Walking or cycling instead of driving a car can reduce usage of fossil fuels.

- Energy ratings for new products such as cars and washing machines encourage the use of more energy efficient machinery.

- Reduced use of air travel.

Activity

3 a Discuss the ways in which international cooperation can help to reduce future greenhouse gas emissions in an attempt to reduce the impact of global warming.

b Suggest why these policies are not implemented by some nations.

Did you know?

At present 862 wind turbines produce over 412 MW of electrical power, enough to supply more than 260,000 homes. The Cefn Croes, near Aberystwyth will supply 40,000 homes.

The government subsidises wind power by 3p a unit for renewable energy to encourage its usage.

Links

Find out more about responses to global warming at climatecrisis.net/takeaction

In this chapter you will have learnt:

■ that the sun is the source of nearly all the energy on the planet, and there is a balance of incoming and outgoing energy

■ that the atmosphere has a sharp pressure gradient which decreases with increasing altitude, it can be divided into a number of layers with distinct characteristics

■ that some parts of the Earth experience marked seasonal variations in the amount of energy received by the atmosphere and the surface

■ that horizontal and vertical movements of energy are responsible for redistributing energy from areas of surplus to areas of deficit

■ that ocean currents operating near the surface and at depth help to redistribute around 20 per cent of the available energy around the planet

■ the British Isles experiences great variability in its weather as a function of its mid-latitude, edge-of-continent location

■ that an air mass is a body of air with largely uniform characteristics, and how five major air masses influence the weather and climate of the British Isles throughout the year

■ that Britain is affected by low-pressure weather systems called depressions that bring unsettled weather, especially from autumn to spring

■ that the South East Asian monsoon is a seasonal reversal of pressure and winds and associated heavy rainfall

■ that tropical revolving storms are intense storms with wind speeds over 119 km/hr, which (along with drought) are responsible for most deaths attributed to natural hazards; they are largely restricted to the tropics

■ how urban microclimates can significantly alter local conditions in terms of temperature, humidity, wind speed and air quality

■ that these changes, especially in terms of the build-up of pollutants, have important social, economic and ecological effects

■ that evidence for enhanced global warming comes from many sources that increasingly appear to point to a link with greenhouse gas emissions resulting from human activities during the recent past

■ that responses to global warming include reducing activities seen to be harmful to the atmosphere, adapting to changing climatic conditions

■ why changes to the nature of the climate in countries affected by the South East Asian monsoon and in the British Isles may be profound

■ why international action and cooperation is increasingly seen to be essential if the problems associated with rising temperatures are to be addressed effectively.

3 Ecosystems: change and challenge

The nature of ecosystems

For some people the study of **ecology** is the most fundamental study in the world today. The **ecosystems** on which we as a species depend for our survival are under a lot of stress and are being changed by human activities all over the globe. If we as a species do not understand ecosystems and guard them well, we are doomed to destroy our **environment**. Managing ecosystems to cope with change is a massive challenge for this and future generations.

The first stage in understanding ecosystems is to understand the terminology used by ecologists, and to ensure that we use these terms correctly. The Key terms define some of the most fundamental terms, and Fig. 3.1 shows how ecosystems can be arranged into a hierarchy of units.

Key terms

Ecology: the study of communities of living organisms and the relationships among the members of those communities and between them and the physical and chemical constituents of their surroundings.

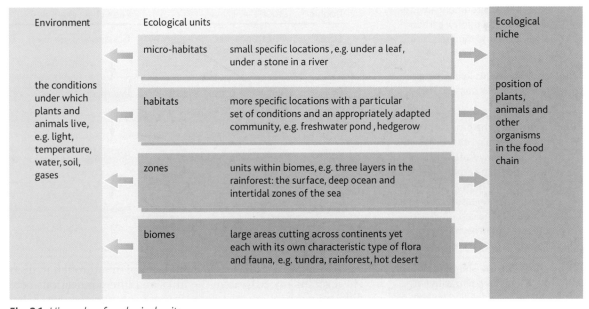

Fig. 3.1 *Hierarchy of ecological units*

The diagram shows:

Environment — the conditions under which plants and animals live, e.g. light, temperature, water, soil, gases

Ecological units:

- **micro-habitats** — small specific locations, e.g. under a leaf, under a stone in a river
- **habitats** — more specific locations with a particular set of conditions and an appropriately adapted community, e.g. freshwater pond, hedgerow
- **zones** — units within biomes, e.g. three layers in the rainforest: the surface, deep ocean and intertidal zones of the sea
- **biomes** — large areas cutting across continents yet each with its own characteristic type of flora and fauna, e.g. tundra, rainforest, hot desert

Ecological niche — position of plants, animals and other organisms in the food chain

Key terms

Ecosystem: system in which organisms interact with each other and with their environment. There are two parts: the entire complex of organisms, or biome, living in harmony and the habitat in which the biome exists.

Environment: everything that surrounds us, including ourselves.

■ Energy flows in ecosystems

The sun is the main driving force of all ecosystems. It provides the heat that warms up plants, animals and their **abiotic environment**, and the sun's heat also drives the water cycle and other crucial flows of the ecosystem. However, the sun's light energy is just as important for the functioning of the ecosystem because this light provides the energy for **photosynthesis**.

Once the food has been used to build the plant, that plant then becomes available as food for other organisms which, in their turn, become available to other organisms. This flow of energy through plants and animals, then back into the soil, is called a **food chain**. The flows in the chain are shown in Fig. 3.2.

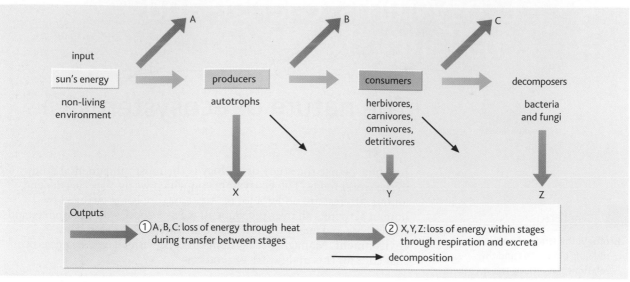

Fig. 3.2 *Stages in food chains*

Each stage of the food chain is also known as a **trophic level**. *Trophe* is Greek for food, and so a trophic level just describes a position in the food chain.

Trophic	Process	Food chain examples	
Level 1	Autotrophs produce energy by photosynthesis	Grass (dead/decomposed)	Leaf
Level 2	Herbivores consume plant material	Worm	Caterpillar
Level 3	Carnivores consume animals	Blackbird	Shrew
Level 4	Large carnivores or omnivores consume smaller animals	Hawk	Fox

Fig. 3.3 *Trophic levels*

Fig. 3.3 shows a simple food chain from plants through to decomposers. However, in any ecosystem the links and interconnections between the different types of organism are far more complicated. Fig. 3.4 shows some aspects of the **food web** in an English deciduous woodland.

At each trophic level in the food web there is a loss of energy from the web due to respiration, excretion and a general transfer of heat to the atmosphere. This loss of energy means that at each higher level fewer individual organisms can be supported. What is more, the organisms at the higher levels are usually more complex and this also means that more lower-level organisms are needed to support each higher-level organism, producing the trophic pyramid shown in Fig. 3.5.

Key terms

Decomposer: organism that takes the remains of dead plants and animals, as well as their excreted waste, and converts them back into carbon dioxide and nutrients. This releases raw nutrients in a chemical form usable to plants and algae, which incorporate the chemicals into their own cells.

Trophic level: an organism's position in the food chain. Level 1 is formed of autotrophs (plants), which produce their own food. Level 2 is formed of primary consumers that feed on the Level 1 plants. Level 3 feeds on Level 2, and so on.

Food web: more complex than a food chain, but more common as simple food chains are rare. In a food web there are a variety of different sources of food at each trophic level and most animals in the web have more than one source of food, and/or provide food for more than one consumer in the level above.

Fig. 3.4 *Part of a food web in an oak woodland*

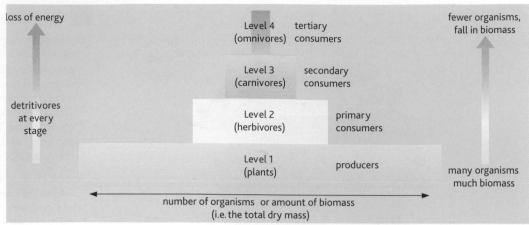

Fig. 3.5 *The trophic pyramid*

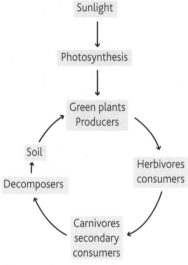

Fig. 3.6 *The energy cycle*

■ Material cycling and stores in the ecosystem

One of the most fundamental points to understand about ecosystems is their role in recycling various materials. The energy cycle has been described above and can be summarised as shown in Fig. 3.6.

Other essential cycles in the ecosystem include the nitrogen cycle, the carbon cycle and the nutrient cycle.

Nitrogen cycle: the simple form is shown in Fig. 3.7. Nitrogen is necessary for the construction of plant and animal matter. It is present in the atmosphere and can be fixed in the soil by some plants. Then it is taken up by the roots of other plants, passes through the ecosystem, and is returned to the soil by decomposition.

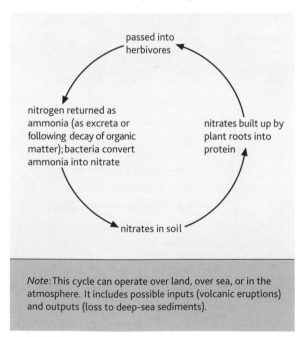

Note: This cycle can operate over land, over sea, or in the atmosphere. It includes possible inputs (volcanic eruptions) and outputs (loss to deep-sea sediments).

Fig. 3.7 *The nitrogen cycle*

Carbon cycle: this is shown in more complexity in Fig. 3.8. In recent years there has been growing concern that human activity is disrupting the carbon cycle. Over millions of years large amounts of carbon have been extracted from the environment and stored in the ground as peat, coal, oil and gas. In addition, large amounts of carbon are in temporary stores in plants, animals and the soil. The burning of fossil fuels and the destruction of forests and peat deposits has released much of this carbon back into the atmosphere as carbon dioxide – one of the main greenhouse gases that are believed to be responsible for global warming and climate change. An understanding of the place of carbon in the ecosystem is an important step in understanding the causes of climate change.

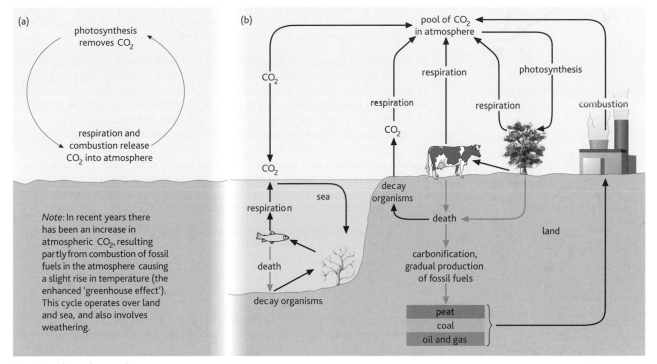

Fig. 3.8 *The carbon cycle*

Nutrient cycle: this has been referred to throughout this chapter up to this point, but only in very general terms. In fact, the flows in the nutrient cycle vary from place to place in their quantities, in how they are stored and in the speed that they move from store to store. The flows through the system can be illustrated in a diagram showing separate 'compartments' – soil, biomass and litter.

■ The soil compartment contains minerals that come from weathered rock, and humus that comes from decomposed plant and animal materials.

■ The biomass compartment contains all the living plant and animal material in the ecosystem. It takes in energy and carbon from the atmosphere and minerals from the soil.

■ The litter compartment is found on the top of the soil and is composed of dead and decaying plant and animal material.

Nutrients are transferred between these different compartments as flows.

Nutrient cycles can be drawn for different environments, with the size of the compartments and arrows drawn to represent the amount of nutrients stored in each compartment or flowing between compartments as seen in Figs 3.9–12.

Cycles have been drawn for the **biomes** that have been dealt with in later stages of this chapter – equatorial forest (pp125–8), tropical grasslands (pp113–25) and temperate deciduous forests (pp96–7).

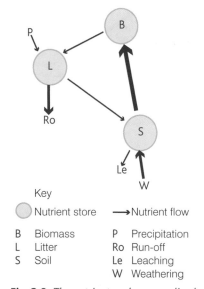

Fig. 3.9 *The nutrient cycle, generalised. Note: in diagrams for particular environments, which follow, the size of the stores and flows represent their comparative importance in that environment*

Key

○ Nutrient store   → Nutrient flow

B   Biomass   P   Precipitation
L   Litter   Ro   Run-off
S   Soil   Le   Leaching
               W   Weathering

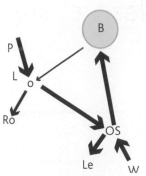

Fig. 3.10 *Tropical rainforest cycle*

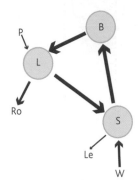

Fig. 3.11 *Savanna cycle*

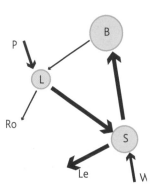

Fig. 3.12 *Deciduous woodland cycle*

The equatorial climate is ideal for plant growth. Growth is so rapid that the biomass stored in the plants contains a huge proportion of the nutrients available. When litter falls to the surface it is broken down quickly in the hot and humid conditions, so the litter store is very small. So, too, is the store of nutrients in the soil, because they are taken up so quickly by plant growth. The heavy rainfall can also **leach** minerals out of the soil and carry them away from the area. This means that if the forest cover is destroyed, by burning for instance, most of the nutrient supply is lost from the ecosystem and the soil soon becomes infertile.

In the tropical grasslands there is much less biomass in the vegetation. The fact that the grasses die back in the dry season means that there is no possibility of huge amounts accumulating as happens in the rainforests. However, the dead grasses rot more slowly, partly because the area lacks moisture to speed up the decomposition and partly because the grasses are so tough, so this means that the proportion of the nutrients in the litter layer is higher than in the rainforests. As plant growth is seasonal and does not occur all year round, there is a greater accumulation of nutrients in the soil than there is under the rainforests. Leaching is at a low level because the low rainfall and high evaporation mean that little water flows away through the soil.

The deciduous forest ecosystem shows a pattern of nutrient flows and storage that appears to be midway between the previous two. The forest cover is neither so dense nor so high as in the rainforests, so there are fewer nutrients stored in the vegetation. However, the autumn leaf fall decays fairly slowly in the lower temperatures found here and so there is a comparatively large store in the litter layer. The nutrients from this layer can then be carried down into the soil by the activity of decomposers such as worms, so the store in the soil is quite important.

Activity

1 The diagrams in Figs 3.9–3.12 are important. Each summarises a lot of information. It could be very useful to draw them in an exam; it is a quick and efficient way to show a lot of precise information, but it only works if you **know** the diagrams. So …

 a Learn the four diagrams.

 b Practise drawing them.

 c Check that you drew them correctly.

 d Repeat stages 1 to 3 until perfect.

 e Revise, just before the exam.

Key terms

Biome: a major, world-scale ecosystem. It is the climatic climax vegetation across an area of continental size, with one dominant vegetation type.

Leaching: occurs when rainwater, which is slightly acidic, drains through the soil, dissolving basic minerals and carrying them away in solution. They may be deposited lower down in the soil or washed away to the rivers and lost to the ecosystem.

Ecosystems in the British Isles – change through time

In this section you will learn:

■ how ecosystems change through time, with particular reference to psammoseres and hydroseres.

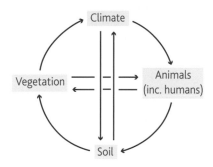

Fig. 3.13 *Interactions between different elements in the ecosystem*

Activity

1 Fig. 3.13 shows the influence of each element in the ecosystem on the others. Discuss examples to show some of the ways in which each of these interactions take place. (Note, though, that some of the interactions are much stronger than others.)

Key terms

Seral progression: the move from one sere to another.

Sere: a stage in the development of the vegetation of an area over a period of time.

Climatic climax vegetation: the vegetation that is thought to evolve in a climate region if the seral progression is not interrupted by human activity, tectonic processes, impeded drainage, etc.

Dominant plant: the largest, most complex and tallest species present in a community.

Vegetation succession

Ecosystems are not static; they evolve over time. The interactions between different elements in the system mean that climate affects vegetation, vegetation affects soil, changes in the soil can affect drainage, and so on.

The most obvious way that these changes can be seen is through the progressive development of the vegetation community in an environment, which is known as a **seral progression**. The vegetation at each stage is known as a **sere**.

The first sere in an area is called the **pioneer community** and it develops on a newly exposed surface.

This might be on:

■ bare rock, after a volcanic eruption, exposure of the bedrock due to a landslide or some other cause; this then leads to the development of a **lithosere**

■ sand, for example sand dunes, leading to a **psammosere**

■ a wet, salty surface, such as a marine salt marsh, leading to a **halosere**

■ freshwater wetland, such as a pond that has been filled in by sedimentation, leading to a **hydrosere**.

The theory of the **climatic climax vegetation** says that the initial surface becomes colonised by a small number of species that are particularly adapted to the difficult conditions for plant growth that are presented by the surface. Then those species gradually change the surface by adding nutrients to form soil, increasing the height of the surface through adding the bulk of decaying plant matter, possibly by aiding the development of a mature drainage system, and so on. This allows new plants to invade the area – and to develop a new sere.

Each sere in the progression is named after the **dominant plant** in the community. Each successive sere has taller dominant plants than the preceding sere. (See psammosere on pp90–92 and hydrosere on pp93–95.)

Eventually, possibly after thousands of years, the climatic climax community develops – where the vegetation is completely adapted to the climate and where there is little change in the community. The community is usually layered with the dominant species sheltering lower sub-dominants and even lower layers of shrubs, grasses and ground-level plants, all surviving in equilibrium with each other, with the climate and soil, and with the animal life that is there.

Unfortunately, conditions rarely stay stable for long enough for the climax community to develop. Tectonic processes and erosion and deposition may change the structure and drainage of an area, and climate change has always happened, even without the intervention of human processes. But it is the intervention of humans that has had the biggest effect on vegetation communities in most parts of the world. Deforestation and reafforestation, ploughing, burning, draining and flooding and such processes all affect vegetation in some areas; and human-induced climate change is affecting it everywhere now.

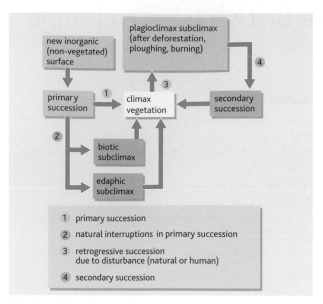

1 primary succession

2 natural interruptions in primary succession

3 retrogressive succession
due to disturbance (natural or human)

4 secondary succession

Fig. 3.14 *Alternatives to the climax vegetation model*

As a result, the simple idea of a **prisere** progressing from a bare surface to the climatic climax community has been adapted to take account of the various interruptions that can occur.

■ Human interruptions to the succession can produce a **plagioclimax community**, which is then maintained by management. These can include the heather moorlands in Britain and the grasslands of the tropics that are managed by herders to provide pasture for their animals.

■ If the arresting factor is then removed, a **secondary succession** develops.

■ Natural interruptions, such as impeded drainage or regular deposition of fresh river sediment in an area can produce an **interrupted succession** and a **subclimax community**.

Heather moorland, a plagioclimax community

Heather moorland is one of the major components of the vegetation of the British Isles, especially in upland areas, but it was probably never a major part of the primary succession that followed the retreat of the ice at the end of the last Ice Age, about 20,000 years ago. It owes its present extent to human interference and the clearance of upland forests.

The woodland was probably first cleared to allow crops to be grown or to provide grazing, but once the trees had been removed there were no deep roots to bring nutrients to the surface and renew soil fertility. Instead the heavy rainfall in the uplands allowed nutrients to be washed (or leached) out of the soils. So these upland areas

were often colonised by bracken, grasses, scrub woodland and heather.

As long as the moorlands were grazed heavily this mixed moorland vegetation was maintained. However, in many areas, such as the North York Moors, parts of the Pennines and large parts of the Eastern Scottish Highlands, there is a deliberate management policy to maintain the land under heather moorland. The young shoots of the heather provide ideal food for red grouse, which are used as the basis for the very lucrative shooting industry in these areas.

To encourage the growth of new shoots, the old, woody heather plants must be burnt off every three or four years. Estate

managers burn off sections of their moor in rotation, so that at any time the moor has a variety of different habitats, with some areas of new heather providing food supplies and areas of older heather providing good cover for the grouse.

If the burning stops and if the heather moor is not grazed by cattle or sheep the heather grows old and woody. It can be invaded by scrub and woodland. On the other hand, overgrazing can lead to destruction of the young heather shoots and invasion by bracken or by mat grasses. This seemingly natural vegetation community is, in fact, a plagioclimax community, only maintained by human management.

■ Psammoseres

Psammoseres can be seen developing in many places around the coast of the UK where sand dune systems are being or have recently been formed. Ainsdale Dunes between Liverpool and Southport and Studland Dunes between Poole and Swanage are typical.

These are dynamic geomorphological environments where the dunes have been formed by wind blowing sand inland off the beach. A series of stages in the seral progression can all be seen in a cross-section across the dunes (see fig 3.17), moving inland from the shoreline across the most

Key terms

Prisere: the whole process from a pioneer community to the climax vegetation.

recently formed dunes to the older and more stable dunes a few hundred metres or so inland.

Shore and foredunes

If any plants grow on the edge of the beach they have to be very tolerant of salty conditions, so occasional examples of sea couch grass and glasswort may be found.

Mobile dunes

The first vegetation that is encountered in many dune systems is marram grass. This is found almost exclusively on the first line of dunes. Its extensive systems of underground stems, or rhizomes, allow it to thrive under conditions of shifting sands and high winds. The various species of marram grass are examples of **xerophytes**, which are plants that can withstand arid conditions such as deserts or sandy beaches. It thrives under these conditions because of:

■ deep roots that help bind the sand together and stabilise the dune

■ its tolerance for moderately salty soils

■ the tough blades that are adapted to stand up to the regular strong winds

■ its adaptations to reduce water loss from their surfaces – important on rapidly draining sand

■ its ability to thrive in very poor soils which are very alkaline due to the presence of shell fragments.

Marram grass is native to North Atlantic coastal areas but it is so well adapted to conditions in the mobile dunes near the sea that it has been introduced into sand dune areas around the world to help stabilise them.

Fig. 3.15 *Marram grass growing on a sand dune*

Fixed dunes

Over time, the mobile dunes become stabilised by the roots of the grasses and soil starts to improve as humus from the decaying plants is added. Gradually a brown surface layer of up to 10 cm deep is formed. This is able to retain some moisture, unlike the sand of the mobile dunes. Other plants are able to colonise this soil and these start to out-compete the marram grass. These include other grasses, creeping fescue and sea spurge, and some low shrubs such as heather.

Dune heathlands

Further addition of humus means that at a distance inland the soils become very acidic. Heathland plants now colonise the area. These can include heather, gorse, bracken, holly and buckthorn. The dominant species are now considerably taller than the grasses on the mobile dunes. If left free from human interference these plants allow the soil to develop further and so trees start to invade the area.

Fig. 3.16 *Dune heath*

Climax community

Finally, oak woodland would develop. However, in many areas of dune in the UK, plantations of conifers have been grown on the dunes. They are partly to act as a windbreak to protect inland agriculture and housing, partly to further stabilise the dunes and stop sand blowing, and partly for commercial timber and/or wildlife reserves.

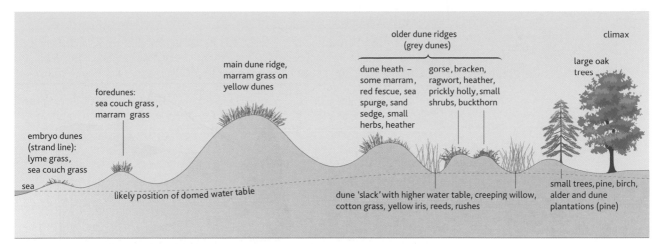

Fig. 3.17 *Transect of a typical sand dune system*

Activity

2 **a** Draw a sketch cross-section through a dune system. Add arrows to show how the following change as one moves across the system:

- stability of the surface
- water retention by the soil
- salinity
- height of the vegetation
- acidity of the soil
- complexity of the vegetation.

b How might the vegetation succession on a dune system be interrupted by human activity in the area?

c Winds blowing over the dunes can erode sand and form low areas called 'blow-outs' between the dunes. These hollows might be low enough to reach the water table, causing shallow pools or areas of marsh to develop at the bottom of the slack. How would these affect the development of the vegetation?

Key terms

Carr woodland: forms when shallow water or fen is left unmanaged and small shrubs and trees start to grow.

Case study

East Chevington Nature Reserve – hydrosere or plagioclimax?

Hydroseres develop on land that has been formed by the silting-up of a former area of fresh water, such as a lake, a pond, a swamp or a river flood plain.

The following quotes describe the ecosystems at East Chevington Nature Reserve near the Northumberland coast. The reserve has been developed on former open-cast mining land.

Extract from Druridge Bay Coastal Management Plan – Northumberland County Council

Druridge Bay is a low-lying plain where water is never far away. Mining has profoundly altered the natural hydrology and ecology of watercourses and wetlands, and has created new wetlands through subsidence and restoration. The wetlands in the coastal fringe form a very valuable refuge for breeding and migratory birds as well as for plants, invertebrates and amphibians. In addition to open water habitats there are water meadows, reed bed and swamp communities, mudflats and **carr woodlands**. Many of the wetland areas are also surrounded by important areas of drier semi-natural habitat such as woodland, scrub and rough grassland.

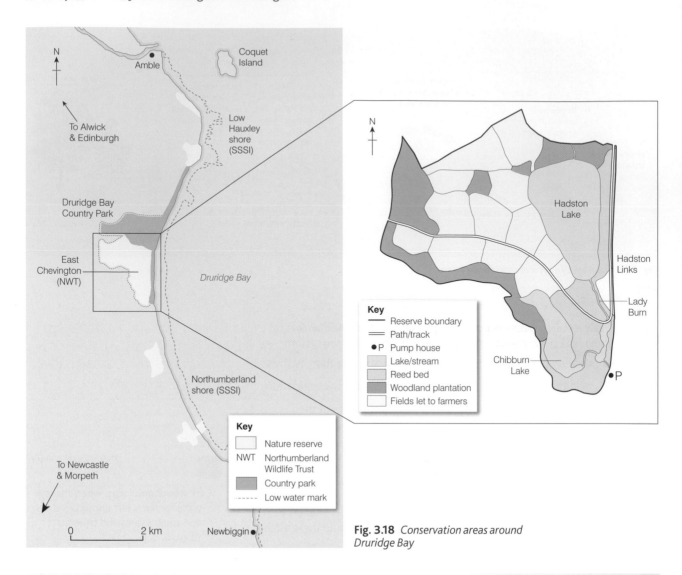

Fig. 3.18 *Conservation areas around Druridge Bay*

Extracts from interview with Northumberland Wildlife Trust volunteer at East Chevington reserve

I have done quite a lot of work on reed beds. Their ecology is fascinating. They form naturally as part of seral progression in shallow water round the edges of lakes. A stream flows into a shallow lake or pond. It deposits sediments in the pond and enriches the water with nutrients. Algae and mosses start to grow in the water, then water lilies, pond weed and submerged plants start to grow in the shallow water. As they die they enrich the organic content of the bed of the pond. Because the litter is covered in water there is no oxygen there to allow decomposition and this means that a layer of peat builds up on the lake bed. As this increases and the water becomes shallower, bulrushes, sedges and reeds can grow in and around the edge of the water.

It is this reed bed community that is particularly attractive to a wide range of insects and birds, forming an interesting but fragile ecosystem. As the reeds thicken they trap more sediment and the pond shrinks in size. Shrubs and trees, such as alder and willow, start to colonise the beds. Their roots help create new soil, and litter fall speeds up creating conditions where oak and ash can come in, creating a climatic climax community.

So what do the volunteers do to alter this progression? Essentially we interfere with the progression to maintain a plagioclimax community, which suits the needs of the area's management plan. We cut the reeds and bulrushes at the end of their growing season so that they do not fall and rot on the bed of the lake, and this slows down the formation of a litter layer that helps to fill up the lake bed. Then, every two years we try to clear out all the saplings and little shrubs, to stop them growing and out-competing the reeds. If they were allowed to develop they would block the light from the reeds and eventually stop them growing.

We feel that the reed bed here should be extensive enough to allow bitterns to colonise the area. A few years ago this species of bird was threatened with extinction in this country. Now it is becoming re-established on many reed-beds, just like the one we are trying to create here.

Activity

3 Make a copy of Fig. 3.19.

Annotate it to show the stages of development of a hydrosere on this land.

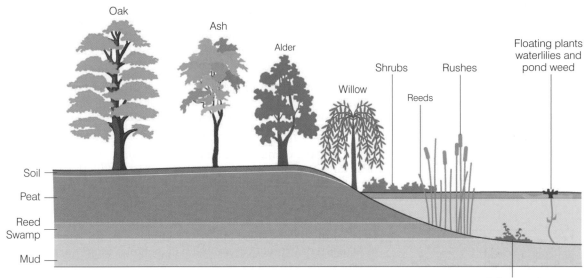

Fig. 3.19 *Seral progression on the edge of a lake or pond*

Soil	Sand and shells Not consolidated No organic content No moisture retention	Sand and traces of humus No water retention	Brown surface soil layer 5 cm – 10 cm Some water retention	Black humus-rich soil up tp 30 cm deep Quite good water retention
pH	8	8	6–5	4
Percentage bare ground	98–100	85–50	10–5	0
Number of species observed	1	1–3	8–20	12

Activity

4 Explain why the volunteer refers to the reed beds as a 'plagioclimax community'.

The climatic climax in the UK – the deciduous woodland biome

In this section you will learn:

- about the temperate deciduous woodland biome in the UK.

Links

Attempts are being made, with government backing, to reintroduce deciduous forest into the country wherever possible. To find out about major schemes go to: www. nationalforest.org and www. communityforest.org.uk

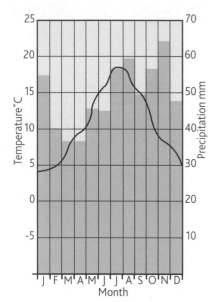

Fig. 3.20 *Climate graph for London*

The location of the temperate deciduous woodland biome is shown on the map, Fig. 3.32 on p114. However, it will be obvious to any geographer that this is a fairly theoretical map. It shows the vegetation that probably covered large parts of this area before humans started to remove it for farmland, pasture, buildings, roads, plantations of coniferous forests and many other uses. The remnants of the natural forest biome that survive in this country are few and far between.

The biome is a result of the interaction of the cool temperate western margin climate and the major soil type of the area, known as a brown earth. (Note that a soil type that is more or less consistent over a major continental or subcontinental area, like this one, is called a **zonal soil**.)

Over time, the climate, soil and vegetation have interacted so that, in many areas, interrupting factors that were stopping the progression to a climatic climax vegetation have been removed.

Deciduous forest has a high productivity. That is, it produces a large amount of organic matter for each square metre of area that it covers. In fact it is the second most productive biome after the equatorial forest, although it only produces around half as much material as the equatorial forest.

The dominant species is oak. Other common trees that grow almost as tall include beech (which is often dominant in forests with thinner soils formed on chalk or gravel), sycamore, ash (common on lime-rich soils) and chestnut. They all have broad, thin leaves which can absorb the maximum amount of sunlight with the smallest possible expenditure of energy. They all shed their leaves in winter. This adaptation to climate has come about because they cannot photosynthesise during winter so leaves are unnecessary then. It is more efficient for the tree to shed worn out and damaged leaves in autumn and to grow new ones in spring. The loss of leaves also slows transpiration and this has the added advantage of stopping the tree becoming desiccated (or dried out) at a time when moisture may not be easily available because the soil might be frozen.

Below the canopy formed by the dominant and sub-dominant trees there is often a shrub layer consisting of holly, hazel, hawthorn and smaller oak, etc., which are striving to grow upwards to reach the canopy.

Then, on the floor, there is often a layer of undergrowth – shrubs, bracken, ferns, grass, etc. In spring there might be many flowering plants on the woodland floor, with bluebells being the most characteristic. This undergrowth layer can be so thick and varied because plenty of light can penetrate in spring and early summer, before the leaf canopy has fully developed.

The food web in a deciduous woodland is complex (see Fig. 3.4).

The brown earth soils of the deciduous forest biome are mainly deep and fertile. There is a good supply of litter, particularly from the leaf fall. This decomposes fairly quickly because of the humidity – but not as quickly as litter decomposes in the rainforest biome, where temperatures are much higher. The rich variety of decomposers in the soil then helps to incorporate humus, from the decomposed litter, downwards into the soil.

The layer of dead material – leaves, twigs, etc. – on the surface is called the litter layer (or L horizon).

Then, beneath the litter is a layer where material has begun to decompose, due to the action of bacteria, etc. However, the shapes of leaves and twigs are still recognisable. This layer is called the fermentation layer.

With time this becomes a black, amorphous mass of organic material called the humus. This forms another distinct layer below the fermentation layer and above the mineral-rich A horizon.

Some humus can be carried downwards (or translocated) by the action of water percolating down into the soil. Soil organisms such as worms can also carry humus downwards. This helps to give the next layer of the soil (called the A horizon) its characteristic brown colour, as the humus stains the mineral content of the soil.

Through most of the year precipitation exceeds evaporation in the temperate climate regions, so there is a net downwards movement of water through the soil. This leaches base minerals out of the top layers of the soil and carries them downwards. Often they are redeposited lower down, forming a reddish layer where iron oxides have been deposited (the B horizon).

Finally, a layer of partly weathered parent material (the C horizon) is reached, merging with unweathered rock. This layer is often quite deep compared with soils in other biomes. Deep chemical weathering can take place here because of the abundance of water that flows through the soil down to this layer. In addition, this water is often mildly acidic, having dissolved some carbon dioxide from the atmosphere to form a weak solution of carbonic acid, or some humus, forming humic acid. Deep penetration of roots can also help to weather the C horizon.

Fig. 3.21 *The deciduous woodlands biome*

Did you know?

A single oak tree can be home to more than 400 different species of insects. They all find ecological niches, consuming different parts of the tree, or consuming other insects. In turn, all these insects attract birds and mammals to predate on them. The dead and decaying litter from the tree and its inhabitants attracts fungi, beetles, earthworms, microbes and other decomposers to the soil beneath the tree. An oak tree is the heart of its own separate ecosystem.

Activity

1 Compare what you have read here – about the theory of the temperate deciduous forest biome – with the reality of woods that you know. Discuss:

- any information that you can discover or deduce about the age of the woodland

- the different species of trees and other plants that you can see there

- any evidence that is available of other species – birds, mammals, insects, fungi, etc.

- whether the woodland has the layered structure expected in the model forest

- whether there is any evidence of the woodland regenerating itself – with new trees growing from seed, in the form of saplings, perhaps filling spaces left by dead or dying specimens

- what pressures have been put on the forest by human activities which may have made it into a plagioclimax community rather than a true climatic climax community

- whether any attempts have been made to conserve the forest.

Links

See how the seral progressions in a psammosere and in a hydrosere both move towards creation of deciduous woodland – pp89–93.

Ecosystem issues on a local scale

In this section you will learn:

- how urbanisation has produced a variety of specialised ecosystems in the UK

- about urban nature reserves in London and Bristol.

Changes resulting from urbanisation

As has been seen in the earlier parts of this chapter, the study of ecosystems involves, among other things, a study of:

- the colonisation of bare areas

- energy flows

- nutrient cycles

- species interactions, particularly the interactions in the food chain between three categories of organisms:
  - producers, or plants that are capable of photosynthesis
  - consumers – primary consumers (herbivorous), or secondary consumers (carnivorous)
  - decomposers – which break down the remains of other species

- the dynamics and changes in the system

- successions, leading towards stability in the ecosystem.

Any study of urban ecosystems needs to consider those same aspects but in a context where human influence is much stronger than in any other ecosystem. The increase in impervious surface area in urban areas affects both geomorphological and hydrological processes; it changes flows of water, nutrients and sediment. Urbanisation's use of energy gives out waste heat that is often stored in the atmosphere for longer because the pollution given off by urban areas traps the heat and does not allow it to be radiated away. Urbanisation's building density alters the flow patterns of the air, producing wind flows, turbulence and areas of shelter. All these alterations produce changes that influence the whole structure of urban ecosystems – the flora and fauna in niches throughout the urban area and beyond.

Table 3.1 shows how it is estimated that urban climates differ from surrounding areas.

Table 3.1 *Comparison of urban/rural climatic conditions*

Climatic or atmospheric factor	In comparison with surrounding area
Atmospheric pollution	10–25 times more
Solar radiation	15–20% less
Mean air temperature	0.5–1.5 °C higher
Air temperature on clear days	2–6 °C higher
Relative humidity (winter)	2% less
Relative humidity (summer)	8–10% less
Total rainfall	5–10% more
Cloudiness (periods of overcast sky)	5–10% more

What makes urban regions different from many other ecosystems is that in these regions humans are a dominant component – or an even more dominant component than in other regions. Cities evolve as the outcome of myriad interactions between the individual choices and actions of many human agents (e.g. households, businesses, developers and governments) and biophysical agents such as local geomorphology and climate. These choices produce different patterns of development, land use and infrastructure density. They affect ecosystem processes both directly (in and near the city) and remotely through their use of resources, and generation of emissions and waste.

There are many different land-use types (including industrial, commercial, mixed use, dense inner-city residential, less dense suburban residential and open space), all of which show different land-cover composition and patterns and all of which offer different opportunities and constraints on the development of the ecosystem.

More than that, human interference means that urban ecosystems are subject to more change and more rapid change than more natural ecosystems. It is far less likely that urban ecosystems will be left unaltered for long enough to move towards stability. Changes in drainage, micro-climate and the composition of the surface material, the introduction of new species either accidentally or deliberately, and the removal of established species for one reason or another mean that it is unlikely that the communities in these areas will achieve stability.

The effects of urbanisation are not just confined to built-up areas. Changes on the rural/urban fringe and beyond also result from the urbanisation process. Urban sprawl has important economic, social and environmental costs. It fragments forests, removes native vegetation, degrades water quality, lowers fish populations, and demands high mobility and an intensive transport infrastructure.

Moreover, urbanisation causes environmental changes at larger scales. Today's cities are sustained by a socioeconomic infrastructure on a global scale; the ecologically productive area required to support an urban area can be 100 to 300 times larger than the urban region. A city's footprint, its ecological impact, can be very far-reaching and have very profound effects even in areas that seem very 'rural'.

Fig. 3.22 *Buddleia growing on waste ground*

Human-dominated landscapes have unique biophysical characteristics. Humans redistribute organisms and alter the flows of energy and materials. The effects are both obvious (e.g. pavements, car parks) and subtle (e.g. acid rain, accidental introduction of non-native plant species); both immediate (e.g. dams drown river valleys) and long-term (e.g. new major roads direct and promote city growth on 20- to 100-year scales). All cities produce a complex mosaic of biological and physical patches in the midst of infrastructure, human organisations and social institutions.

The transformation of land cover favours organisms that are more capable of rapid colonisation, better adapted to the new conditions, and more tolerant of people than are many endemic, sensitive, locally specialised organisms. As a result, urbanising areas often have novel combinations of organisms living in unique communities. Mixes of native and non-native species interact in complex communities.

Some of those changes are outlined below.

■ Colonisation of wasteland

Wasteland is particularly associated with inner-city areas, though it is found in all but the most affluent parts of a town, and includes unused or vacant land such as areas of former industrial or mining land, abandoned factories and other large building areas such as demolished houses, and former railway land such as sidings and disused trackways. These are areas generally ranging from 0.1 to 10 hectares in size that have essentially been left to nature.

Plant colonisation on these areas of wasteland represents a seral progression – probably a lithosere – with the surface of the land being, in some ways, like a newly exposed bare rock surface.

This kind of wasteland often represents a temporary land use, since many such areas are scheduled to be redeveloped for other uses. Wasteland is found on such a wide range of **substrates** and soils that a wide variety of ecological communities may form. Plants might colonise newly created wasteland by dispersing from similar sites elsewhere; they might arrive in dumped soil; and they might germinate from the seed bank associated with previous land uses. Bare substrate is not uncommon, and there tends to be an abundance of pioneer lichens and mosses, annual and biennial plants (often of an ephemeral nature), and garden escapes.

Invertebrate life here can be abundant and species-rich. Common invertebrates in the early stages of succession include ground predators such as spiders, harvestmen and beetles, as well as moths, butterflies, etc. visiting nectar-producing flowers. As the site ages, earthworms and other soil-dwelling invertebrates become commoner, enhancing soil development. A few vertebrates might use these areas for breeding, especially where size and isolation permit. It is for feeding, however, that wasteland habitats are, perhaps, most important for birds and mammals – ranging from feral pigeons to peregrine falcons, from rats to urban foxes.

Many wasteland sites are eyesores that attract abuse from the public, such as fly-tipping and bonfires. Nevertheless, they have an intrinsic value to local and regional biodiversity and conservation, and with low levels of care many could be turned into sites of importance for local communities (see London Wildlife Trust). Some conservationists even say that the term 'wasteland' should be avoided, as the areas might be viewed more positively if they were called 'urban commons'.

After demolition of buildings, sites are left as slightly domed areas of rubble and finer material which is dominated by lime-based mortar, producing neutral to alkaline soils (pH values typically 6.5–8.0). Such sites are generally free-draining, well-aerated and low in organic matter. Fertility will vary. Substrates based on previously industrial land can also be alkaline – for example, over slag – but acid conditions can occur, and these differences will be reflected in the flora and vegetation. Post-industrial sites might also be heavily polluted, especially by heavy metals, and the flora will be limited to pollution-tolerant species and varieties. Many post-industrial sites have a varied micro-topography which, in turn, varies in permeability. A common result is a patchwork of different plant communities on mounds, in permeable depressions, and in impermeable dips in the surface.

Many wasteland sites are temporary, and the land is often redeveloped within a few years. If succession is allowed to take place, a series of stages can often be seen:

■ An initial annual/biennial/short-lived perennial stage, the plants colonising an often bare inorganic substrate containing at best a few small patches where organic detritus or a thin soil is found. Nitrogen-fixing plants increase the amount of available nitrogen. Wind-blown species are characteristic.

■ After perhaps 3–6 years, as the soil cover becomes greater in extent and depth, and with an increase in organic matter and available nutrients, the vegetation often becomes dominated by tall perennial herbs. Rosebay willow herb is particularly common. Woody species begin to colonise, whether scrambling species such as bramble, shrubs such as buddleia, or small trees. Numbers and cover at this stage remain low.

■ With time, the proportion of grass in the vegetation increases, and after 8–10 years or so, tall herb communities may give way to grassland, though a grassland in which some perennial plants may persist, as well as woody species. As more and more woody plants enter the tall herb or grassland community these might eventually be replaced by scrub woodland.

Urban nature reserves managed by London Wildlife Trust

Gunnersbury Triangle (near Chiswick Park Underground station, on a triangle of land between railway lines) became one of the London Wildlife Trust's first reserves when it was saved from development by a campaign run by local people. Since the end of the Second World War the woodland here has grown up naturally and the reserve has become a sheltered birch and willow woodland with attractive pond, marsh and meadow. Hidden away, the reserve opens up before you – so follow the nature trail, listening out for birds or the rustle of a hedgehog and look out for the tunnels of field voles or interesting spiders and ladybirds.

The Ripple, set amid the industrial landscape of Barking Reach, and once a dumping area for pulverised fuel ash, the 10-hectare site provides a fascinating example of how nature can reclaim industrial wasteland. Hundreds of orchids, including the southern marsh and common spotted orchids, provide the major attraction of the site and can be seen dotted throughout the birch woodland floor between May and June. The silver birches stand next to a new meadow boasting a wide range of native wildflowers and grasses, attracting a range of butterflies, hoverflies and bees.

■ Links

Further details about these three sites can be found at: www.wildlondon.org.uk (type in 'Wasteland' and follow the links)

Camley Street Natural Park is the most urban of all London's nature reserves. Lying between King's Cross Station and Regents Canal the patch of land had been used for industry for around 200 years. It had been an ironworks, a rubbish tip, part of it had even been a poorhouse. From the late 1800s until 1970 the site had been used as a coal drop – coal was dropped off from the railway on to canal barges which distributed it around London. This practice had become obsolete by the late 1960s and the site had become derelict. It was a typical post-industrial urban wasteland. So the GLC wanted to tarmac this land over, while the local eco group wanted it to be saved for wildlife.

King's Cross fox

London Wildlife Trust volunteer Shaun Marriott took this picture of a sleek **fox** peering into the pond at **Camley Street Natural Park** in King's Cross. Foxes are thriving in the city, mainly due to their amazing adaptability.

Fig. 3.23 *The King's Cross fox*

■ Ecosystems along routeways

Routeways through and between urban areas have their own special ecosystems that are affected by many processes and flows that are different from other parts of the urban or semi-urban areas through which they pass. Among these processes and flows are:

■ construction techniques that make the surface quite different from elsewhere

■ drainage systems that are quite different from most other areas and which help create a varied patchwork of niche ecosystems

■ maintenance that involves some management of the ecosystem, and some total neglect

■ a constant linear movement of traffic along the routeways, often carrying and dispersing seeds, etc.

■ an absence of people from the verges and embankments, reducing one kind of human interference

■ the addition of large amounts of salt (and other substances) to reduce the risk of ice in winter

■ pollution from traffic fumes and litter.

Two aspects of routeway ecosystems will be considered here:

1 the development of communities on motorway verges

2 the railways and the spread of Oxford ragwort.

The development of communities on motorway verges

Most modern roads and their verges tend to be about 100 years old or more, stemming from the invention of tarmacadam, but quite a few are much older still. However, the first section of motorway was only completed in 1959, so even the oldest is still only just 50 years old. The ecology of a motorway verge is influenced by local climate and soil conditions and by the planting and management policies of the Highways Agency that is responsible for the upkeep of the road and its verges.

The soil that is excavated from the bed of the motorway is generally piled up on the sides, forming banks. These act as sound deflectors as well as creating a barrier for any vehicles that leave the carriageways.

The geology of a given area affects the size, shape and gradient of the bordering verge, and the development of the soil. These are influenced by

Fig. 3.24 *Vegetation on a motorway verge*

the hardness, durability, stability and rate of weathering of the local rock structure. Rocks such as chalk, limestone or granite are very stable and relatively hard, so the gradient can be steep and soil formation is quite slow. Clays and sandstones form lighter soils with higher weathering rates, so the gradient will be lower and the roots of the verge plants are needed to hold the structure together and create a stable environment.

During the construction of a motorway, the soil verges are appropriately prepared to make a good seedbed prior to seeding, which is then done as soon as possible to avoid soil erosion. The seed mixtures that are used are basically of two types, grass seed mix and flower meadow mix. The flower meadow mix will have native wild flower seed with very little or no grass seeds in. The grass seed mix will have four to six species of grass seed and usually some white clover as a nitrogen fixer.

As well as herbaceous plants, trees and shrubs are also planted. The Forestry Commission and the Department for Environment, Food and Rural Affairs (Defra) choose suitable areas for planting, with preferences for sites that hide unsightly objects, soften hard outlines of structures such as bridges and help to deaden noise levels in built-up areas.

The most common tree species planted are field maple, sycamore, silver birch, Scots pine, oak, beech and ash. Common shrub species planted are hazel, goat willow, hawthorn, blackthorn and elder.

Soon after the initial planting and seeding, the community starts to be penetrated by other plant species. The rate and extent of this invasion depends on the nature of the terrain, the number of dormant seeds present in the topsoil, the introduction of seeds from elsewhere (wind-blown seeds from surrounding areas or seeds carried on passing traffic and/or birds) and management methods. Of particular interest is the spread of halophiles (salt-loving plants) along the motorway networks. Because of the salt spread on major roads in winter, seaside species can be found spreading inland along many main roads and motorways. These include Danish scurvy grass (ground-hugging plants whose whitish flowers border hard shoulders in April and May), lesser sea-spurrey, and buck's-horn plantain and grass-leaved orache (both found on the M5).

The grassland, scrub and woods beside the country's major roads now contain 60 Sites of Special Scientific Interest and harbour some rare plants such as the Deptford pink, green-winged orchid and yellow rattle. They are also home to black hairstreak and white admiral butterflies, and mammals such as Daubenton's bats and muntjac deer, water voles by the M26 and greater horseshoe bats by the A38. In fact, the small mammal populations of mice, shrews and voles tempt so many kestrels to hover over verges that the bird is virtually an emblem of the road network; and the red kites of the Chilterns are a noted feature for many travellers on the M40. One reason for their presence is the abundance of carrion (or roadkill) in the area.

Did you know?

The Highways Agency (HA) is actually the second biggest planter of trees in the country: there are 32 million of them on England's motorway and trunk road network. Last year the HA planted its 50 millionth tree since the Second World War, and it has now put up 1,000 bat boxes and miles of badger fencing, as well as otter runs and ponds for great crested newts.

Blogging about biodiversity

I used to survey motorway verges – not a lot of fun you know … I've not seen anything that rare I suppose, highlights would be: tree sparrows, waxwings, adders, slow worms, lizards, common spotted orchids, pyramidal orchids and another orchid I couldn't ID probably lots of other interesting plants but I wasn't there to look for them … but yes they can be very useful as green corridors for small terrestrial animals and plants as often the land immediately behind the Highway Agency Boundary is intensively managed arable. Unfortunately they are often too attractive to barn owls …

From blog on www.wildaboutbritain.co.uk

Fig. 3.25 *Oxford ragwort colonising waste ground*

The vortex of air following the express train carries the fruits in its wake. I have seen them enter a railway-carriage window near Oxford and remain suspended in the air in the compartment until they found an exit at Tilehurst.

George Druce, botanist and Mayor of Oxford, 1927

Key terms

Ecological niche: the place of each species within an ecosystem. This includes the space that it occupies and also the role it carries out within the community and its relationship with the other species living around it.

■ The planned and unplanned introduction of new species

The spread of Oxford ragwort along the railways

Oxford ragwort is a member of the *Senecio* genus. Senecio is a yellow-flowered herbaceous plant, native to mountainous, rocky or volcanic areas. It was introduced into Britain from Sicily, where it lives as a native on volcanic ash. It was brought in 1700 to the Duchess of Beaufort's garden at Badminton and was later transferred to the Oxford Botanic Garden. It probably 'escaped' into the wild in around 1720 and grew in the stonework of Oxford colleges and many of the stone walls around the city of Oxford. This gave the plant its common name, 'Oxford ragwort'.

Since then it has managed to find other homes on man-made and natural piles of rocks, war-ruined neighbourhoods and even on stone walls that resemble its well-drained, rocky homeland. Oxford became connected to the railway system in the mid-1800s and the plant gained a new habitat in the railway lines' clinker beds, gradually spreading via the railway to other parts of the country. The process was accelerated by the movement of the trains and the limestone ballast that provides a similar growing medium to the lava-soils of its native home in Sicily.

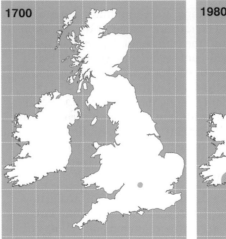

Fig. 3.26 *Spread of Oxford ragwort, 1700–1980*

The two maps in Fig. 3.26 show how Oxford ragwort has spread over a period of 180 years.

■ Ecosystems at the rural/urban fringe

Like any other part of the urban area, the rural/urban fringe generally consists of a mosaic of ecosystems, each existing in its own small **ecological niche**.

On the rural side there might typically be a mixture of intensive agriculture, market gardening for the nearby urban market, hedgerow, pastoral land, small woods, nature reserves, wasteland, patches of housing with gardens, etc.

On the more urban side of the fringe the mixture might contain an increased percentage of new gardens, established gardens, parks, playing fields, roadside and railway verges, allotments, derelict land, etc.

Sometimes the edge of the urban area is defined by planning laws. Green-belt legislation, for instance, makes it very difficult to obtain planning permission to build beyond a certain line, and even when there is no green belt, local land-use zoning can still make it difficult to obtain planning permission in the rural parts of the fringe zone.

Urban blight

Urban blight can affect rural areas just beyond the limits of a town or city. It can happen that agricultural land near to a city starts to deteriorate and to be less well farmed. This can be due to a variety of causes, including:

- vandalism caused by urban dwellers (including fly-tipping)
- pressure of tourist and leisure demands on the farmland, leading to diversification away from traditional farming
- tourism and leisure making farming more difficult because of pressure from walkers, dog-walkers, off-road cyclists, canoeists, etc.
- pollution from traffic, housing, litter, etc. damaging farmland.

However, one of the biggest pressures leading to the decline of farmland can be caused by farmers not bothering to invest in improving their land because they expect that it might be bought up in the fairly near future for building development. Indeed, much of the farmland around some towns and cities has already been bought by developers, building companies or just by land speculators in the hope of a future profit when the planners allow the land to be developed. Such owners might continue to farm the land through tenants on short-term contracts, but they do not encourage investment for long-term development by farmers.

All these influences on the land beyond the edge of the city can affect the ecology. They can even lead to a more varied ecology as any reduction in the intensity of farming and the use of chemical fertilisers and pesticides is likely to lead to an increase in biodiversity.

Fig. 3.27 *Newcastle Great Park*

Garden creation

Gardens created on the rural/urban fringe can range through:

- paved areas and patios where the ecosystem is deliberately destroyed and where rapid run-off of rainwater is deliberately encouraged, adding to potential flooding problems in, and downstream from, urban areas

'Wildlife corridors' are the prime means of physically linking wildlife habitat and allow some species to move between otherwise isolated areas. This can help to replenish isolated populations. Ideally, the corridor itself also meets some or all of the need for shelter, protection, food and breeding sites – a simple concept but one which can occur in a variety of settings and habitat – urban as well as rural.

From Shared Earth Trust: www. shared-earth-trust.org.uk

■ **Did you know?**

Wildlife corridors on a completely different scale are now being planned in parts of Amazonia, to link up surviving areas of rainforest in burnt regions to isolated patches where species might not survive without links to other patches.

- lawns, which when 'well kept' become monocultures, free from weeds and treated with chemicals that limit the number of plant and animal species there, even limiting the development of worms and the birds that feed on them

- gardens where large numbers of exotic (imported from outside the country or region) plant species are introduced; these can then escape into the surrounding environment (see Oxford ragwort) and compete with indigenous species; they might also discourage wildlife species, as they are not adapted to survive on and around such exotics

- 'wildlife gardens' where planting patterns are designed to encourage species of insects, butterflies, birds and small mammals; ponds and damp areas are managed to attract further varieties of insects along with frogs and other amphibians; areas are designed for hedgehogs to hibernate, birds to nest and feed; chemical use is kept to a minimum or avoided altogether, to encourage the widest possible variety of species of all kinds.

Creation of new habitats and wildlife corridors

The concept of 'urban wildlife corridors' is a vital one for everyone concerned with the conservation of urban ecosystems. Within any urban area there are patches where wildlife can continue to exist. Small and medium-sized areas develop either by chance, because they are ignored or because individuals and groups have made deliberate efforts to develop and maintain them. Unfortunately, these areas are often isolated from each other within a matrix of different land uses. This makes them less viable because species become isolated and, existing in small groups, can easily be wiped out by disruptions to the ecosystem. Other species cannot survive in the small patches because they need a bigger range to survive and cannot find enough food, however suitable that patch might otherwise be.

Wildlife corridors through farmland are important in rural areas. These can include hedgerows, streams and their banks, earth banks, footpaths, set-aside strips and field edges, and so on. In urban areas these more traditional corridors have to be replaced by other features that can play a part in the wildlife distribution network. Railway lines and motorway verges offer security from human disturbance, with the wildlife quickly adapting to the noise and wind generated by passing trains and vehicles. Industrial sites can also provide vital links, through peripheral waste ground and overgrown run-off ditches, in what otherwise would be a wildlife 'desert'. As 'greenfield' sites are developed, gardens and school grounds can take on increasing significance as stepping stones for wildlife between areas of countryside.

Corridors can be non-continuous. For example, clumps of habitat not too far apart, such as groups of gardens, derelict buildings and patches of wasteland enable some species to cross areas that they would otherwise find difficult. Such 'stepping stones' can help to link patches of richer habitat. Some species might not even need stepping stones of the same habitat type, but just a more friendly environment that provides food or shelter, over which to travel.

Many planning authorities in urban areas are now deliberately developing wildlife corridors in their areas. Milton Keynes was planned as a New Town and, right from its inception in 1967, it was built around a grid system of roads that intersected more or less at right angles. Built alongside this road system was a grid of green corridors along rivers, through parks and linked by roadside verges, footpaths and the earth banks that separated housing areas from employment areas.

In 2002 part of the green belt around Newcastle upon Tyne was taken out so that development could go ahead on it. One of the conditions for developers was that the areas around the developments had to be landscaped. The landscaping usually involved the planting of native species of plants that would be attractive to the indigenous wildlife. And the landscaped areas were linked together by streams. These streams ran into the Ouseburn, which flowed from the newly developed area into the older, built-up areas of the city.

In fact, the Ouseburn forms a green corridor that runs from the countryside to the north, right through Gosforth, Jesmond and Byker, to the old industrial heart of the city. From the Newcastle Great Park the river runs through the Garden Village, Jesmond Dene, Jesmond Vale, Byker City Farm and the Ouseburn Redevelopment Area, all of which include areas with wildlife friendly ecosystems (see *AQA AS Geography*, pp191–5).

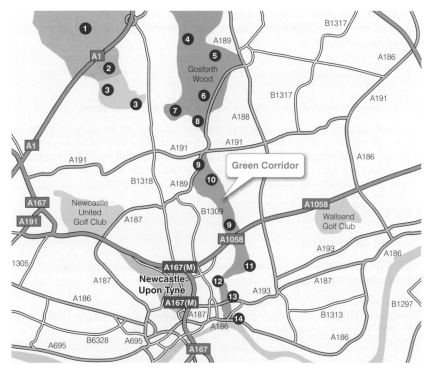

Key

1 Newcastle Great Park – some early development shown in blue ⎫
2 Newcastle Great Park – new housing in landscaped park ⎬ Ouse Burn flows through both parts
3 Golf course
4 Race course and park
5 Nature reserve
6 Farmland
7 Cemetery
8 Allotments and public open space
9 Jesmond Dene – deeply incised valley with steep wooded slopes
10 Playing fields
11 Victorian park with bandstand, etc.
12 Playing fields
13 Byker city farm
14 Confluence of Ouse Burn and River Tyne

0   1 km
approx scale

Various open spaces
Golf courses
Newcastle Great Park – former green belt

Fig. 3.28 *Ouseburn green corridor*

Links

See the Scottish Environment Protection Agency leaflet on Watercourses in the Community showing how urban waterways can become green corridors at www.sepa.org.uk/water/water_publications/habitat_enhancement_initiative.aspx Ouseburn green corridor.

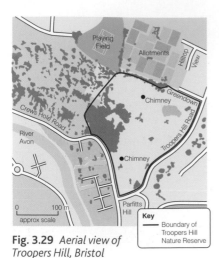

Fig. 3.29 *Aerial view of Troopers Hill, Bristol*

■ Links

The aerial photo of the Troopers Hill site came from: www.multimap.com – go to the site and click on 'Bird's Eye' to see photos of the site in more detail.

The full Management Plan can be downloaded from: www.bristol.gov.uk

Go to 'Parks and open spaces' then 'Nature reserves' then 'Troopers Hill' and the Management Plan link is at the bottom of that page.

■ Case study

Troopers Hill – urban conservation case study

Troopers Hill Local Nature Reserve lies about 1 km east of Bristol city centre, on the northern valley side of the River Avon. In the past this was the scene of mining and industrial activities, but now it is an important and much-loved nature reserve and local amenity. The land is owned and managed by Bristol City Council, but local people are actively involved in caring for the area and in planning for its future. The reserve has two main aims:

■ to provide an area for recreation for local people

■ to serve as an ecological conservation area and to conserve its special ecosystem that has evolved and adapted to fit this urban environment and which is home to several rare species.

In January 2007 a new Management Plan was adopted for the reserve. The plan looks to the future, but includes an ongoing review process:

> The plan was implemented from the start of the financial year, 1 April 2007.
>
> The plan is to inform policy-making with a view of over 50 years.
>
> It contains a fiveyear work plan that will be reviewed annually as part of the process of creating an annual action plan. This is because it identifies a number of longer-term proposals that cannot be implemented until financial resources have been identified. It will also make it more responsive to, for example, changes in wildlife populations.
>
> The whole document will be reviewed after five years, in April 2012.

Site description

This description is based on material from the Troopers Hill Management Plan.

Troopers Hill is a hillside facing south and west, providing spectacular views across the city and towards the Mendip Hills. The top is an uneven plateau which slopes steeply down towards the River Avon to the south-west. The site is mainly surrounded by suburban roads, but to the north-east part of the boundary lies adjacent to 'The Farm' allotment site. The site has been extensively worked for minerals in the past. It is uneven and very steep in places, with mainly very poor soils. There is some bare rock on the steeper slopes and there are some areas of mining spoil heaps, which are eroded by gullies in places.

The flora of Troopers Hill is very interesting. The top of the ridge and tops of the spoil heaps are generally clothed with fine grasses and mosses. There is occasional ling and heather in places. It is difficult to decide if this is a remnant of wider areas of heath or new heath colonising the grass. The tops of the slopes have heath, sometimes with broom or gorse. Lower down is often bramble with bracken which diffuses into hawthorn and woodland trees at the bottom of the slopes and especially around the boundaries of the site.

History of the site

In the 18th century a copper-smelting industry was established near Troopers Hill. Copper ore was brought by boat, mainly from Cornwall and north Devon, and coal was sourced locally. The chimney that still dominates the site (and is now a Grade II listed structure) was probably built in the 1790s for a copper works. The smelting of both copper and lead in the Avon Valley throughout the 18th century might have had an effect on the natural environment of the hill. Both produce smoke laden with sulphur, which could have increased the acidity of the soil in the surrounding area.

In the early 19th century there was some quarrying of sandstone for use as building material, but the most significant development was the opening of Troopers Hill pit. The colliery mined coal from the early 1800s and closed before 1845. All that remains of the colliery is the area's second chimney, also now a Grade II listed structure.

Fig. 3.29 *Troopers Hill, heath in spring*

In 1830 Elisabeth Emra, the parson's daughter, described the area:

> ... the barren and quarried hill, with its yellow spots of gorse and broom, and its purple shade of heath, raising itself above the dark heaps of dross on our own side; and then the river, the beautiful, soft flowing river that we have all loved so well ...

(*Dross* meant heaps of waste from the smelting industry.)

Then, in 1843, a chemical works was built at the foot of Troopers Hill to make creosote and tar to treat the railway sleepers being used to build the new Great Western Railway. Production of chemicals probably continued until the late 19th century, and sandstone quarrying until slightly later. The site lay derelict until it was bought by Bristol Council in 1932. In 1912 the vegetation of the area had been described as:

> the trees are low in stature, as if stunted by fumes and smoke from collieries and chemical works; and the few remaining portions of old Kingswood Chase are sprinkled with heather, broom, needle-whin, and uncommon forms of bramble.

Recently a survey said:

> Troopers Hill LNR supports the only significant area of Lowland Heathland and Lowland Acidic Grassland in the Bristol area. Both of these habitats are identified under the UK Biodiversity Action Plan (www.ukbap.org.uk) as UK Priority Habitats.

Vegetation communities and their management

Several vegetation communities have been identified on the Troopers Hill site. Their special nature arises mainly from the fact that the bedrocks are sandstones, producing an acid soil that contrasts with the more basic soils formed on the Carboniferous limestones that underlie most of the Bristol area.

Each community has a distinct set of management priorities.

Acid heath

Ling and bell heather are both found on the site, growing in a matrix of acid grassland. This is considered to be the most important part of the site because it is the only heath within the city of Bristol.

Acid grassland

This grows on the very poorest soils with minimal maintenance. In places there is very sparse vegetation cover and mosses colonise the area. Bare soil is evident in many places and this is important for many of the invertebrates.

Current management

The heathland and acidic grassland are the most important habitats on the site. Therefore, no other species are allowed to invade this area. Until now, little management has been necessary other than preventing invasion by bramble, bracken, scrub and trees.

However, parts of Troopers Hill now have relatively old heather and ling plants, and in future it might be necessary to consider cutting back these areas to encourage regrowth and new seedlings to emerge. The situation will be monitored annually along with the five-year work plan.

Flower meadow

There is an area within the site that has more fertile soil than most other parts. It has a flora more akin to a meadow, with both vigorous grasses and flowering plants, as in the traditional hay meadow where the grass was only mowed by farmers in late June or July. This allowed flower species to bloom and seed before they were cut down, producing a very attractive mix of grasses and flowers. Modern farming techniques and early mowing mean that such meadows are increasingly rare.

Current management

Troopers Hill is mown annually, with the arisings (or cut grass) removed from the site to encourage as diverse a range of plant life as possible.

Trees

While there are some sizeable oaks there are no really large mature trees on Troopers Hill. This is probably due to the previous industrial use of the site. It is impossible to know if any trees have ever been planted here. It is assumed that the trees have all arrived through natural regeneration, probably from the well-wooded slopes of the adjacent site. The main group is oak; there is also a group of birch and a scattering of willow.

Current management

'Native' trees are allowed to colonise parts of the boundaries of Troopers Hill. This forms a useful barrier giving privacy to adjoining properties and shelter for birds. It also screens the adjacent allotment site.

Non-native species are removed when still young. All seedling trees are removed from areas of heath and grassland in order to conserve those important environments. Trees are checked every two years as part of the risk assessment regime.

Scrub

Scrub is an important component of the Troopers Hill landscape and provides very important wildlife habitats. It includes all stages, from scattered bushes in grassland to closed-canopy (where the ground is not open to the sky) vegetation, dominated by shrubs and tree saplings, usually less than 5 m tall, occasionally with a few scattered trees.

Links

Much of the management is carried out by Friends of Troopers Hill. Their site is excellent. It can be found at: www.troopers-hill.org.uk

Of particular interest is the Photo Survey which shows in great detail how the site has developed over the period between 1994 and 2006. There are many other photos on other parts of the site, but the sequences in the survey are particularly interesting because they show ecological changes so well.

There is an increasing amount of bramble, hawthorn and bracken scrub present on Troopers Hill. Some scrub patches have more wildlife value than others – low, dense scrub is of maximum value for most invertebrates and nesting birds. The benefits of scrub include:

■ as a landscape feature to frame views or block intrusive views, e.g. the adjacent allotment site

■ to provide variation and relief from the very open grassland landscape

■ to provide habitat for insects, birds and plants that do not inhabit open grassland

■ to provide warmth, shelter and variations in grassland habitats by acting as a windbreak and casting shade

■ to add educational interest.

Scrub is a transitional landscape between grassland and woodland and will disappear if not managed. The spaces between the woody plants are just as important as the woody plants themselves. This is true from both a landscape and wildlife perspective. If it is not managed, the spaces in between the shrubs disappear first (loss of some herbaceous species) and then the larger woody types (trees) dominate, with a consequential loss of some small woody species and herbs. The existing landscape character will be lost and the diversity of 'wild' species will be diminished if scrub is not managed.

Current management

Heathland-type scrub with broom is managed to maintain the presence of typical species on site.

Hawthorn scrub is managed to prevent it from developing into woodland.

Bramble is managed to prevent encroachment onto open areas of heath or grassland and paths.

Japanese knotweed is present in places. This is sprayed with herbicide twice a year. The objective is to remove this non-native, invasive species completely.

Invertebrates

Many species of bird and mammal can be seen on Troopers Hill, but it is the invertebrate species that make this site particularly special. The following passages from the Friends of Troopers Hill website and from the Management Plan illustrate this.

◀ ▶   File   Edit   History   Bookmarks   Print   View   Window   Help

Invertebrates

Troopers Hill is alive with butterflies in the spring and summer. Common blues, holly blues, small coppers, marbled white and the beautiful brimstone are all regularly seen. The grassland is home to thousands of crickets and grasshoppers that can be heard as well as seen.

In addition to butterflies there are many smaller less noticeable invertebrates on Troopers Hill and for many of these it is the most important site of its type in the Bristol region. There are a large number of local rarities and an endangered species, the mining bee was found in 2000. This and other more common bees nest in the areas of erosion on the hill making these areas of bare ground one of the most important habitats on the site.

The importance of the site for invertebrates has been confirmed by a series of surveys carried out by local expert David Gibbs, which can be downloaded from www.troopers-hill. org.uk/Flora/DGibbs2007.pdf
Just four visits in 2007 yielded 262 species of which 30 are considered to be of conservation significance and 6 have Red Data Book (RDB) or equivalent status. RDB status means that the invertebrates are considered to be rare in this country.

Links

The full Management Plan can be downloaded from: www.bristol.gov.uk

Go to 'Parks and open spaces' then 'Nature reserves' then 'Troopers Hill' and the Management Plan link is at the bottom of that page.

The 2006 survey identified a species of particular interest as it was recorded here for the first time in Great Britain. This tiny leafmining fly (*Phytomyza sedi*) is a European species so far known from France, Germany, Spain and Yugoslavia. Its host plant is stonecrop (*Sedum*) where it mines the leaves. At Troopers Hill it is associated with the extensive patch of stonecrop. This is not a native species in Britain. It is impossible to know if it is an introduced species associated with garden stonecrops or a previously undetected native.

Activity

1 a Study the text on Troopers Hill, and the linked websites. Write summaries to show how:

- the ecosystem has been affected by geology

- the ecosystem has been affected by past industrial activity

- the vegetation of the area has evolved over the period from 1994 to the present

- invasive species have the potential to affect the ecosystem and how/why these invasions are being resisted by the managers of the site

- local communities can change the ecology of the site in both positive and negative ways.

b Discuss the reasons for keeping areas like this, in heavily built-up areas, as both nature reserves and open spaces for public recreation. Are these two different uses of the land compatible? Can a real nature reserve exist when the area is well used for general recreation?

c Should areas like this have management plans that are designed to slow down or stop the natural seral progression and keep the ecosystem in a particular state rather than evolving naturally?

The tropical grassland biome

In this section you will learn:

- how climate, soils, vegetation, animals and man interact in the tropical grasslands biome

- how attempts are being made to conserve the ecosystems of the Serengeti grasslands in Tanzania and the rainforests of Amazonia.

The map in Fig. 3.31 shows the distribution of the world's major biomes. The tropical grassland or savanna grassland biome generally lies between about 5° north or south of the equator and 23° north or south, on either side of the tropical rainforest biome. The one major exception to this pattern comes in East Africa, where the grassland spreads right across the equator, connecting the northern and southern grassland areas.

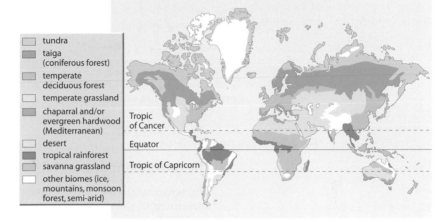

Fig. 3.31 *World biomes*

The climate of the tropical grassland region

The tropical grassland region lies close enough to the equator to experience high temperatures throughout the year. However, the apparent migration of the overhead sun gives the region a distinctly seasonal climate.

The formation of the ITCZ rainfall belt

The origin of most of the rainfall in the tropical regions is an area known as the **inter-tropical convergence zone** (**ITCZ**). It forms as a result of intense solar heating.

Warm air is able to hold more water vapour than cool air can. When the air at the surface is heated it can hold large quantities of water vapour that has been evaporated from the surface or has transpired from the surfaces of plants. Then, as the air rises and cools, it is less able to hold water vapour. Some of that water vapour condenses to form microscopic water droplets, but these droplets coalesce (join together) to form larger and larger particles. If the air rises high enough, condensation will continue to add to the number and size of water droplets so that thick clouds will form, eventually leading to rain. Because the air is moving in convection currents, this type of rainfall is known as **convectional rain**.

At the ITCZ the heating is so intense and the convection currents so strong that they dominate the climate of the whole tropical region. The air rises, cools and brings rain. The cooler air then flows polewards, away from the equator. Then, at about 30° from the equator, the cooled air starts to sink back towards the surface.

As the air sinks it warms again, due to compression. However, because the air has lost its moisture (which fell as rain at the ITCZ), the warming process is more rapid than the cooling as the air rose. This means that

Key terms

Inter-tropical convergence zone (ITCZ): a result of the heating of part of the Earth's surface, caused by the concentrated insolation from the overhead sun. This leads to heating of the air lying on that surface. The heated air becomes less dense and rises. This draws in cooler air that flows across the surface to replace the rising air. Air streams are drawn in from both north and south of the equator and they meet in the area from which the air is rising.

areas of hot, dry, high-pressure air form at about 30° north and south of the equator. It is air from these high-pressure air masses that is drawn back in to the ITCZ as surface winds.

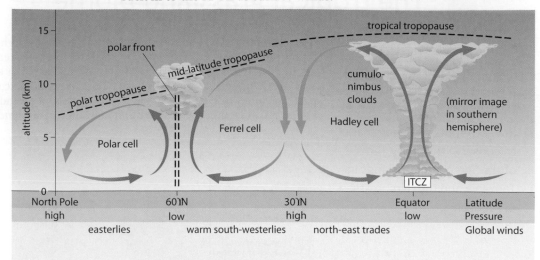

Fig. 3.32 *Atmospheric circulation*

The movement of the ITCZ

The seasonal nature of the tropical climate is due to the apparent movement of the overhead sun. This, in turn, leads to the migration of the ITCZ and its associated rain belt. The sun appears overhead at the equator on or around 21 March and 21 September. During summer in the northern hemisphere the sun appears to migrate north of the equator, and in the northern winter it appears to migrate south of the equator. As the overhead sun migrates, so does the area of maximum insolation and maximum heating of the surface; so, too, does the ITCZ.

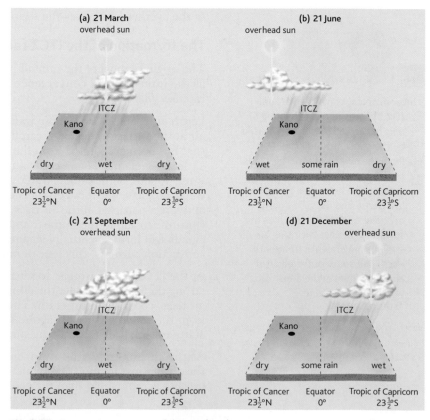

Fig. 3.33 *Apparent movement of the overhead sun*

This means that places such as Kano, near to the tropic, have one season of the year when the sun is overhead and the ITCZ dominates the area and brings intense rainfall. For the rest of the year Kano's climate is dominated by the tropical high-pressure air mass and is dry.

Closer to the equator the wet season gets longer and rainfall totals get higher, until the tropical climate merges with the equatorial climate. Moving the other way, towards the poles, the rainfall season gets shorter and the rainfall totals get lower, until the tropical climate merges with the hot desert climate.

The combined pattern of rainfall and temperature leads to the area's **soil moisture budget**.

During the wet season, from May to September in the case of Kano, there is usually an excess of rainfall over evaporation. There is plenty of water available to infiltrate the soil where it is available for plant growth.

During the dry season there is an excess of evaporation over precipitation so little water percolates down through the soil. Indeed, some water is drawn back to the surface where it then evaporates so little water percolates down through the soil. Evaporation, combined with water being used by plants, steadily reduces the soil's store of moisture until it is dry. From this point on there is no moisture available for plant growth and so most plants stop growing and enter a dormant period. This is known as the period of 'soil moisture deficit'.

Then, at the start of the next wet season, the first rains that infiltrate the soil (that is, that do not get evaporated by the sun, used by plants or animals or run off to the rivers) go to recharge the pore spaces in the soil. This is known as the period of 'soil moisture recharge'.

If a point is reached when the pore spaces are all filled and there is still an excess of rainfall over evaporation, the excess water will flow through or over the soil to the rivers or to the water table in the rock below.

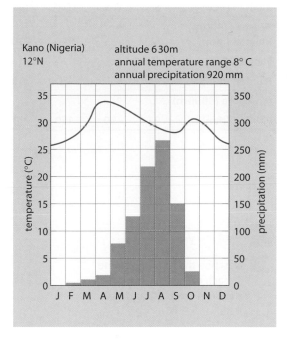

Kano (Nigeria)
12°N

altitude 630m
annual temperature range 8° C
annual precipitation 920 mm

Fig. 3.34 *Climate of Kano*

■ The situation in East Africa

The map (Fig. 3.31) shows that South America and West Africa both have two areas of tropical grassland, one north and one south of the equator. However, in East Africa the grassland spreads right across the equator and there is no area of equatorial rainforest or equatorial climate dividing this biome into two parts. This is a result of the relief of this area.

Large parts of East Africa lie at over 1,000 metres above sea level. There are extensive ranges that are at more than 2,000 metres; the highest peaks, Kilimanjaro and Kenya, are 5,985 and 5,199 metres respectively.

The height of this land has the effect of moderating the temperatures, even when the sun is overhead. The whole pattern of circulation of the winds is affected by this, and by monsoonal influence. As a result there is no area of year-round rainfall (producing an area of equatorial climate and rainforest vegetation) as might be expected at this latitude. This leads to the tropical grassland spreading right across the equator in East Africa.

Within Tanzania there is enormous variation in rainfall amount and seasonal distribution. Mean monthly rainfall data for four stations in Tanzania is set out in Table 3.2.

Table 3.2 *Rainfall at four stations in Tanzania*

	Jan	Feb	Mar	Apr	May	June	July	Aug	Sept	Oct	Nov	Dec
Musoma (1130 m) Rainfall (mm)	55	85	120	195	105	20	15	15	30	50	105	75
Arusha (1400 m) Rainfall (mm)	65	75	140	230	80	10	5	5	10	20	105	95
Tanga (20 m) Rainfall (mm)	45	35	110	230	255	80	55	60	75	105	130	70
Morogoro (9000 m) Rainfall (mm)	95	90	150	210	90	35	10	5	10	30	60	90

Activity

1 Describe the **rainfall regime** at each of the four stations shown in Table 3.2 and Fig. 3.35.

Consider how the seasonal pattern and the totals at each station are influenced by:

- ■ distance from the equator
- ■ height above sea level
- ■ distance from the coast.

Key terms

Rainfall regime: the distribution of rainfall throughout the year at a particular place.

Fig. 3.35 *Map of Serengeti and surrounding areas*

■ Characteristics of the tropical grassland biome

In many ways the tropical grassland can be seen as a transition between the equatorial rainforest and the hot deserts, as shown in Fig. 3.36.

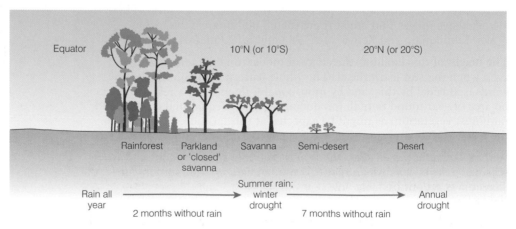

Fig. 3.36 *Rainforest/grassland desert transitions*

Towards the poleward edge of the rainforest the trees gradually become lower and fewer and grow less closely together. The continuous canopy of branches and leaves that characterises the true rainforest becomes more broken until the trees form a discontinuous cover, separated by stretches of grassland.

This is known as **parkland** or **closed savanna**. The area receives insufficient rainfall for the continuous cover of trees. The trees that do survive compete with each other for the more limited water supply. Their roots need to spread out to collect moisture from a wider area, and so there are spaces between the individual trees where there is insufficient water to allow new competing trees to grow to maturity. Instead, grasses, flowering plants and shrubs grow in the spaces between the trees. They are adapted to survive on the seasonal rains. After the summer rains the grasses grow quickly, reaching up to 3 m high in some cases. Then they produce seeds that can lie dormant until the next rainy season and the blades of the grass dry out and die down, leaving a protective layer over the surface which protects the roots from drying out during the hot, dry weather that follows.

On the outer edge this gives way to **savanna** grassland which has a continuous cover of grasses with occasional clumps of trees, especially along the watercourses or in hollows where water might accumulate close to the surface. The grasses often form tussocks, or tufts which spread because vegetative growth from the roots is more important than growth of new plants from seeds. These tussocks provide extra protection to the roots and help to conserve the soil moisture from evaporation. The blades of the grasses are tough, with waxy leaves that reduce transpiration, and silvery surfaces that reflect light.

The tough surfaces of the grasses also offer some protection from some grazing animals. It is only when the new shoots are growing at the start of the wet season that these grasses are easily available to grazers. For this reason there has been a long history of herdsmen burning off the old dead grasses at the end of the dry season to encourage the growth of new, succulent shoots for their animals. The possible effects of this burning will be discussed later.

Fig. 3.37 *Elephants in the Serengeti*

The trees that do survive in the savanna grasslands also have to be well adapted to the conditions. Two that are particularly notable are the baobab and the acacia tree. The baobab (or bottle tree) has a very thick trunk, up to 10 metres in diameter. It can store water in its trunk, for use in the dry season. Its bark is tough to cut down on transpiration and to resist fires. It has a fairly sparse network of branches when compared with the deciduous trees of temperate countries such as the UK, and it has a very small number of small, tough leaves – again to reduce transpiration.

Acacia trees also have fire-resistant bark, narrow leaves and sparse networks of branches. Their roots tend to grow much deeper than those of the baobab and to spread less widely. This means that acacias can grow in groups, unlike baobabs which need much wider areas from which to gather water and so deter the growth of local competitors.

Fig. 3.38 *Baobab tree in the Serengeti*

The savanna grasslands, particularly those of East and southern Africa, are home to spectacular herds of herbivorous animals such as elephants, zebras, wildebeest, giraffes and many species of deer. They graze on the grasslands – and sometimes on the trees. However, they have to move from place to place because of the seasonal nature of the grasslands and of the water supply. They migrate constantly, seeking supplies of fresh grazing. In good years their numbers multiply dramatically, but in poor years, when the rains fail or are in short supply, their numbers are adjusted downwards by the lack of food.

It is also well known that the herbivores attract carnivores – predators such as lions and leopards, and scavengers such as hyenas and vultures. Their numbers, too, are subject to fluctuations from season to season, largely depending on the rainfall and the supply of herbivores.

Fig. 3.39 *Grove of acacia trees*

Fig. 3.40 *Serengeti wildlife*

Each species in the system occupies its own particular spot, with the termites and a range of beetles playing an important role as the decomposers of the dead vegetation and the animal remains. Microbes must be present in the soil to complete the process of decomposition.

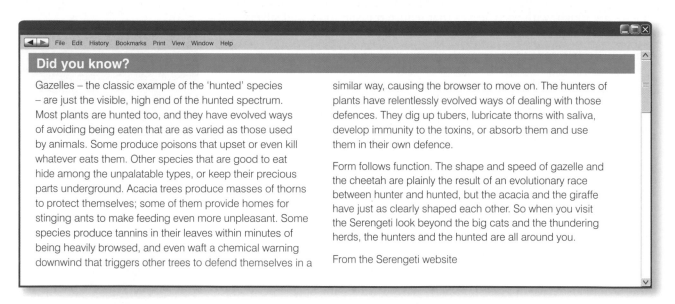

Did you know?

Gazelles – the classic example of the 'hunted' species – are just the visible, high end of the hunted spectrum. Most plants are hunted too, and they have evolved ways of avoiding being eaten that are as varied as those used by animals. Some produce poisons that upset or even kill whatever eats them. Other species that are good to eat hide among the unpalatable types, or keep their precious parts underground. Acacia trees produce masses of thorns to protect themselves; some of them provide homes for stinging ants to make feeding even more unpleasant. Some species produce tannins in their leaves within minutes of being heavily browsed, and even waft a chemical warning downwind that triggers other trees to defend themselves in a

similar way, causing the browser to move on. The hunters of plants have relentlessly evolved ways of dealing with those defences. They dig up tubers, lubricate thorns with saliva, develop immunity to the toxins, or absorb them and use them in their own defence.

Form follows function. The shape and speed of gazelle and the cheetah are plainly the result of an evolutionary race between hunter and hunted, but the acacia and the giraffe have just as clearly shaped each other. So when you visit the Serengeti look beyond the big cats and the thundering herds, the hunters and the hunted are all around you.

From the Serengeti website

Open savanna or **semi-desert scrub** gradually takes over from the true savanna on the poleward margins, adjacent to the true deserts. The trees almost disappear from this vegetation type and the tussocks of grass become more and more scattered, with wide areas of bare soil.

The characteristic features of the soils of the biome are a result of the seasonal rainfall, the high temperatures and the abundant grass-based litter provided during the drought seasons.

■ During the wet season there is usually an excess of rainfall over evaporation. Moisture can percolate into the soil and, in the hot conditions, it dissolves the more soluble salts from the upper layers and carries them downwards.

Links

The adaptations of this vegetation become more like the adaptations of desert plants, described in *AQA AS Geography*, pp132–3.

■ This leaves the upper layers with a concentration of the less soluble oxides of iron and aluminium. These are red in colour (like ferric oxide, more commonly known as 'rust'), giving savanna soils their characteristic colour.

■ As the grasses die back they are readily broken down by the action of termites and soil microbes, which act quickly in the hot conditions. This gives a layer of dark brown/black humus lying on top of the red, oxidised layer.

■ This humus layer is rich in nutrients but it is usually only thin and it can easily be lost to erosion if it is exposed by overgrazing or the burning of vegetation.

■ The vegetation and litter layers at the top of the soil tend to protect it from drying out during the dry season. However, when water is drawn back to the surface by evaporation it can carry many of the dissolved salts to the surface. Then, when the water evaporates, the salts are precipitated at or close to the surface. This can form a hard, cement-like layer called a laterite.

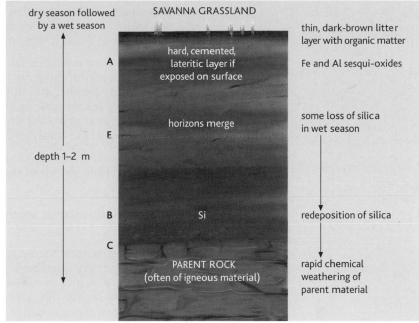

Fig. 3.41 *Laterite soil profile*

■ The formation of laterite surface layers can leave the lower layers very soft and crumbly. When laterites are eroded in places the soft rocks below are very vulnerable to erosion. This can leave a very broken landscape with patches of uneroded surface protected by caps of laterite, with deeply eroded gullies and ravines in between.

■ Human activity and the tropical grasslands

The tropical grasslands have long been attractive to pastoralists. Grasslands in Africa have been used by a variety of different peoples, mainly nomadic herders who keep cattle, moving round on a seasonal pattern of migration, following the rains, their source of water and of the new grass that provides the best pasture.

However, the activities of the herders have led to a major debate among ecologists over the extent to which the grasslands are 'natural' and the degree to which they have been affected by the burning of grasses. This takes place in many areas at the end of the dry season to remove dead grass and to speed the growth of new grasses in the following wet season.

The fires are normally quite well controlled. They burn off the dead grass that covers the surface, but the fires are not allowed to burn hot enough or long enough to destroy the roots of the grasses. These quickly recover when the rains come and send up new shoots, which make good fodder for the herds. In fact, the roots might even benefit from the burning because it provides ash which is an easily accessible form of fertiliser.

The grass roots are protected and can regrow, but this is not the case with young trees that are growing in the same area. If new seedlings or saplings are growing in the grass, they are often destroyed by the fires.

Their roots cannot produce new growth. If the part of the tree above the surface is burnt the whole plant is destroyed. As explained above, some trees such as the baobab and acacia are adapted to resist fire – but they are only able to do so once they have reached a certain stage of maturity. Young specimens will not have developed the necessary thickness of bark, and even members of these resistant species are generally destroyed if subjected to fire in the first three or four years of their growth.

So the debate among ecologists is: To what extent would the tropical grasslands be forested if the areas were not subjected to regular burning by cattle herders? Another question, linked to this, is: Do animals, both wild and herded, destroy young trees before they can become established, thus keeping areas as grassland when some form of forest would become established without the animals' intervention?

Some of the answers to those questions are provided by the following extract, adapted from a study of the Serengeti National Park.

Serengeti Woodlands Study (adapted from www.serengeti. org)

Today the Serengeti National Park has areas of open plains and areas of woodland. The woodlands cover the majority of the northern part of the park and the western part of the park. The Serengeti was not always like this, and in fact shifted from being almost entirely open plains to dense woodlands twice in the last century. If visitors to the park look carefully, they can see the product of these changes. Scattered throughout the landscape are a few very large, old Acacia trees that began life in a burst of growth in 1900. Spread throughout the park are areas of dense bush and trees that began life in a similar burst during the late 1970s. This is a story of disease, hunting, weather, illegal poaching, and is one of the most dramatic stories of the ecology in the Serengeti. While there are many factors which affect a tree, the two most important appear to be fires and grazing by animals.

Fire

Every year, fires burn inside the Serengeti National Park. Fire is an integral part of the ecology of savannas, and is not necessarily a bad thing in the right quantities. During the dry season (May–November), the lush green grasses of the wet season dry out and become perfect fuel for bush fires. A hot fire, such as those at the end of the dry season, can kill small trees. The trees fight back as they get old, growing a thick layer of insulating bark, while at the same time removing the water and sunlight that grass needs to grow around the tree, thus reducing the temperature of the size of escape, at which point they are no longer damaged by fires. Thus, for the Serengeti to have changed from grassland to woodland there must have been a few years in its history in which there were no fires.

Animals

Trees are eaten by a variety of animals throughout their lifetimes. This is because trees are generally more nutritious and easier to digest than grasses. While trees are seedlings, they are eaten by Thomson's gazelle, herds of impalas and other small browsers. As trees grow larger, they are eaten by giraffe. All through trees' lives, they are eaten by elephants, from the seedling stage to the adult stage. In order to grow to become a tree, a seedling must avoid being eaten by all of these animals. While each of these animals can limit the number of seedlings that grow larger, the most important seems to be the elephants, mostly because of the number of seedlings that they eat. Thus, for the Serengeti to have changed from grassland to woodland there must have been a period without elephants.

Why the Serengeti changed

The Serengeti changed from a grassland state to a woodland state twice in the last century. The few old, very large scattered trees dotting the Serengeti landscape started life about 1900, followed by a slow decline in tree numbers mainly due to elephants, fire and disease, leaving the few that we see today. The second group of smaller trees established itself during the period 1976–83, and these trees are still growing in abundance today. Both of these groups were able to grow because for two periods in the Serengeti there were no elephants and no fires.

Rinderpest

Rinderpest is a cattle disease that came to East Africa in about 1896. The effect on both the wild animals and the cattle of native peoples in the area was devastating. Most of the Serengeti wildebeest died in a few short years, as did the cattle of the people surrounding the park. With no cattle, a famine and rapid emigration from the area took place. With no people in the area, there was no one to light fires, and, for a few years, the Serengeti went un-burned.

At the same time, the trade in ivory was at its peak, decimating the elephant numbers all over East Africa. With no fires and no elephants, young trees were able to grow and flourish. This was the first big establishment of the century.

The effect of Rinderpest lasted for many years, with the wildebeest not regaining their current high numbers until the 1970s, seventy years after the disease was first introduced. Elephants were only reported to re-enter the Serengeti during the 1930s.

Weather

During the late 1970s and early 1980s, the weather patterns in and around Serengeti changed. The seasonal rains became more spread-out, meaning that the grasslands did not dry and were unable to burn during the 'dry season'. During this time there was, unfortunately, an enormous upswing in the illegal ivory trade. Elephants were killed or fled to safer areas. With both fire and elephants removed, the trees again established themselves in a burst. These trees are now about 30 years old and range from two to five metres tall, forming both dense thickets and standing singly.

Recent situation

Today, the woodlands of Serengeti are growing taller, as the trees which started during the mass-establishment of the 1970s mature. The trees of the 1900 establishment are growing older and dying.

There are interesting questions being asked about the trees today, including 'what us the effect of all this vegetation change on the animal species of Serengeti?'

There has been a large increase in the number of impala inside the park. These animals seem to be much more successful in the woodlands than in the grasslands, and have increased as the woodlands have increased. These and other changes may only be the tip of the ecological iceberg of woodland-related change which scientists are studying today.

In the past, elephants and fire have controlled the establishment of new trees. Today, both elephants and fire are monitored closely. Fire is monitored and controlled through the Park Ecology Department which burns fire breaks to stop the spread of large fires, and conducts 'cool' early-burns in fire-prone areas. Elephants have recovered since the heavy illegal poaching during the 1970s; it appears both by re-entering Serengeti and by breeding quickly. Most female elephants in the park have several offspring with them, forming large family groups.

Activity

2 Prepare yourself to answer a question on this topic.

There is no easy answer to the main question that might be asked about the extent of human influence on the grasslands. However, you should be prepared to discuss some of the possibilities even if you are not in the position to reach a final conclusion.

Whatever happens, be prepared to support your argument with evidence.

Development issues in the Serengeti

It is important to consider the potential for sustainability of the ecosystems studied during the course. The issue of sustainability is seen particularly clearly in the Serengeti where a number of conflicting groups have interests in the area. All want to use the area now, but also need to sustain the area so that it is still available in the future. This is a fragile environment where the balance between climate, soils, vegetation, animal life and people could easily be upset and the ecosystem destroyed.

The competing interest groups include:

- the indigenous people of the area, including the Masai
- the authorities and the conservationists who set up the National Park – at first the National Park was mainly supported by white people of European origin, but in recent years many black Tanzanians have also come to support the conservationist aims of the park
- tourists, both the officially sanctioned ones and the illegal big game hunters
- the Tanzanian government which sees the area as a source of food for the people and of revenue from tourism.

The ecosystem can only be conserved if these groups can find some compromises that favour long-term sustainability.

The Masai people had been grazing their livestock in the open plains known as the Serengeti (between modern Tanzania and Kenya) for over 200 years when the first European explorers visited the area. The first known Briton to enter the Serengeti was Stewart Edward White, who camped in the area for three months in 1920. During this time he and his companions shot 50 lions.

Because the hunting of lions made them so scarce, the British colonial administration decided to make a partial game reserve in the area in 1921 and a full one in 1929. This became the basis for the Serengeti National Park, which was established in 1951. As part of the creation of the park, and in order to preserve wildlife, the resident Masai were moved to the Ngorongoro highlands.

In recent years the park authorities have changed their attitude to their task radically. Now, rather than a top-down approach to management that took little notice of the needs of local people, they have adopted a cooperative approach to the people living in and around the park. They realise that if local residents do not benefit from the park, it will not survive. What is more, the areas around the Serengeti are important parts of the migration cycles of the herds that roam the plains, so these must have some degree of protection. The current policy of game management allows the people living around the edges of the park to do some controlled and licensed hunting of game. This hunting is now seen as an important part of controlling the herds, keeping them in balance with the grassland resources. Hunting can stop the tendency to overgraze the area that can arise if the number of animals grows too high.

A balance must also be kept between grazing land, for wild and domestic animals, and the use of land in areas around the park for growing crops. Crop production is essential to feed the growing population, but the authorities try to keep a balance between the needs of the animals and the needs of the people to grow food.

Finally, it has been realised that local people will support tourism and recognise the importance of wildlife conservation if they benefit economically from the tourist industry. It is seen as essential to offer local people jobs in wildlife management and policing of the park, and in the hotels, safari lodges and transport facilities provided for tourists. Some villages are becoming tourist sites in their own right and benefiting from money paid by visitors to see traditional Masai culture and buy locally produced goods.

Links

You can see details of migration patterns on the map at: www.serengeti.org/gfx/img_map_migration.gif

Extract from the UN Environmental Programme website (see Links)

The human population to the west of the park has expanded rapidly over the past 30 years, wildlife and livestock populations have grown, and demand for land is high. Grazing land is becoming scarce as pasture land is converted into cropland. Local people are vulnerable to external development and large-scale agricultural schemes which do not benefit local communities. Open landownership has also resulted in local people overexploiting common resources. Agriculture has encroached on park boundaries and former subsistence poaching has now become large-scale and commercial.

An estimated 200,000 animals are killed annually, resulting in large falls in the numbers of several species: warthog, giraffe, eland, topi, impala and buffalo. The rhinoceros have been decimated. The rise in demand for meat has been partly driven by the growing local population and in-migration as wildlife and fuelwood are depleted elsewhere. The need for bushmeat has also been exacerbated by the relatively low contribution that tourism has made to the local economy and the resulting antagonism felt by the excluded local population.

The work of the various departments of the National Park is described in extracts from the website (see Link).

Ecology Department

Understanding Park Ecology

… collecting important ecological information to help us understand this remarkable ecosystem. We have a long-term rainfall monitoring programme that covers 65 sites in the park. We are involved in aerial surveys to monitor the distribution and numbers of large mammals.

Assessing environmental impact

We monitor the impact of tourist developments in the park including such varied activities and threats as campsite development, and the invasion of exotic species … ensuring

that the ecological regulations and restrictions outlined in the management plans for the park are upheld.

Managing the effects of fire

… preventing wildfires by controlled burning early in the season and firefighting late in the season. … critical habitats and habitation at risk from fire are protected.

Coordinating ecological research

We work to ensure that current ecological information is used to guide the management and conservation of this great resource.

Tourism Department

Providing high quality visitor services and facilities

We provide trained park guides for game viewing, interpretive sites like the Visitor Centre, and information including brochures, bird checklists and road signs. We patrol and survey game viewing tracks, monitor visitor use and keep campsites clean. We monitor visitor satisfaction … improving the services and facilities provided for

you. The money from park fees is the lifeblood that keeps our national parks alive. We ensure this crucial resource is collected and cared for.

Protecting the environment

We make sure that Park rules and regulations are enforced. This plan is designed to minimise the ecological impact of visitors to the Park while improving your experience.

Links

For a detailed analysis of the ecosystem and its management go to: www.unep-wcmc.org/sites/wh/pdf/Serengeti.pdf

The Serengeti's own website is excellent and is worth exploring carefully at: www.serengeti.org

Law Enforcement Department

Maintaining law and order

… primary mission is to protect the Park's resources and people … eliminate poaching, stop cattle rustling, secure park boundaries, and provide security to visitors.

Protecting priority species

In order to safeguard the survival of some threatened species like the black rhino, patrols are organised.

Veterinary Department

Identifying Wildlife Diseases

... identify wildlife diseases and their sources in the Serengeti. ... investigate reports of sick animals. Determine causes of death, and monitor any disease outbreaks.

Aiding injured animals and endangered species

Death is a cold fact of life here but in some cases our help is required. For example, we have removed poacher's snares from suffering animals like lions and hyenas, elephants and giraffes. We monitor, treat, and translocate individuals if necessary.

Assisting animal research

The Serengeti has attracted many research projects. We ensure proper animal handling techniques and ethics. We help immobilise animals like lions and cheetah to attach radio collars, take samples for analysis and assess reasons for death.

Developing links for disease control

The spread of disease, whether in domestic or wild animals, is a concern to us all. As disease knows no political boundary, we work to develop effective monitoring and control procedures that require partnerships nationally and internationally.

Community Conservation

Building a bridge between the park management and the local population

Community-based wildlife conservation is a broad range of activities which enhance the involvement and participation of rural people in wildlife conservation ... ensure that the benefits of conservation are shared with local communities in appropriate ways. We work with local communities to meet their development goals, secure alternatives for resources people need from the park and discuss shared problems.

Educating the public

... conservation clubs in 74 primary schools surrounding the park ... educational materials for students and hold regular teacher-training workshops. Adults and school groups are brought to the park to experience the Serengeti first hand. A regular newsletter keeps groups and individuals informed of what is happening in the park.

Sharing the benefits

A percentage of park fees is used to assist in projects initiated by neighbouring communities. We have helped to safeguard water supplies and build schools and dispensaries. We are working with local communities to secure resources traditionally used from the park and are constantly striving to improve our relations with our neighbours.

Activity

3 Study all the resources provided on the Serengeti National Park and the surrounding area and then answer the following:

- ■ Explain why this can be considered a fragile environment, taking into account some of the threats to that environment.

- ■ Outline what is being done by the park authorities to encourage biodiversity.

- ■ Discuss the extent to which the present management regime is sustainable.

■ A contrasting case study

■ Case study

Jaú National Park – Amazonia

Jaú National Park is another area with potential for either sustainable development or unsustainable exploitation. This is another fragile ecosystem that could easily be destroyed, but at present the park authorities are attempting to balance conservation and development. However, like many parts of Amazonia, Jaú is

Fig. 3.43 *Location map – Jaú National Park*

Fig. 3.44 *Dense tropical forest – Jaú National Park*

threatened by those who wish to exploit its resources for short-term gain and who could easily destroy the delicate structure of the ecosystem.

Lying approximately 200 km north-west of Manaus, Jaú is the largest national park in the Amazon Basin and a region of great biodiversity.

The ecosystem

Jaú has a humid, tropical climate where the rain falls in two seasons, with around 1,750 mm between July and September and 2,500 mm between December and April. Annual temperature ranges are usually less than the diurnal (or daily) range. The annual average range is only between 26°C and 26.7°C.

There are three main vegetation types in the park:

- ■ **Dense tropical forest**, mainly on unflooded land, generally very stratified, with a layer of tall emergent trees and averaging 180 plant species per hectare.

- ■ **Open tropical igapó** – seasonally flooded forest. This is characterised by low trees with thin trunks, with many orchid epiphytes; it grows on sandy, nutrient-poor soils and averages 108 plant species per hectare.

Fig 3.45 *Tropical igapó forest – Jaú National Park*

- ■ **Campinarana** – a tall, dry shrub-woodland mosaic restricted to the Rio Negro region which grows primarily in well-drained uplands. It is dominated by tall trees and epiphytes and lianas are very rare.

Within each of these micro-habitats is a variety of vegetation types, including chavascai swamp and grassland.

Jaú Park protects an impressive range of fauna. There is high diversity with 120 species of mammals, 470 birds (said to be approximately two-thirds of the birds recorded from the Central Amazon), 15 reptiles and 320 fish, which represents about two-thirds of the fish species recorded in the Rio Negro basin. Mammal species considered locally threatened include the long-haired spider monkey, woolly spider monkey, blackheaded uakari monkey, giant anteater, giant armadillo, bush dog, small-eared dog, giant otter, longtailed otter, jaguar, puma, ocelot and Amazonian manatee. Threatened reptiles are the terrestrial yellow-footed tortoise, 10 species of freshwater turtles and black caiman.

Human geography

Brazil's federal government owns 98.3 per cent of the park. The rest consists of 31 legally held properties which are to be repossessed by the state and presented to the Brazilian Institute of the Environment and Natural Resources (IBAMA) which manages the park. About 1.5 per cent of the land is settled by 183 families without ownership title. These are mainly descendants of Portuguese settlers, originally attracted by rubber collecting. They live in traditional style by manioc cultivation, hunting, fishing, gathering turtles and ornamental fish, and the collection of timber, rubber, nuts, oils, resins and gum. No indigenous people live in the park.

There is no road access to Jaú Park and it is only accessible by river, usually by rented boats. The journey from Manaus to the park entrance takes up to 18 hours, or 8 hours by speedboat. Visitors need prior authorisation from the park director at IBAMA headquarters in Manaus. At the entrance, there is a recently built visitors' centre, a houseboat for the park guards and housing for researchers and visitors.

Conservation

Jaú Park is one of the few conservation units in the Brazilian Amazon with a management plan that is both complete and being implemented. This was evolved between IBAMA, local government, research institutions and members of the mining and tourism industries. To integrate local residents with conservation initiatives there are periodic meetings with residents to disseminate planning decisions, provide training for environmental education professionals and research on the economic valuation of natural resources. One example is the Fibrarte Project, set up to stimulate the use of natural fibres such as aruma to produce high-quality handicrafts. Action has been taken towards resolving remaining conflicts over land-ownership titles.

The management plan has three sections:

1 Protection, minimising of impacts and integration with neighbours

Deforestation is currently the main threat in the Amazon region. Only 3.5 per cent of the total area of the Brazilian Amazon is officially designated as protected areas. These include national parks, within which people are not allowed to live. However, this law is unenforceable, and all protected areas in the Amazon region have people living in them.

The park is in good condition, the grass fires, blow-downs and floods that do occur being part of the natural order of the forest. But there are around 250 families who fish the area's river quite intensively. The park has also been invaded by people from the surrounding area and is in great need of better basic infrastructure. For instance, there are only three park rangers at the entrance, making it easily invaded by outsiders who remove fish and turtles, which may affect future stocks. However, in the surrounding region no development projects such as hydroelectric dams, gas pipelines, power lines, highways, logging or mining exist or are foreseen.

2 Research into and protection of biodiversity

The Vitória Amazônica Foundation (FVA) has carried out multidisciplinary research in the park since 1992, recording the fauna and flora, soils and landscape. Ongoing research on the resident population is focused on analysis of land use and activities, trends in demography, subsistence and environmental impacts. FVA stores the data in a computerised database, as an information centre about the park. Geographic information systems are used to generate landscape maps, land-use maps and other images.

3 Specific activities

These include programmes for the regulation of the use of park resources (such as turtles and ornamental fish), public use, recreation and education about the natural processes of the area, public relations, encouragement of crafts, management training for local people, and the provision of sponsorship. The primary sources of funding are the Worldwide Fund for Nature (WWF), the EU, the Government of Austria and 15 other institutions. The funding available to the project amounts to nearly US$47 million.

A zoning plan for Jaú Park defines four management zones:

- **primitive** – of great natural value – minimum intervention and maximum protection

- **extensive use** – some human activity – work with the people to minimise their impact on the environment and encourage sustainable use of resources

- **intensive use** – already altered by humans

- **special use** – the park services core.

Jaú Park has a staff of four people: the Head of Conservation and three rangers. This is not yet adequate, although 26 volunteer guards have received training. FVA has a staff of 26 people, including 2 ecologists and 3 sociologist researchers, 3 IT experts, 2 educators, 2 technical staff responsible for alternative economic activities such as the Fibrarte Project, 11 people in administration and 2 in charge of the institutional development of the foundation.

Activity

4 Read all the information about Jaú National Park and then answer the following:

a Outline the ecology of the Jaú National Park.

b List the threats to the Brazilian rainforest in general and to Jaú Park in particular.

c Describe the management scheme for the park.

d Discuss whether this management plan seems adequate to meet:
  i the present needs of the area's environment
  ii the possible future needs of the environment.

In this chapter you will h ave learnt:

- how to describe and analyse ecosystems
- how vegetation succession tends to move vegetation communities towards the climatic climax
- how human activity can interrupt this succession
- about psammoseres, hydroseres and temperate deciduous forest in the UK
- about urban ecosystems, along routeways, on wasteland and on the urban fringe
- how conservation is helping to conserve some urban ecosystems for the benefits of people and of the natural world
- the main characteristics of the tropical grassland biome
- how human activity has affected and is affecting that biome
- how attempts are being made to conserve fragile environments in Tanzania and in Brazil.

4 World cities

Megacities, world cities and millionaire cities

In this section you will learn:

- how geographers define world cities.

Key terms

Megacity: metropolitan area with a total population in excess of 10 million people. The population density is usually over 2,000 persons/km². A megacity can be a single metropolitan area or two or more metropolitan areas that converge upon one another.

World city: a city that acts as a major centre for finance, trade business, politics, culture, science, information gathering and diffusion, publishing and mass media, and all the associated activities – serving not just a country or a region but the whole world. New York, London and Tokyo are the three pre-eminent world cities although there are some others that could be considered 'important multinational cities'.

Millionaire city: a city with over a million inhabitants.

Urbanisation: the growth in the proportion of a country's population that lives in urban as opposed to rural areas. The word is also used, less accurately, to describe the actual process of moving from a rural to an urban area.

The **urbanisation** of the world's population was one of the major geographic, demographic, economic and social changes of the 20th century, and it is continuing or even accelerating in some areas in the 21st century.

Fig. 4.1 *The bright lights of Shanghai, China*

The World Gazeteer is a website that lists the world's biggest cities. (The list includes some cities and some conurbations.) At the end of February 2008 this list included:

- 1 city (Tokyo) with over 30 million people – actually more than 37 million

- 5 cities with between 20 and 30 million (New York, Mexico City, Seoul, Mumbai, São Paulo)

- 21 cities with 10–20 million

- 41 cities with 5–10 million

- 31 cities with 4–5 million

- 38 cities with 3–4 million

- 81 cities with 2–3 million

- 360 cities with 1–2 million

- 380 cities with 0.5–1 million.

Activities

1. Put the World Gazeteer figures on a scatter graph with size in millions on the *x*-axis and number of cities in the category on the *y*-axis. Can you see a pattern in the table of the world's biggest cities of 2008?

2. Visit www.worldkit.org/population which provides a GIS map to show which cities reached millionaire status between 1775 and 1975.

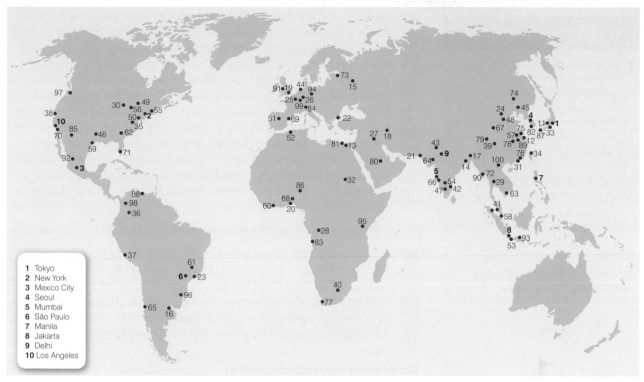

1 Tokyo
2 New York
3 Mexico City
4 Seoul
5 Mumbai
6 São Paulo
7 Manila
8 Jakarta
9 Delhi
10 Los Angeles

Fig. 4.2 *Map showing world's top 100 cities*

At least until the middle of the 20th century, the biggest cities in the world were in the most developed countries. New York and London were, on most measures, the world's two biggest cities, with Paris, Berlin, Rome, Tokyo, Chicago and Los Angeles also near the top of the list.

In the 1950s, New York, or the New York region, was recognised as becoming the world's first megacity. London and some of the other big cities in developed countries might also have qualified for such a description. However, since 1950 many cities in developing countries, propelled by high rates of natural increase and very high rates of rural-to-urban migration, have joined them. In 1960, 9 of the world's 19 biggest cities were located in developing countries; by 2008, 48 out of the 68 cities with a population over 5 million were in developing countries.

Peter Hall, a geographer who is Professor of Planning at London University, first developed the idea of world cities. In a lecture in 1997 he explained how they grow.

In the first lecture of the series Peter Hall referred to:

> the phenomenon of **globalisation** and its impact on the urban system, coupled with what can be called the '**informationalisation**' of the economy, the progressive shift of advanced economies from goods production to information handling, whereby the great majority of the workforce no longer deal with material outputs … this is the fundamental economic shift of the present era, as momentous as the shift from an agrarian to an industrial economy in the eighteenth and nineteenth centuries.

He went on to explain that globalisation has led to a shift of manufacturing from its traditional centres in the developed world – cities such as Manchester and Detroit – to lower-wage economies in China, India, etc.

> Thus, as production disperses worldwide, services increasingly concentrate into a relatively few trading cities, both the well-known

Links

Peter Hall's lecture and others in the series, which began in 1997 and continue today, can be found in full in the archive at: www.megacities.nl

Key terms

Globalisation: at AS-level globalisation was defined as a set of processes leading to the integration of economic, cultural, political and social systems across geographical boundaries. It refers to increasing economic integration of countries, especially in terms of trade and the movement of capital.

Informationalisation: the increasing importance of the information-based sector of the economy which relies on electronic data transfer.

'global cities' and a second rung of about 20 cities immediately below these, which we can distinguish as 'sub-global'. These cities are centres for financial services (banking, insurance) and headquarters of major production companies; most are also seats of the major world-power governments. They attract specialised business services like commercial law and accountancy, advertising and public relations services and legal services, themselves increasingly globalised, and related to controlling headquarters locations. In turn this clustering attracts business tourism and real estate functions; business tourism allies with leisure tourism because both are in part drawn to these cities because of their cultural reputations, with effects on the transportation, communication, personal services and entertainment-cultural sectors. There is intense competition between such cities.

As an illustration he describes the growth of foreign banks in London.

Thirty foreign banks were already established in London before 1914. Another 19 became established between the two world wars, and another 87 by 1969. Then the pace accelerated: 183 in the 1970s, 115 in the first half of the 1980s. In all, between 1914 and the end of 1985 the number of foreign banks in London grew more than 14-fold, from 30 to 434. Both London and New York now have more foreign than domestic banks.

World cities are resource centres

Cities grow because they are resource bases. Companies need access to knowledge in order to grow, and in cities they find access to temporary or semi-permanent networks of knowledge. When the right combination of knowledge resources is available at the right time, innovation and entrepreneurship flourish. There are two kinds of knowledge: codified knowledge, which is carried and spread by technology such as the internet and so is available to anyone anywhere in the world; and tacit knowledge, whose development depends on discussion and face-to-face contact.

World cities are learning centres

If companies can learn, they enter cycles of growth and development. To allow this, they must be part of the networks of learning that consist of clusters of universities and other education institutions, policymakers, company research bases, and so on. World cities may be seen as 'learning regions', 'smart cities', 'science cities' or 'creative hubs'.

World cities are centres of spatial proximity

Tacit knowledge is particularly likely to exist, develop and grow in certain areas of cities, such as Central Business Districts (CBDs), university campuses, science parks. Such places are cradles of innovation. Meetings and contacts take place on a regular basis, providing – sometimes by design and sometimes by chance – the spark for the new ideas. This is far more likely to occur in an area with a high concentration of people and activities where there are many opportunities for interaction and knowledge sharing.

World cities may be characterised in three ways:

■ they have shed a lot of their routine, low-value activities – manufacturing, distribution, routine services – to other cities or countries

■ they have high levels of **synergy** in their economic structures

Key terms

Synergy: a term originally used in biology to describe the way that two organisms or two systems work together to produce a better result or output than they could alone. The term is now applied in economics when two or more companies, groups or individuals achieve mutual benefits by working closely together.

■ they offer a wide range of jobs but there is a tendency towards a polarised labour force. At the top end are jobs that demand a high level of education, training and personal skills – and high rewards. To support these jobs there is a wide range of semi-casual and low-paid work with few career prospects. This can lead to an increasing spatial differentiation in the distribution of types of residential area in the cities.

■ Europe's urban hierarchy?

Cities increasingly tend to compete and a distinct hierarchy exists, which is particularly evident in Europe but is developing elsewhere too. In western Europe the only indisputable world city is London, with Paris perhaps also qualifying, although Paris could still be classified as a (smaller) megacity.

Below them come the national capital cities (see Fig. 4.3) as well as a number of specialised cities which effectively act as commercial or cultural capitals. They are all smaller: typically, their metropolitan areas have populations between about 1 million and 4 million. They compete with the world cities in their specialised functions, such as Brussels, Rome and Geneva for government, Frankfurt and Zurich or Amsterdam for banking, or Milan for design.

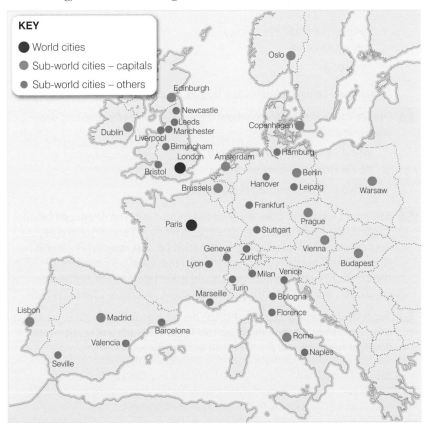

KEY
● World cities
● Sub-world cities – capitals
● Sub-world cities – others

Fig. 4.3 *Map of Europe's urban hierarchy*

The Eurocities form a tight inner circle forming what the EC's Europe 2000+ report calls the National Capitals Region – all within convenient radius for face-to-face contact by air and, increasingly, by high-speed train. So it seems certain that they will constitute an effective central core of the European urban system. In turn, they will be connected by regular and frequent air services to a number of key regional cities which effectively form an outer ring some 500–700 km distant, including

Copenhagen, Berlin, Vienna, Zurich, Milan, Madrid, Dublin and Edinburgh. These places will also be connected by high-speed train to cities within their own 500-km radii: Milan with Turin, Venice and Bologna; Berlin with Hanover, Hamburg and Leipzig; Madrid with Seville and Barcelona – and will thus form the points of contact between the European and the regional urban systems.

With their typical population range of 1 to 4 million, these national capitals and commercial capitals overlap in size with the major provincial capitals of the larger European nation states (such as Manchester and Birmingham, Lyons and Marseilles, Florence and Naples. These places typically serve as administrative and higher-level service centres for mixed urban–rural regions. Most, though not all of them, are prosperous, and they have shown considerable dynamism in adapting to their loss of traditional manufacturing and goods-handling functions. They are all millionaire cities in their own right, or they can be classified as such when taken to include the densely populated urban regions that surround them.

Activities

3 List the main features of:
- millionaire cities
- world or global cities
- sub-world cities
- megacities.

Name three cities, preferably the biggest, in each category.

4 Draw a concept map to show how the ideas are linked in the sections above, entitled:
- World cities are resource centres
- World cities are learning centres
- World cities are centres of spatial proximity.

5 At present the world cities are found in countries of the developed world. Suggest why some cities from countries that have been described as 'less developed' or 'developing' might soon join the ranks of the world cities. (Shanghai and Mumbai are the two most likely contenders for this status.) In your answers you should make reference to globalisation; population size and growth; the development process in China and India.

6 Suggest why some people predict the development of a single European megacity called the 'National Capitals Region? If such a megacity does develop, where do you predict it will be? Justify your answer.

Economic development and the effects of urbanisation

In this section you will learn:

- about the contemporary urbanisation process in countries at different stages of development.

Urban functions

- trading
- administration
- transport
- religion
- education
- health care
- arts and entertainment
- manufacturing
- insurance
- banking
- publishing
- media
- science
- defence
- policing
- diplomacy
- … and so on.

Links

Reread the section entitled 'What makes cities grow' in Chapter 5 of *AQA AS Geography*, pp184–7.

In the previous section we saw how the present growth of cities has been a result of economic forces coming together in particular places at particular times to create a synergy and dynamic process that has caused huge urban growth. This is not a new phenomenon.

Cities have always been the places where surplus wealth can be created and/or stored. They started as centres for organising agricultural production, trading surplus agricultural produce and administering the rural area round about. Then, over time, as cities grew, they attracted further functions as labour became more specialised and jobs became more precisely differentiated.

Most of these functions can only take place in a large community where division of labour is possible and where not everyone has to concentrate on producing food and shelter for most of their time. On the other hand, as cities grow and attract more and more people they can develop an increasingly wider range of functions, with jobs that become more and more specialised.

In Europe, during the Industrial Revolution of the 18th and 19th centuries a number of developments occurred around the same time that allowed cities to grow larger than they ever had in the past. These included:

- the agricultural revolution and the enclosure movement which led to loss of work on the land but also produced a surplus of food that could be transported to the towns to feed their growing population

- the invention of industrial processes that led to the development of the factory system, where production was concentrated close to sources of power, drawing in labour from the countryside

- new forms of power, so that coal took the place of water power, concentrating industry in the mining areas rather than having it spread along rivers

- improved transport systems: canals at first, followed by railways and later by motorised road transport

- gradual improvements in medicine, hygiene and public health, which allowed large numbers of people to live in close proximity without leading to the inevitable spread of disease.

These processes led to the rapid urbanisation of the populations of many of the countries of western Europe and North America. Unfortunately the processes did not all operate in a smooth, synchronised way. Urbanisation often led to great hardships and to dreadful conditions for people in both the new towns and the countryside. At some stages the loss of jobs in farming led to large numbers of rural poor; at other times migration to the towns outstripped the demand for labour or produced a swollen workforce and depressed wage rates. Rural-to-urban migration led to massive overcrowding and slum housing. Some of the problems of 19th-century urbanisation are shown in Fig 4.4.

Fig. 4.4 *Conditions in 19th-century UK cities*

Since the mid-20th century, urbanisation has been taking place most rapidly in South America, Asia and Africa. New megacities include Mexico City, São Paulo, Mumbai, Shanghai, Cairo and Nairobi, and there are many other millionaire cities.

As with cities in Europe during the Industrial Revolution, urbanisation in the developing world has not been a smoothly planned process. Many people have been pushed from the countryside by poverty, unemployment, hunger and lack of opportunity; and pulled to the cities by the hope of well-paid jobs, or at least the hope that they would be able to survive in the informal economy. Unfortunately, there is often a shortage of work or, at best, only very poorly paid work, and there is still a lack of housing and other infrastructure such as education, health care, sewers and water supply.

Fig. 4.5 *Conditions in 21st-century developing cities: São Paulo, Bangkok and Mumbai*

However, in many cities of the developing world, urbanisation has provided opportunities for economic development, as shown in the study of Mumbai.

Case study

Mumbai

Mumbai (formerly known as Bombay) is not the capital of India, but it is the country's biggest city, with 14,350,000 people. It is also India's financial centre, a major port and industrial area and, as home of the 'Bollywood' movie industry, a centre of culture.

Mumbai illustrates many of the big problems faced by cities in developing countries. In particular, it shows how city authorities struggle to keep pace with rapid growth as people are drawn in from the countryside seeking work, and as the growing economy needs more and more people to work in a whole range of jobs, from the most highly skilled to the most menial.

In some ways these problems are made worse by Mumbai's site. It was originally a series of fishing villages that became a port, and at first, its site encouraged its development. This early growth was concentrated at the end of a peninsula, with access to the sea on both sides. Now this site restricts development and poses a massive challenge to urban planners. The hybrid map/satellite image in Fig. 4.6 shows the site of the original city and some of its growth. If you use the Link provided you can zoom in to see large parts of central Mumbai in great detail and the whole of greater Mumbai at a smaller scale.

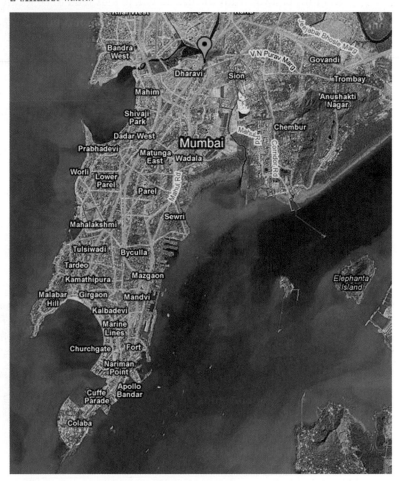

Fig. 4.6 *The site of Mumbai, India*

The British colonial administration in India developed the peninsula and the sheltered inlet into a major port. It was the closest port of entry to the subcontinent for travellers from Europe. The port and its surroundings became known as the Gateway to India. The area around the port became industrialised, processing goods for export and handling imports. A whole variety of services grew up around the port, causing the city to grow during the period of British rule and, even more rapidly, after the British left in 1947.

The banking, finance and insurance sectors that were associated with the port allowed Mumbai to become India's major centre of finance. As India's economy grows and becomes increasingly part of the globalised economy, Mumbai is becoming a world city.

Links

You can find a copy of the hybrid image of Mumbai at: www. maplandia.com/india/maharashtra/greater-bombay/dharavi/

Use the tools provided to look at the whole of Mumbai and to focus in on small parts of the city. You can find out a lot of detail about the city's site, structure, development and urban issues.

Unfortunately, the site that was becoming crowded and inadequate 50 to 100 years ago is now desperately overcrowded. The price of land in the central business district has rocketed, making it one of the most expensive cities in the world. Meanwhile, tens of thousands of people from surrounding rural areas and across India move to Mumbai every year, seeking a share of the wealth that the city now generates.

Some of the migrants are uneducated, with few skills that are needed to make a living in a modern city. Others do have the education and skills to obtain jobs, but even for them housing is in short supply and is expensive. So the influx of people leads to:

■ the spread of **suburbs** of cheap and poorly built housing, further and further away from the centre where jobs tend to be located

■ consequent massive overcrowding on the trains and buses that carry commuters into the centre

■ the development of squatter settlements where the shelters are frequently built from recycled waste material, often in dangerous areas such as on railway land and on marshland close to the rivers – and these are home, not just to the very poorest, but also to some people in regular employment who can afford nothing better.

In the 1970s a major plan was developed to move many of the port, market and industrial functions, and many of the people who worked in these sectors, out of the old city to Navi Mumbai (New Bombay) on the mainland to the east. The plan was only partly successful, and central Mumbai is still desperately crowded, as are the transport routes – especially the trains – that bring people into the centre every day. The focus of the problem is now seen to be in the area of Dharavi (see Fig. 4.7).

Dharavi – the problem?

Dharavi is sometimes called 'the biggest slum in Asia'. It is home to more than 600,000 people, most of whom make their living there. Spreading over 2 km², it has a vast range of cottage industries that are estimated to generate almost US$40m worth of business every year. But, as Fig 4.6 shows (and as can be seen from the satellite images quoted in the Link above), it lies just north of central Mumbai and restricts its growth almost completely. Dharavi lies across a narrow part of the peninsula and across the routes that bring hundreds of thousands of commuters into the CBD from the northern suburbs. It seems inevitable that Dharavi will be redeveloped, but equally inevitably this will lead to conflict between residents and developers.

Fig. 4.7 *Dharavi's shanty towns*

Madhukar, a 60-year-old leather goods maker, was born in Dharavi, where five generations of his family have made their living. He remembers when Dharavi was just marshland, and how after school he would help his grandfather and his father fill up the soil with cement to build their home and their leather workshop.

'Why should we go? We won't go,' Madhukar says. 'We are the ones who made Dharavi. All those developers, the government, they didn't make it. We built Dharavi. We are not leaving.'

'Dharavi sits right in the middle of Mumbai,' says Pranay Vakil, property consultant at Knight Franks. 'And the centre of gravity in India's financial capital is moving north, towards Dharavi. Right next to it sits Mumbai's new corporate district, the Bandra Kurla Complex. And there's no more room to build in this city. Dharavi is the most important location in Mumbai today.'

Dharavi – the solution?

The governments of Mumbai and Maharashtra state are now planning wholesale development of the Dharavi slum. Housing is set to be cleared in stages. As each section is cleared, some of the population will be rehoused in temporary accommodation; then all one- and two-storey houses will be replaced with seven-storey tenements. Any family that can prove they have been living in Dharavi since 1995 will receive free housing in the new blocks. The rest of the housing will then be sold or let on the open market.

The Dharavi Redevelopment Project is experimenting with a new way of dealing with slums, where an entire slum is redeveloped as an independent self-sufficient 'township.' Thus the five segments of the 2 km² of Dharavi will be developed so that each has housing, health care, civic amenities, and industries …

The developer will have to provide not just the buildings to resettle the slum dwellers living in the particular area but also all the infrastructure including roads, drainage, water supply, municipal office, hospital, school, industrial estate, open spaces for recreation, etc.

To entice developers, the government has had to modify the Development Control Rules for this project. … So even with the additional burden of providing infrastructure, developers stand to make substantial profits under the scheme. …

Why Dharavi? It is the value of the land on which Dharavi is located that marked it for this experiment. Dharavi sits just south of the Mithi River, a stone's throw away from the swank and futuristic Bandra Kurla Complex (BKC) that has emerged as the major business hub for Mumbai. Last year, the lack of foresight in planning BKC became evident when the entire area went under water during the July 26 deluge. In the course of developing this business district, the Mithi River was diverted resulting in a serious adverse impact on natural drainage in the area. In comparison Dharavi, which was once a swamp but has been gradually filled up by the very people who live there, escaped unscathed from the flooding as it is now on higher ground.

This has enhanced Dharavi's attractiveness and its real estate value. Ideally, the developers would like to raze all structures in the slum and start from scratch, the way they have been able to do in Mumbai's textile mill district. But politically this is impossible. So the compromise is to find a way to accommodate those who live in Dharavi while converting it into a 'world class cultural, knowledge, business and health centre.' …

It has been estimated that there are 4,500 'industries' — basically small to medium industrial units producing leather, ready-made garments, jewellery, foodstuffs, soap, pottery. Under the scheme, people with such enterprises are entitled to 225 sq ft free and can purchase additional space at market rates. Some of the bigger units would be able to afford this but thousands of smaller units that work out of lofts will be forced to shut shop. Also, all polluting industries like soap making or leather tanneries will have to close. Kumbharwada, the large potters' colony that is a landmark in Dharavi, is being treated as a special case.

From *The Hindu, 6 October 2006*

Fig. 4.8 *Part of Bandra Kurla complex, Mumbai*

The project cannot go ahead unless a majority of the registered residents agree to it – which means that the views of many unregistered people will be ignored. Moreover, some community leaders claim that the government and developers have used underhand tactics to try to make people sign agreements. They also fear that, as development proceeds, financial pressures will mean that the planned housing might well be replaced by more valuable developments of commercial and office premises for the growing business area.

Bandra Kurla Complex to be extended

In 2007 'The Mumbai Metropolitan Regional Development Authority' (MMRDA), the planning authority for BKC, announced that the area of land available for development was to be doubled. The additional area is expected to bring in an estimated Rs 300,000 million, which the MMRDA wants to use for the Metro rail projects and the Mumbai Urban Transport Project (MUTP).

Property experts said this would make available the much-needed office space which is now restricted to saturated areas like Nariman Point and Worli.

'It's a great move as eventually land supply in BKC would have dried up. We can now compete with international business centres like Canary Wharf in London, which is spread over a large area …,' said Anuj Puri, chairman and country head of global real estate consultants JLL Meghraj.

Activities

3 Read the Mumbai case study.

a Explain why Mumbai seems to be growing to be India's first world city.

b Write summaries to compare the types of development planned for Bandra Kurla Complex and Dharavi.

c Suggest, with reasons, how the following people might react to the plans to develop Dharavi that are outlined in the Case study:

■ a resident of the area who has lived there since 1991

■ a resident who has lived there since 1997

■ a resident who runs a medium-sized business in the area processing leather from skins bought from the slaughterhouse

■ a resident who runs a small business making sweets for sale in the neighbourhood

■ a businessman who specialises in finding commercial premises and apartments for foreign companies moving to Mumbai

■ a planner on the railways, who is responsible for the lines running from the north of Mumbai into the CBD

■ a planner for the Mumbai water authority – who has to consider flood control and also provision of fresh water supplies to housing areas

■ a doctor who works in Dharavi as a general practitioner.

4 Refer back to the whole of this section on world cities. Write a summary of the consequencs of urbanisation in:

■ countries of western Europe

■ countries at a later stage of economic development.

You should refer to economic, social and environmental consequences.

Contemporary urbanisation processes

Is Great Britain still urbanising?

Figures for the 2001 census (the last full census in the UK) showed that the country's population was broken down as shown in Table 4.1 below.

Table 4.1 *The UK population at the 2001 census, showing rates of urban change*

Type of district	Population in thousands	% of GB population	% Change 1991–2001
London	7,308	13	7.0
Metropolitan areas*	12,542	22	−2.1
Large non-met. cities	3,629	6	−1.0
Small non-met. cities	2,202	4	3.3
District with industrial areas	7,866	14	1.7
District with new town	2,950	5	4.3
Resort/port/retirement	3,447	6	3.8
Urban/rural mixed	10,798	19	5.1
Remoter/mainly rural	6 621	12	6.1
Great Britain	**57,363**		**2.7**

* = Clydeside, Tyne and Wear, West Yorkshire, Merseyside, Greater Manchester, South Yorkshire, West Midlands

Links

The first in a series of briefs by CASE on the 2001 census, which presents findings on population, on changes in the size and distribution of minority ethnic groups, on tenure and household change and on employment change, can be found at: www.lse.ac.uk/collections/pressAndInformationOffice/PDF/census%20brief%201%20for%20web.pdf

Activities

1 Answer the following questions, making detailed reference to the data in Table 4.1.

a Is the UK an urbanised country?

b Which types of area are:
- gaining population at well above the national average?
- gaining population at slightly above the national average?
- gaining population more slowly than the national average?
- losing population?

c With reference to your answers above, is the UK still urbanising?

2 Fig. 4.9 shows the situation in the non-metropolitan cities in more detail. It shows which cities are losing and which are gaining population.

a Compare the rates of change in the large cities with those in the small cities.

b Study the locations of the non-metropolitan cities on a map of the UK. Is there a geographical pattern to the rate of change?

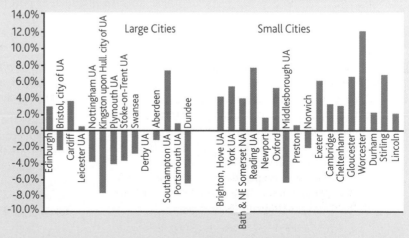

Fig. 4.9 *Population change in non-metropolitan cities (1991–2001)*

■ Is the rest of the world urbanising?

The data in Table 4.2 show how the percentages of urban and rural population in different regions have changed over the last 60 years – and how they are predicted to change in future. Study the table to see how the proportion of urban population has changed and also to see how rates of change differ between rural and urban areas. This will give you a fuller view of the rates of urbanisation.

Table 4.2 *Percentage changes in rural/urban population since 1950*

	More developed regions			Less developed regions			Least developed countries		
	Urban %	Rural GR%	Urban GR%	Urban %	Rural GR%	Urban GR%	Urban %	Rural GR%	Urban GR%
1950	52.5	−0.12	2.33	18.0	1.63	3.83	7.3	1.78	4.60
1960	58.7	−0.44	2.08	21.7	1.78	4.15	9.5	2.01	5.49
1970	64.6	−0.58	1.47	25.3	1.90	3.67	13.1	2.14	4.84
1980	68.8	−0.23	0.93	29.6	1.30	3.86	17.3	2.10	4.55
1990	71.2	−0.27	0.74	35.1	1.06	3.19	21.0	2.20	4.41
2000	73.1	−0.34	0.61	40.2	0.57	2.68	24.8	1.83	4.10
2001	75.0	−0.77	0.52	45.3	0.32	2.39	29.4	1.49	3.99
2002	77.5	−1.27	0.46	50.5	−0.09	2.07	35.0	0.99	3.70
2003	80.6	−1.63	0.36	56.0	−0.57	1.74	41.5	0.46	3.28
2004	83.5	−1.75	0.23	61.6	−0.95	1.42	48.4	−0.03	2.80
2005	86.0	−1.80	0.19	67.0	−1.14	1.26	55.5	−0.29	2.55

* GR = Growth rate per year

The data came from the UN World Urbanization Prospects website.

The site defines:

■ more developed regions as 'all regions of Europe plus North America, Australia/New Zealand and Japan'

■ less developed regions as 'Africa, Asia (excluding Japan), Latin America and the Caribbean and the Pacific Island groups'

■ least developed countries as 'the 50 poorest countries of which 34 are in Africa, 10 in Asia, 1 in the Caribbean and 5 in Oceania' (note that these are also included as part of the less developed regions).

■ Links

Data for urbanisation rates in individual countries can be found at this site: esa.un.org/unup/index.asp?panel=1

■ Activity

3 Use the data from Table 4.2 to construct two line graphs.

a On your first graph show the changing percentages of the population that is urban in the three regions.

b On your second graph show the rates of change of the rural and urban populations in the three regions. This graph will have to show rates of change that are both positive and negative.

c On each of your graphs use three different colours to represent the three different regions.

d Explain what your graphs show about the pattern of world urbanisation from 1950 to the present, and predicted changes up to 2050.

If you use the website in the Link above you can select individual countries and draw individual profile graphs to illustrate their rates of urbanisation. For example, you could compare the urbanisation histories of Japan, Singapore, South Korea, India and China to see how patterns have varied as economic development has taken place at different rates.

Suburbanisation, counter-urbanisation and re-urbanisation

Suburbanisation

Many residents of towns and cities no longer live and work within the central urban area, choosing instead to live in suburbs and commute to work by car or public transport. Others have taken advantage of technological advances to work from their homes, in an environment they consider more pleasant than the city centre. This process of **suburbanisation** is most common in more economically developed countries. The US is believed to be the first country in which the majority of the population lives in the suburbs, rather than in central cities or in rural areas. Similar figures are not available for the UK, but it is obvious that the process is very advanced here too.

Suburbanisation can be linked to a number of different push and pull factors. Push factors include:

- the congestion and population density of city centres
- pollution caused by industry and high levels of traffic
- a general perception of a lower quality of life in city centres.

Pull factors include:

- more open spaces and a perception of being closer to 'nature'
- lower price of land and housing in comparison to the city centre
- the increasing number of job opportunities in the suburban areas
- a general perception of better opportunities for education than in central city areas.

Race is also documented as playing a role in American suburbanisation. During the First World War, African Americans from the rural southern states migrated heavily to the cities of the north in search of work. Many settled in inner-city areas, while white families moved to the suburbs, which they perceived as safer places to live and raise a family. This movement was known as 'white flight'.

A similar trend has been observed in some cities in the UK from the 1960s onwards. This is partly a result of white flight and partly a result of the desire for members of immigrant communities to live closely together for social and economic support.

Suburbanisation could not have happened without the improvements in transport infrastructure which allowed the development of commuting to the nearby town or city centre to work. Developments in railways, bus routes and roads are the main improvements that make suburbanisation more practical. The development of the London Underground and other such mass-transit systems have been crucial in this respect.

Recent developments in communication technology, such as the spread of broadband services, the growth of e-mail and the advent of practical home video conferencing, have enabled more people to work from home rather than commuting. Although this can occur either in the city centre or in the suburbs, the effect is generally decentralising. Similarly, the rise of efficient package express delivery systems, such as Federal Express and UPS, which take advantage of computerisation and integrated transport, also eliminates some of the advantages of working in the city centre. The overall effect of these developments is that some people and small

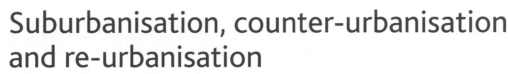

Fig. 4.10 *Suburban living and the development of the Underground system*

businesses now see an advantage to locating further from the city centre, where the cost of buying land, renting space and running their operations is cheaper than in central areas.

This has led to another recent phenomenon: the advent of 'edge cities' in suburban areas, with clusters of office buildings built around suburban business districts and shopping malls. With more and more jobs for suburbanites being located in these areas rather than in the main city, core traffic patterns – which for decades centred on people commuting between the city centres and the suburbs – have become more complex, with the volume of intra-suburban traffic increasing tremendously.

Suburbanisation clearly offers many lifestyle improvements. However, it also causes problems. Many planners consider that it is important to reduce or even reverse the process of urban sprawl which, they argue, leads to inner-urban decay and a concentration of lower-income residents in the inner city.

In effect, suburbanisation means the transfer of the middle-class population out of the inner cities and into the suburbs, sometimes with devastating effects on the viability of city centres. Many urban areas in the UK, and some in the US, have adopted 'green belt' policies that limit growth in the fringe of a city, in order to encourage more growth in the urban core. It is now generally accepted that a certain level of population density in the centre of a city creates a good, working urban environment.

It is also apparent that suburbanisation and the growth of commuting can lead to a huge increase in the use of cars, with increased emissions of greenhouse gases and other pollutants. Commuting by car has also caused pressure to design cities to cope with cars, sometimes at the expense of pedestrians and cyclists.

■ Counter-urbanisation

The data in Table 4.1 show that areas classified as 'Urban/rural mixed' increased their population by 5.1 per cent between 1991 and 2001 and those classified as 'Remoter/mainly rural' increased by 6.1 per cent.

Meanwhile 'Metropolitan areas' decreased by 2.1 per cent and 'Large non-met. cities' by 1.0 per cent, while 'Districts with industrial areas' only increased by 1.7 per cent – less than the rate of natural increase.

'Resort towns' and 'New towns' were also growing at above the rate of natural increase.

So these data suggest that there was an element of **counter-urbanisation** in the UK's population – but London was still the fastest-growing region in this period, so the movement was not simple or straightforward.

There are age-related and social group-related elements in these changes.

■ Some people retire and move to the countryside, the seaside or to a small town.

■ Young people go to universities which are usually in the bigger towns and cities.

Activity

1 Reread the study of suburbanisation in Newcastle upon Tyne (see Link) and compare this area with an area that you know which has been suburbanised.

Links

In *AQA AS Geography*, Chapter 5 'Population change', the sections on Jesmond (pp193–4) and Gosforth (pp195–6), along with the statistics on p90, provide a case study of suburbanisation in Newcastle upon Tyne.

■ Many people seek their early jobs in cities and live as close to their work as possible.

■ When people start families they often move outwards, towards suburbs, small towns or rural areas.

■ Some successful urban dwellers buy second homes in the country and this may distort the census figures.

■ Immigrants often settle in inner urban areas because of access to jobs, availability of cheap housing and the support available in neighbourhoods based on the group's origin.

Case study

Whitley Bay

Whitley Bay is a town in North Tyneside, part of the Tyneside conurbation. It is on the North Sea coast with a fine stretch of golden sand beach, forming a bay stretching from the rocky St Mary's Island in the north to Cullercoats and Tynemouth in the south. The town, which has a population of about 35,000, became a holiday destination for the people of north-east England in the late 19th and early 20th centuries and remained popular until the 1980s. The town is now widely seen as a dormitory town for Newcastle upon Tyne.

In 1904 the electric suburban railway linked Whitley Bay to Newcastle and first allowed it to become a commuter town, providing housing for people who worked in the city but wanted more spacious, less polluted conditions in which to live and bring up their families. When the electric railway became the basis for the development of the Metro light railway system in 1980, the town became even more popular with commuters, encouraging further counter-urbanisation from the city.

Quite clearly, there is a complex pattern in the UK today. Some towns and cities are growing while others are declining; rural areas in general are increasing their populations, but some more remote or less attractive rural areas are losing population. The processes of urbanisation and counter-urbanisation seem to be taking place at the same time in different parts of the country for different reasons. Still other areas show signs of **re-urbanisation** taking place.

■ Re-urbanisation

Since the 1970s there have been many initiatives aimed at regenerating the inner areas of towns and cities in the UK. These are the areas where the growth linked with industrialisation took place. Industry, housing, transport and other services became concentrated here in the 19th and the first half of the 20th centuries.

Activity

2 Reread the study of Long Horsley in *AQA AS Geography* (pp197–8). Then study the mini-case study of Whitley Bay below.

a Combine these two studies to write a summary of counter-urbanisation in north-east England.

b Compare this case study with examples of counter-urbanisation in an area near you.

AQA Examiner's tip

Do not think that 'suburbanisation', 'counter-urbanisation' and 're-urbanisation' are three quite distinct processes that occur in a clear succession. It is often possible to see elements of all three processes taking place in one city or one region at the same time.

From the 1950s the urban infrastructure became outdated and deteriorated rapidly. Both housing and industry were considered to be no longer fit for purpose and large areas were abandoned or allowed to deteriorate, attracting a variety of economic, environmental and social problems.

Since the 1980s there has been a general view that these areas could best be improved by encouraging housing, jobs and services back into the centres – to produce mixed-use development.

In the past 30 years many different initiatives have aimed to:

■ bring derelict land and buildings back into use

■ improve housing conditions

■ bring new jobs

■ improve the chances of local residents to apply for these jobs, through education and training

■ encourage private-sector investment in these areas

■ encourage self-help to improve the social fabric of the areas

■ improve the quality of the environment.

All these initiatives are designed to improve conditions for residents to encourage them to stay in the inner cities and also to encourage people to move back into cities.

Initiatives to encourage re-urbanisation

Initiatives have included:

■ **Urban Development Corporations (UDCs)** were set up to regenerate areas that contained large amounts of derelict land. London Docklands and the Merseyside Development Corporation were set up in 1981, and a further 11 followed between 1986 and 1993. The UDCs had power to acquire land, clear it and provide infrastructure; then they were to encourage the private sector to develop the area. It is generally agreed that they brought economic development to these areas, but local needs were often ignored in the interests of outside investors. Subsequent developments (such as the UDCs involved with planning the Thames Gateway) have tried to take local needs into account.

■ **Enterprise Zones (EZs)** were also created in 1981 to try to stimulate development in areas of high unemployment by reducing taxes on businesses and easing planning restrictions. They had some success in attracting businesses into areas, but many of them were not new start-ups but just moved location to take advantage of the tax breaks.

■ **Inner-City Task Force (1987)** was a temporary scheme to provide training opportunities. It was credited with creating 50,000 new jobs.

■ **Single Generation Budgets (SGB – 1997)** were set up after a change of government. Local authorities (LAs) had to bid for regeneration budgets for run-down housing areas. It was felt that the LA involvement would give local people a bigger say in how the money was spent.

■ **English Partnerships** is now the **national regeneration agency** in England. It is based in the government department of Communities and Local Government (CLG). They work with a wide range of partners including local authorities, the Housing Corporation, regional development agencies and the Commission for the Built Environment (CABE).

The English Partnerships website describes their aims as follows:

```
◄ ▶   File  Edit  History  Bookmarks  Print  View  Window  Help
```

English Partnerships – What we do

English Partnerships is the national regeneration agency helping the government to support high quality sustainable growth in England.

We focus on three core areas of work to deliver our business objectives:

> unlocking and increasing the supply of land to meet housing and other growth needs

> creating and sustaining well-served mixed communities where people enjoy living and working

> improving quality of life and enhancing the environment through innovation and raising standards

Links

Updated details of each of those objectives can be accessed through links to 'About us' on the website at: www.englishpartnerships.co.uk

This also has links to case studies of projects that they have supported. One of these is at Park Hill in Sheffield.

A lot of further information about the Park Hill project, including video, audio and photos can be found on the BBC South Yorkshire website at: www.bbc.co.uk/southyorkshire/places/park_hill

Activity

3 Five different types of regeneration initiative have been described above. As you read the case studies of Park Hill, Sheffield, Thames Gateway, Merry Hill and Touchwood (below), try to see which of these initiatives has been used to help the development. What were the strengths and weaknesses of each, as applied in the case studies?

Urban decline and regeneration

- about the causes and consequences of urban decline
- about attempts to regenerate urban areas.

Key terms

Housing association: independent non-profit-making organisation for managing, building and renovating housing. Funded by central government through the Housing Corporation they can also receive funds from local authorities.

AQA Examiner's tip

At the time of writing, the Park Hill scheme is at an early stage of development. If you expect to use this case study in your exam you are strongly advised to research up-to-date material to see how the scheme is progressing.

Case study

Park Hill, Sheffield

Sheffield used to be a classic example of a city dependent on heavy industry. This had developed because of the area's natural resources: iron ore, water power and coal. Local entrepreneurs and inventors also played a major role in the growth of the area's industry.

Park Hill in Sheffield is a huge estate of flats, built in the 1960s and designed to replace some of the slums left from the late 19th and early 20th centuries that had housed Sheffield's factory workers. The new flats had many advantages, with modern amenities such as hot and cold running water and inside toilets, which had been lacking in many of the houses that they replaced. The style of construction also helped to preserve the sense of community, which was lost in some 1960s developments. However, after 40 years the flats had become run-down and dilapidated.

In parallel, as Park Hill aged, local industry went into steep decline. Many parts of Sheffield's city centre were devastated by the loss of industry and jobs. Unemployment, environmental blight, social problems and poverty all afflicted the area. Renewal of the flats was complicated by the fact that they were no longer all owned and let by the local council. Renewal of the old brownfield industrial sites was particularly difficult because the ground was polluted by the waste from the iron and steel making, requiring a massive investment to clean up the area before any redevelopment could take place.

The current plan is a good example of a partnership scheme where the local authority, a **housing association** and private developers work together. The regeneration of Park Hill is part of a widespread renewal of large areas of inner-city Sheffield and the Don Valley. However, the area has gradually been redeveloped through a combination of public and private investment. Developments planned and built during the period of urban renewal include:

- Meadowhall shopping complex
- the nearby Robin Hood International Airport
- Sheffield's tram system of urban transport
- the Don Valley stadium international sports venue
- the Advanced Manufacturing Park built by a partnership including Boeing and the University of Sheffield
- a new city economic development company, Creative Sheffield, which has been established to bring a variety of developments where art and commerce are linked to provide jobs.

As this economic change is taking place, Sheffield needs to consider how to redevelop its housing stock.

File   Edit   History   Bookmarks   Print   View   Window   Help

Park Hill, Sheffield

A £146m transformation of the Park Hill estate in Sheffield got the go-ahead in January 2007 with an agreement between English Partnerships, Sheffield City Council and developer Urban Splash.

Completed in 1961, the Park Hill estate was the most ambitious inner-city development of its time and is recognised as **Europe's largest Grade II listed building**. Covering some 13 ha, the estate contains around 1,000 flats as well as shops, pubs and

Fig. 4.11 *Architect's model of proposed redevelopment of Park Hill flats*

other community facilities. But to meet the needs and aspirations of the broader housing market renewal partnership, an overhaul of this historic estate was needed.

In a **unique funding arrangement**, the Housing Corporation committed £9.85m up front to underpin the affordable housing for rent and **shared equity** units, while English Partnerships agreed a £14.8m grant towards the cost of redeveloping the remainder of the estate. This forward funding has allowed the refurbishment plans to progress more speedily and an additional £5.5m from Transform South Yorkshire (the Housing Market Renewal Pathfinder) is covering the cost of tenant rehousing during the programme. English Heritage has also contributed £500,000 towards project costs.

Urban Splash has submitted detailed plans to modernise the total estate and, along with Manchester Methodist Housing Association, to create a more balanced community.

The **public commitment** has brought in more than £100m investment from the developer who is confident that it will see significant returns from Park Hill as it strives to return the estate to its former glory and restore the pride of the community.

Case study

The Thames Gateway

The Thames Gateway is one of four growth areas identified in the UK government's Sustainable Communities Plan published in February 2003. The plans for redevelopment of the area provide a good example, in some parts, of property-led redevelopment where investment in buildings or transport infrastructure is designed to stimulate an area and attract further development, jobs and residents. Some of the areas in the Gateway are being managed by Development Corporations. In other areas the development is managed by Partnership Agreements with many different organisations, as the following statement from the government shows.

> The Plan sets out a long-term programme of action for delivering sustainable communities in both urban and rural areas. It aims to tackle housing supply issues in the south-east, low demand in other parts of the country and the quality of our public spaces.
>
> The programme of action aims to focus the attention and coordinate the efforts of all levels of government and stakeholders in bringing about development that meets the economic, social and environmental needs of future generations as well as succeeding now.

The Thames Gateway area is 70 km long and up to 32 km wide, and covers 200,000 hectares of land. It was the industrial and

Links

For London TGDC go to: www.ltgdc.org.uk

For Thurrock TGDC go to: www.thurrocktgdc.org.uk

trading heart of the southern region and of the country, but loss of heavy industry and changes in shipping led to its rapid decline as a production centre. The Thames Gateway area represents a major opportunity to address the shortage of affordable homes in London and the south-east, and the regeneration of the eastern corridor into London and out along the Thames Estuary. Major investment is needed in infrastructure and reinstatement of damaged former industrial land.

Responsibility for delivering the plans for the area's redevelopment has been passed to a series of delivery organisations – Development Corporations and Partnerships – shown on the map in Fig. 4.12.

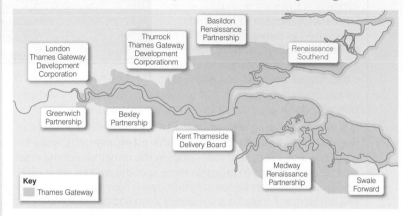

Fig. 4.12 Thames Gateway location

Links

The map in Fig. 4.12 came from www. ltgdc.org.uk (the webpage can be used to access each of the delivery organisations' websites).

Links

The Delivery Plan can be read at: www.communities.gov.uk

In November 2007 the Thames Gateway Delivery Plan was published. It stated:

'Through this Delivery Plan we are backing our vision with clear cross-government priorities and funding commitments. The Plan provides a framework for making the best use of public investment, local ownership, big project expertise and private sector entrepreneurship. It sets out a proposed spending programme for 2008–11 which includes £500 million for regeneration and £100 million for local transport improvements within a total Government investment commitment of over £9 billion.

The Plan is structured around three driving forces for positive change in the Gateway:

■ a strong economy,

■ improvements in the quality of life and

■ the development of the Gateway as an eco-region.'

The Gateway – economy and housing

The first two of those driving forces are illustrated in Figs 4.13 and 4.14.

Fig. 4.13 shows the four major 'strategic transformers' or key economic development projects that will be at the heart of the creation of jobs and wealth that the Gateway hopes to encourage. The key investments in these Strategic Transformers will come from national government sources. These transformers show many aspects of property-led development.

Fig. 14.4 shows the 10 biggest housing sites and the 10 biggest job-generating programmes in the Gateway. These will be supported by the Department of Communities and local government, in partnership with the local authorities in the areas concerned, and other key players.

The Olympics and Stratford City

Regeneration of the area at the heart of the 2012 Olympics bid. The Olympic park is being designed as a sustainable showpiece area for the whole Gateway. The London Development Agency has set up an employment and skills action plan designed to get 70,000 Londoners into work through the Games. Stratford City is a £4 billion retail-led, mixed-use urban regeneration project. It will create 5,000 jobs by 2016 and up to 20,000 by 2025 in new office, retail and leisure.

London Gateway

Regeneration of a 1,500-acre former oil refinery site to provide the largest deep-water port in Europe. It will be able to handle the largest container ships and will link to road, rail and sea connections through one of Europe's biggest logistics parks. The owners, DP world, will invest £15 billion (the 2nd largest inward investment ever) in the port to create 14,000 new jobs by 2025. They will also build an Innovation and Learning Centre for Ports and Logistics to train local residents and to provide a skilled workforce.

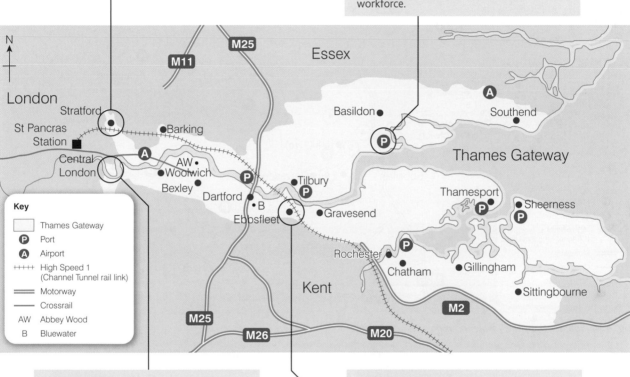

Canary Wharf

This global finance centre will be the main economic driver of the Thames Gateway. Already it employs 90,000 people and four new sites are planned, bringing over 100,000 new jobs by 2016. Crossrail will link Canary Wharf to Maidenhead to the West of London and to Heathrow. It will extend east to Abbey Wood – with links to Ebbsfleet international station. This eastern link will make it easier for residents of East London to access the jobs at Canary Wharf. A new commercial and retail scheme is to be designed by Richard Rogers Partnership, bringing 10,000 jobs to the area.

Ebbsfleet Valley

This will be a new community on brownfield sites around Ebbsfleet International station. High-speed train link Ebbsfleet to Paris and Brussels – but also to St Pancras (17 mins) and Stratford Olympic site (12 mins) over 500,000 m² of new offices should bring 10,000 new jobs by 2016. A new fast-track bus system (£35 million in government funding) links Ebbsfleet to Dartford, Gravesend and the Bluewater shopping centre.
In 2007 the government agreed to pay £74 million towards a £166 million programme to invest in roads and other transport measures. This allowed planning permission to be given for 25,000 new houses and 36,000 new jobs in Kent Thameside by 2026.

Fig. 4.13 *Thames Gateway – strategic transformers*

Top 10 housing sites supported by communities and local government

1. Lower Lea Valley and Stratford	23,400
2. The Royals and Canning Town	18,900
3. Greenwich Peninsula	13,300
4. Thurrock	12,200
5. Barking – Riverside and Town Centre	10,500
6. Medway – Waterfront and Chatham	8,100
7. Basildon	6,700
8. Woolwich	6,100
9. Kent Thameside Waterfront	5,700
10. Ebbsfleet Valley	3,700

Top 10 job generating programmes supported by communities and local government

1. East Greenwich Peninsula	9,971
2. Belvedere	8,000
3. Sittingbourne	7,486
4. West Thurrock/Lakeside	7,311
5. Kent Thames Waterfront	7,098
6. Basildon Business Economics	6,500
7. Basildon Town Centre	6,250
8. Central Southend	5,542
9. Chatham Centre and Waterfront	5,000
10. Grays	4,290

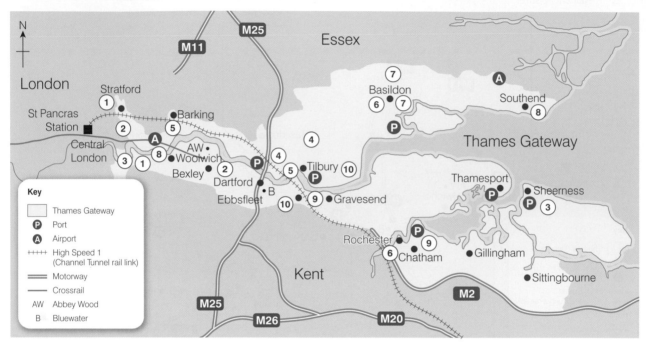

Fig. 4.14 *Thames Gateway – major housing sites*

Eco-quarter: bids will be invited from local authorities for £15 million to '**retrofit**' existing homes with energy-saving measures. Carbon-neutral shops, offices, etc. will be built alongside these houses to make a section of a town very energy-efficient.

Retrofit: make changes to improve the structure of buildings to incorporate technological advances that were not available when the buildings were originally constructed.

The Gateway as eco-region

One of the challenges, recognised in the Delivery Plan, is to combine increased economic growth with a concern for the environment and efforts to tackle climate change. It is hoped that the Gateway will 'pioneer new environmental technologies and lead the way with environmental jobs, greater use of renewables and environmental improvements to existing homes'.

The Plan tries to promote schemes to:

■ cut carbon emissions

■ conserve water

■ reduce waste

■ protect people against flood risk.

Studies have already been started to ensure that these schemes can be put into place. The Plan also announces the following:

■ They will invite proposals to set up at least one '**eco-quarter**' within an existing town.

■ Eighty per cent of new homes will be built on brownfield sites.

- They will carry out a study of feasibility of a 'zero construction waste' target.

- Waste heat from Barking power station will be used to heat neighbourhood homes.

- A 'closed loop' recycling facility for food-grade plastic will be established in Dagenham.

- Support will be provided for an environmental innovation park to harness research expertise.

- A 'green grid' of parklands and heritage sites throughout the area will be established and developed.

It must be noted though that much of the land that is designated for development in the Thames Gateway lies on the flood plain of the Thames and its tributaries. One important aspect of the planning process is to ensure that the area is made as 'flood-proof' as possible. To this end it is clear that the Green Grid is not only planned as an amenity for the residents but as an area where water can be absorbed and stored during periods when the area is at risk of flooding by water from either land or sea.

Activity

1 The details about Thames Gateway were correct at the time of writing (May 2008). However, this is a very dynamic area and development is very much ongoing. You must keep up to date through study on the internet and in the press. For instance, you could research the following:

- Have the plans been affected by changes in political control – for instance, the change of mayor from Livingstone to Johnson?

- Have the plans been affected by changes in economic conditions? For instance, at the time of writing house prices are falling and it is important to know how this might affect house-building programmes.

- Is the Environment Agency being funded well enough to provide adequate protection from flooding in an area of major flood risk?

- Is the development of the Olympic site going according to plan?

... and so on.

Links

See reference to sustainable transport in the Thames Gateway on p167.

■ Gentrification

Gentrification is the improvement of housing in an area that was formerly poor and run-down. It is mainly carried out by the residents themselves in a piecemeal way. Individual home owners make repairs and improvements to their own property and, over time, if enough houses are improved, the nature of the whole area improves and draws in more people with the money to invest in their own properties.

As the standard of the housing improves so does the wealth of the neighbourhood. This, in turn, attracts different kinds of business – shops and services with a more up-market appeal. 'Greasy spoon' cafés might be replaced by trendy coffee shops, local pubs by wine bars or gastropubs, cheap grocery stores by delicatessens, charity shops by estate agents, and so on, and the value of all the property in the area goes up.

Newington Green in North London is one small area that has been gentrified since the 1990s. The influx of professional people into this once run-down area has led to the development of the Newington Green Action Group, to improve the public spaces in the area.

Fig. 4.15 *Newington Green – gentrified London*

Links

The NGAG Newsletter can be accessed at: www.n16mag.com

Issue 16 is particularly interesting, at: www.n16mag.com/issue20/p13i20.htm

An article written by a resident journalist can be found at: www.guardian.co.uk/society/2005/apr/20/communities.guardiansocietysupplement

But not everyone necessarily benefits from gentrification. What happens to the former residents of areas that become gentrified?

If they own houses that they can sell, they obviously make a profit; and the decision to sell and move is theirs alone to make.

But many of the residents of such areas are in properties that they rent. They might include many single-parent families, unemployed people, low earners, retired people, recent immigrants, mentally ill people and so on. It might well be that their landlords see a greater potential profit in selling their houses to incomers or in redeveloping the properties so that they can be let at much higher rents.

In some cases they probably put pressure on tenants to move out of their homes – a process known as **displacement**. Studies (including one carried out by the National Census authority) have suggested that 2–10 per cent of tenants renting houses in the UK are harassed each year by their landlords or by people thought to represent landlords.

Links

See: www.radstats.org.uk/no069/article2.htm

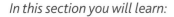

Retailing and other services

In this section you will learn:

- how retail areas are changing and developing in cities in the UK.

Key terms

Comparison goods: goods that are bought less often than everyday 'convenience goods'. They include things such as clothes, shoes, electrical and household goods, for which people make special shopping trips so that they can compare prices, styles, etc.

Did you know?

Note that even Metro Centre is tiny on a world scale. The world's biggest out-of-town-centre shopping centre is the South China Mall in Dongguan, China (890,000 m²). The next four biggest are all in Asia, as are 12 of the world's top 20. The biggest in North America is the West Edmonton Mall in Canada (570,000 m²); the biggest in Europe is Cevahir Mall in Istanbul, Turkey (420,000 m²); and the biggest in the US are the King of Prussia Mall in Pennsylvania and the Mall of America in Minnesota (numbering 15 and 16 on the world's biggest list; both over 390,000 m²).

In the past there were recognisable hierarchies of retail and service centres in all towns and cities in the UK, ranging from small neighbourhood shops providing mainly convenenience goods for a local population, to the city-centre shops selling specialist and **comparison goods** and providing a wide range of specialised services for the whole urban area and beyond.

From the 1970s onwards, the pattern changed radically. Out-of-town-centre shopping has developed on a large scale, following patterns first seen in the US and other examples pioneered in France. These changes have been made possible by widespread car ownership which allows people freedom to choose where to go for major shopping trips, rather than leaving them dependent on town centre locations accessible by public transport.

Most cities and major towns now have their own out-of-town-centre shopping centres, the biggest of which are regional shopping centres that draw their custom from well beyond the city in which they are located. There are now about 10 such regional shopping centres in the UK. They include:

- Metro Centre on Tyneside (at 165,000 m², the biggest in western Europe)
- Trafford Centre in Greater Manchester
- Meadowhall in Sheffield
- Merry Hill in the West Midlands
- Bluewater in Kent
- Cribbs Causeway at Patchway near Bristol
- Lakeside at Thurrock.

Almost all these regional centres:

- were built on the edge of a major conurbation, where land is cheaper than in the centres
- were built on land that was derelict – this made the land comparatively cheap and planning permission comparatively easy to gain; however, there were often big costs in cleaning up the land, but these costs were sometimes met, at least in part, by government
- are close to major road transport networks, motorways or major bypass roads
- have plenty of space for car parking that is usually free or at least much cheaper than in the centre
- already had, or soon developed, public transport links by train, bus or new urban transport system
- early in their development attracted one or more major 'big-name' stores which, in turn, served to attract other smaller stores
- combine shopping with leisure facilities such as cinemas, bowling alleys, mini fun-fairs, etc. and with a variety of cafés, restaurants, bars, food courts, etc.
- are built close to housing areas from which they can draw much of their staff

■ expect to attract individuals and families for whole-day shopping and leisure experiences, building on the fact that some people have come to regard shopping as a leisure activity!

However, planning laws now make it unlikely that any similar regional shopping centres will be built in the UK in the near future. They do cause problems, such as the following:

■ They compete with local shopping centres, both in town centres and in suburban areas and have been blamed, at least in part, for inner-city decline and urban blight.

■ They contribute to the sprawl that afflicts many parts of the rural–urban fringe.

■ They can cause severe congestion on the nearby motorways, often leading to long tailbacks on linked sections of the road network at peak periods.

■ They can be seen as socially divisive. Town centres, with their public transport systems, are accessible to virtually everyone; the out-of-town centres can be difficult and expensive to get to for those without cars. Therefore, they can exclude the poor, the elderly, the under-17s who cannot drive or get lifts, single-parent families, and so on.

Once the out-of-town centres developed, there was a reaction from the old urban areas. Three key responses to the regional out-of-town centres are:

1 Redevelopment of town centres – see the Touchwood case study below (p156).

2 The growth of 'outlet centres' where large brand-name manufacturers and sellers sell their own goods (often seconds or old lines) direct to the public at lower prices than are available in the main stores. These centres are smaller than the regional centres, have fewer units and are not all under one roof. They have their own car parks and some additional facilities, but do not provide the full shopping-as-leisure experience.

3 The development of smaller shopping centres in suburbs, such as outlet centres and the small centres, sometimes known in North America as 'box malls'.

■ Box malls

Although this expression is not currently in widespread use in the UK, it is quite descriptive. These shopping centres are not 'all under one roof' like the major centres. Instead, they usually consist of a number of 'box-shaped' retail outlets. These often sell specialised goods, such as furniture, DIY materials, consumer electricals or 'white goods', computers and electronic goods. They do not specialise in 'comparison goods', such as fashion clothes and shoes, which tend to concentrate in larger city centres or major out-of-town shopping centres.

Sometimes these malls are built close to a group of leisure attractions, particularly multiplex cinemas.

Greenbridge Retail and Leisure Park is one such development near Swindon.

Fig. 4.16 *An example of a box mall*

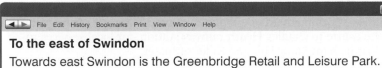

To the east of Swindon

Towards east Swindon is the Greenbridge Retail and Leisure Park. Covering several acres, the facilities include large-store facilities for a range of household brands like Boots, Mothercare, Argos, PC World, Currys and JJB – to name but a few! The complex also has a range of leisure activities such as an Empire Cinemas 12-screen multiplex cinema, a Gala Bingo Club, a private health and fitness club and many restaurants and fast-food outlets.

Extract from *the Swindon Council's shopping guide*

Links

The following website gives more details about Swindon's different types of shopping, with links to both out-of-town and town centre shopping: www.swindon.gov.uk/leisuresport/shopping

Case study

Merry Hill, West Midlands

Out-of-town retailing

Merry Hill is a retail facility which was built between 1984 and 1989, with extensions ongoing today. These extensions and new developments show how all kinds of retail developments have to respond to developments elsewhere. It is quite clear that the development of the Touchwood shopping centre in Solihull (see below, pp160–1) was partly a response to the competition from out-of-town-centre retail developments. Now, though, Merry Hill is having to respond and redevelop its facilities in order to keep up with new town-centre developments. These two case studies should be considered together as part of an ongoing process of reatil competition.

Merry Hill occupies a site of over 50 ha, with two levels of covered mall shops, a retail warehouse park, a 10-screen multiplex cinema and 10,000 car parking spaces. The lettable floor area is 148,000 m². Areas of the various elements of Merry Hill are approximately:

- Covered shopping – 100,000 m²
- Multiplex cinema – 371.6 m²
- Retail warehouse – 2,787 m²
- Other retail – 929 m²

The covered malls provide over 185 shops and kiosks, a department store, several large variety stores, two supermarkets and 24 catering outlets providing 2,200 seats.

Depending on the method of measurement, it is probably the third-largest facility of its type in the UK, after Bluewater in Kent and Tyneside's Metro Centre.

As well as its retail and cinema functions, Merry Hill provides banks and building societies, post office, tourist information centre and a range of community facilities such as senior citizens' clubs, careers service and a Citizens Advice Bureau. There are also plenty of toilets and baby-changing rooms.

Fig. 4.17 *Merry Hill retail facility*

Some statistics:

- Car parking spaces: 8,000
- Customer visits: 21 million pa (approx.)
- Demographics: Catchment area in excess of 3 million

Merry Hill has been served by a bus station since 1986, giving direct connections to towns including Dudley, Halesowen,

Stourbridge, West Bromwich and Cradley Heath, as well as the cities of Birmingham and Wolverhampton. The bus service connects the centre to Cradley Heath railway station, for local services to Birmingham Snow Hill and Kidderminster.

Merry Hill is in Brierley Hill, West Midlands. The first businesses moved into the complex in 1985 and the original centre was fully occupied by 1989. Several expansion projects have taken place since then.

Merry Hill is home to a multiplex cinema and a number of larger shops such as Primark, Next, Marks & Spencer and Debenhams. Adjacent to the main shopping site is The Waterfront, which overlooks the canal and provides offices – among the occupants are Virgin Media and HM Revenue and Customs – and has a marina area with a number of bars and restaurants.

There was an elevated monorail in operation at Merry Hill from 1991, but this closed in 1996 as a result of a combination of technical problems and safety concerns (especially the difficulty of evacuation), exacerbated by a dispute between the owners of Merry Hill and The Waterfront which at this time were owned separately.

Construction

In the 1980s the government created a number of Enterprise Zones (EZs) which gave incentives to firms wishing to set up in areas affected by a downturn in manufacturing. The Brierley Hill area had suffered the loss of the Round Oak Steelworks, and it was hoped that other manufacturers would be encouraged to move into the area. EZ incentives included relaxed planning rules and a 10-year period exempt from business rates. Developers took advantage of the lack of restrictions by making a shopping centre, rather than the industrial units originally envisaged by the EZ policy.

The EZ encompassed both the former steelworks site and a large open green space known as Merry Hill Farm. This was well used for recreation by local people and was a haven for wildlife. There was much hostility when building of the first phase of the shopping centre commenced on the green space, rather than on the former steelworks site. Despite protests from local citizens, the Merry Hill Farm site was destroyed in the first phase of development. The steelworks site was not built on until later stages of the Merry Hill/Waterfront Project.

Planning consent had been granted, some time before the closure of Round Oak Steelworks in December 1982, for the land of the farm to be used for the tipping of steelworks waste. The perimeter of the site had been landscaped with embankments and tree planting to mask the tipping from neighbouring housing. The first phase of building not only destroyed the farm, which would soon have been covered by waste in any case, but also removed the new landscaping and threatened the stability of the canal embankment on the hillside above the site. This resulted in the closure of the Dudley Canal to traffic for several years.

Effect on surrounding towns

When the Merry Hill Centre opened, a number of large retail chains decided to move their stores from surrounding towns into the new shopping centre. This left a number of large empty premises behind, which, in turn, meant many shoppers abandoned town centres for the Merry Hill Centre, which led to a large downturn in trade for remaining shops, affecting their viability. Most affected was Dudley, the largest nearby town; Halesowen and Stourbridge were also hit.

A further blow came when Dudley Council announced that it was bringing in parking charges; this turned more shoppers away from local towns and towards the Merry Hill Centre, where parking remained free. However, parking charges will be introduced in 2008, in response to local council requirements that a shopping centre of its size implement charges similar to those in local town centres. Meanwhile, other nearby towns have responded to the Merry Hill development by redeveloping their own town centres, as shown in the Touchwood case study (see pp160–61).

Recent and planned developments

Merry Hill has been forced to respond to the complaints from local towns that have suffered retail decline because of the out-of-town-developments and to the competition that has come from town centre redevelopment in Solihull, Birmingham centre and elsewhere. The owners and local council leaders have stated their aim to better connect and integrate Merry Hill with the traditional town-centre of Brierley Hill. To this end, the Dudley Canal has been rerouted, and a number of new flats and houses have been built around the site, with more expected to follow. A new line of the Midland Metro tram system will reach the site in 2011. It will terminate a short distance south of the centre in Brierley Hill town centre, and will give direct light-rail links to the towns of Dudley, Tipton and Wednesbury.

For summer 2010 a replacement cinema (16–20 screens) will be built on the vacant land behind the existing cinema, along with the construction of numerous other leisure facilities, including a bowling alley, comedy club, outdoor performing area, many restaurants and bars and a proposed casino. This 'leisure plateau' will begin the integration of Brierley Hill town centre with the Merry Hill shopping centre, with a direct walkway between the two. The entertainment area will be in a newly created public square. Further expansion is expected along the entire canal to turn it into an entertainment district that could even rival city locations. The redevelopment of the centre is intended to achieve high levels of 'green' efficiency, with Merry Hill being the first retail development in the country to be awarded BREEAM (Building Research Establishment Environmental Assessment Method) accreditation.

Many local factories and establishments are discussing closing down or relocating (including all factories on the Brierley Hill side of the canal) to make way for more modern apartments, multi-storey car parks and businesses.

The extracts on p160 are taken from a West Midlands Planning document Regional Spatial Strategy for the West Midlands – Draft Phase 1 Revision. The full document can be consulted at the weblink provided.

… Brierley Hill/Merry Hill will have significant potential to assist the regeneration of the Black Country. The case for designation of Brierley Hill/Merry Hill as a strategic centre is therefore now very clearly established through the Draft Revision and the evidence in support fully justifies this approach.

[We must] recognise the dynamic nature of networks of centres over time. Some centres will decline and others will rise to become more significant in the regional or a sub-regional network. Brierley Hill/Merry Hill has already supplanted Dudley town centre as the main retail centre in this part of the sub-region and in its own right is a very significant retail destination in the region as a whole. Dudley town centre does not have the physical capacity to meet the demand for additional comparison retail floorspace identified in the period up to 2021 and evidence is clear that there is a lack of market confidence.

The decline in the fortunes of Dudley town centre has meant there is currently a significant deficiency in the network of existing strategic centres in the Black Country. This deficiency is a weakness in the economic prospects for the sub-region and has led to an unbalanced Regional network of centres.

A prosperous, appropriately developed Brierley Hill/Merry Hill, as part of a package approach to regeneration across the Black Country, will attract more people to live in the area and retain retail expenditure to the benefit of the whole sub-region. Sustainable regeneration requires the effective harnessing of commercially available market-driven opportunities.

The designation of Brierley Hill/Merry Hill as a strategic centre is an important element in the strategy for economic growth and urban renaissance in the Black Country.

It is also one of the aims of the draft revision to create a situation where the trend of increasing leakage of retail expenditure out of the Black Country is reversed and the growth of the four strategic centres enables more sustainable patterns of travel to develop and longer journeys to other centres outside the sub-region to be reduced. Brierley Hill/Merry Hill has a very important role to play in achieving this …

Evidence clearly shows that Dudley has ceased to function as a strategic centre but its heritage and tourism functions could give it long-term potential.

Links

The full West Midlands planning document 'Regional Spatial Strategy for the West Midlands – Draft Phase 1 Revision' can be found at: www.planning-inspectorate.gov.uk/pins/rss/west_midlands/documents/WMRAandBCC95and76S6.pdf

Activity

1. Read the case study and write a summary of ways in which Touchwood illustrates Solihull's response to out-of-town retail developments such as Merry Hill, and in which new developments at Merry Hill illustrate their response to town-centre redevelopments. (This might take the form of a flow diagram.)

Case study

Touchwood, Solihull

Urban centre redevelopment

Touchwood is a shopping centre in Solihull, on the south-east of the West Midlands conurbation – the opposite side from Dudley. It is on redeveloped land in the town centre, close to the bus and railway stations, and with its own multi-storey car park.

While Dudley is one of the less prosperous parts of the West Midlands, Solihull is one of the more prosperous. Its area includes the National Exhibition Centre and Birmingham International Airport. It has less derelict industrial land than Dudley and has far more employment in growing sectors of the economy. However, by the 1990s the town centre seemed rather old-fashioned and was struggling to compete with regional out-of-town developments such as Merry Hill. The Touchwood centre was the response.

File   Edit   History   Bookmarks   Print   View   Window   Help

What is Touchwood?

A successful combination of retail and leisure

The 60,000m² Touchwood shopping and entertainment destination in Solihull, which opened on 5 September 2001, has become the new blueprint for in-town development, and its innovative design has truly integrated it into Solihull's town centre.

Touchwood's success has been proven, with the winning of UK Retail Destination of the Year and Best Major New Shopping Centre. Touchwood created over 2,000 retail jobs, a significant contribution to employment in the Solihull region.

Close partnerships have also been developed with key retailers, Solihull Metropolitan Council, the John Lewis Partnership, Jobcentreplus, Birmingham and Solihull Learning and Skills Council and local businesses in order to maximise Solihull's potential. As a result, Solihull's status as a subregional town has catapulted to a top 50 shopping venue in the UK.

The vision

Touchwood was designed to reflect the architectural features and heritage of Solihull with its naturally lit arcades, leafy courtyards and open spaces. The complex is comprised of John Lewis's only department store in the West Midlands at 265,000 sq. ft, plus 80 other stores, over 20 restaurants and a Cineworld nine-screen multiplex cinema. It is ideally located, with Junctions 4 and 5 of the M42 linking directly into the town, and with 6,000 car parking spaces.

Fig. 4.18 *Inside Touchwood's shopping centre*

Solihull is the new retail destination of choice for the West Midlands.

The design

Touchwood's design integrates seamlessly with the existing high street, reflecting the heritage of Solihull in a contemporary style. It echoes the detail of the town's architectural features, such as an intricacy of brickwork, gables and box bay windows. Special finishing touches include natural limestone flooring, timberwork, brick arches, geometrically designed ceilings, internal planting and uniquely designed lighting.

Unlike any other retail destination in the UK, Touchwood features the largest collection of retail arcades ever built in the UK, and the greatest number of open courtyards and publicly accessible gardens.

The Three Arcades

Touchwood's three arcades each have a different look and feel, borrowing from the graceful display of cabinet windows, ornamental ceilings, elegant shop fronts and controlled lighting of London's great arcades.

The concept architecture blends the intimate atmosphere of traditional English arcades with the modern retailer's requirements for large stores of up to 40 metres in depth. By integrating open courtyards and publicly accessible gardens Touchwood creates a unique, contemporary environment.

Internal courtyards

Touchwood features two internal courtyards, Ivy Court and the Map Room. Inspired by the vaulted roofs of Sir John Soane's Bank of England, these atria are impressive rooms, that act as focal points and meeting places for shoppers, with comfortable seating for resting and relaxing.

Ivy Court: situated outside the entrance to the John Lewis store, it has a countryside theme. Its ceiling features a beautiful canopy of leaves specially designed and made from stainless steel.

The Map Room: the ceiling here is a map of the British Isles denoting market towns of a similar size to Solihull.

Four new gardens

Touchwood has created four new gardens with hundreds of new trees in Solihull. The new gardens provide moments of respite from a morning's shopping or a long day's work.

Encircled by the Library, Public Theatre and Touchwood, **Library Square** is a paved courtyard featuring a grove of ornamental flowering.

Golden Jubilee Gardens comprises a network of paths leading up a gently sloping tree-lined hill and encircling a grass amphitheatre outside the Homer Road entrance to Touchwood. A circle of cherry trees adjacent to the Register Office creates a picturesque area for bridal parties.

Manor Square Gardens follows in the tradition of great town gardens with extensive seating under a canopy of trees. **Magistrates' Garden** is a peaceful cloister from the hustle and bustle of the town centre.

Contemporary sustainability issues in urban areas

Waste management and recycling in cities

In this section you will learn:

- about sustainability issues, linked to waste management and transport systems, in contemporary cities.

If cities are to be sustainable, they must manage their waste efficiently and cause the least possible damage to the environment. How is this done? Consider Fig. 4.19:

Most favoured option

Least favoured option

Prevention
Minimisation
Reuse
Recycling
Energy recovery
Disposal

Fig. 4.19 *Waste management hierarchy*

The waste hierarchy refers to the '3 Rs': reduce, reuse and recycle, which classify waste management strategies according to their desirability in terms of waste minimisation. The waste hierarchy remains the cornerstone of most waste minimisation strategies. The aim is to extract the maximum practical benefits from products and to generate the minimum amount of waste.

Dealing with the waste produced by any town or city is a huge issue. There is a political as well as an environmental dimension, for two reasons:

1 The EU and the UK government have produced targets for all local authorities (LAs) to reduce the waste buried in their landfill sites and to increase the proportion that they recycle. (See below for targets.) LAs that do not reach their targets will be fined for burying more than their quota of waste in landfill sites.

2 The government suggested that LAs should consider charging households that throw away (without recycling) more waste than average and rewarding households that throw away less than average. A very loud campaign was mounted against this by certain parts of the press, so the government appears to have backed down from this suggestion. However, it is clear that the problem of waste will not diminish and some alternative approach will be needed.

Waste management methods vary widely between areas for many reasons, including type of waste material, nearby land uses and the area available. Fig. 4.20 shows the **total diversion rates** for each of the London boroughs. The key compares the rates of the boroughs with the rates in all the LAs in the UK.

Key terms

Total diversion rate: the amount of material (in kg/household/yr) that is recycled and/or composted instead of going to landfill.

Key: kilograms of waste/
household recycled/year

	<199
	200–249
	250–299
	300–349
	>350

*265 kg is the average UK performance

Fig. 4.20 *London borough recycling rates*

■ **Activities**

1 Study the map in Fig. 4.20.

  a Describe the spatial pattern shown.

  b Suggest reasons for the pattern shown.

  c Suggest why such a high proportion of boroughs fall below the
    national average for recycling.

2 The cost of transporting material to landfill sites is particularly high for
London. Suggest why. Then explain why it would seem to be particularly
important for London to increase its recycling rates.

3 Visit the Wrap (Waste and Resources Action Programme) website and
research the recycling records for your own area. Compare them with the
London rates (or Londoners, compare your rates with an area outside
London, perhaps Cambridge and Peterborough).

■ Waste management methods

Disposal

Disposing of waste in a landfill involves burying waste, and many
landfills were established in disused quarries or mines. Properly designed
and well-managed landfills can be a hygienic and relatively inexpensive
method of disposing of waste materials. When badly managed, they can
create adverse environmental impacts, such as wind-blown litter, vermin
and liquids leaching out to pollute groundwater. Other common by-
products of landfills are gases, mostly methane and carbon dioxide.

Modern landfills include methods to stop leaching, such as clay or plastic
lining material. Deposited waste is normally compacted to increase its
density and stability, and covered to prevent attracting vermin. Many
landfills also have landfill gas extraction systems installed to extract the
landfill gas. Gas is pumped out of the landfill using perforated pipes and
flared off or burnt in a gas engine to generate electricity.

■ Links

The Wrap website has an interactive
map and GIS at: www.wrap.org.uk/
local_authorities/online_recycling_
information_system_oris/mapping.
html

Many other resources can be seen on
other parts of the site.

Incineration

Incineration involves combustion of waste material. Incinerators convert waste materials into heat, gas, steam and ash. It is recognised as a practical method of disposing of certain hazardous waste materials (such as biological medical waste), but it is controversial due to issues such as emission of gaseous pollutants. Some facilities burn waste in a furnace or boiler to generate heat, steam and/or electricity.

■ Recycling methods

The process of extracting resources or value from waste is generally referred to as recycling, meaning to recover or reuse the material. There are a number of different methods by which waste material is recycled: the raw materials might be extracted and reprocessed, or the calorific content of the waste might be converted to electricity.

Physical reprocessing

The popular meaning of 'recycling' in most developed countries refers to the widespread collection and reuse of everyday waste materials. These are collected and sorted so that the raw materials from which the items are made can be reprocessed into new products. Material for recycling may be collected separately from general waste using dedicated bins and collection vehicles, or sorted directly from mixed waste streams.

The most common consumer products recycled include aluminium drink cans, steel cans, plastic bottles, glass bottles and jars, paperboard cartons, newspapers, magazines and cardboard. These items are usually composed of a single material, making them relatively easy to recycle. Recycling more complex products (such as computers and other electronic equipment) is more difficult, due to the additional dismantling and separation required.

Biological reprocessing

Waste materials that are organic in nature, such as plant material, food scraps, and paper products, can be recycled by composting. The resulting organic material is then recycled as mulch or compost for agricultural or landscaping purposes. In addition, waste gas from the process (such as methane) can be captured and used for generating electricity. There is a large variety of composting and digestion methods and technologies, varying in complexity from simple home compost heaps to industrial-scale enclosed-vessel digestion of mixed domestic waste.

Energy recovery

The energy content of waste products can be harnessed directly by using them as a direct combustion fuel, or indirectly by processing them into another type of fuel. Recycling through thermal treatment ranges from using waste as a fuel source for cooking or heating, to fuel for boilers to generate steam and electricity in a turbine.

■ Waste reduction methods

An important method of waste management is the prevention of waste material being created, also known as waste reduction. This might be done by reusing second-hand products, repairing broken items instead of buying new, designing products to be refillable or reusable (such as cotton instead of plastic shopping bags), encouraging consumers to avoid using disposable products (such as disposable cutlery), and designing products that use less material to achieve the same purpose (for example, lightweighting of beverage cans).

> ### ■ Did you know?
>
> Glass is 100 per cent recyclable but only 30 per cent of glass bottles and jars used in the UK are currently recycled. The energy saving from recycling one bottle will power:
> - a 100-watt light bulb for almost an hour
> - a computer for 25 minutes
> - a colour TV for 20 minutes
> - a washing machine for 10 minutes.

The UK Department for the Environment, Food and Rural Affairs (Defra) is trying to reduce waste through setting targets for local authorities. These are explained on its website, an extract from which is provided below.

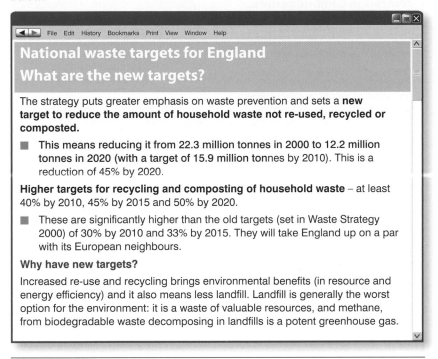

National waste targets for England
What are the new targets?

The strategy puts greater emphasis on waste prevention and sets a **new target to reduce the amount of household waste not re-used, recycled or composted.**

- This means reducing it from 22.3 million tonnes in 2000 to 12.2 million tonnes in 2020 (with a target of 15.9 million tonnes by 2010). This is a reduction of 45% by 2020.

Higher targets for recycling and composting of household waste – at least 40% by 2010, 45% by 2015 and 50% by 2020.

- These are significantly higher than the old targets (set in Waste Strategy 2000) of 30% by 2010 and 33% by 2015. They will take England up on a par with its European neighbours.

Why have new targets?

Increased re-use and recycling brings environmental benefits (in resource and energy efficiency) and it also means less landfill. Landfill is generally the worst option for the environment: it is a waste of valuable resources, and methane, from biodegradable waste decomposing in landfills is a potent greenhouse gas.

www.defra.gov.uk/environment/waste/strategy/factsheets/targets.htm

In order to encourage local authorities to reduce their landfill and increase rates of recycling, the government has designated certain authorities as Beacon Authorities for Waste Disposal. Cambridgeshire and Peterborough is one of those. This area includes some rural areas as well as the contrasting towns of Cambridge (an ancient university town which has grown very rapidly as a centre of high-tech industry in the last 30 years or so) and Peterborough (which has also grown very rapidly since being designated as a new town in 1967).

Two of their schemes are described here and a third is referenced in the link box. These range from a major authority-wide initiative to very locally based work. The two schemes discussed here are:

1 their major new recycling plant

2 EARP – the scheme to recycle electrical appliances.

Links

Further details of this scheme can be found at: www.recap. co.uk/news/newsitem. aspx?action=view&id=1431

Links

Further details of EARP can be found at: www.cambridgeshire.gov.uk/ NR/rdonlyres/15BCFE68-36DA-487F-AA97-91C54C66DFF1/0/ EARPforweb.pdf

You can also find details about Cambridge's Master Composter scheme at: www.cambridgeshire. gov.uk/NR/rdonlyres/4A85F49D-6F62-4EE2-8213-063448746DA4/0/ Mastercompostercasestudyforweb. pdf

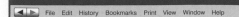

File   Edit   History   Bookmarks   Print   View   Window   Help

11/04/2008 – Sign of the times … major £730 million recycling contract in Cambridgeshire

A £730 million contract that will see thousands of tonnes of Cambridgeshire waste composted or recycled was signed this week.

The new 28-year contract between Cambridgeshire County Council and local company Donarbon Waste Management Limited will see the most modern recycling facilities in the eastern region built at Waterbeach to help reduce the waste from Cambridgeshire's growing population.

The Council has been successful in attracting £35 million in Government PFI credits to help pay for the scheme.

The centrepiece of the plans is a state-of-the-art Mechanical Biological Treatment (MBT) plant which sorts 'black bag rubbish', removing material for recycling before producing a compost-like material. But waste chiefs made it clear that this technology should not be seen as an alternative to using existing kerbside recycling services as kerbside sorting results in higher quality materials for recycling. It is instead a way of capturing materials that are harder to separate at the kerbside.

The scheme will also include a visitor centre where people, including local children, will be able to learn more about recycling and find out about the MBT plant, which uses environmentally friendly methods to treat waste.

Cambridgeshire has topped national league tables for recycling and composting since 2003–2004 and is on track to exceed its target of 50% for 2007–2008. But it still has to spend £7 million each year landfilling thousands of tonnes of rubbish that cannot currently be treated, a figure that is set to rise by another £1 million in 2008–2009 due to recent Government landfill tax increases.

Cambridgeshire County Councillor John Reynolds, who was instrumental in bringing the PFI contract to fruition as the previous Lead Member for Planning and Regional Matters, said, 'Helping to secure a greener future for our children and grandchildren has always been at the heart of this contract. We are very pleased to have laid the foundations for managing Cambridgeshire's waste over the next 28 years.'

www.recap.co.uk

File   Edit   History   Bookmarks   Print   View   Window   Help

RECAP Case Study – Peterborough EARP (Electrical Appliance Recycling Programme)

Residents of Peterborough generate approximately 300,000 old electrical items (e.g. fridges, freezers, washers, dryers, computers, kettles, hoovers, etc.) for disposal each year. Forward thinking and our proactive approach to the proposed Waste Electrical and Electronic Equipment (WEEE) Directive resulted in the opening of our innovative **Electrical Appliance Recycling Programme** in partnership with a registered community-based charity, Compass (Peterborough) Ltd. This project, the only one in the country, takes a holistic view to waste minimisation, emphasising collection, reprocessing and education. It has a working group consisting of Peterborough City Council, Compass (Peterborough) Ltd, Ukceed (research & development), Hewlett Packard and Merloni (manufacturers). Our role is:

- white goods and small electrical items are collected from households by means of take-back schemes through manufacturers, bulky waste collections and four small electrical banks situated around the city.

- to comply with future WEEE legislation, each item is bar-coded to enable easy auditing and ensuring quality control for items reused in the community.

- the first process is establishing the condition of each appliance and whether to reuse or recycle. Items for reuse are tested for faults in our test areas, repaired by our workstation trainees and finally PAT tested by our fully qualified electrician.

- Those for recycling are broken down into components, e.g. light iron, aluminium, copper and plastic. All components are sent for reprocessing except for plastic, which is further sorted into types before being granulated in one of our three granulators.

The project acts as a catalyst for community volunteering and provides training for disadvantaged people.

www.cambridgeshire.gov.uk

■ Sustainable transport schemes

The study on the Thames Gateway developments (pp149–53) stated:

> this delivery plan ... provides a framework for making the best use of public investment, local ownership, big project expertise and private sector entrepreneurship. It sets out a proposed spending programme for 2008–11 which includes £500 million for regeneration and £100 million for local transport improvements.

One of the key priorities in the delivery plan is the development of an integrated and sustainable transport network. This extract from the London Development Authority website describes how this network will develop. Study it alongside the maps of the Thames Gateway on pp150–2.

A vibrant and sustainable Thames Gateway requires a sustainable and integrated transport system offering access to town centres, employment areas, local communities and regional destinations through a real choice of transport modes. The vision for public transport requires extensive, efficient, reliable, safe and convenient connections at regional and sub-regional levels.

Fig. 4.21 *Sustainable transport is available in many British towns and cities*

Walking and cycling will be the preferred options for local access and use of the car and road-based freight will be carefully managed to balance the priorities of economic efficiency, environmental protection and social inclusion. Land use and transport will be carefully integrated to reduce the need to travel and create a built environment that enhances people's lives and daily experience.

Quick and efficient access to international travel and markets will be available from City Airport, Stansted, Eurostar services at Stratford International and Ebbsfleet, and the fast access to Heathrow Airport provided by Crossrail. Crossrail will form the rail spine of Thames Gateway London,

providing a fast, high-capacity link to and through London's three central business districts at Canary Wharf, the City and the West End. Development will be focused at Crossrail stations, which will also be fed by integrated public transport feeder services including the Docklands Light Railway (DLR), the transits and high quality buses.

Extensions of the DLR through London City Airport, across the Thames to Woolwich and eastwards through London Riverside will increase the accessibility of these areas. Options for enhancements to the North London Line corridor through the Lower Lea, including a proposed conversion for DLR operation, are being investigated jointly with the Strategic Rail Authority.

At a local level the public transport system will be knitted together by the two transit schemes' (Greenwich Waterfront Transit and East London Transit) key bus routes, providing a high quality and accessible bus-based network unhindered by the unreliability caused by traffic congestion. Linked together via the Thames Gateway Bridge, these transit schemes will radically enhance orbital public transport travel and connect the area's major town centres and rail networks.

Good quality interchanges, integrated with safe, convenient and comprehensive local pedestrian and cycle networks will complete the system.

www.lda.gov.uk

Links

The Thames Gateway plans may be seen in full at: www.lda.gov.uk/upload/rtf/thames_gateway.rtf

Smart Growth USA

Smart Growth is an organisation in the US. It was formed by a group of planners, architects, and academics with an interest in developing more sustainable ways of living in cities. Some of their ideas could well be useful for cities in the UK and elsewhere. Some of their projects can be seen following the Links below.

The Goals of Smart Growth

Healthier, safer communities

Protecting the environment

Better access, less traffic

Thriving cities, suburbs and towns

Shared benefits

Lower costs, lower taxes

Keeping open space open

The 10 principles of smart growth

1　Provide a variety of transportation choices

2　Mix land uses

3　Create a range of housing opportunities and choices

4　Create walkable neighbourhoods

5　Encourage community and stakeholder collaboration

6　Foster distinctive, attractive communities with a strong sense of place

7　Make development decisions predictable, fair and cost-effective

8　Preserve open space, farmland, natural beauty and critical environmental areas

9　Strengthen and direct development towards existing communities

10　Take advantage of compact building design and efficient infrastructure design

■ Links

You can read the Goals and the Principles in detail at: www. smartgrowthtoolkit.net

Then you can follow the links to the case studies and to other aspects of their work.

One of the principles is explained below:

1　Provide a variety of transportation choices

Most communities built within the last 40 years are designed so that residents are almost completely dependent on driving. With no other options, we have to take our cars to run every errand (going to the store, going to school, going to a park, etc.). Many places don't allow us to take even short walks to nearby shops because there are no pavements. Providing a variety of transportation options – like safe and reliable public transportation, pavements, bike paths and walking trails – promotes and improves our health, conserves energy and safeguards the environment. We can only reduce our dependency on automobiles if there are other attractive and convenient ways to get where we want to go.

There are also many members of our communities who can't drive or don't have access to a car. Providing transportation options creates communities where our seniors, young people below driving age and the disabled can all live comfortably.

Activities

4 The Smart Growth Goals and Principles were developed for use in the US.

  a Are they also applicable to this country?

  b How would they need to be adapted?

  c Consider how they could be applied to transport in a local area that you have studied to produce an 'integrated, efficient and sustainable' transport system.

5 Visit the Sustrans website and find examples of how that organisation is trying to provide safe and efficient cycling routes in cities in the UK. Make notes on one such example.

Contrast these small-scale approaches with the much larger-scale attempts to produce an integrated transport system in London and the Thames Gateway.

Links

Sustrans is at: www.sustrans.org.uk

In particular you should follow directions to 'Liveable neighbourhoods' and 'Safe routes to schools' (in the 'Sustrans Projects' section).

In this chapter you will h ave learnt:

- about the world distribution of millionaire cities, megacities and world cities

- how urban development and economic growth are linked

- how Mumbai's growth has occurred and how its future growth is being planned

- about the contemporary growth of cities in the UK, and their development, decline and regeneration

- how patterns of retailing in cities are changing and about the planning process involved

- how planners are trying to ensure the sustainability of cities in the future.

Development and globalisation

Describing and classifying levels of development

In this section you will learn:

- how development is defined, measured and mapped.

Key terms

Gross domestic product (GDP): the value of all the goods and services produced in a country during a year, in $US. This is often given as GDP per capita, that is, an average for each person in the country. Total GDP is divided by the number of people in the country. The figures are further adjusted to take account of the purchasing power of money in each country rather than simply using exchange rates to convert local currency into $US. Figures converted like this are called GDP.

Development can be defined as a process of social and economic advancement, in terms of the quality of human life.

Most geographers would agree that development involves people becoming better-off in material terms but that it also involves change in:

- the demographic structure of a country or region's population (see *AQA AS Geography*, pp162–7)

- the nature of society, with a move towards a more equal distribution of wealth, education, health care and opportunities for advancement

- the political structure, with increased participation and democracy

- the culture of the society, with more education, greater levels of literacy, more equal rights for women, and so on.

However, some people would argue that this view of development implies a dominant Western world view, involving such elements as a belief in progress, the inevitability of material growth, the solution of problems by the application of science and technology, and the assumption of human dominance over nature. Alternative philosophies are suggested by the use of terms such as 'sustainable development' or 'participatory development'.

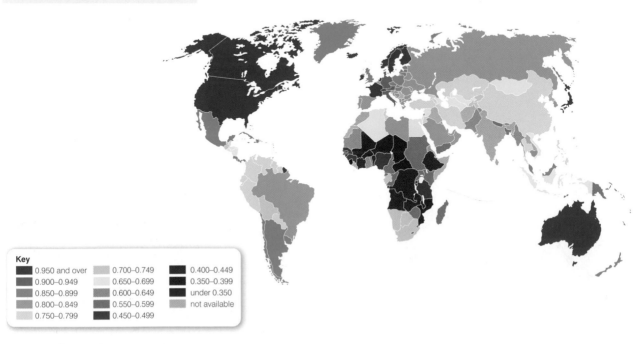

Key
- 0.950 and over
- 0.900–0.949
- 0.850–0.899
- 0.800–0.849
- 0.750–0.799
- 0.700–0.749
- 0.650–0.699
- 0.600–0.649
- 0.550–0.599
- 0.450–0.499
- 0.400–0.449
- 0.350–0.399
- under 0.350
- not available

Fig. 5.1 *The Human Development Index for 2007*

Some people even hold the view that this 'Western' form of 'development' can be destructive to traditional cultures and ways of life. In fact, some groups, in areas such as the mountain regions of Afghanistan and the rainforests of Brazil, suggest that Western-style development is so damaging that it ought to be resisted by armed conflict, if necessary.

There are many ways of describing and classifying development levels in countries around the world. Two of the most useful are **gross domestic product (GDP)** and the **Human Development Index (HDI)**.

Tables showing the top and bottom ranked countries for these two measures are shown on p172 along with definitions of the two measures.

Maps showing the world distribution of HDIs and GDP are shown on pp170–71.

Key terms

Human Development Index (HDI): a comparative measure of life expectancy, literacy, education and standards of living. It is a standardised way to compare well-being, especially child welfare, in different countries. It can be used to measure the impact of economic policies on the quality of life of people in the country.

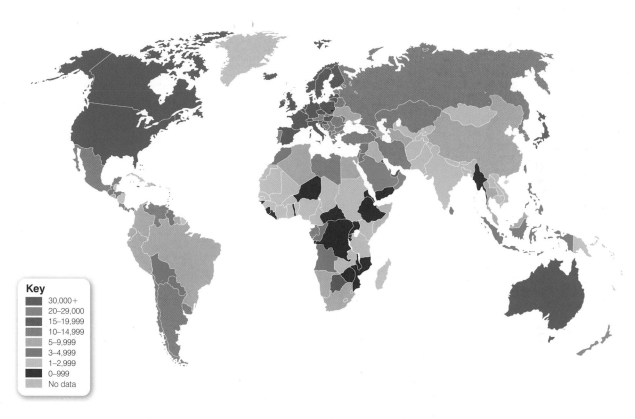

Key

- 30,000+
- 20–29,000
- 15–19,999
- 10–14,999
- 5–9,999
- 3–4,999
- 1–2,999
- 0–999
- No data

Fig. 5.2 *GDP PPP per capita in $US, 2007/2008. From the International Monetary Fund*

Links

Several other maps showing aspects of economic development are available at: www.en.wikipedia.org/wiki/LEDC

You can find a full list of the world's countries, ranked by both GDP and HDI at: www.en.wikipedia.org/wiki/List_of_countries_by_GDP_(PPP)_per_capita; and: www.en.wikipedia.org/wiki/List_of_countries_by_Human_Development_Index

Table 5.1 *Countries at the top and bottom of the HDI league, 2004/2005*

Rank	HDI change from 2004–2005	Country	HDI in 2005 (compared to 2004 data)
1	▲ 2	Iceland	0.968
2	▼ 1	Norway	0.968
3	– 0	Australia	0.962
4	▲ 2	Canada	0.961
5	▼ 1	Ireland	0.959
6	▼ 1	Sweden	0.956
7	▲ 2	Switzerland	0.955
8	▼ 1	Japan	0.953
9	▲ 1	Netherlands	0.953
10	▲ 6	France	0.952
11	– 0	Finland	0.952
12	▼ 4	US	0.951
13	▲ 6	Spain	0.949
14	▲ 1	Denmark	0.949
15	▼ 1	Austria	0.948
16	▲ 2	UK	0.94

Rank	HDI change from 2004–2005	Country	HDI in 2005 (compared to 2004 data)
168	▼ 1	Democratic Republic of Congo	0.411
169	▲ 1	Ethiopia	0.406
170	▲ 1	Chad	0.388
171	▲ 1	Central African Republic	0.384
172	▼ 4	Mozambique	0.384
173	▲ 2	Mali	0.380
174	▲ 3	Niger	0.374
175	▼ 3	Guinea–Bissau	0.374
176	▼ 2	Burkina Faso	0.370
177	▼ 1	Sierra Leone	0.336

Table 5.2 *The countries at the top and bottom of the GDP PPP ranking (2005)*

Country	Rank	GDP in US$/capita
Luxembourg	1	79,985
Norway	2	53,701
Singapore	3	50,299
US	4	45,790
Ireland	5	42,978
Switzerland	6	39,244
Netherlands	7	38,144
Austria	8	38,106
Iceland	9	37,277
Denmark	10	36,223
Canada	11	35,729
Sweden	12	35,622
Finland	13	35,124
Australia	14	34,882
Belgium	15	34,780
UK	16	34,105

Country	Rank	GDP in US$/capita
Malawi	158	756
Timor-Leste	159	740
Central African Republic	160	714
Sierra Leone	161	677
Niger	162	628
Guinea-Bissau	163	477
Eritrea	164	403
Liberia	165	358
Burundi	166	341
Democratic Republic of Congo	167	298

Activity

1 Study the maps in Figs 5.1 and 5.2 and the data in Tables 5.1 and 5.2. You will need to use an atlas to check names and locations of countries.

Describe the patterns that you observe. Comment on:

a The geographical distribution of countries with both high and low scores on the GDP map.

b The geographical distribution of countries with both high and low scores on the HDI map.

c Any significant differences that you observe between the two maps.

d Whether there are any countries in the 'highest' and 'lowest' lists that you did not expect.

e The reasons for your observations in each of the four patterns.

■ Classifying development

Looking at the lists of countries in the Link on p171, you might have been struck by the differences between the richest and poorest countries or between the more developed economies and the less developed ones. You might also have noticed that it is very difficult to draw a dividing line between different sets of countries. Simplistic divisions are misleading. You might be familiar with terms such as:

■ **First World**, **Second World** and **Third World**, once used to describe the developed capitalist countries, the developed communist countries and the less developed countries, respectively

■ **The North** and **The South**, used by the Brandt Commission in the 1970s to highlight the differences between more developed and less developed countries.

At one time it was common to define countries as **developed**, **less developed** and **least developed**. Then the terms **more economically developed** and **less economically developed** were used, because countries can be economically poor but very highly developed culturally.

However, all these terms have one major fault: not all countries can be neatly categorised like this. Instead, they form a continuum from highly developed to those with a very low level of development; and countries can change – as shown by the Asian Tigers and now by the newly industrialised countries (NICs). (See below, pp180–6).

The Brandt Commission, led by the Chancellor of West Germany in the 1970s, divided the world into the 'Rich North' and the 'Poor South', with a line that roughly circled the world at 30°N, passing between North and Central America, north of Africa, India and China, but dipping south so as to include Australia and New Zealand in the 'North'.

The fall of the Soviet bloc countries and their further poverty weakened the expression 'North–South divide', since many Soviet bloc nations now fall into the developing category. On the other hand, many nations previously considered 'developing', such as the Asian Tigers, are now developed by any standards. Other newly industrialised countries appear to be crossing over the divide.

Some maps still show the North–South divide even though it is now quite outdated. The North–South divide has more recently been named the **development gap**. This places greater emphasis on closing the evident gap between rich and poor countries.

AQA Examiner's tip

You need to be well aware of the **continuum of development** and able to discuss 'countries at different stages of development'.

Links

See www.en.wikipedia.org/wiki/ Image:North_South_Divide_3.PNG for a map of the revised north–south divide.

Key terms

Development gap: the difference in the level of economic development between richer and poorer countries.

The processes of globalisation

Did you know?

The concept of the 'global village', based on the replacement of visual (print) culture by electronic media, was formed as far back as the early 1960s by the Canadian philosopher Marshall McLuhan. He wrote about what he called 'electronic interdependence', based on electronic media, which would cause humankind to move from individualism and fragmentation to a collective identity, with a 'tribal base' of shared technology.

Flows of information and capital

You should already have thought carefully about globalisation during your AS human option course. The concept should have formed an important basis to your study of food supply, energy or health issues.

One of the most important factors that have allowed globalisation to occur as it has done in the late 20th and early 21st centuries has been the development of information and communications technology (ICT). This allows cheap, reliable and almost instantaneous communications between almost all parts of the world, permitting the sharing of information, the transfer of capital and marketing to take place far more quickly and easily than has ever been possible before.

Fig. 5.3 *Computers allow links between stock markets, banks, stock traders and currency dealers throughout the major countries in the world so that trade and the movement of funds can take place around the world, 24 hours a day, 365 days a year*

Table 5.3 *Statistics for internet use around the world. Usage in the Middle East and Africa is growing exponentially*

World regions	Population (2008 est.)	Internet users, Dec 31 2000	Internet usage, latest data	% population (penetration)	% usage of world	% usage growth 2000–8
Africa	955,206,348	4,514,400	51,065,630	5.3	3.5	1,031.2
Asia	3,776,181,949	114,304,000	578,538,257	15.3	39.5	406.1
Europe	800,401,065	105,096,093	384,633,765	48.1	26.3	266.0
Middle East	197,090,443	3,284,800	41,939,200	21.3	2.9	1,176.8
North America	337,167,248	108,096,800	248,241,969	73.6	17.0	129.6
Latin America/ Caribbean	576,091,673	18,068,919	139,009,209	24.1	9.5	669.3
Oceania/ Australia	33,981,562	7,620,480	20,204,331	59.5	1.4	165.1
WORLD TOTAL	6,676,120,288	360,985,492	1,463,632,361	21.9	100.0	305.5

Activity

1 a Describe and explain the present pattern of internet usage and percentage penetration rates shown in Table 5.3.

   b Describe and explain the trends in the growth of internet usage shown.

   c Consider the implications of these trends for:

   ■ the ICT industry

   ■ education

   ■ the globalisation of trade

   ■ the development of people in the poorer regions of the world.

Did you know?

The rapid growth of the internet and mobile phone use in Asia, the Middle East and Africa is partly explained by the ability of many countries in these regions to bypass older internet and fixed-wire technology and infrastructure. Economic growth in Asia and in many urban areas of Africa also allows vastly more people to get online or on cellphone networks.

■ Flows of goods and people

The second set of changes that have supported the flow of information and allowed globalisation to occur are linked to improvements in transport for both people and goods.

Again, it is worth referring back to your optional human module studied at AS to see how food, or fuel, or medical drugs move around the world. These movements have been made possible by the reduced costs and increased efficiency of transport systems. Such systems include:

■ the increased size of aircraft, allowing more people and goods to be moved, and reducing unit costs per person or item moved

■ integrated air movement networks, often based on major international hubs feeding national and regional services

■ the growth of low-cost airlines and airfreight companies

■ the container revolution that allowed the integration of freight movements by sea, rail, road and even air

■ the handling revolution that allowed containerisation to become so efficient

■ new computerised logistics systems for all forms of transport

■ high-speed rail networks.

Some people think that we have already passed the point when the world's production of oil has peaked. If this is so, how will the globalised system of trade cope? Can it adapt to a world after 'Peak Oil'?

The movement of people around the world has also increased with improved transport and increased globalisation. This growth includes increases in:

■ international and intercontinental tourism

■ movement of specialised workers on a temporary or a permanent basis, including both people who work for a company or organisation and who are moved to work elsewhere for the same company, and people who move to a different country or region because either they have been offered work with a new organisation or they are seeking new employment

■ unskilled workers, who are increasingly forced to migrate illegally as richer countries try to protect their populations from an influx of workers who would be willing to accept lower wages and poorer working conditions

Fig. 5.4 *Aerial view of Newark International Airport*

Activity

2 a As part of your AS course you studied some aspects of world trade in your optional topic. Now go back to your AS book and read about world trade in either food (pp202–9) or energy (pp236–46).

   b The specification says that, for Paper 3, you need to look at patterns of:

   ■ production

   ■ distribution

   ■ consumption

and how these have been affected by globalisation. Ensure that you have good notes available on this topic.

Fig. 5.5 *Mobile phones now provide communications and also access to information in most of the world. As phones get more functions they have potential to bring enormous economic and social changes*

Did you know?

On an individual level, access to the internet, satellite TV networks and mobile phones means that information about products and services and the opportunity to purchase is available to almost everyone, from inhabitants of world cities such as New York and London to the inhabitants of villages in India and China, and to people in remote wilderness areas such as the Vugut Gwitchin in Old Crow Flats, Yukon. (See *AQA AS Geography*, pp70–4.)

Key terms

Transnational corporation (or multinational corporation) (TNC/MNC): at its simplest level, this is a corporation that has production establishments or delivers services in at least two countries. However, some TNCs have grown so large that they have budgets that exceed those of many countries in which they operate.

refugees from conflict. It should be noted though, that such refugees usually travel to the nearest possible safe refuge. In areas of conflict such as Iraq, Afghanistan, Zimbabwe and Congo the countries that have received by far the biggest numbers of refugees are neighbouring countries such as Jordan and Syria, Pakistan and Iran, and Rwanda and Burundi, respectively. The press often emphasises the number of refugees coming to the UK, but the proportion of refugees who are able to travel so far is really very small.

Finally, as capital, information, products and people are increasingly moving from country to country as a result of globalisation, services are moving too. The following section, on Global marketing, shows how the advertising industry has become globalised. However, the globalisation of services is covered in more detail in the case study of India on p185.

■ Global marketing

Have you ever noticed how, in car adverts on TV and at the cinema, the car being advertised is left-hand drive? Have you also spotted that the scenery often suggests that the ads have been shot somewhere around the Mediterranean, or in the Alps, or in Scandinavia? Do you wonder why?

It could be to give the car a sophisticated continental image, or it could be because the ad was made as part of an international marketing strategy whereby the same film is used to create the same image of the car across the EU or even further afield. Similar strategies are used for huge numbers of the products of **transnational corporations (TNCs)**.

For instance, Cif is a household cleaner produced by Unilever, a UK-based TNC. In the UK there was a controversy some years ago when Unilever changed the name of its cleaner from 'Jif' to 'Cif' in order to fit in with its international marketing strategy. These comments from the Cif webpage show that this was part of a complex process:

> File Edit History Bookmarks Print View Window Help
>
> **A history of innovation**
>
> The arrival of Cif in 1969, first in France and later rolled out in 45 countries, heralded the end of scouring powders. Initially, the brand focused on cream cleansers for the kitchen and bathroom, underpinned by its famous 'Skater' ads, which highlighted how scouring powders can 'scratch like skates on ice'.
>
> **Flexible & convenient**
>
> More recently, Cif has extended its core strength – its 'strong yet gentle' cream heritage – into new arenas, giving consumers greater flexibility and convenience. In India, we've developed a specialist protective coating for our hand dishwash bar that prevents it turning 'mushy' when it's left in water. In the UK Cif has sponsored a popular prime-time TV programme, How Clean is your House …
>
> **Key facts**
>
> ▶ Cif is sold in 51 countries around the globe.
> ▶ Cif is the number 1 abrasive cleaner in the world.
> ▶ Asia is Cif's fastest-growing market and India its largest.

The advantages for TNCs of such international strategies are:

- the cost of research and development of products can be spread across many more sales, reducing unit costs and increasing profits

- brand loyalty can be encouraged as people move from one country to another

- manufacturing can move to countries and regions where production costs (particularly wages) are cheaper, without needing to change the basic product which is internationalised.

File Edit History Bookmarks Print View Window Help

TOP PROGRAMME

TOP stands for The Olympic Partner programme. Created in 1985, the TOP programme, managed by the International Olympic Committee (IOC), is the only sponsorship with the exclusive worldwide marketing rights to both Winter and Summer Games.

As an event that commands the focus of the media and the attention of the entire world for two weeks every other year, the Olympic Games are one of the most effective international marketing platforms in the world, reaching billions of people in over 200 countries and territories throughout the world.

Sponsor support is crucial to the staging of the Games and the operations of every organisation within the Olympic Movement. Commercial partners also provide vital technical services and product support to the IOC, Organising Committees (OCOGs) and National Olympic Committees (NOCs).

TOP PARTNERS

TOP Partners for the Beijing 2008 Olympic Games included Coca-Cola, Johnson & Johnson, Kodak, Mc Donald's, Omega, Panasonic, Samsung and Visa.

Activity

3 Go to the Olympic website at www.olympic.org/uk/organisation/facts/programme/sponsors_uk.asp to find out how one or more of these Olympic Partners uses the Games as part of a global marketing strategy.

The four 'Asian Tigers'

The term **Asian Tigers** started to be used widely in the 1970s and 1980s to refer to the economies of **Taiwan**, **South Korea**, **Hong Kong** and **Singapore**. From the 1960s onwards they had all followed similar patterns of development, and by the start of the 21st century the four Tigers had reached fully developed status.

In the 1960s the conventional wisdom was that the development process was best started by import substitution – putting up tariffs to reduce imports of consumer goods and allowing a country's own industries to develop. Instead, the four Asian Tigers pursued an export-driven model of industrialisation and development, with the production of export goods aimed at the highly industrialised nations of Europe and North America. Now their model of development is being followed by other Asian economies which are experiencing rapid economic change and growth.

During their period of most rapid growth the four Asian Tigers had a number of characteristics in common:

- All four territories had a strong degree of Chinese influence. South Korea had a population that included 65 per cent ethnic Chinese, Singapore had 75 per cent, Hong Kong had 95 per cent and Taiwan had 98 per cent.

- They were relatively poor during the 1960s and had an abundance of cheap labour.

- They had non-democratic and relatively authoritarian political systems during the early years, so the governments could drive through their plans for economic development fairly easily.

- They focused their development drive on exports to richer industrialised nations rather than focusing on import substitution, which meant that they built up trade surpluses with the industrialised countries.

- The Tigers singled out education as a way of improving the productivity of the labour force. They ensured that all children attended primary school, then secondary school. They also invested heavily in the development of their university systems and in sending students to foreign universities.

- Domestic consumption and purchase of consumer goods was discouraged at first, often by placing a high tariff on imports.

- The high tariff on imports this meant that high savings rates were encouraged, allowing investment in selected areas of industry.

- Trade unions were discouraged, but governments encouraged managers to provide job security and other benefits in a paternalistic type of industrial organisation.

- They were able to sustain double-digit rates of growth for decades.

- While industry was developing, agriculture was protected by subsidies and tariffs on non-essential imports. Land reform ensured that small and medium-sized farmers had security of tenure, which encouraged them to invest in their land. This stopped rural discontent and also allowed investment in mechanisation of agriculture, releasing rural workers to allow further industrialisation.

Fig. 5.6 *A consignment of cars ready to be exported to the West*

Are the Tigers a good model for other countries?

Some economists and geographers criticise the four Tigers because their economies focused mainly on exports at the cost of home demand. As a result, the Tigers rely on the economic health of their targeted export nations. In addition, these nations have met difficulties after they lost the initial competitive edge provided by their cheap, productive labour. India, China and much of South East Asia have now emerged as fast-growing economies based on cheap labour, largely replacing the Tigers.

In the 1990s a setback occurred for the Asian Tigers. Their economies had expanded too fast, and the prices of property and stocks and shares had become overvalued. Several of the stock markets crashed and a worldwide financial crisis followed. This caused social unrest and political instability, requiring help from the International Monetary Fund.

Since the 1990s crisis most of the Tiger economies have become financially stable, with stronger companies and regulatory frameworks in place to prevent another crisis. This has also shown many Asian governments that the easy and predictable prosperity of export-led growth and cheap labour costs will not last for ever. In order to compete with the emerging manufacturing giants such as China and India, they will have to create new industries that add more value and create stronger service sectors to help provide strong demand at home.

Fig. 5.7 *Hong Kong waterfront*

179

Newly industrialised countries (NICs)

NICs are countries whose economies have not yet reached developed or First World economic status but have outpaced other developing countries in terms of their economic growth. This growth is usually export-oriented. Ongoing industrialisation is an important indicator of an NIC. In many NICs, social upheaval can occur as primarily rural, agricultural populations migrate to the cities, where the growth of manufacturing concerns and factories can draw many thousands of workers and people looking for work.

Table 5.4 presents the list of countries in each continent consistently considered NICs by a variety of geographers and economists.

Table 5.4 *The NICs*

Continent	Country	GDP (Millions of $US, 2007)	GDP per capita ($US, 2007)	Human Development Index (HDI, 2007)	GDP growth rate (% per year)
Africa	South Africa	467,089	5,906	0.674 (medium)	4.50
North America	Mexico	1,346,009	8,478	0.829 (high)	3.00
South America	Brazil	1,835,642	6,937	0.800 (high)	5.40
Asia	China	6,991,036	2,460	0.777 (medium)	11.10
	India	2,988,867	977	0.619 (medium)	9.70
	Malaysia	357,391	6,947	0.811 (high)	5.40
	Philippines	299,626	1,624	0.771 (medium)	7.50
	Thailand	519,362	3,736	0.781 (medium)	4.40
Europe	Turkey	360,985,492	1,463,632,361	0.775 (medium)	5.20

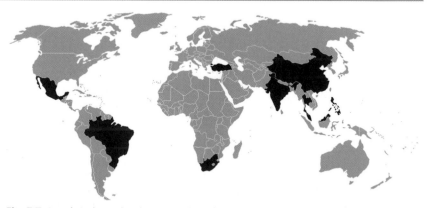

Fig. 5.7 *Newly industrialised countries in 2007*

Activity

1 a Examine the map in Fig. 5.7. Describe the global pattern of NICs. Suggest what these countries might have in common which is helping them to industrialise.

   b Suggest, with reasons, how the patterns shown on the map might change in future.

   c Discuss whether growth in GDP might be linked to changes in HDI.

In both China and India, the huge populations (each with over 1 billion people) means that per capita income will remain low even if these economies surpass that of the US in overall GDP.

Brazil, China, India, Mexico and South Africa meet annually with the G8 countries to discuss financial topics and climate change (due to their economic importance in today's global market and environmental impact) in a group known as G8+5.

Some experts think that some other countries could also be considered NICs, but there is no agreement on any of them. The list includes Egypt, Pakistan, Indonesia and Jordan.

NICs benefit from comparatively low labour costs. This means that it is often easier for producers in NICs to outperform and out-produce factories in developed countries, where the cost of living is higher, wages are higher, unions are better organised and there is more legal protection of workers' rights and of the environment.

Common factors of NICs

These NICs have several characteristics in common, but each is also unique due to its special factors. Among the common factors are:

■ a large population that provides a big internal market and is a resource that attracts investment

■ an openness to globalisation, involving movements of capital, labour and trade

■ a recent switch from agricultural to industrial economies

■ large national corporations based there but also operating in several continents

■ strong political leadership and some elements of state planning to ensure development

■ an education system that is strong enough to produce a core of well-educated people.

The special factors that are helping some of the NICs to develop include the following:

Special factors of NICs

■ **South Africa** has huge resources of minerals – gold, diamonds, coal and many more – that draw in investment, provide jobs and incomes and so boost spending power.

■ **Mexico** lies next to the US and so has many trading advantages. US-based TNCs are keen to locate in Mexico to take advantage of the cheap labour supply. At the same time many Mexicans have migrated, temporarily or permanently, and send home remittances that make a major contribution to the Mexican economy. The US government is keen to ensure that the Mexican economy is reasonably prosperous both to ensure political stability on its southern border and to help to reduce the flow of illegal migration.

■ **Brazil** has a big resource base with minerals, forest resources and agricultural land. It also has one region, the south-east around São Paulo and Rio de Janeiro, that became industrialised from the 1950s onwards and has provided a dynamic area that has driven Brazilian development, providing a market and generating capital. Development has spread outwards from this region.

> ■ **Did you know?**
>
> In 2001 Goldman Sachs, a New York-based investment and banking group, published a review of emerging economies that introduced the idea of the BRIC economies – later adapted to BRIMC (Brazil, India, Mexico and China). This predicted that by 2050 the largest economies in the world will be:
>
> 1 China   2 US
> 3 India   4 Japan
> 5 Brazil   6 Mexico

Fig. 5.8 *Seri Wawasan Bridge, Cyberjaya, Malaysia*

Links

The MSC website is at www. mscmalaysia.my

The Cyberjaya site is at www. cyberjaya-msc.com

The Planetizen site is at www. planetizen.com

To find out more on Dubai's rate of development visit www. metropolismag.com and search for 'Beyond the Spectacle'.

■ **Turkey** has taken advantage of its crucial strategic position to become a major trading nation. It has a mainly Muslim population, but its leadership has tried to maintain a secular government and to encourage the development of a strong economy with links to the West as well as to the Islamic world. Recent moves towards joining the EU have also helped to strengthen the economy. Trading opportunities with the EU are already developing, even though negotiations for membership are at a fairly early stage.

■ **Malaysia** has a reasonably strong resource base and a dynamic, multiracial population. The large ethnic Chinese community has provided an entrepreneurial class; and neighbouring Tiger economies, particularly that of Singapore, have provided a good source of investment. The most interesting area of development is the Multimedia Super Corridor (MSC) which runs from the Twin Towers skyscraper in the capital, Kuala Lumpur, out to the International Airport. Within the MSC is Cyberjaya (or Cyber City), which is one of the most imaginative and dynamic developments in the whole of South East Asia.

■ **Dubai** is a much smaller country than the NICs described above and it already has a far higher GDP per person than any of them – and higher than most developed countries. Dubai is an interesting example of the way that new technologies, new markets and well-invested oil revenues can transform the fortunes of some countries. The following extract is taken from the Planetizen website. (Planetizen is a US-based planning and sustainable development network.)

Fig. 5.9 *Construction work in Dubai*

The megacity of Dubai will be the new economic and cultural capital of the world, spanning its neighbouring emirates of Abu Dhabi, Sharjah, and beyond in one urbanised mass, rich in the biggest source of renewable energy – sunlight – a pioneer in sustainability and new technology, and conveniently located within easy travel distance of a population of more than 2 billion in the Middle East, Europe, India, and Africa …

… for the real substance behind the city you have to look beyond the spectacle of its thousand skyscrapers, malls, resorts, islands, and theme parks … The more than US$310 billion in total construction under way or planned over the next decade includes a financial centre, an academic hub, an information-technology centre, a free media zone, and a minicity devoted to the worldwide distribution of humanitarian aid, as well as environmentally friendly projects such as self-powered buildings, a solar water-desalinisation plant, a subway, and a light-rail system. The tourist spectacles are great publicity and a growing part of the economy, but they're mainly distractions from the … doubling in size of Jebel Ali port, the building of a new international airport, and the launch of the Dubai stock market two years ago, which are more telling signs of Dubai's long-term goal of positioning itself as the central economic hub between London and Singapore.

China

During the Second World War, China, which was already a weak and divided country, was invaded by Japan, which left it in an even worse state after the war. Then, in 1949, China became Communist and developed a centralised economic system, in which the state had a large degree of control over the economy at both national and local levels. Agriculture was collectivised and the state started to invest in heavy industry. Economic progress was not smooth, and there was a serious famine in the late 1950s followed by a period of political upheaval known as the 'Cultural Revolution' in the 1960s that disrupted industrial and agricultural output.

However, in 1978 a period of 'economic reform' started, still under centralised control by the Communist regime. At first this mainly affected farming, with private producers being encouraged to compete with the state-owned and managed collective farms. Then, in the 1990s, industry was liberalised and private companies and TNCs were encouraged to develop in some sectors of industry.

Today, some heavy industries and products of national strategic importance remain state-owned, but an increasing proportion of lighter and consumer-oriented manufacturing firms are privately owned, either by local communities or run as joint ventures. Major state industries are iron, steel, coal, machine building, armaments and textiles. These industries completed a decade of reform (1979–89) with little substantial management change.

The energy industry

Since 1980 China's energy production has grown dramatically, as has the proportion allocated to domestic consumption. Eighty per cent of all power is generated from fossil fuel at thermal plants, with about 17 per cent from HEP stations and about 2 per cent from nuclear energy, mainly from plants located in Guangdong and Zhejiang provinces in the south. China has rich overall energy potential, but most sources have yet to be developed – and those that have been developed are often inefficient and polluting. In addition, the geographical distribution of energy puts most of these resources relatively far from their major industrial users: the industrialised regions around Guangzhou and the Lower Yangtze region around Shanghai have too little energy, while there is relatively little heavy industry located near major energy resources in north-east, central and south-west China.

Although electricity generating capacity is growing rapidly, it still falls considerably short of demand. This is partly because energy prices have been fixed so low that industry has few incentives to conserve. In addition, it has often been necessary to transport fuels (especially coal) great distances from the mines to consumers.

The manufacturing industry

The automobile industry has grown rapidly since 2000, as has the petrochemical industry. Machinery and electronic products became China's main exports. China is the world's leading manufacturer of chemical fertilisers, cement and steel.

The **steel industry** is important in any country aiming to industrialise, as it is the basis on which many other sectors depend for their raw materials. During the 1960s Chinese government policy was to develop blast furnaces and steel-making facilities on a small

Links

For information on China's population policies from the 1950s to the present, see *AQA AS Geography*, pp172–4.

Links

Statistics for China's energy production can be seen in *AQA AS Geography*, p235.

Did you know?

China's 11th Five-Year Programme (2006–10) called for greater energy conservation measures, including development of renewable energy sources and increased attention to environmental protection. Guidelines called for a 20 per cent reduction in energy consumption per unit of GDP by 2010. Moving away from coal towards cleaner energy sources including oil, natural gas, renewable energy and nuclear power is an important component of China's development programme. Beijing also intends to continue to promote the use of clean coal technology.

China has abundant hydroelectric resources; the Three Gorges Dam, for example, will have a total capacity of 18 gigawatts when fully online (projected for 2009). In addition, the share of electricity generated by nuclear power is projected to grow from 1 per cent in 2000 to 5 per cent in 2030. China's renewable energy law, which went into effect in 2006, calls for 10 per cent of its energy to come from renewable energy sources by 2020.

scale, spread throughout the country, so as to spread the growth of manufacturing employment. Unfortunately, this policy, despite its good social objectives, did not produce an efficient and competitive industry. In the period of economic reform the industry has become more concentrated, with the construction of some huge new plants, particularly at Anshan.

Steel production, an estimated 142 million tonnes in 2000, was increased to 426 million tonnes in 2006. However, despite modernisation, much of the country's steel output still comes from a large number of small-scale producing centres.

The government's planners made the main focus of development in the **petrochemical industry** the expansion of the output of fertilisers, plastics and synthetic fibres. This was to encourage improvements in farm productivity and to stimulate the growth of industries such as textiles and clothing. The growth of this industry has placed China among the world's leading producers of nitrogenous fertilisers.

However, it is the **motor industry** that shows most clearly how China's economy has changed since the economic reforms and, particularly, in the first few years of the 21st century. Total production of vehicles (including lorries and cars) and exports is shown in Table 5.5.

In the **consumer goods** sector the main emphasis is on textiles and clothing, which also form an important part of China's exports. Textile manufacturing, a rapidly growing proportion of which consists of synthetics, accounts for about 10 per cent of the gross industrial output and continues to be important, but less so than before. The industry tends to be scattered throughout the country, but there are a number of important textile centres including Shanghai, Guangzhou and Harbin.

Fig. 5.10 *China's eleventh five-year plan aims to reduce pollution*

Table 5.5 *Production in China's motor industry*

Year	Units produced	Units exported
1975	139,800	n.a.*
1985	443,377	n.a.
1992	n.a.	1,100,000
2001	n.a.	2,300,000
2002	n.a.	3,250,000
2003		4,440,000 (Honda factory built at Guangzhou, solely for export market)
2004	78,000	5,070,000
2005	173,000	5,710,000
2006	340,000 (now 3rd largest producer after US and Japan; 2nd largest consumer after US)	7,280,000
2007	n.a.	9,000,000 (est.)

*Note: * n.a. = not available*

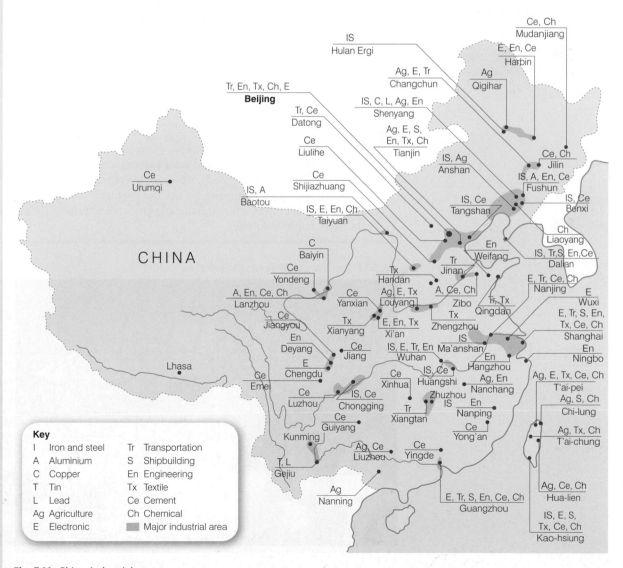

Fig. 5.11 *China–industrial areas*

Key

I	Iron and steel	Tr	Transportation
A	Aluminium	S	Shipbuilding
C	Copper	En	Engineering
T	Tin	Tx	Textile
L	Lead	Ce	Cement
Ag	Agriculture	Ch	Chemical
E	Electronic	▨	Major industrial area

The service sector

China's service sector ranks seventh worldwide, but in the long term this sector seems almost certain to expand rapidly. In 2005 the services sector produced 40.3 per cent of China's annual GDP, second only to manufacturing. However, its proportion of GDP is still low compared with the ratio in more developed countries, and the agricultural sector still employs a larger workforce. Since the economic reforms of the 1980s, retail trade has expanded quickly, with urban areas now having many shopping malls, retail shops, restaurant chains and hotels. Public administration has remained a main component of the service sector, while tourism has become a significant source of employment and of foreign exchange.

The biggest possible boost to the industry was China's hosting of the 2008 Olympic Games, but future growth has to depend on a variety of other attractions throughout the country. At present there are approximately 15,000 natural, cultural and man-made places of interest which are classed as national or international attractions. Investors based in Hong Kong have been the main participants in the establishment of tourist attractions in China, but foreign investment in the tourist industry is now being sought.

According to the plan by China National Tourism Administration, the number of inbound tourists and foreign exchange earnings from tourism are targeted to have annual growth rates of 4 per cent and 8 per cent, respectively, in the next 5–10 years. It is also forecast by the WTO that China's tourism industry will take up to 8.6 per cent of world market share to become the world's top tourism industry by 2020.

Did you know?

Economic liberalisation has not always been matched with political freedom in China. There are many issues that concern observers of China, such as:

■ internet censorship

■ suppression of religions that are not officially sanctioned, especially evangelical Christianity

■ lack of minority rights, especially in Tibet and the western provinces where there is a large Muslim population

■ strict limits on freedom of speech and freedom to publish dissenting views.

Activity

2 The 2008 Olympic games in China were superbly well organised, with a large number of foreign visitors. However, the number of Chinese attending was a little disappointing. Use the internet to research the overall success of the Games in attracting tourists and helping the growth of China's tourist industry.

Fig. 5.12 *The Olympic 'Bird's Nest' Stadium*

The globalisation of services

Key terms

Service sector: economic activity that does not produce goods but provides services, including services to companies such as marketing, advertising, banking or services to individuals such as leisure, tourism, financial or transport services.

Offshore outsourcing: the practice of hiring an external organisation to perform some business functions in a country other than the one where the products or services are developed or manufactured.

Links

You can see the full list of India's advantages at: www.blr.stpi.in/indiaglance_advantages.htm

Then you navigate from here to see the specific advantages of Karnataka state in general and of Bangalore in particular.

Did you know?

India ranks first in the world in terms of financial attractiveness, people and skills availability and business environment. This is revealed in A.T. Kearney's 2007 Global Services Location Index.
(A.T. Kearney is one of the world's leading financial consultancy firms.)
See: www.atkearney.com/res/shared/pdf/GSLI_2007.pdf

Case study

India

There are those who think that the modern Indian **service sector** is based on call centres. In fact, the Indian service sector and its involvement in **offshore outsourcing** is huge, and call centres are only a tiny part of a rapidly growing industry.

India has many advantages for the location of firms involved in the transnational service sector. One website, published by STPI, an organisation funded by the Indian government, lists 26 'competitive advantages'. Some of these are technical, financial and legal points; they include:

- the second-largest English-speaking human resource in the world
- investment-friendly and supportive government policies
- adaptability to new technologies
- a world-class infrastructure in line with the developed countries for power, transport and data communication
- the world's third-largest brain bank, with around 2.5 million technical professionals
- a stable democratic environment with over 50 years of independence
- a large market size with a middle-class population of 250–350 million, with increasing purchasing power reflected by a huge increase in the purchase of consumer durables in recent years
- special investment and tax incentives given for exports in certain sectors such as electronics, telecom, software, and research and development activities
- legal protection for intellectual property rights.

The site then goes on to explain why Karnataka state and its capital city of Bangalore developed into India's leading centre for ICT, and why this centre has become so dominant in the world's offshore outsourcing of ICT-linked services. Some of the advantages for the area are as follows:

- The state was the first in India to set up engineering colleges.
- It was also the first to set up a technology university.
- It introduced a statewide policy to promote the IT industry with grants and tax incentives.
- In 1991 it established a software technology park in Bangalore which now covers 140,000 m^2.
- It now has six further technology parks with a total area of around 560,000 m^2.
- It has the best telecom infrastructure in the country.

■ In 2008 there are plans to build:

- a new Green Park, for research into environmentally friendly building design and construction (to be built using investments from Saudi Arabia)
- a NanoPark for research into nanotechnology (technology dealing with matter on a molecular size scale of nanometres (1 billionth of a metre)
- a biotech park for research into new medical, veterinary and plant technology.

Infosys – a Bangalore-based TNC

Infosys, with its headquarters in Bangalore, is one of the largest software companies in India.

From the Infosys website:

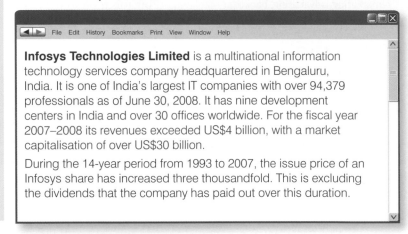

File Edit History Bookmarks Print View Window Help

Infosys Technologies Limited is a multinational information technology services company headquartered in Bengaluru, India. It is one of India's largest IT companies with over 94,379 professionals as of June 30, 2008. It has nine development centers in India and over 30 offices worldwide. For the fiscal year 2007–2008 its revenues exceeded US$4 billion, with a market capitalisation of over US$30 billion.

During the 14-year period from 1993 to 2007, the issue price of an Infosys share has increased three thousandfold. This is excluding the dividends that the company has paid out over this duration.

■ Links

The Infosys website is at: www. infosys.com

The company is also described and promoted at: www.youtube.com

Type Infosys into the search engine and peruse the result.

Fig. 5.13 *Infosys headquarters in Bangalore*

Infosys was founded in 1981 and moved to Bangalore in 1983. In 1987 it got its first foreign client, Data Basics Corporation from the US. Then, in 1992, it opened its first overseas sales office, in Boston, US. This was followed by offices in Milton Keynes (1996), Toronto (1997), France and Hong Kong (2000), UAE and Argentina (2001), Netherlands, Singapore and Sweden (2002), and so on.

Now it is a truly transnational corporation, operating in most of the world's leading industrial countries and with wholly owned subsidiary companies in many countries. Still, about 45 per cent of the company's workforce is based in Bangalore, and well over half are in India.

There is a clear awareness that India's labour cost advantages might be only temporary as other developing countries try to move in to the same market area, so Infosys is developing more sophisticated aspects of the industry to add greater value in the face of possible low-cost competition. It has developed business units to provide a full range of ICT services in industries such as:

- banking and capital markets
- communications media and entertainment
- aerospace and avionics
- energy, utilities and services
- insurance, health care and life sciences
- manufacturing
- retail, consumer product goods and logistics.

The company is also heavily involved in education, both of its own workforce and of its potential workforce and customers through a variety of initiatives to support university and school education in Bangalore and the rest of Karnataka.

The International Technology Park – Bangalore

A large part of the Infosys Bangalore operation is based at this park.

The company that owns and manages this park describes it like this:

> File Edit History Bookmarks Print View Window Help
>
> The International Tech Park Bangalore (ITPB) is the icon of India's IT success story, and continues its contribution to the development of Whitefield as a major IT hub in India's Silicon Valley. Located just 18 km from the city centre, ITPB catalysed the growth of a burgeoning suburban city at Whitefield.
>
> Managed by Ascendas, ITPB epitomises the finest of the Ascendas Advantage offering: Quality Business Space, Reliable Solutions and an International Business Lifestyle second to none. Its world-class business infrastructure amidst wide green spaces provides the optimal environment for TNCs and leading local corporations located at the Park.
>
> Enjoy hassle-free set-up at ITPB. Simply plug-and-play in a complete office space. ITPB's professional in-house property management team ensures your business continuity round-the-clock with efficient services and infrastructure such as security and fire protection systems, seamless telecommunication networks, optical fibre connectivity and a dedicated power plant.
>
> At ITPB, all your business and employee needs are taken care of. These include comprehensive lifestyle amenities, regular shuttle bus services covering more than 80 routes, ample parking and all the conveniences you need in India's most complete work-live-play business space.

Did you know?

One of the guiding principles of Infosys's Global Delivery Model is 'to combine the best of the local world with the best of the global world'.

The company provides services to deal with:

- consulting
- enterprise solutions
- infrastructure management services
- product engineering services
- systems integration.

While these may involve some low-level, call-centre jobs, they also provide a full service to design and manage the software, hardware and personnel at both ends of the chain – in the client country and in Bangalore itself.

Links

For more details of ITPB go to: www.intltechpark.com

A promotional video for the park can be found at: www.intltechpark.com/videos/ITPB_high.html

For a different, and slightly less professional video of the park, go to: www.youtube.com/watch?v=Uffu2lzhUPc

The park contains six major office blocks supported by a dedicated power plant (20 MW), an in-house dedicated telephone exchange system of 3,000 lines with capacity to expand by another 10,000 lines, full high-speed Wi-Fi connectivity, parking, water storage and sewage treatment facilities. Round-the-clock, state-of-the-art security is provided along with climate control, ventilation and fire protection.

Activities

1 From your study of Bangalore and other parts of your A Level course to date, consider:

  a How is Bangalore similar to and/or different from major cities that you have studied in countries at a higher level of economic development?

  b How is Infosys similar to and/or different from TNCs that you have studied that are based in countries at a higher level of economic development?

  c How might Bangalore, Karnataka state and Infosys develop in the next 25 years or so? Justify your suggestions, referring to other case studies and theories that you have studied.

2 The BRIMC countries and others might soon become major world economies. Most NICs have a number of factors in common, such as a well-educated core workforce and a large internal market.

How well do India, Karnataka and Bangalore fit these criteria for development?

Global social and economic groupings

In this section you will learn:

 the importance of groupings of nations.

We live in an increasingly globalised world where information, trade, capital and people can move more and more easily across frontiers. However, at the same time that globalisation is taking place, other groupings of nations are forming. Some of these aim to improve trade between member states, or to negotiate trade advantages for members, while others have far larger aims – with some working to a very high level of social and economic integration between members. Most global groupings are designed to help their members to achieve economic and social development by:

- making trade between members flow more easily, increasing profits
- allowing freer movement of people, bringing advantages of a more flexible labour market
- sharing knowledge to allow growth in all members, etc.

In this section three groupings will be considered. These are:

- the World Trade Organization (WTO)
- the Group of 77 and China
- the EU.

You can find out more about some other world groupings by going to the BBC website, which describes:

- the Asia/Pacific Economic Cooperation group (APEC)
- the Cairns Group of agricultural exporting nations
- the EU
- the G20 group of rapidly industrialising nations, set up to challenge the power of the EU and the US at the WTO talks
- the North American Free Trade Association (NAFTA).

Links

A guide to world trade blocs can be found at: news.bbc.co.uk

The World Trade Organization

The WTO can be described as a liberalising organisation, set up by the major capitalist, market-oriented economies to organise world trade. It aims to reduce barriers to trade, allowing trade between members to increase. The organisation describes its aims below:

Essentially, the WTO is a place where member governments go, to try to sort out the trade problems they face with each other. The first step is to talk. The WTO was born out of negotiations, and everything the WTO does is the result of negotiations. The bulk of the WTO's current work comes from the 1986–94 negotiations called the Uruguay Round and earlier negotiations under the General Agreement on Tariffs and Trade (GATT). The WTO is currently the host to new negotiations, under the 'Doha Development Agenda' launched in 2001.

Where countries have faced trade barriers and wanted them lowered, the negotiations have helped to liberalize trade. But the WTO is not just about liberalizing trade, and in some circumstances its rules support maintaining trade barriers – for example to protect consumers or prevent the spread of disease.

www.wto.org/english/thewto_e/whatis_e/tif_e/fact1_e.htm

At its heart are the WTO agreements, negotiated and signed by the bulk of the world's trading nations. These documents provide the legal ground-rules for international commerce. They are essentially contracts, binding governments to keep their trade policies within agreed limits. Although negotiated and signed by governments, the goal is to help producers of goods and services, exporters, and importers conduct their business, while allowing governments to meet social and environmental objectives.

The system's overriding purpose is to help trade flow as freely as possible – so long as there are no undesirable side-effects – because this is important for economic development and well-being. That partly means removing obstacles. It also means ensuring that individuals, companies and governments know what the trade rules are around the world, and giving them the confidence that there will be no sudden changes of policy.

■ Member countries of WTO

Fig. 5.14 *Members of the World Trade Organization*

Despite the good intentions of the WTO, it is clearly a divided organisation. Many developing countries felt that, in its early years, it was dominated by the developed countries, particularly the US and the EU. That is why the G20 was set up, with the object of arguing together in the interests of the poorer countries.

■ The 'Group of 77' developing countries and China

The Group of 77 was set up at the UN to represent the interests of the poorest countries. China has always been an important ally of this group although not a formal member. Of course, it has some interests in common with the 77 nations, but it also hopes to increase its influence in world affairs by this alliance. On its website the Group defines its aims:

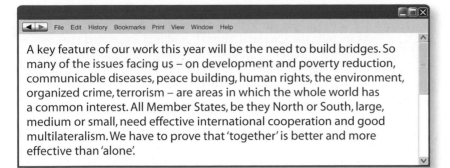

File   Edit   History   Bookmarks   Print   View   Window   Help

A key feature of our work this year will be the need to build bridges. So many of the issues facing us – on development and poverty reduction, communicable diseases, peace building, human rights, the environment, organized crime, terrorism – are areas in which the whole world has a common interest. All Member States, be they North or South, large, medium or small, need effective international cooperation and good multilateralism. We have to prove that 'together' is better and more effective than 'alone'.

■ The European Union

The EU was first set up in 1956 with six member states and was known as Benelux (named after Belgium, the Netherlands and Luxembourg, the original members). Expansion since then has produced a current total of 27 members, with a number of others at various stages of negotiations to join. The sites mentioned in the Link give details of the EU's growth.

The EU was first set up after the Second World War, when its main objective was to integrate the economies of the main European powers so that a further war became impossible. Since then it has developed many other key policies including the following:

Single market: The original core objective of the EU was the development of a single market between its member states. This involves the free circulation of goods, capital, people and services within the EU and the creation of customs union with a common external tariff on all goods entering the market.

Monetary union: On 1 January 1999 the euro was launched by 11 of the 15 member states of the EU. The Eurozone has since grown to 15 countries, the most recent being Cyprus and Malta which joined on 1 January 2008. All other EU member states, except Denmark and the UK, are legally bound to join the euro when the economic conditions are met. Public opinion in these countries is, however, often against joining.

The euro is designed to help build a single market by easing travel of citizens and goods and eliminating exchange rate problems. It is also intended as a political symbol of integration and as a stimulus for more.

Agriculture: The Common Agricultural Policy (CAP) is one of the oldest policies of the EU and was one of its core aims. It has the objectives of increasing agricultural production, providing certainty in food supplies, ensuring a high quality of life for farmers, stabilising markets and ensuring reasonable prices for consumers. It accounts for around 35 per cent of the EU's annual budget.

The CAP's price controls and market interventions led to considerable overproduction, resulting in so-called **butter mountains** and **wine lakes**. In order to dispose of surplus stores, these were often sold on the world market at prices considerably below their cost of production; the system has been criticised for undercutting farmers in the developing world, and also on environmental grounds in that it encourages environmentally unfriendly intensive farming methods.

Since the beginning of the 1990s the CAP has been subject to a series of reforms to make it more responsive to market demands and less environmentally damaging.

Links

An animated map of the growth of the EU can be found at:
europa.eu/abc/history/animated_map/index_en.htm

The following site gives a timeline:
news.bbc.co.uk/1/hi/world/europe/3583801.stm

Infrastructure: The EU is working to improve cross-border infrastructure, for example through the Trans-European Networks (TEN). TEN projects include the Channel Tunnel, and it is estimated that by 2010 the network will cover 75,200 km of roads; 78,000 km of railways and many airports and harbours. The eastwards expansion of the EU has increased the demand for new infrastructure.

Regional development: There are a number of funds to support development of underdeveloped regions of the EU. Such regions are primarily located in the new member states of eastern Europe. These funds provide support for candidate members to transform their country to conform to the EU's standard. For instance, Poland has benefited from:

- structural fund investment to help move from a state-controlled economy towards greater market orientation

- infrastructure funds to improve the road system, particularly its links to its EU neighbours, including Germany

- CAP funding for the development of its agriculture

- free movement of its people (although only Ireland, Sweden and the UK allowed this at first) for work and training.

At an earlier stage in its evolution the Integrated Mediterranean Programme was a policy designed to modernise farming in member countries around the Mediterranean. It involved money for education of farmers, modernisation of their practices, including mechanisation and irrigation, and creation of industrial and service jobs in rural areas. The programme was responsible for much development of rural areas in Spain, Portugal, Italy and Greece.

The European Development Fund (EDF): This fund directs aid from the EU to developing countries. In the period 2008–13 it is expected to allocate over 10 billion euros of aid, mainly to former colonies of the EU member states.

Environment: The EU's environmental policy addresses issues such as acid rain, the thinning of the ozone layer, air quality, noise pollution, waste and water pollution.

In 2007, member states agreed that the EU is to use 20 per cent renewable energy in the future and that it has to reduce carbon dioxide emissions in 2020 by at least 20 per cent compared to 1990 levels. It is considered to be one of the most ambitious moves of an important industrialised region to fight global warming. Renewable energy is a priority in transnational research activities supported by the EU.

The EU's attempts to cut its carbon footprint have also been aided by an expansion of Europe's forests which, between 1990 and 2005, grew 10 per cent in western Europe and 15 per cent in eastern Europe. During this period they soaked up 126 million metric tonnes of carbon dioxide, equivalent to 11 per cent of EU emissions from human activities.

Links

For more details about the changes that have been brought to Poland since it joined the EU, see Chapter 8.

Activities

1 Read all the information on the development of the EU. Then discuss the extent to which the EU has helped to:

- integrate European economies

- develop the economies of Europe and other countries

- increase globalisation

- ensure food security in Europe

- protect the environment

- make Europe a more peaceful place than it was in the 19th and early 20th centuries.

2 With reference to at least two groupings of nations, explain how such groupings have assisted the members of the groups to develop their economies.

TNCs, globalisation and development

Links

There are also many references to TNCs in *AQA AS Geography*. Of particular importance are:

- the world trade in food, pp205–6
- TNCs and the oil trade, pp245–6 (especially Table 7.6 on p246)
- TNCs and health care, pp270–6.

Poland's development and the role of TNCs and FDI are also discussed in some detail in Chapter 8 of this book.

Did you know?

Not all multinationals are large.

Enabled by internet-based communication tools, a new breed of multinational companies is growing in numbers. These multinationals start operating in different countries from the very early stages and are being called **micro-multinationals**. Some of them, particularly software development companies, have been hiring employees in multiple countries from the beginning of the internet era. But more and more micro-multinationals are actively starting to market their products and services in various countries. Internet tools such as Google, Yahoo!, MSN, eBay, Skype and Amazon make it easier for the micro-multinationals to reach potential customers in other countries.

Facebook is a perfect example. It started out as a 'dispersed virtual business' with employees, clients and resources located in various countries. Its rapid growth is a direct result of being able to use the internet, cheap telephony and low travel costs to create a unique business opportunity.

Transactional corporations (TNCs) are an important area of study. Because of their size TNCs can have a powerful influence on both local economies and international relations. TNCs have played, and are continuing to play, an important role in globalisation.

There are many reasons for TNCs to locate to other countries.

- One reason is to escape trade tariffs. For example, the decision made by Nissan to produce cars in Sunderland was almost certainly to gain access to the EU market without having to pay tariffs.

- Other TNCs may be seeking the lowest cost location for their production facilities (such as the location of Nike sportswear manufacturing in Vietnam) or be attracted by an abundance of skilled or cheap labour (and this includes Infosys and its corporate partners setting up in Bangalore – see pp188–90).

- Others might want to reach foreign markets more effectively; for example Marks & Spencer, McDonald's, Tesco and BAT (see *AQA AS Geography*, pp273–6). These overseas developments do not just increase sales but they can also help to reduce the unit costs of each item produced or sold worldwide.

- Of course, other TNCs are forced to develop operations overseas in order to exploit mineral and other resources found in those countries. The oil TNCs are examples of this. (See *AQA AS Geography*, pp245–6).

Problems and benefits of TNCs

Many TNCs are large in relation to the income of the countries in which they are located. This means that it can be hard for governments to enforce national laws on TNCs. Generally speaking, governments want investment from the TNCs because they generate jobs and incomes, train local workers in new, transferable skills and bring new technology. The taxes that TNCs pay can be an important stimulus to economic development.

As for the TNCs themselves, the prospects of cheap labour, cheap land, cheap and abundant resources and a 'good business environment' are big attractions. (Note: 'good business environment' is a euphemism that can be used in some TNCs to mean a low level of trade union activity and/or weak anti-pollution legislation.)

In fact, TNCs and the foreign direct investment (FDI) that they can bring have become so important to many economies, both rich and poor, that countries must compete against one another for their investment. Countries and regions sometimes offer incentives such as tax breaks, pledges of governmental assistance or improved infrastructure to attract TNCs. When this happens in an extreme form it can be characterised as 'a race to the bottom', or a competition to attract investment by offering even lower wage rates and even less strict controls than other low-wage/low-regulation economies.

However, some geographers and economists argue that TNCs are engaged in a 'race to the top'. While multinationals certainly regard a low tax and/or low labour costs as an advantage, there is little evidence to suggest that major TNCs deliberately seek lax environmental regulation or poor labour standards. In fact, TNC profits are tied to operational efficiency, which includes a high degree of standardisation across the company's

Links

To read the whole of Palmisano's article go to: www.ibm.com/ibm/governmentalprograms/samforeignaffairs.pdf

Activities

1 a Read about globally integrated enterprises.

  b Then reread the section on Infosys on pp188–90

  c To what extent does Infosys appear to be a globally integrated enterprise?

2 TNCs are so big and powerful that they obviously have a huge effect on all countries where they are located. Summarise these effects by constructing a table to show the positive and negative effects of TNCs on the social, economic and environmental geography of both the host country and the country of origin (where relevant).

AQA Examiner's tip

Palmisano's article is a detailed discussion of the history and present form of many TNCs. You might try to read it if you are aiming for a top grade in geography, if you are planning to study geography at university, or if you are also studying economics or politics. If you are just hoping to get a grade D or E you would be better advised to work on your more basic studies rather than visiting this site!

different operations. TNCs are therefore likely to keep to similar standards across the countries in which they operate. This can mean that standards rise towards those that have to be met in the best regulated countries in which they operate.

As for labour costs, while TNCs clearly pay workers in, say, Vietnam, much less than they would in the UK or the US, it is also the case that they tend to pay wages between 10 and 100 per cent higher than local rates.

Finally, it has been suggested that TNCs behave irresponsibly, shifting investment from place to place in search of ever-lower costs. However, the costs of establishing plant, training workers, etc. can be very high; so most TNCs research their location decisions very carefully and, once they have located, they are likely to remain committed to that location for as long as possible. Indeed, TNCs can be vulnerable to predatory practices from the host countries – such as expropriation, sudden contract renegotiation, the arbitrary withdrawal of 'licences', etc. (See *AQA AS Geography*, p246 for references to Shell in Russia.)

It can be easy to overstate either the benefits or the problems caused by TNC investment. At this point in the 21st century the range of different types and sizes of TNC is enormous, as is the range of reasons for their development and the range of countries and regions in which they operate. Predatory TNCs exist; more idealistic TNCs based on the principles of sustainable development also exist. Each TNC must be considered as a separate identity and discussion of the advantages and disadvantages that it can bring must be based on clear factual analysis.

Globally integrated enterprises

In 2006 Sam Palmisano, CEO of IBM Corporation, coined the phrase 'globally integrated enterprise'. He used it to denote a company that fashions its strategy, its management and its operations, in pursuit of a new goal: the integration of production and value delivery worldwide. State borders define less and less the boundaries of corporate thinking or practice.

Palmisano argues that in the 19th century, most big companies were centred in their home country, with only elements of sales and distribution happening overseas. The MNC of the 20th century – in which companies created small versions of themselves in each country – was a response to the trade barriers that arose after the world wars. This was a successful model because it enabled the company to grow in those markets, understand local customer requirements and cultivate local talent. But it also created waste because each country had its own back-office functions (e.g. supply, procurement, finance and human resources).

Now the globally integrated TNC can locate functions anywhere in the world, based on the right cost, skills and environment, argues Palmisano. (IBM now has one supply chain, for example.) This new organisational form has emerged because, in the globalised world, everything is connected, and work can move to the place where it is done best. The barriers that used to block the flow of work, capital and ideas are weakening.

Development issues in countries at very low levels of economic development

In this section you will learn:

- about countries at very low levels of development.

Links

The UN factsheet entitled 'Facts about Least Developed Countries (LDCs)' can be found at: www.unohrlls.org/UserFiles/File/Publications/Factsheet.pdf

Links

For selected statistics on population and development see *AQA AS Geography*, p158.

Activity

1 Draw a concept diagram to show how the factors that characterise low development, like those mentioned in this section, are interrelated.

AQA Examiner's tip

In your exam you should be prepared to discuss these interrelationships **and** to quote statistics and other details about countries that you have studied.

The UN classifies a country as a least developed country (LDC) if it meets three criteria:

- low income (three-year average income per capita of less than US$750)

- human resource weakness (based on indicators of nutrition, health, education and adult literacy)

- economic vulnerability (based on instability of agricultural production, instability of exports, economic importance of non-traditional activities, handicap of economic smallness and percentage of population displaced by natural disasters).

The current list of LDCs includes 49 countries: 33 in Africa, 15 in Asia and the Pacific and 1 in Latin America. These countries are shown on the map in Fig. 5.15.

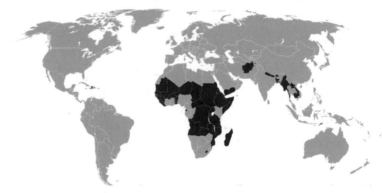

Fig. 5.15 *Least developed countries (LDCs)*

Developing countries, in general, have not achieved a significant degree of industrialisation and have, in most cases, a medium to low standard of living. There is a strong correlation between low income and high population growth, low education standards, low life expectancy, etc.

Case study

Bangladesh – the present situation

Key population facts:

- Total population: 144.2 million (in 2005)

- Annual population growth rate: 1.7 per cent

- Total fertility rate (births per woman): 3.2 per cent

- No. of people living below US$1 a day: 36.0 per cent

- No. of people living below US$2 a day: 82.8 per cent

- Gross national income per capita: US$400

- Life expectancy at birth: 63.3 years

- Infant mortality rate: 41/1,000 live births

- Human Development Index rank: 137 out of 177 countries

■ Links

The DfID Bangladesh site can be seen at: www.dfid.gov.uk/countries/asia/bangladesh.asp

Facts about Bangladesh can be found at: www.dfid.gov.uk/countries/asia/Bangladesh–facts.asp

There are references to the work of ActionAid in Bangladesh in *AQA AS Geography*, pp218–19.

Key economic facts:

GDP real growth rate   7.0% (2006 est.)

	GDP – composition by sector (%)	Labour force – by occupation (%)
Agriculture	20.5	65
Industry and mining	26.7	10
Services	52.8	25

The following is an extract from the UK's Department for International Development (DfID) website.

The UK expects to spend £114 million on aid to Bangladesh in 2008/9. This is broadly the same level as in recent years. Future spending is subject to decisions about UK public expenditure plans for the next three years, but we stand ready to increase our aid to Bangladesh if we judge it can be used effectively.

The UK's long-term goal is for Bangladesh to be a stable, prosperous and moderate Muslim majority democracy, playing a positive role in the global community. Our objectives are to embed democratic values; enable prosperity for all; and engender stability.

The UK's development programme is a significant part of the UK's relationship with Bangladesh. Over the past three years we have spent over £350 million, and helped to:

- lift more than half a million people out of extreme poverty
- raise more than 20,000 flood-prone homesteads on Char islands above 1988 flood levels
- construct 14,000 new classrooms, and recruit 12,000 new teachers
- provide basic education to 4.5 million children, through a non-government programme
- ensure 14 million urban dwellers have access to basic health services
- enable more than 100,000 farmers to gain improved access to markets.

The UK remains fully committed to working with the government and people of Bangladesh to support their economic, social and political ambitions by helping to:

- build better governance
- reduce extreme poverty and vulnerability to climate change, and eliminate seasonal hunger;
- increase jobs and incomes through private sector development
- improve the availability and quality of basic social services for the poor.

This will continue to involve a range of development interventions: technical assistance, sector support, and targeted programmes. It will also require a significant increase in the effectiveness of external aid, building on the Joint Strategy approach developed by the four largest donors to Bangladesh: Japan, Asian Development Bank, World Bank and the UK.

Bangladesh – development priorities

Bangladesh is developing, but it is not growing as fast as some of its neighbours and poverty remains widespread, especially in rural areas. Among the most serious of the country's problems are:

■ the widespread indebtedness of poor farmers, which arose partly because of attempts by the farmers to commercialise their farming by using more fertilisers, pesticides and machinery (see below); however, in an area where frequent floods and cyclones can destroy a farmer's whole crops for a season, this often led to an inability to pay back debts; what is more, commercial banks often charged particularly high levels of interest to poor farmers, because it was felt that loans were insecure

■ social problems, including poor provision of education and health care (see below)

■ the position of women in this Muslim society; in many areas women find it very difficult to find work outside the immediate confines of the home.

The UK and other partner governments and NGOs are working together to tackle some of the country's problems. Their main priority is described as **pro-poor growth or growth that is targeted at the poorest sections of the population.**

From independence until about 2000, development spending has concentrated on a number of different priorities.

■ In the 1970s, the emphasis was on market interventions to try to reduce the cost of food for the poor, and large capital spending on flood control, irrigation and drainage projects.

■ In the 1980s, most public expenditures focused on broad agricultural development, with relatively low emphasis on rural infrastructure.

■ In the 1990s, the development of small-scale infrastructure – roads, bridges, culverts and market places – was singled out as the major element of the new rural development strategy.

The road development projects, connecting 1,400 of the 2,100 growth centres/markets, contributed to increasing farm and non-farm output, employment and income, especially of the rural poor and women. Moreover, the landless and small farmers gained a larger share of the increase from crops, wages, livestock and fisheries.

In the 21st century, investment has concentrated on four main areas of development:

■ **Education:** The greater emphasis on primary education, especially girls' education, has been a consistent feature of the successive regimes since transition to democracy in 1991. Spending on education has been the largest single item in the revenue and development budget, and has become an important part of the programmes of all the main parties.

■ **Health care:** Bangladesh has achieved impressive gains in life expectancy, child mortality and reproductive health. Bangladesh has lower child mortality, higher access to drinking water and sanitation, lower maternal mortality and higher contraceptive use than its neighbour, India. The national health programme has, over the years, focused on the provision of affordable rural primary health care (through Family Welfare Centres) and

Activity

2 Referring to the information given on p196, write a summary paragraph or two to describe the state of development in Bangladesh.

Links

The issues of the role of women in the family, education, farming development and the provision of loans for development are all dealt with in *AQA AS Geography*, pp218–19.

Fig. 5.16 *Education for all*

■ Links

For more details of high-yielding varieties see *AQA AS Geography*, pp211–13.

■ Key terms

Grameen Bank: a micro-finance organisation and community development bank started in Bangladesh that makes small loans to the impoverished without requiring collateral.

■ Links

Further details of the Grameen Bank can be found at: en.wikipedia.org

The bank's own website is at: www.grameen-info.org

on developing partnerships with NGOs. NGOs have been an extremely important source of health successes in Bangladesh, especially in the area of family planning and immunisation services.

■ **Agricultural development:** especially through provision of loan facilities for all farmers, even the poorest, and liberalisation of the market. This means that now high-yielding variety seeds have spread to about 65 per cent of rice-cropped area, and irrigation facilities are available to over 40 per cent of the cultivated area. Fertiliser use has grown by 10 per cent per year over the last 30 years. Some of the most important developments have been in the production of 'dry-season' rice varieties. As floods can destroy crops during the rainy season this fall-back crop has been vital in increasing food security for the poor.

■ **Micro-finance projects:** these have become widespread throughout Bangladesh. The **Grameen Bank** is the biggest of these, but several others are run by NGOs such as ActionAid (see *AQA AS Geography*, pp218–19). The range of enterprises that are supported by such loans is enormous and many are linked to farm production, processing and marketing. However, the biggest proportion is in the garment industry, often producing clothes for export. One recent estimate suggests that the total number of borrowers is about 5 million, of whom about 90 per cent are women. As most of them are rural poor their enterprises play a vital part in stabilising their family economies. It is important that the work can take place in and around the home because of the need for modesty among Muslim women.

The system of this bank is based on the idea that the poor have skills that are underutilised. A group-based credit approach relies on peer pressure within the group to ensure the borrowers conduct their financial affairs with strict discipline, ensuring repayment eventually and allowing the borrowers to develop good credit standing. A distinctive feature of the bank's credit programme is that a significant majority of its borrowers are women. The bank was founded in 1976. The organisation and its founder, Muhammad Yunus, were jointly awarded the Nobel Peace Prize in 2006.

Among many different applications of micro-credit by the bank, one is the Village Phone programme, through which women entrepreneurs can start a business providing a wireless payphone service in rural areas. This programme earned the 2004 Petersberg Prize, worth 100,000 euros, for its contribution of Technology to Development. The press release announcing the prize said:

> Grameen has created a new class of women entrepreneurs who have raised themselves from poverty. Moreover, it has improved the livelihoods of farmers and others who are provided access to critical market information and lifeline communications previously unattainable in some 28,000 villages of Bangladesh. More than 55,000 phones are currently in operation, with more than 80 million people benefiting from access to market information, news from relatives, and more.

Bangladesh – industry and trade

Agriculture in the remoter rural areas of Bangladesh needs aid from the Bangladesh government, foreign governments and NGOs if it is to develop and feed the growing population. However, the country's

Textile exports are number 1 and still rising!

Bangladesh's textile industry, which includes knitwear and ready-made garments along with specialised textile products, is the nation's number one export earner. The sector, which employs 2.2 million workers, accounted for 75 per cent of Bangladesh's total exports of US$10.53 billion in 2005–6, in the process logging a record growth rate of 24.44 per cent. However, since May 2006 the industry has been plagued by ongoing industrial unrest, as textile workers, who are among some of the most lowly paid in the world, have staged regular violent demonstrations in a bid to achieve a higher minimum wage, regular rest days and safer working conditions.

The Bangladesh Garments Manufacturers and Exporters Association (BGMEA) has predicted textile exports will rise from US$7.90 billion earned in 2005–6 to US$15 billion by 2011. In part this optimism stems from how well the sector has fared since the end of textile and clothing quotas, under the Multifibre Agreement, in early 2005.

According to a UN Development Programme report 'Sewing Thoughts: How to Realise Human Development Gains in the Post-Quota World', Bangladesh's expansion has mainly been a result of the reduction of trade restrictions, brought about by negotiations through the World Trade Organization.

'Last year we had tremendous growth. The quota-free textile regime has proved to be a big boost for our factories', BGMEA president S.M. Fazlul Hoque told reporters, after the sector's 24 per cent growth rate was revealed.

industry is developing quickly – from a very low base. This development has come about largely because of trade liberalisation.

The Bangladesh government continues to court foreign investment, something it has done fairly successfully in private power generation and gas exploration and production, as well as in other sectors such as cellular telephony, textiles and pharmaceuticals.

The government has also set up a number of export processing zones (EPZs) around the country. Companies operating in these areas are granted big reductions in taxes and in bureaucratic restrictions as long as all production is exported from the country. It was hoped that the EPZs would help attract foreign direct investment in industry. However, the AFL-CIO (the main trade union organisation in the US) has asked their government to deny Bangladesh preferential access to US markets. They cite Bangladesh's failure to meet promises to allow trade unions to operate in EPZs. They are concerned that un-unionised companies will undercut prices in those countries where workers are allowed more rights.

Activity

3 Study all the information on Bangladesh.
a Describe how both trade and aid are helping Bangladesh to develop.
b Discuss the view that trade and aid have to go hand in hand to ensure that Bangladesh develops for all its people, including the very poorest.
c Discuss how environmentally sustainable Bangladesh's development is.
d Compare Bangladesh's road to development with that followed by India, China and/or the Asian Tigers. Refer in particular to the roles of trade and aid in stimulating development.

Sustainable tourism and development

In this section you will learn:

- about development issues such as trade, aid and sustainable tourism.

Did you know?

Economic, social and environmental aspects of sustainable development must include the interests of all stakeholders, including:

- indigenous people
- local communities
- visitors
- tourist industry
- government.

What is sustainable tourism?

Sustainable development is development that meets the needs of the present without compromising the ability of future generations to meet their own needs.

The goal of sustainable development is to enable all people throughout the world to satisfy their basic needs and enjoy a good quality of life, without compromising the quality of life of future generations.

Sustainable tourism is about refocusing and readapting the traditional approach to tourism. A balance must be found between limits and use to ensure that tourism can be managed without damaging the physical or human environments that provide the initial attraction. This requires thinking long term (10–20 plus years) and realising that change is often cumulative, gradual and irreversible.

Case study

The Kasbah du Toubkal, Morocco

The Kasbah du Toubkal in the High Atlas Mountains is an extraordinary venture, the product of an imaginative Berber and European partnership. The idea for the development came from Mike McHugo, a British trekker.

'We had noticed the crumbling ruin of an old kasbah – originally the summer home of a local feudal chief', recalls McHugo. 'We decided to buy it.' He had read that direct foreign investment in Morocco was being encouraged and was apparently going to become easier. It was also seen to be the key to the country's development. He thought that he had a 'safe pair of hands' to do something useful and sustainable with the special site.

Between 1989 and 1995 McHugo bought the property, restored it and opened Kasbah du Toubkal for paying guests. It was not a straightforward project as he wanted to create a comfortable and spectacular environment in a style that was simple and vernacular. Village labourers used traditional building techniques and local materials in its construction, with everything having to be carried in by hand or on the backs of mules. Power tools could not be used, as electricity didn't arrive in this remote region until 1997.

Then he wanted to be sure that the development brought benefits to the local community. A local villager and his wife manage the property, employing a team of 32 staff from nearby villages. They share McHugo's belief that the beauty of the Toubkal National Park should be accessible to all who respect it.

Fig. 5.17 *The Kasbah du Toubkal courtyard (left) and site (right)*

Today, there are eight rooms with en suite bathrooms, a three-bedroom family house and separate dormitory accommodation with a conference centre for study groups. The rooms are rustic yet comfortable, with simple Berber adornments such as hand-woven carpets, blankets, intricate carved woodwork and oleander branch panelled ceilings.

Many of the staff come from the nearby village of Imlil, with a population of just 1,500. Its location is at the end of the main road system, beyond which narrow footpaths and precipitous mule tracks are the only channels of communication with the outside world. To ensure the Kasbah retains its close links with the local community, Discover Ltd was instrumental in setting up the Imlil Village Association, funded by the levy of 5 per cent on all accommodation.

The Association has created and manages the following:

■ a rubbish clearance and disposal by small local incinerators

■ a 4×4 ambulance service

■ a community *hammam* or bath-house (shared on a timetable between men and women)

■ the provision of accommodation in Asni (a nearby town) for school children to attend school

■ the provision of improved safe water to outlying villages

■ the provision of téléboutique and internet café

■ the promotion and adoption of design code of practice to preserve architecture.

The Kasbah's benefits to the local community are wide-ranging – the building is carried out by local inhabitants, staff are recruited locally, mule transport that is a significant service is distributed around the more than 100 local muleteers, meat and vegetables are bought locally, as are most services. Extensive training has taken place to create the world-class team.

McHugo said, 'Such a project would not be possible without close and deep local ties. I also believe that due to our correct behaviour and respect for the local population they have come to respect us and also accept some of our differences.'

Fig. 5.18 *Imlil village*

Links

The Kasbah du Toubkal site is at:
www.kasbahdutoubkal.com

Typical excursions include:

Aguersioual, south of the Kasbah

1-day trek (good level of fitness required)

After trekking up to the Tizi n' Tamatert col, descend into the stunning Imane valley. Walk by the village of Tinerhourhine and around to the village of Aguersioual, follow river courses, cross seguias (traditional irrigation canals) and rivulets, past terraces and through walnut groves. Picnic en route.

Duration: 6–7 hours' walking time.

Full-day camel excursion

08.00hrs: Depart from Marrakech or the Kasbah du Toubkal early morning. Approx. 1 hours' drive to nearby village (Amizmiz or Tahanoute). Spend a full day trekking with camels. Lunch provided.

16.00hrs to 17.00hrs: Return to Marrakech or the Kasbah du Toubkal.

Fig. 5.19 *Trekking through a village south of the Kasbah*

Case study

Cuba

In recent years Cuba has struggled to redevelop its tourist industry. This has been difficult because it has suffered an economic blockade led by the US, so there has been a shortage of tourists and a shortage of capital to develop the infrastructure. In 2008 it appeared as though things might be about to change as the Cuban government was changing its political stance and there was some possibility of the blockade being lifted.

During the years of the blockade Cuba–partly out of necessity and partly out of fundamental beliefs–developed several resorts that were more or less based on sustainable development principles – one of the sustainable resorts is Las Terrazas is described opposite.

Tourism in Cuba has not developed as much as it has in many parts of the Caribbean, therefore there are many areas on the coast and inland that are still unspoilt and could become very important conservation areas. On the other hand, Cuba lies very close to the USA and, if tourism were to develop in an unrestrained way, these areas could be overwhelmed.

The following is taken from the Worldwide Fund for Nature and the Environment (WWF) website:

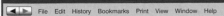

◄ ► | File   Edit   History   Bookmarks   Print   View   Window   Help

Sustainable tourism in Cuba

The biggest threat to marine conservation in Cuba is the current high volume of tourists, attracted to the beautiful beaches and pristine waters of the ocean. The prospect of a massive growth in mass tourism, should the US lift its embargo, could have serious impacts on marine conservation.

Having made marine conservation a priority for WWF Canada's work in Cuba, this project will directly contribute to securing and ensuring effective management of a network of marine protected areas (MPAs). Canada is the single largest source of tourists, so there is both strong responsibility and leverage to ensure sustainable tourism in Cuba. Effective relationships with Canadian tourism operators may also provide some revenues to support these goals.

Background

Beachside mega-hotel complexes offering packaged 'sun and sand' vacations are the dominant tourism model in the Caribbean, Mediterranean and other tropical locations. In fact, package deals to destinations such as Acapulco, Cancun and Barbados account for most of the tourism industry's annual trillion dollar revenues.

Cuba's return to the tourism industry since the 1970s has followed much the same model. Attracted by the sun, beautiful beaches, aquamarine ocean and affordable all-inclusive deals, more and more tourists are flocking to several intensively developed areas including Varadero, Cayo Largo and Holguin.

Cuba is now host to approximately 1.5 million tourists per year. The official plan is to attract 10 million tourists by 2010, mainly by building major hotel complexes at already developed areas like Varadero, and at new locations such as the southern keys.

In dramatic contrast to most of its Caribbean neighbours, Cuba's beaches, mangroves, coral reefs and sea grass beds remain relatively well conserved. However, the ecological implications of Cuba's ambitious plans for growth in the tourism sector are significant since tourism infrastructure and tourist use are fundamentally tied to these coastal and marine ecosystems.

WWF has a long-standing interest and involvement in tourism issues, stemming from a 30-year history of parks creation, forest and coastal zone conservation and recovery/management of endangered and migratory species. WWF has worked worldwide with the tourism industry to drive forward local engagement in conservation. In areas where mass tourism has caused a negative impact on wildlife species or ecosystems, WWF has offered advice and advanced alternatives.

WWF's position on tourism recognises that tourism, including mass tourism, will continue to grow, and focuses on three key areas for action:

1   Minimise the impact of mass tourism through appropriate siting of new facilities, infrastructure (re)design, reduced consumption and waste, and sensitivity to the local natural and social environment, with application to both existing and new developments.

2   Significantly increase the proportion of true ecotourism which inflicts minimum impact on the local environment and culture.

3   Ensure tourists and local tourism operators contribute substantively to conservation.

Objectives

Establish laws, policies, economic instruments, infrastructure, educational mechanisms and behaviour that reduce the impact of current and future tourism operations on Cuba's marine and coastal ecosystems and advance a network of effectively managed MPAs.

Given that tourism designations primarily involve beaches and reefs, the potential for impact on Cuba's relatively well-conserved marine and coastal ecosystems is high. WWF is taking a positive approach to advance the sustainability and domestic value of tourism and reduce the overall tourism footprint by working with the tourism sector to define and implement 'greening' policies and practices, setting criteria for the implementation of real ecotourism and helping Canadians be responsible tourists in Cuba.

www.panda.org/about_wwf/where_we_work/latin_america_and_caribbean/
country/cuba/index.cfm?uProjectID=CU0012

One of the main destinations for nature tourism is western Pinar del Río province, where a project combines sustainable development and tourism in Las Terrazas. Las Terrazas is situated in Sierra del Rosario, which was designated a Biosphere Reserve by the United Nations Educational, Scientific and Cultural Organization (UNESCO) in 1985.

The area was originally settled in 1792 by colonists who planted coffee. After the failure of the plantations, local people turned to forestry and charcoal burning until, by the time of Castro's revolution, the ecosystem was totally degraded. In 1971 Las Terrazas was founded as part of a reafforestation project. Now it is a community of 1,200 people who mostly live in a model village built on the edge of a lake.

People live by farming, mainly fruit and vegetables and tobacco for Cuba's cigar industry. As in all of Cuba the farming is classified as organic. (The definition of organic is rather different from in the UK, but they do not use most manufactured fertilisers or pesticides.) There is also a thriving craft industry of potters and woodworkers.

The area's main hotel, La Moka, was built to fit in with the environment – so much so that trees have been left, growing up through the building in several places. All the tourist guides and the workers at the hotel are from the local community and the hotel uses almost entirely local produce in the restaurants.

The area's main attractions are the birds (over 70 species), animals and trees of the forest, along with the spectacular natural scenery – and so the tourist industry depends enormously on the conservation of the ecosystem. There is a small ecological research station in Las Terrazas too.

Activity

1 **a** To what extent are the two tourism projects at Las Terrazas and the Kasbah du Toubkal helping to sustain the local environment and the local economic and social systems?

   b The WWF fears that tourism development might damage the marine environment off the coast of Cuba. Suggest how.

   c How might such damage affect both the local economy and the ecosystem of the wider area?

   d Can tourism from the UK to Morocco or from Canada to Cuba ever be environmentally sustainable? Can tourist developments like the two case studies described here ever hope to cater for the demands of mass tourism or is this just a niche market? Should we, therefore, bother with ecotourism?

In this chapter you will h ave learnt:

■ how development is defined, measured and mapped

■ about the processes of development and globalisation and about the patterns of development produced, with particular reference to:
   • the Asian Tiger economies
   • newly industrialised countries
   • the development of service industries
   • the impact of new technology

■ the importance of groupings of nations to the development process

■ about countries at very low levels of development, with reference to Bangladesh

■ the role of transnational corporations in the development process

■ about development issues, including:
   • trade and aid
   • economic sustainability and environmental sustainability
   • sustainable tourism.

AQA Examiner's tip

The issue of 'economic sustainability versus environmental sustainability' does not come under a specific heading in this book. However, the issues are considered in both the sections on sustainable tourism and on trade and aid in Bangladesh.

Think about how you could use this material to answer questions on the sustainability topic. **Make your case studies work for you.**

6 Contemporary conflicts and challenges

The geographical basis of conflicts

In this section you will learn:

■ about the nature of conflict, and about how conflicts are often rooted in particular locations and arise from the geographical attributes of those locations.

 Key terms

Conflict: a state of opposition, disagreement or incompatibility between two or more people or groups of people, which is sometimes characterised by physical violence. The disagreements are based on incompatible goals, needs, desires, values, beliefs and/or attitudes.

The AQA A Level Geography Specification states that you must study the 'nature and origin of **conflict**'. This could lead to a very deep discussion on the nature of humanity.

■ Is it part of human nature for individuals and groups to come into conflict with each other?

■ Is life without conflict possible?

■ Is that even desirable, or does conflict lead to progress and development?

You will probably spend some time thinking about these questions and discussing them in your class while you are studying this chapter. However, as a geographer studying conflict, you need to consider conflicts linked to specific places, including those based on:

■ nationalism, regionalism and localism

■ ethnicity and culture

■ resources, including territory

■ ideology linked to places.

Having defined the type of conflicts that you should be studying, you need to be concerned with:

■ the different 'expressions of conflict'

■ why conflicts arise

■ what the results of the conflicts are

■ how they might be better managed in future.

The word 'conflict' implies a state of disagreement between two or more parties. This might be expressed in many different ways, which can be seen as stages in the escalation of a conflict. The stages can involve some or all of:

■ discussion, argument, political and diplomatic activity

■ legal action

■ boycotts, threats, posturing and manoeuvring short of violence

■ physical violence through seizure of property or land, terrorism (or freedom fighting, depending on your point of view), insurrection or war.

There are several ways in which people can work towards conflict resolution. Sometimes this can involve the removal of the causes of the conflict, but more often it involves negotiating to allow all parties to live with some sort of compromise over the problem. Conflict resolution usually consists of a gradual process of talking and building trust which, in turn, tends to require an outside mediator.

Many tools are available to people trying to resolve or to manage conflict, including negotiation, mediation, community building, diplomacy,

Fig. 6.1 *President Clinton tries to mediate in the Arab Israeli conflict*

teaching, prayer and counselling. In real-world conflict situations, which range in scale from primary school bullying to genocide, practitioners will creatively combine several of these approaches as needed.

Conflict resolution is highly sensitive to culture. In Western cultural contexts, successful conflict resolution usually involves fostering communication among disputants, problem solving and drafting agreements that meet their underlying needs. In these situations, conflict resolvers often talk about finding the *win-win* solution, or mutually satisfying scenario, for everyone involved.

In many non-Western cultural contexts, such as Afghanistan and Iraq, it is also important to find *win-win* solutions; however, in these contexts, direct communication between disputants that explicitly addresses the issues at stake in the conflict can be perceived as very rude, making the conflict worse and delaying its resolution. Rather, it can make sense to involve religious, tribal or community leaders, communicate difficult truths indirectly through a third party, and make suggestions through stories. Intercultural conflicts are often the most difficult to resolve because the expectations of the disputants can be very different, and it is easy for misunderstanding to occur.

The geographical similarities that allow all these conflicts to be studied together include:

■ competition for space

■ competition for resources

■ the existence of group identities that have often existed for many decades or even centuries

■ strongly held beliefs and cultures that define groups of people, but which can also separate them from other groups

■ changes in the size and power of different groups that can result from changing birth and death rates, migration, etc.

Finally, and in some ways most importantly, there are conflicts that arise from the challenge of global poverty. In some ways these conflicts are conflicts for resources, but the poverty of some groups of people increases their desperation; if they have nothing to lose their reactions can become more desperate or more extreme. Sometimes the poor are forced to migrate to seek resources and they will travel in ways that seem quite appalling to those of us who have never been in their position. In other situations they are forced to fight, again in ways that seem desperate. Sadly, the fighting is often made worse because sophisticated, high-tech weaponry, coming from the more developed world.

It is important to look for such themes and similarities while studying the conflicts that follow. Do not view each case study in isolation but try to understand how each conflict can teach lessons that might be applied to other conflicts in different areas and at different scales.

Did you know?

Some geography graduates have been welcomed into postgraduate courses in conflict management. The study of geography is considered to develop skills in seeing all sides and opinions about issues and in looking for wise compromise solutions.

AQA Examiner's tip

Geographical conflicts arise at a lot of different scales and from a lot of different causes. In the AQA course it is essential to look at conflicts at different scales: local, national and global.

It is also essential to consider conflicts caused by people coming together to share the same space, as with multicultural societies, and by people wanting to separate from each other.

Conflict over local resources

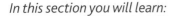

In this section you will learn:

- how conflicts can arise over the use of local resources, and about the planning processes that operate to try to reduce or manage the conflicts, with particular reference to conflicts over Black Mountain outside Belfast.

Links

The PAS site can be seen at: www.pas.gov.uk

The Planning Portal is another organisation set up by the government, but they work with individual members of the public rather than with local authorities. Their website is at: www.planningportal.gov.uk

On a local, regional or even national level, it is easier to avoid conflict over local resources because everybody is subject to the same laws. Planning laws are put in place by local authorities to prevent a chaotic approach to development and use of resources, and to minimise ensuing conflict about the impact of these on different segments of the population. When conflict does result, it is more likely to lead to litigation than to warfare.

Geographers sometimes refer rather carelessly to 'planning', when what they really mean is 'spatial planning'. In England, the Planning Advisory Service (PAS) is a government-funded body that advises local authorities about the planning process (or should that be 'the spatial planning' process?). The plans that they deal with can range from a plan to extend a house by building a bedroom over the garage, to a plan to develop a new shopping centre.

> Planning could also be described as an attempt to resolve conflicts between people and groups with different views about how land should be used.

The above statement from the PAS website gives a good definition of what the planning process is all about.

The system of planning in England and Wales

England and Wales follow a 'plan-led system'. This means that local authorities have a legal duty to prepare plans that set out what can be built and where, within the boundaries of each authority. This system was updated by an Act of Parliament in December 2004. It is also followed, with some slight variations, in Northern Ireland and Scotland.

The plans

There are two main levels of plan:

- **Regional Spatial Strategies** – each Regional Planning Body (such as the south-west of England) is preparing a Regional Spatial Strategy. These set out things such as how many homes are needed to meet the future needs of people in the region, or whether the region needs a new major shopping centre or an airport. Certain areas within the authority are 'zoned' for particular types of development, or for protection from development.

- **Local Development Frameworks** – each local planning authority within the region is preparing a Local Development Framework. This is a folder of documents that sets out how the local area might change over the next few years.

These different types of plan are usually available from local libraries.

All plans must take account of the sustainable needs of future communities. They must take account of the environment as well as setting out the sorts of development needed to help people live and work in the area. In the plans some areas have **special protection** against certain developments because they contain attractive landscape (e.g. national parks) or interesting plants and wildlife, or because the spread of towns and villages into open countryside needs to be controlled (e.g. the greenbelt). Some smaller areas of land also contain ancient monuments that must not be damaged. Some buildings are specially protected or listed because of their architectural or historic interest.

Public involvement in the plans

Individuals and communities are encouraged to get involved during the preparation of the plans. Local planning authorities must set out how they will involve the local community by making a Statement of Community Involvement.

The local plans are first published as 'draft' plans and people and groups are encouraged to comment on these and suggest changes. Draft plans are also examined at inquiries by independent inspectors from the government, and everyone has an opportunity to put their views to the inspector.

When the drafts are being finally approved, the councils (which are subject to democratic control through elections) have to take all comments into account before giving their final approval to the plan.

Planning permission for development

Most people only come into contact with the planning system when decisions have to be taken about whether something can be built in their area. Most new buildings or major changes to existing buildings or to the local environment need consent – known as planning permission.

Each application for planning permission is made to the local planning authority for the area. If the planning application is in line with the approved plan, householders can usually expect to receive planning permission within eight weeks. Approval for larger, commercial developments often takes longer.

When an application has been made, local residents must be told about the application. They must have the opportunity to give their views for or against the planned development. Then the elected members of the authority, advised by their professional planning officers, have to decide whether to grant permission and allow the development to go ahead.

Fig. 6.2 *Buildings and areas of historical and/or architectural interest, like this one in Bath, are protected by planning laws*

Appeals against refusal of permission

If the local authority refuses permission, the person applying can appeal to the government. Appeals are dealt with by the planning inspectors. Most appeals are dealt with in writing; some go to a hearing in front of a tribunal; a small number go to a full public inquiry if the matter is serious enough and affects a large number of people.

Different people and organisations in the community will have different views on most planning matters and these must all be taken into account.

Achieving balance

Good planning, by local authorities or by planning inspectors, involves balancing different views and finding a way of resolving conflict. It is essential that the decisions:

- take account of all views, including those of the poor and those lacking in power

- recognise that a few people or groups might make a lot of noise about a conflict but that this should not be allowed to drown out the views of those who do not express their views so strongly

- consider the long-term needs of a sustainable environment, as well as the short-term needs of particular groups

- balance the views of a small number of people, who might be very seriously affected, with the views of the large number of people who might only be affected in a small but still significant way

- balance economic considerations against quality of life considerations

- recognise that some people might win and others might lose when a planning decision is made, but try to minimise any losses that might arise.

Case study

Black Mountain Quarry and the Belfast Metropolitan Area Plan (BMAP)

At the edge of the built-up area of West Belfast stand Divis (478 m high) and Black Mountain (390 m). They are formed from limestone with some beds of basalt – an extrusive igneous rock, formed from lava (at the surface) rather than magma. Belfast is a crowded city, with little public open space, so Black Mountain has always provided an important area for open-air recreation, as well as giving dramatic views from almost anywhere in the city. You can gain some impression of its scenic importance by visiting the panorama site shown in the Link.

However, there is conflict over the future of some of the land on Black Mountain. As well as recreational and conservation use, the land is also farmed, although most of it is of comparatively low agricultural quality. In addition, a quarrying and construction company has permission to quarry an outcrop of basalt (around the locale of GR 280723 on Fig. 6.5) to produce roadstone.

The quarry provides around 40 jobs (in quarrying, processing the quarried materials and transport) and produces materials for one of Ireland's most successful building and civil engineering companies. Planning permission was granted more than 20 years ago. This allows the company to develop the site and to spread outwards as well as downwards. Estimates suggest that the quarry has the capacity to continue producing for another 20 years before it becomes exhausted.

Activities

1 Try to get hold of your area's Regional Spatial Strategy and your own authority's Local Development Framework to see just how they see your area developing over the next few years.

You might be able to find draft versions of the plans on the internet, and then see how they were altered as a result of the consultation process.

2 Study your local papers, or enquire of your local council to find out some of the applications for planning permission that have been made in your area recently.

Most of these will be minor matters that involve little, if any, conflict. However, you should try to find at least one application that has aroused strong opinions and conflict between different groups of people. Then follow the progress of the application, by studying either press reports or council minutes and other official documents. Many of these will be published on the internet.

Try to discover:

- the reasons for the conflict
- the attitudes of different groups of people to the conflict
- how the conflict has been resolved, or might be resolved in future.

Links

The panorama view of the Black Mountain is at: www.virtualvisit-northernireland.com – type 'Divis and Black Mountain' into the search box.

You can find out much more about recreation in the Belfast Hills at: www.belfasthills.org

Fig. 6.3 *Black Mountain, viewed from Belfast*

Fig. 6.4 *Black Mountain quarry*

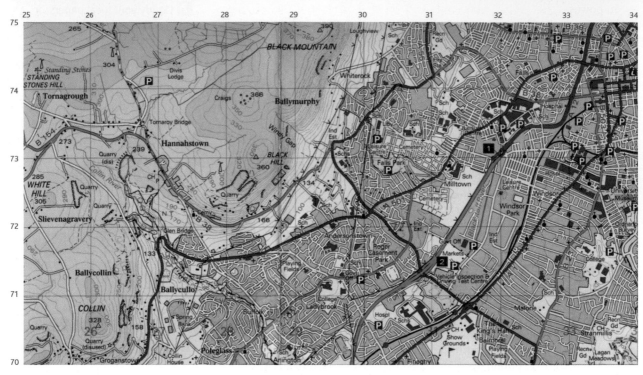

Fig. 6.5 *West Belfast and the Black Mountain*

Quarrying not only removes an interesting geological site but also damages a variety of ecosystems. It makes land unavailable for recreation and causes noise and visual pollution to a wider surrounding area. The only way out of the quarry for stone and other products is by lorry, along roads through densely built-up areas.

Other quarries in the area that have been worked out and abandoned have become important conservation and recreation sites (e.g. Glenside Community Woodland at GR 271727).

Links

See details of Glenside at: www. belfasthills.org/minisite/adult_ version/goexplore_glenside.html

In 2001 there was a debate in the Northern Ireland Assembly on conservation in the Black Mountain area, introduced by Sinn Fein leader and Assembly Member for West Belfast, Gerry Adams. He stated:

> I welcome the opportunity to discuss the urgent need to conserve the Black Mountain. It is essential that the Assembly support the preservation of the Black Mountain and the Belfast Hills. I invite the Minister of the Environment, Mr Foster, to visit the Black Mountain with me to see, at first hand, the gaping chasm and sheer cliffs that make up the quarry, and to understand why it is vital that his Department takes the necessary steps to end quarrying. … I hope that today's discussion will be informative and signal a beginning of the end for quarrying on the Black Mountain and real moves towards preserving the Belfast Hills.

Meanwhile, the government of Northern Ireland and Belfast Council had been preparing the Belfast Metropolitan Area Plan 2015. This is designed to be the basis for all planning and development decisions made up to 2015, when the plan will need to be revised.

Drawing up of the plan began in 2000 and was formally announced in 2001, with notice given to all citizens and other interested parties that consultations would take place and that views should be submitted by all who wished to influence the final plan. In December 2001 an Issues Paper was published.

The extract below shows how consultation was expected to take place.

To facilitate comment and discussion following publication of this Issues Paper, a series of public meetings will be held throughout the plan area.

These events will be advertised in the local press and will be arranged and chaired by the consultants appointed by the Department. The consultants will submit a report to the Department presenting a collation of the views expressed during the various meetings.

Plan Programme

8.5 The programme for the preparation of the Plan is as follows:

- Publication of Issues Paper – December 2001.
- Publication of Draft Plan – end 2002.
- Public Inquiry held by Planning Appeals Commission to consider objections – 2003/2004.
- Adoption of Plan following consideration of Inquiry report – 2004/2005.

Plan Monitor

8.6 The Plan will be subject to a revision after 10 years to consider if major changes of direction are required in the light of new trends and circumstances. After five years, there will be a focused assessment to identify any aspects where in course adjustments might be appropriate.

■ Links

The full text of the debate can be read at: www.niassembly.gov.uk/record/reports/010430e.htm

■ Did you know?

In the debate Mr Adams referred to the Black Mountain being easily accessible to the people of 'West Belfast'. Other speakers referred to it being accessible to the people of 'North Belfast'. Some referred to it being accessible to the people of 'both West and North Belfast'.

People who are not familiar with Northern Ireland might not realise that West Belfast is a predominantly Nationalist (Roman Catholic) community, while North Belfast is predominantly Unionist (Protestant).

It is interesting to note that in Belfast the issue of access to recreational land might still involve some aspects of inter-communal conflict – and that efforts to resolve the conflict included providing recreational facilities that could be enjoyed by all.

Note that, as of August 2008 the Planning Appeals Commission is examining the plan in the light of submissions that have been received. It is hoped that they will report in early summer 2010 and the final BMAP will be published soon after that.

One set of issues raised in the Issues Paper, on which discussion was to be encouraged, was headed 'The Countryside'. Several of the issues raised here could be seen as relevant to the consideration of Black Mountain and its quarries. These incuded:

7.1   While the plan area may be dominated by the large urban areas, it nevertheless has a significant rural component. It is a unique landscape containing significant areas of high environmental quality. The rural economy and agriculture in particular have been subject to considerable change …

7.2   The rural landscape is also experiencing change as a result of pressures from urban type uses and associated impacts, particularly around the urban fringes …

7.4   BMAP will seek to support the aim of the Regional Development Strategy which is 'to develop an attractive and prosperous rural area, based on a balanced and integrated approach to the development of town, village and countryside in order to sustain a strong and vibrant rural community.'

> In what ways could the Plan assist the diversification of the rural economy and the development of countryside recreation and rural tourism in an environmentally sensitive manner?

> Are the measures currently in force to protect the rural environment considered to be effective or should the Plan identify special areas of landscape quality for additional protection? If so in what way could they be justified? Are there further ways in which the Plan could help enhance the rural landscape?

After the consultation period the Draft BMAP was published. In it, proposals for the countryside areas were listed under the headings COU 1 to COU 11. These included the following statements:

Designation COU 6
Areas of High Scenic Value

Areas of High Scenic Value are designated in the following areas as identified on Map No 1 – Overview … Belfast Basalt Escarpment …

The above Areas of High Scenic Value are also designated as Areas of Constraint on Mineral Development.

Policy COU 8
Area of Constraint on Mineral Development

Planning permission will not be granted for the extraction and/or processing of minerals within Areas of constraint on Mineral Development.

Exceptions may be made where the proposed operations are short term and the environmental implications are not significant. In such cases the on-site processing of the excavated material is unlikely to be permitted.

Policy COU 7
Areas of High Scenic Value

Planning permission will not be granted to development proposals that would adversely affect the quality, character and features of interest in Areas of High Scenic Value. Proposals for mineral working and waste disposal will not be acceptable.

A Landscape Analysis must accompany development proposals in these areas to indicate the likely effects of the proposal on the landscape.

… the Belfast Basalt Escarpment – Area of High Scenic Value is situated within the Metropolitan Urban Area … .

All AOHSV are also designated as Areas of Constraint on Mineral Development in the Plan. This will restrict new or extended mineral operations to those locations and proposals, which will minimise conflict with amenity, recreation and conservation interests in the Plan Area.

When the Draft BMAP was published, the owners of the Black Mountain Quarry objected to all the above policies. Their objection included the following statement:

> The Department has not sought in drafting policy COU8 in BMAP to balance equitably the aim of sustaining and diversifying the rural economy against protecting the natural environment. It is noted that the Planning Service Minerals Unit did not refer to the strategic rural economy guidelines when drafting [BMAP] and they focused solely on the protection of the natural environment. This is a significant omission …

> The Department however ignores the contribution that the mineral extraction industry makes to the economy of Northern Ireland and disadvantages quarry operators in the Belfast Metropolitan Area by limiting the potential growth of existing facilities …

> … [The Department] is of the opinion that there is a strong sustainability argument for the continued use of existing mineral quarries to limit the need for new quarry sites and the detrimental impacts these can cause. It is also recognised that sites which are located in close proximity to existing established markets in the most densely populated region of Northern Ireland with the need to reduce the unsustainable long distance road haulage of minerals brings additional sustainable environmental benefits. To this end … extensions to existing mineral workings which minimise environmental disturbance in the countryside will normally be preferred to green field sites.

At the time of writing it appears that the Draft BMAP has not been altered to meet these objections. However, consultation is ongoing and the final version of the BMAP should now be published in summer 2010. Then it will be placed on the planning website for Northern Ireland (www.planningni.gov.uk) and the draft plan will be removed shortly thereafter.

Links

The BMAP can be seen at: www.planningni.gov.uk

Go to 'View Development Plans and Policies', and choose the BMAP Draft Plan from the A–Z Index. Part 3 of the Plan and then to the section on Countryside and Coast.

The objections to the restraints on quarrying can be seen at: www.pacni. gov.uk/bmapstage1/objections/ BMAP 2030.doc

Activities

4 a From your study of the text, documents, photos and maps in this section on Black Mountain, evaluate the importance of the area for:
   i   outdoor leisure and conservation of the natural environment
   ii quarrying to provide jobs and income for the area.
   b To what extent does the quarrying that is taking place at present seem to threaten the area's suitability for outdoor leisure and conservation?
   c Do you think that the planners who produced the BMAP went through a satisfactory process of consultation?
   d Do you think that they were justified in imposing limits on the future development of quarrying in the area? Justify your answer.

5 Draw a timeline with dates to show the planning process for this quarry so far.

The geographical impact of international conflicts

In this section you will learn:

▪ how international conflicts arise, with particular reference to conflicts in the Middle East between Israel and the Palestinians, and in the Caucasus between Russia and Georgia.

The title of this section could be considered slightly misleading. It implies that conflicts exist first, and then they have an effect on the geography of the areas in which they occur. However, many people would argue that much of the basis of the conflict is geographical: that is, based in a particular place with competition for farmland, water and mineral resources, strategically important land, access to ports or other routes, and so on.

Nowhere is this more obvious than in the Middle East, with the conflict between Israel and the West Bank Palestinians and with other Arab neighbours. The political map of the area illustrates the complexity and the instability of the political boundaries in the region.

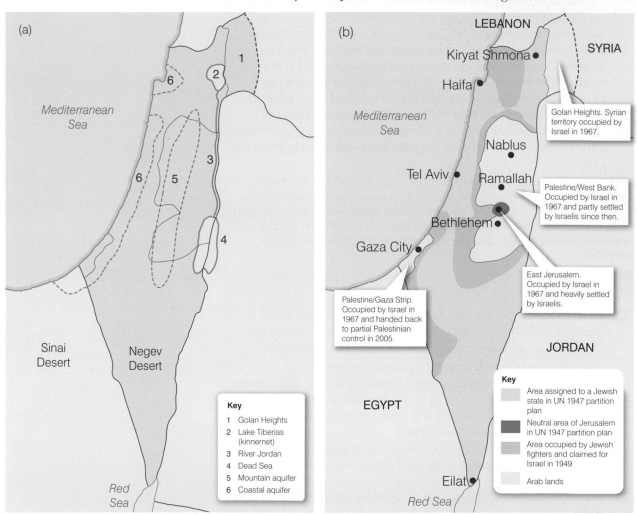

Fig. 6.6 *(a) Israel/Palestine – water resources; (b) Israel/Palestine – political*

Conflicts between Israel and Palestine

The West Bank barrier which separates Israel and some areas of Israeli settlement – the West Bank – from the rest of Palestine/West Bank has replaced the Berlin Wall (1961–89), symbol of the Cold War, as a symbol of a divided world. Begun in 2002, it is being built gradually along a route of approximately 725 km and prevents entry into Israeli territory except through designated checkpoints, which require a permit to pass through. In open country the barrier is 50 m wide and constitutes a gated electric fence topped with barbed wire and constantly patrolled by Israeli security forces; in heavily populated areas it is a tall concrete wall with observation posts and small doors to allow access. The barrier currently keeps 10,000 Palestinians out of Israel and is expected to restrict another 50,000 when it is complete.

Even more drastically, the barrier cuts off access between Palestinian homes and their schools, places of work, agricultural land, hospitals and other essential services. In many places it cuts people off from their livelihoods and divides families.

Fig. 6.7 *The Israel–Palestine barrier*

Why was the West Bank barrier built?

Israel's stated reason for building the barrier was to prevent attacks on Israeli citizens by suicide bombers from Palestinian settlements in the West Bank (occupied by Israel in the Six Day War of 1967). Militant Palestinians from the West Bank were crossing into Israeli territory and blowing themselves up on buses, in restaurants, in markets and in other crowded places. These bombs often killed dozens of people at a time and were designed to destabilise Israel.

Putting up a barrier at the West Bank allowed Israel to perform identity checks on everyone entering its territory. This was intended to keep out the bombers and gunmen, or at least to make it far more difficult for them to enter. It has been a source of enormous frustration to the Palestinians that the barrier also severely restricts the movements of civilians, most of whom are not bombers or gunmen.

Also, at the same time as improving security, the barrier has encroached onto Palestinian territory that was not previously considered part of Israel and is now being settled by Israelis. This surreptitious extension is seen by the country's enemies as a second and quite cynical reason for the siting and construction of the barrier. As well as encroaching on Palestinian land, the barrier causes hardship to Palestinians who do not have free movement and access to jobs, public services and shops.

Links

There is an excellent slide presentation on the barrier at: www.guardian.co.uk/world/interactive/2008/jul/07/israelandthepalestinians

You can also see a BBC helicopter tour of Israel and occupied lands at: news.bbc.co.uk/player/nol/newsid_7110000/newsid_7114100/7114144.stm?bw=bb&mp=rm&asb=1&news=1&bbcws=1

Why were the bombers attacking Israel?

The Palestinians believe that much of Israel belongs to them, having been seized by Jewish settlers even before Israel was created. The UN Partition Plan in 1947 would have legalised this occupation. However, in 1948 Israel proclaimed independence without waiting for international agreement. Then further land was seized in the Arab-Israeli War of 1949 which was ended by the creation of the state of Israel.

More land was occupied after the Six Day War of 1967. Some of this was later returned to the Palestinians, but there has been a steady spread of Israeli settlements onto much of the occupied land of the West Bank and East Jerusalem since then.

Some Palestinians just want a settlement that allows the two groups of people to live at peace; others want their land back; and others want to see the State of Israel 'wiped off the map'. Whatever their views, the Palestinians feel powerless. They have no country, no government, no army and few resources – so they resort to bombing to make their point.

Why did the Jews seize the land that is now Israel?

In biblical times the Tribes of Israel were nomadic people who settled in Palestine. At the time of the Roman Empire there were many Jews living in and around Jerusalem, their main holy site. According to the Old Testament Bible, this land had been promised to them by God and they had settled there after their periods of wandering. However, in the second century AD the Jews staged and lost a rebellion against Roman rule and were deprived of their land. Most went into exile, travelling widely and settling across Europe and the Middle East – the 'Jewish diaspora'. Wherever they lived, Jews maintained their culture, religion and identity into modern times. Unfortunately, their cultural separateness often caused them to be persecuted, and anti-Semitism was common.

As a response to the Jews' long history of persecution, the Zionist movement began in Europe in the late 19th century, dedicated to setting up a separate Jewish state. Most Zionists saw Palestine – the land promised to the Jews in the Bible – as the natural location for such a state. Zionism encouraged Jews to move to Palestine with the long-term aim of forming the nucleus of the future state of Israel. After the end of the Second World War the rate of immigration (both legal and illegal) accelerated, as survivors of the Holocaust sought refuge there.

A wide spectrum of groups came, from socialist Zionists (who believed in setting up cooperative ways of living with a community in a settlement called a kibbutz, at peace with their Arab neighbours), to ultra-religious Zionists who believed that the Jews were entitled, by the word of God, to all the land of biblical Palestine.

Some of the new arrivals settled on land that had no apparent owners, although sometimes this land was part of a nomadic farming system that was visited from time to time by herdsmen. Other settlers bought their land, and some others used force to evict previous occupants.

Following the Second World War and the Holocaust, there was tremendous international sympathy for the Jews and the United Nations helped to establish an independent state of Israel, despite strong protests from the Arab world.

What about the Arabs who lived there before the settlers came?

In 1880 the entire population of Palestine was estimated at 550,000 – approximately 24,000 were Jews and the rest were mainly Arabs. Some of the Arabs were settled farmers and some were nomadic herders.

By 1947 the number of Jews had risen to 630,000 (mainly through immigration) and the number of non-Jews had risen to 1,310,000 (mainly by natural increase).

When the state of Israel came into being in 1948, many of the Arab inhabitants fled, as **refugees**, to the West Bank or to the Gaza Strip, which at the time were controlled by Jordan and Egypt respectively. Israel fought and won two wars against its Arab neighbours: the Arab-Israeli War of 1948 and the Six Day War of 1967, each of which added to its territory. Today's occupied areas of East Jerusalem, the West Bank and Gaza (along with the Sinai Peninsula and the Golan Heights) are the legacies of those wars.

In 2008 Israel's population was 7,282,000. Some 5,499,000 of the population (75.5 per cent) are Jews, and 1,461,000 (20.1 per cent) are Arabs.

The Palestinian population of the Gaza Strip stands at approximately 1.4 million, while in the West Bank it is approximately 2.4 million. There are 237,185 Palestinians in occupied East Jerusalem. Many Palestinians and their descendants have emigrated to other Arab countries, to the US, western Europe and elsewhere.

> ### Key terms
>
> **Refugee:** someone who flees for refuge or safety, usually to a foreign country, at a time of political upheaval, economic hardship, war, natural disaster, etc.

Who governs the Palestinian lands of Gaza and the West Bank?

Israel is ruled by an elected democratic government, with the strong support of the US. However, the status of the Palestinian lands remains complex, even since the various peace initiatives of the 1990s which have given the Palestinians limited self-government under the Palestinian Authority.

Gaza is dominated by Hamas, an armed Islamic group that does not recognise Israel and which is not recognised in turn by Israel, the US and most of Europe, or by Egypt and Saudi Arabia.

In the West Bank some urban areas are governed by the Palestinian Authority. The Authority is made up of members of Fatah (a non-religious Palestinian organisation which recognises Israel) and Hamas. However, Israel is still responsible for security in all rural areas of the West Bank and it is completely responsible for the Israeli settlements that are governed as part of Israel.

Most of the revenue of the Palestinian Authority comes from the EU and US. Customs duties on goods coming into the West Bank are collected by Israel and paid to the Authority later.

■ What are the geographical issues?

Geographers are concerned with many issues in the Middle East, all of them interlinked. Four of these are outlined below.

Note also that each issue looks quite different from the different points of view of the parties involved. The comments are one person's attempt to understand the issues.

You will also see that many attempts have been made, and are being made, to move towards solutions of some of these issues. Of course, we can consider our own solutions to the conflicts in the area but, as geographers, we should be very well aware of the complexity of the issues and must avoid the temptation to think that simplistic solutions can ever hope to work.

1 Can a two-state solution be found, whereby Israelis and Palestinians can agree to divide up the land between them and live peacefully?

If this is to happen, both countries must have viable economies.

At present Israel has the strongest economy in the region but is still dependent on economic support from the US government and from private individuals in the US and Europe. A very high proportion of the state's resources go on defence, to protect against both domestic (by Palestinians) and foreign (from hostile Arab neighbours) attacks. In particular, Israel is concerned that Iran might develop nuclear weapons; Iranian leaders have quite recently suggested that Israel has no right to exist.

The West Bank does not have a viable economy. It has few resources beyond its agriculture and its people are often cut off from their land, either because of annexation by Israelis or because of the West Bank barrier or other security checks that make life difficult for farmers. Agricultural development is difficult because of limited water supplies.

Gaza has even fewer resources. It is little more than a refugee camp in the desert.

Fig. 6.8 *People of Gaza collect supplies from a UN relief food store*

Both Gaza and the West Bank used to earn money by sending people to work in Israel. They provided a cheap labour force to develop the Israeli economy, and gained income in return. However, since the 1990s the bombings carried out by Palestinians in Israel have led to a drastic reduction in such cross-border movements. Israel has replaced their cheap labour with immigrants from eastern Europe and elsewhere.

2 Until peace comes (and even when it does), can Israel give up strategically important land?

Many of the Israeli settlements on occupied land in the West Bank are on hilltops. These sites are obviously attractive because of views and the cooling breezes that blow on higher land. However, they are also strategically important. By keeping these sites occupied, Israel prevents them from being used for firing on Israeli settlements or for observing movements of Israeli forces. In the worst case, they could even be used by Israeli forces to help to control the area.

The Golan Heights is another such strategic area. This was Syrian territory that Israel occupied after the Six Day War of 1967. Israel is reluctant to leave this area, which helps fortify its northern borders; if they did abandon the Heights, northern Israel would be easier to keep under Syrian surveillance.

3 How would the water supply be divided up in a two-state solution?

Located on the fringe of a desert, Israel and Palestine are almost wholly dependent on seasonal rainfall for their water supplies. Rarely does the area experience rainfall outside of a five-month winter season from November through to March. The whole area has a chronic water-shortage problem.

Israel has a growing population that maintains a sufficient standard of living that water is not considered a luxury, although Israeli water consumption is low by North American or European standards. On average, annual Israeli water consumption per person is less than half of that in southern California, a region with similar climatic conditions.

The West Bank and Gaza have desperate shortages of water, both for agriculture and for domestic use. A modern infrastructure of supply and distribution is just not available.

Israel's water supply is stored in three main sources, which together comprise the National Water System: Lake Kinneret, the coastal **aquifer**, and the mountain aquifer. Together these can supply 600–800 m³ per year. Current non-agricultural demand has reached the level of 600–700 m³. As a result, Israeli agriculture has become increasingly dependent on recycled sewage and other types of low-grade waters which are unsuitable for drinking.

Key terms

Aquifer: a porous layer of rock that carries water that falls in one area, below the ground surface, so that it becomes available elsewhere, either by flowing to the surface under its own pressure or by being pumped out.

Table 6.1 *Israel – water supplies (million m³)*

Water resources	Annual recharge	Israeli water use	Settlement water use	Palestinian water use	Total water use
Mountain aquifer					
Western	362	344	10	22	376
North-eastern	145	103	5	30	138
Eastern	172	40	35–50	69	144–159
Coastal aquifer	250	260	0	0	260
Gaza	55	0	0	110	110
River Jordan	1311	685	10–20	0	1334–40*
Wastewater	450	450	0	0	450

Note 1: The mountain aquifer is a folded anticline so water flows in three different directions. Pumping stations can transfer water from one area to another though.

Note 2: The River Jordan is largely fed from Kinneret, which acts as a controlling reservoir.

Note 3*: Some water is also taken out of the Jordan (by treaty with Israel) for use in Syria and Jordan.

Note 4: 'Israel' is the land that was occupied as the State of Israel up to 1967.

'Settlements' are the Israeli settlements built on occupied land in the West Bank.

Moreover, there is deterioration in the coastal aquifer, where the level of salting and other pollutants has reduced the quality in numerous sites to below that permissible for drinking water. A similar pattern has begun in Lake Kinneret as well, albeit to a lesser extent. This leaves the mountain aquifer as the primary source of water for Jerusalem, and it is regarded by the Israeli authorities as the most important part of the National Water System.

As one Israeli writer has said:

> The political and strategic significance for Israel is clear. Withdrawing from Judea and Samaria – i.e. the mountain aquifer – or from the Golan Heights would create a situation in which the fate of Israel's water supply would be determined by the Palestinian Authority and the Syrians, respectively. Can Israel really afford to trust her most valuable and irreplaceable national resource in the hands of those who have had a long history of trying to destroy the Jewish State?

How can a viable Palestinian state ever develop without access to reliable and secure water supplies?

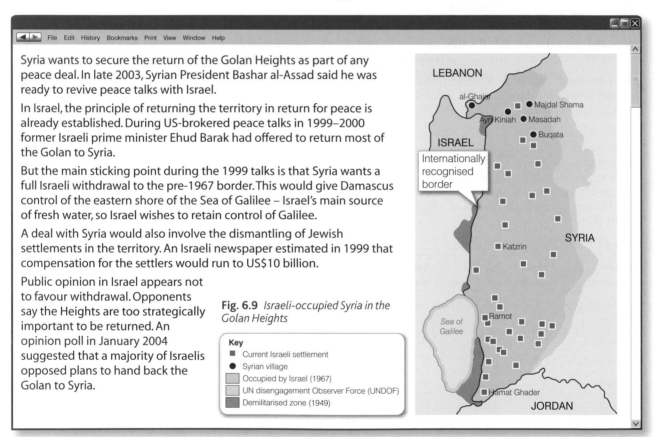

Syria wants to secure the return of the Golan Heights as part of any peace deal. In late 2003, Syrian President Bashar al-Assad said he was ready to revive peace talks with Israel.

In Israel, the principle of returning the territory in return for peace is already established. During US-brokered peace talks in 1999–2000 former Israeli prime minister Ehud Barak had offered to return most of the Golan to Syria.

But the main sticking point during the 1999 talks is that Syria wants a full Israeli withdrawal to the pre-1967 border. This would give Damascus control of the eastern shore of the Sea of Galilee – Israel's main source of fresh water, so Israel wishes to retain control of Galilee.

A deal with Syria would also involve the dismantling of Jewish settlements in the territory. An Israeli newspaper estimated in 1999 that compensation for the settlers would run to US$10 billion.

Public opinion in Israel appears not to favour withdrawal. Opponents say the Heights are too strategically important to be returned. An opinion poll in January 2004 suggested that a majority of Israelis opposed plans to hand back the Golan to Syria.

Fig. 6.9 *Israeli-occupied Syria in the Golan Heights*

Key
- ■ Current Israeli settlement
- ● Syrian village
- ☐ Occupied by Israel (1967)
- ☐ UN disengagement Observer Force (UNDOF)
- ▨ Demilitarised zone (1949)

4 What will happen to Jerusalem?

Jerusalem is a religious site of the utmost significance for Jews, Christians and Muslims, and many of the most important sites for each group are found in roughly the same area. In 1947 the United Nations plan for Palestine proposed that the city would be under international control and open to people of all faiths to visit their sites and worship as they wished.

However, this is not satisfactory to either the Jews or the Muslims. Both Israel and the Palestinians claim the city as their capital. The Israelis seized West Jerusalem in 1949 and then East Jerusalem in 1967. Since then they have made Jerusalem their seat of government and they have embarked on a settlement programme in and around Jerusalem, trying to consolidate their control of the city.

Muslims are still allowed to visit their sites but access is very strictly controlled.

Tzipi Livni was elected leader of her party, Israel's ruling Kadima Party, in September 2008, replacing Prime Minister Ehud Olmert, who had resigned. Attempts to form a coalition in October failed and new elections are expected in 2009.

There are high hopes of Livni's ability to make progress with Palestinian negotiations.

> Livni has been closely involved in the last year of talks with the Palestinians, acting as Israel's lead negotiator, and she is expected to continue those talks if she becomes prime minister, adopting a more dovish stance than some colleagues.
>
> 'I am really happy that Livni won because she is committed to the peace process,' said the Israeli peace activist Yossi Beilin. 'I think the right thing for her to do now is to form a coalition that wants to promote peace rather than a broad government with the right …
>
> 'Because Livni was immersed in the peace process, we believe she will pursue peace moves with us,' said Ahmed Qureia, the chief Palestinian negotiator.

www.guardian.co.uk, 18 September 2008

Activity

1. The Israel/Palestine situation is constantly changing. Try to update yourself on the latest developments. Some possible areas for research are listed below.

   ■ The new US president, Barack Obama, will probably want to start a new peace initiative.

   ■ There are discussions about dismantling some Israeli settlements on the West Bank, but it is likely that, in other areas, new settlements will be under construction.

   ■ Syria and Israel are holding preliminary talks about a settlement between the two countries and these may have progressed … or not.

   ■ The struggle for control of the Palestinian territories between Fatah and Hamas might result in new compromise solutions.

   ■ Israel might start to construct commercially viable desalination plants.

   ■ Relations between Israel and Iran might alter, particularly with regard to Iran's possible research and development of nuclear weapons.

   And you can also be sure that some other factors will have come to prominence and will be exerting an influence on the social, economic and environmental geography of the region.

■ Conflicts in South Ossetia and Abkhazia

In August 2008 a short war took place between Russia (population 142 million; area 17.1 million km²) and Georgia (population 4.6 million; area 69,700 km²).

It is not surprising that Russia quickly achieved its aims, but why did the war break out in the first place? What were the immediate causes and what are the underlying causes?

A study of the area's geography helps to understand what is happening in this area of the Southern Caucasus Mountains in particular and along Russia's western borders in general.

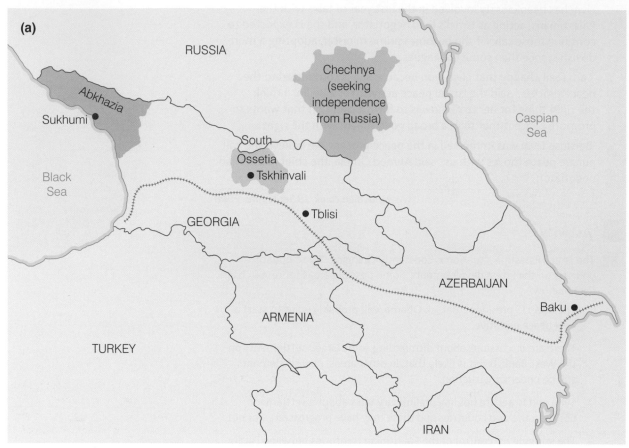

Fig. 6.10 *The Southern Caucasus (a) political; (b) ethnic groups*

You should study the maps here alongside an atlas map of the region. They show that:

■ Georgia lies in a lowland area between the Black Sea and the Caspian Sea.

■ To the east lies Azerbaijan which occupies the rest of the lowland and has access to the Caspian Sea.

■ Georgia is bounded to the north by the Caucasus Mountains (which rise to 5,000 m). The watershed forms a clear physical divide from Russia.

■ To the south lies a highland region that includes Turkey and Armenia.

■ The ethnic composition of the region is complex, with many different linguistic, religious and cultural groups living in close proximity to each other.

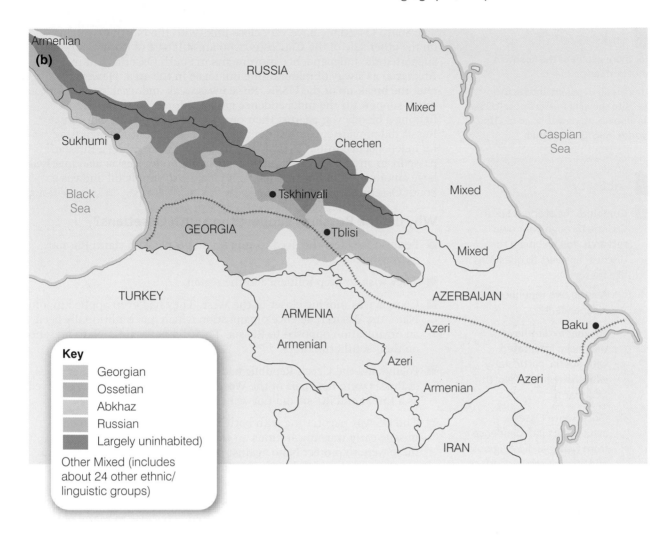

Key
- Georgian
- Ossetian
- Abkhaz
- Russian
- Largely uninhabited)

Other Mixed (includes about 24 other ethnic/ linguistic groups)

- Most of Georgia is occupied by the Georgian **ethnic group**.

- There are also areas occupied by Ossetian peoples in the north/central part of the country in the foothills of the Caucasus and by Abkhaz people in the far west, along the coast of the Black Sea.

- These two ethnic groups mostly live in regions of Georgia called South Ossetia and Abkhazia respectively.

- The Ossetians are linguistically and culturally similar to the Iranians and they speak a language similar to Farsi (the language of Iran).

- The regions of South Ossetia and Abkhazia are also home to some ethnic Georgians.

- The southern border areas of Russia contain a complex mix of different ethnic groups, including Chechens who have been fighting for independence from Russia for the last 20 years or so.

- One of the ethnic groups in southern Russia is also formed of Ossetian people.

From 1998 onwards nationalist groups in South Ossetia started to demand more independence from Georgia. Some wanted full independence and others wanted self-government within Georgia. Militia groups were formed and a civil war broke out from 1991 to 1992. A peace was signed, but tensions remained.

Key terms

Ethnic group: a group that is distinct from the rest of society and identified on the basis of religion, colour, cultural practices and/or national origin.

Did you know?

Until the break-up of the Soviet Union in 1991, Georgia, Azerbaijan and Armenia were all republics in the USSR. During the Soviet period most expressions of nationalist feelings were suppressed, but people (especially in rural areas) had retained their cultural and religious identities and had often continued to hold traditional rivalries with other ethnic groups.

Links

For more details of the Kosovo situation see pp234–6.

There is an excellent, interactive website showing Russia's post-USSR flashpoints at: news.bbc.co.uk/1/hi/world/7596169.stm#map

Activity

3 Complete the story of South Ossetia through your own research. You will need to discover answers to questions like these:

- Are the two republics still independent?

- To what extent have they been integrated with Russia, particularly with the region of North Ossetia?

- Once South Ossetia achieved its independence from Georgia, did religious and ethnic tensions surface which make relations with Russia difficult?

- What is the attitude of the US and Nato to the two republics?

- Have the US and Nato continued to seek alliances with Ukraine or has Russia reasserted its influence there?

- Has Russia used its control over a large proportion of Europe's oil and gas supplies to help it to reassert its influence in the region?

The South Ossetians have very close links with the North Ossetians on the other side of the Caucasus, who are still part of Russia. Russia supported the independence movements in South Ossetia (and in Abkhazia) as a way of maintaining influence in the area. However, after the break-up of the USSR, Russia was weak and unable to provide much support for the independence groups. Moreover, they were fighting a bloody war against their own separatist rebels in Chechnya. Russia did provide encouragement to the rebels to continue agitating for independence from Georgia – for instance, by providing a Russian passport to any South Ossetian who applied for one. Russia also invested large amounts of money in building a pipeline to supply oil and gas to South Ossetia.

Why did the Russians support the South Ossetians?

- Because they feel the need to support all people who claim Russian citizenship.

- They wish to keep influence in the region.

- Georgia was moving closer to the West. They had even applied to join Nato, the Western defence organisation which has traditionally been an organisation opposed to Russia. They did not want a Nato presence on their southern border.

- Poland and the Czech Republic had joined Nato. These former allies of Russia were now part of the Western alliance and so were perceived as a threat and Russia did not want that threat to grow.

- The US was negotiating with both Poland and the Czechs to build missile early warning stations on their territory. The US said that these were to protect Nato against possible missile attack from Iran or other countries in that region. Russia feared that they could also be used to spy on Russia.

- Even more threatening to Russia were the moves by Ukraine to join Nato. Ukraine is a very large country and very close to many of the most populated and industrialised parts of Russia, so this was seen as a great strategic threat.

- Moreover, Russia's Black Sea navy is based in Sevastopol in Ukraine, due to a treaty signed when Ukraine left the USSR. Obviously Russia did not want that threatened.

- Pipelines have been built through Azerbaijan and Georgia to carry Caspian Sea oil and gas to the West. These have great strategic and economic importance and Russia wanted to be close to these links.

Finally, actions by the West in former Yugoslavia influenced a major change in Russian policy. Kosovo used to be part of Serbia, but it sought independence – much as South Ossetia did from Georgia. Russia, a close ally of Serbia, had always supported international laws that respected the integrity of countries within their national borders and pledged to resist breakaway movements.

However, the West supported Kosovo and intervened in Serbia to support the breakaway and to stop Serbia's attempts to preserve its territory. Once Kosovo achieved its independence Russia clearly felt that it was less bound by international law and more able to intervene in South Ossetia.

What happened in the war?

In the 1990s the areas of South Ossetia and Abkhazia had secured a degree of independence within Georgia. Then, in 2004, a new president of Georgia was elected. He made it clear that he intended to bring the two republics back under central control. US advisers started to train the Georgian army in 'anti-terrorist tactics'.

Over the next two years tensions gradually rose with the Georgians trying to reduce Russian influence and assert their own dominance. The South Ossetian militia groups steadily built up their level of armed resistance.

In 2006, two rival elections were held in South Ossetia. To no one's surprise, the region favouring separatism voted for independence. The other region favoured continued links to Georgia.

Posturing and skirmishing increased, with a variety of different forces provoking each other and retaliating. This skirmishing often took the form of attacks by the different ethnic groups on their rivals with the intention of forcing them out of territory – a process often described as 'ethnic cleansing'.

On the eve of the Beijing Olympics (8 August 2008), when the world's attention was elsewhere, Georgia launched a full-scale land and air attack on the breakaway region.

Russia had large detachments of troops close to the border and immediately moved against the Georgians with overwhelming force. They quickly drove the Georgian troops out of South Ossetia and Abkhazia, and continued into neighbouring areas of Georgia itself. Here they destroyed many Georgian military installations before withdrawing a few weeks later under a peace agreement negotiated with representatives from the EU.

What happened next?

Soon afterwards the Russian parliament recognised South Ossetia and Abkhazia as independent states, although few other countries have recognised them.

There was also a lot of ethnic cleansing. Local militia groups drove large numbers of ethnic Georgians out of their homes in South Ossetia while similar processes forced ethnic Ossetians out of Georgia. Amid propaganda from both sides claiming that the militias were supported by uniformed troops, it is difficult to be clear just how organised or extensive such support was.

It is up to you to do your own research to bring the study right up to date.

The challenge of multicultural societies in the UK

In this section you will learn:

■ about the development of multicultural societies in the UK, and about some of the issues that have arisen as a result of those developments.

 **Examiner's tip**

The first definition is the one that you should use for your A Level Geography course. However, you should be aware of the other definitions as you might encounter them in your studies or elsewhere.

'Multiculturalism' and 'multicultural society' can have a variety of meanings, ranging from a simple description to more complex and controversial shades. Here are four definitions that illustrate some of that range.

1 The first describes a multicultural society:
   The status of several different ethnic, racial, religious or cultural groups coexisting in harmony in the same society.

2 The second involves a rather more value-loaded description:
   Multiculturalism refers to a society that recognises values and promotes the contributions of the diverse cultural heritages and ancestries of all the various groups within it.

3 The third has a rather more cynical view of multiculturalism:
   Multiculturalism is a system centred on respect for and the promotion of ethnic diversity in a society. The notion frequently arises that respect for ethnocultural diversity takes precedence over the imperatives of collective integration.

4 And the fourth is very positive:
   Multiculturalism is a state in which an individual has embraced the desire, mastered the knowledge, and developed the skills to feel comfortable and to communicate effectively with people of any culture encountered and in any situation involving groups of people with diverse cultural backgrounds … individuals will have the ability and the desire to acknowledge each person's cultural differences and to celebrate how those differences enrich and strengthen the community in which they both live.

Table 6.2

	Count	Total population %	% of the whole minority ethnic population %
White	54,153,898	92.1	n/a
Mixed	677,117	1.2	14.6
Asian or Asian British			
Indian	1,053,411	1.8	22.7
Pakistani	747,285	1.3	16.1
Bangladeshi	283,063	0.5	6.1
Other Asian	247,664	0.4	5.3
Black or Black British			
Black Caribbean	565,876	1.0	12.2
Black African	485,277	0.8	10.5
Black Other	97,585	0.2	2.1
Chinese	247,403	0.4	5.3
Other	230,615	0.4	5.0
All minority ethnic population	*4,635,296*	*7.9*	*100*
All population	58,789,194	100	n/a

Source: www.statistics.gov.uk

The 2001 census asked people in the UK about their ethnic origin. **Ethnic groups are often self-defining; that is, the members themselves decide whether they belong to the group or not.** The census produced the results shown in Table 6.2.

The census also showed that in Great Britain the minority ethnic population grew by 53 per cent between 1991 and 2001, from 3 million in 1991 to 4.6 million in 2001. (Note this set of data is for GB and not UK because figures for ethnic origin had not been collected for N. Ireland in 1991.)

The commentary on ethnic origins provides some more detail.

London has the highest proportion of people from all minority ethnic groups apart from more who identified themselves as of Pakistani origin, of whom the highest proportion lives in Yorkshire and the Humber (2.9 per cent) and the West Midlands (2.9 per cent).

Two per cent of the population of England and Wales are Indian, with Leicester having the highest proportion (25.7 per cent).

Bangladeshis formed 0.5 per cent of the population of England and Wales, with the highest proportion in the London borough of Tower Hamlets (33.4 per cent).

In England and Wales, 1.1 per cent of people are Black Caribbean, 0.9 per cent are Black African and 0.2 per cent are from Other Black groups.

Black Caribbeans form more than 10 per cent of the population of the London boroughs of Lewisham, Lambeth, Brent and Hackney. Over 10 per cent of Southwark, Newham, Lambeth and Hackney are Black African. More than 2 per cent of people describe themselves as Other Black in Hackney, Lambeth and Lewisham.

Chinese people form more than 2 per cent of the population in Westminster, Cambridge, City of London and Barnet.

The largest proportions of people of Mixed origin are in London, with the exception of Nottingham, where 2 per cent of people are Mixed White and Black Caribbean.

Links

The commentary on ethnic origins can be seen in full at: www.statistics.gov.uk

Did you know?

The census included questions on religion with those on ethnic origin.

At the time the census was carried out, there was an internet campaign that encouraged people, when asked their religion, to answer 'Jedi Knight'. The number of people who claimed to be Jedi was 390,000 (0.7%).

Finding your own data on ethnicity

You can very easily find data on any aspect of the census for your own local area. Use the Neighbourhood Statistics website in the Link.

Links

The Neighbourhood Statistics site is at: www.neighbourhood.statistics.gov.uk

Skills

When you get to the Neighbourhood Statistics site you can obtain a map of the distribution of ethnic groups in your local authority area. The steps below show you how to do this, using the number of ethnic Chinese in London, focusing on Lambeth Borough, as an example.

The site will ask you to enter the details of the area you need. Ask for 'Lambeth' and 'Local Authority'.

From the list of topics you are offered, choose 'Key statistics'.

From the next list of options, choose 'Ethnic group'.

This will give you a table with numbers and percentages for each group. You can print or download the table. Go to the top of the page and click on 'Map this data'.

This will give you a map showing 'All people' in each local authority in London. Click on 'Change variables' and select '% of Chinese'.

You could click on 'Show background' to add some detail about the geography of London.

■ How did the UK's population become multi-ethnic?

Legend – count
- ■ 7,185–71,865
- ■ 71,866–136,546
- ■ 136,547–201,227
- ■ 201,228–265,908
- ■ 265,909–330,587

No. of Divisions ◄ 5 ►

Colour ■ ■ ■ ■

Fig. 6.11 *London – total population by borough, with Lambeth highlighted*

■ Did you know?

In the first decade of the new millennium there has been an increase in the number of people seeking asylum in the UK, due to increased conflict in some areas of the world and easier travel in the globalised world. The main sources of asylum seekers include Iran, Iraq, Somalia, China, Congo and Zimbabwe.

AQA Examiner's tip

For the exam you will be expected to know about recent immigratin into the UK.

The information here is included as background and does not need to be learnt in detail.

Fig. 6.11 *West Indians arriving on the Empire Windrush in 1948*

For hundreds of years there have been small groups of non-white ethnic groups in Britain's cities, mainly in the major ports. Liverpool and Bristol, with their links to the slave trade, have traditionally had a noticeable number of black and mixed-race people and so have parts of London, Glasgow, Newcastle and other ports involved in international trade. Then there was another influx of non-white people during and after the Second World War, when many troops from the colonies fought alongside the British forces; some settled in the UK after the war.

Of course, there had also been some large pockets of white-skinned migrants, most noticeably the Jews from central and western Europe who settled in this country in quite large numbers from the 1880s onwards.

However, at the start of the 1950s there was only a tiny percentage of non-white people living in the UK and they were still concentrated mainly in the inner areas of the largest cities. Many people in rural areas had never seen a non-white person in their lives. Since 1945 there have been several major stages in the migration of people into the country.

On 22 June 1948, the *Empire Windrush* docked at Tilbury in London, delivering hundreds of men from the West Indies. Many had returned to rejoin the RAF. Others had been encouraged to come by adverts offering work. For many people that day marked the start of mass immigration to the UK and the start of the development of a multicultural society.

However, it also caused the start of racial tensions in some areas and at particular times. On the one hand, these men and women had been offered work in a country they had been brought up to revere. On the other, many experienced racial prejudice they had never expected.

For most of the 1950s the main immigrant groups were from the West Indies, but in the late 1950s and early 1960s they were joined by migrants from South Asia: India, Pakistan and Bangladesh.

Legislation allowed people from the Empire and Commonwealth unhindered rights to enter Britain because they carried a British passport.

But, under political pressure, the government legislated three times in less than a decade to make immigration for non-white people harder and harder. By 1972, legislation meant that British passport holders born overseas could only settle in Britain if they (a) had a work permit, and (b) could prove that a parent or grandparent had been born in the UK.

As the government was tightening the entry rules, racial tension meant it had to try to tackle prejudice, and two Race Relations Acts followed.

In 1945, Britain's non-white residents numbered in the low thousands. By 1970 they numbered approximately 1.4 million; a third of these were children born in the UK.

In the 1970s and 1980s the number of new arrivals fell, and most newcomers were wives, children and other relatives, coming to be reunited with their family members who had come to the UK earlier and had now established themselves here.

In the 1990s and 2000s the growth of **asylum seeker** applications contributed to a new increase of immigration to the UK. Between 1998 and 2000, some 45,000 people arrived from Africa, 22,700 from the Indian subcontinent, 25,000 from Asia and almost 12,000 from the Americas. Some 125,000 people were allowed to settle in the UK in 2000.

Then, with the expansion of the EU in 2003, the UK was open to unrestricted migration by citizens of the new EU members in central and eastern Europe. Polish, Hungarian and Czech migrants came in large numbers, although figures for the numbers who came and then stayed or left are unclear and much disputed. However, these people did form a new and quite distinct group. What is more, a significant number of them sought work in rural areas and small towns – and this was often the first time that these areas had experienced large influxes of people with different languages and cultures.

Fifty years after the start of mass immigration to the UK, questions are still being asked about whether or not the UK can become a multi-ethnic society at ease with itself – or whether there is still a long road to be travelled.

Key terms

Asylum seeker: someone who has fled his or her home country to find a safe place elsewhere. Under the 1951 Convention on Refugees, an asylum applicant must be able to demonstrate a well-founded fear of persecution in his or her country of origin for reasons of political opinion, religion, ethnicity, race/nationality, or membership of a particular social group.

Fig. 6.13 *A mosque in a northern industrial town*

Activity

1. Use one or both of the studies mentioned in the Link, or case studies that you have discovered for yourself.

   Find out:

   - where the migrants have come from to settle in the UK

   - why they felt pushed to leave their original home

   - what were the main pulls that attracted them to the UK

   - once they had arrived in the UK, where they settled – and why they chose to settle there (refer both to the town or region where they settled and the particular part of the town in which they settled)

   - what issues they faced as they tried to settle in their new homes (refer to good and bad aspects of their new lives)

   - what issues were faced by the society they lived among (again, refer to good and bad aspects for the society).

   Suggest what the future might hold for the development of a multicultural society in the area that you have studied.

Links

There is a detailed study of Poland, which considers some aspects of Polish migration into the UK, in Chapter 8 of this book.

That section of the book is based on the Advance Information Booklet (AIB) that is provided for the Issue Evaluation exercise. The specimen papers that were published by AQA when this specification was first produced, and the AIB for paper 4B, were based on a study of asylum seekers coming into the UK and settling in Bolton.

Both the specimen papers and the AIB can be used as excellent case studies of migration and the development of multicultural societies – even by students who are not intending to take Paper 4B as an option.

■ Issues associated with multicultural societies

When people move to a new area they often seek familiar people and familiar surroundings. Consider, for instance, how:

■ British migrant workers live in expat communities in the Middle East and do not integrate with local society

■ British communities have developed in Spain, where people have migrated for 'sun, sea and sand' lifestyles

■ British settlers and civil servants in India, in the days of the Raj, settled in close-knit communities where anyone who was considered to have 'gone native' was treated with contempt by their compatriots.

The same process operates with many migrant groups that have settled in the UK. There is a whole range of pressures that encourage people to settle in close-knit communities in particular areas. These include the following:

■ It is comfortable to be near people of the same culture and who speak the same language.

■ Friends from home might help with finding work.

■ They might even provide loans to help set up businesses.

■ It might be possible to rent housing cheaply from other people in the community.

■ Places of worship might be nearby.

■ There are likely to be shops etc. nearby providing goods that you are familiar with and services that you need – such as flights home and money remittance services.

Fig. 6.14 *A fruit and veg stall in London selling a variety of ethnic produce*

■ If the area is an inner-city area

- property will be quite cheap

- jobs in factories, cleaning offices and hotels, working on buses and trains, etc. will be available nearby

- public transport will be more easily available than in the suburbs or rural areas.

■ There might be prejudice that makes it difficult for people of different cultures to spread out and live in the wider community.

These, and other forces, have led to the concentration of immigrant communities in clearly identifiable areas throughout the last 150 years. Examples might include the Jewish community in the East End of London in the 19th century, West Indians in Brixton, Pakistanis in the old mill towns of West Yorkshire, Sikhs in West London near Heathrow and, in the 2000s, African asylum seekers near to the port of Dover and east European agricultural workers in the market towns of East Anglia.

These concentrations of ethnic groups can lead to a number of issues. There are some similarities between the issues facing different communities, but there are a number of common features that affect the communities. You should consider these sensibly and rationally with regard to specific examples that you study.

■ Ethnic communities might become isolated from the society around them and this can lead to mutual hostility between the communities. In the worst cases this can lead to political and religious extremism. (Note that religious and civic groups from both communities often make very strenuous efforts to work together and to reduce the misunderstandings and conflicts.)

■ If it is difficult for people to move out from their communities, for whatever reason, it might be difficult for the members of the community to have full access to education, employment opportunities and housing.

■ Poor immigrant communities often live in close proximity to poor British communities, whose members also often suffer from poor education, employment and housing opportunities. It then becomes quite easy for them to come to think that the immigrant community is responsible for their poor opportunities, leading to open hostility between the communities. This can lead to political extremism developing amongst the white community too.

■ Closed communities often maintain their own language, making it more difficult for their members to take a full part in society. This can be a particular problem for women, as they may be confined to the house and the immediate locality by family commitments and religious and cultural beliefs.

■ Schools in particular neighbourhoods might become dominated by particular ethnic groups. Whatever the quality of education in these schools this can lead to a gulf of understanding and growing suspicions between the young people who do not get to know each other as they might in schools with a mix of ethnic groups.

■ Immigrant groups are often welcomed by their host communities. They can be seen as a positive influence providing much-needed workers, but also having a positive and refreshing impact on diet, music, dress, language, etc. However, from time to time, extreme hostility has developed between immigrants and their host communities and between different groups within the immigrant community. This has shown itself in the form of rioting, persecution, clashes with the police and conflicts between different ethnic groups.

AQA Examiner's tip

The issues surrounding migration and multicultural societies are sensitive and must be approached in a sensible way. Of course, you should feel free to express your own ideas, but **only** do so if you can back them up with clearly verifiable facts. Remember that some of the things printed in some of the newspapers might not be completely reliable. In the past some of the tabloid papers have been known to write in an exaggerated way about issues surrounding immigration, asylum seekers and refugees. Take care that your sources of information are sound, or avoid quoting them in your exam.

Separatism

In this section you will learn:

- how separatism can create stresses that can lead to the loosening of national ties, or even the break-up of countries, with particular reference to the former Yugoslavia and the UK.

Key terms

Separatism: a move, by a minority group or a region within a country, towards greater independence or 'separation' from the country that governs them.

Activity

1 Study Fig. 6.15 and:
   a Describe the physical geography of the former Yugoslavia.
   b Describe the sizes, shapes and location of the countries that have been formed from the break-up of Yugoslavia.
   c Consider whether the new boundaries appear to be related to physical geography.
   d Look at them with an atlas map of south-eastern Europe and consider how the new countries fit in with the wider political geography of the region.
   e Try to decide whether the geographical position of the area has influenced the tendency of the area to break up into a series of separate countries.

In the early years of the 21st century, globalisation seems to be bringing places closer together, to be causing economies throughout the world to become more integrated and to be allowing people, capital, goods and jobs to move more and more easily around the world. At the same time, in Europe there are moves towards greater political integration as the EU has expanded eastwards and has grown from 15 member countries in 2000 to 27 in 2008, and with several more countries in negotiations to join.

However, in some parts of Europe there are also pressures towards **separatism**. For instance, in the 1990s the former Republic of Yugoslavia split into a number of separate, independent countries. The area had a long history of ethnic conflict between Serbs, Croats and Muslims. The term 'Balkanisation' has long been used to describe the tendency of some areas to split up into separate small countries, and it was first used in this area – the Balkans.

Separatism in the Balkans

Yugoslavia was a state that was formed at the end of the First World War and had been ruled by a strong, centralised Communist Party since the end of the Second World War. The country was originally brought together as part of the peace treaties to try to create a reasonably-sized, economically viable, stable state in a region that had been noted for its inter-ethnic rivalries for many centuries. Yugoslavia was composed of six separate republics in a federal structure. Unfortunately, each of the different republics contained a mix of people from each of the different ethnic groups.

Fig. 6.15 *Countries of the former Yugoslavia*

Yugoslavia was ruled by Marshall Tito from 1945 to 1980. When he died, one of the main forces holding the country together was removed and separatist pressures re-emerged. The main pressures for separatism came from:

- ethnic rivalries

- memories of the genocide carried out during the Second World War, by Croats and their German allies, against the Serbs and others who resisted German occupation, and other earlier conflicts

- fear felt by the smaller ethnic groups that the Serbs, the biggest ethnic group, would seek to dominate Yugoslavia if it became a democracy with 'one person one vote'

- the greater fear that Serbian nationalists would try to set up 'Greater Serbia' to include all the land that had any population of Serbs, even where they were in a minority, leading to Serb domination of the area

- the fact that the Serbs had close links with Russia, while Slovenes and Croats had close links with Germany and the Muslims in Bosnia and Kosovo had close links with Albania

- realisation that small states could well be economically viable and successful if they could become part of the EU (Slovenia joined in 2004; Croatia is negotiating to join).

Consequencies of separatism

In 1991 Croatia and Slovenia declared independence from Yugoslavia and, between then and 2008 the country has split into six or seven separate countries. Consequences that have arisen from the separatist pressures and the dissolution of Yugoslavia have included the following:

- Readjustment of state boundaries was attempted, such as when the Serbs of Krienia declared independence from Croatia when they saw that Croatia was planning to withdraw from Yugoslavia.

- Ethnic cleansing took place, as people from each of the separate republics tried to expel those of different ethnic groups and consolidate the territory of the different groups. In some instances the ethnic cleansing led to massacres of rival ethnic groups.

- At various times US, EU or UN troops entered parts of the former Yugoslavia as peacekeepers.

- The worst fighting took place in Bosnia where the population was probably most mixed (with 44 per cent Muslims, 33 per cent Serbs, 18 per cent Croats). The fighting included attempts by minority groups of Serbs and Croats to break away from Bosnia, but escalated as these groups and their supporters tried to claim more and more of the territory. (Sometimes the conflicts were to try to unite small areas that were occupied by people from the same group, by driving out different groups from the intervening areas; sometimes they were attempts to reoccupy land that a group had occupied at some period in the past; sometimes they were just struggles for strategically important positions such as hilltops or mountain passes.) Ethnic cleansing on a large scale took place and UN peacekeepers were often unable to intervene as dreadful atrocities occurred.

- When Kosovo tried to become independent from Serbia (including using guerrilla war tactics) the Serbs reacted with the use of military force. Nato planes, led by the US, then proceeded to bomb Serbia until the government withdrew all its troops from Kosovo.

Links

For further details of the dissolution, and an animated map of the gradual breakup of the country go to: en.wikipedia.org/wiki/Breakup_of_Yugoslavia

■ Links

For more details of the South Ossetia breakaway see pp224–7.

■ Activity

2 As in all sections of the chapter, you should try to find out how things have developed in at least some parts of the former Yugoslavia since 2008.

In particular, it should be interesting to see how the desire of many of the new countries to join the EU has affected their social and economic development.

■ When the West finally recognised an independent Kosovo, Russia, Serbia's ally, was deeply offended and this is often given as one of the reasons for Russia's support for the breakaway of South Ossetia from Georgia.

■ Slovenia is the economic front-runner of the countries that joined the EU in 2004 and was the first new member to adopt the euro on 1 January 2007.

■ Croatian has a stable market economy. The country is preparing for membership in the EU, its most important trading partner.

■ Serbia's economy was severely damaged by war, UN sanctions and Nato bombing during the 1990s. However, since 2000 the economy has been recovering quickly and the country has been called a 'Balkan Tiger' because of its rapid growth rate of around 6.5 per cent. However, there are still severe political tensions between 'modernisers' who look towards EU membership and development of a market economy, and 'Serb Nationalists' who still look towards Russia, favour more central control of the economy and still dream of a Greater Serbia. At present, the modernisers seem to be in the ascendancy.

■ Bosnia is now a federation of two republics – Republic of Serbskja which covers 49 per cent of the country and the Federation of Bosnia and Herzogovina which covers 51 per cent. The country has two main problems: rebuilding a war-shattered economy and reducing its reliance on the armaments industry, which had been concentrated in Bosnia during the period after the Second World War.

■ Separatism in the UK

Compared with problems of separatism in the Balkans and former Yugoslavia, the issues involved in separatism in the UK seem rather less fraught and to have less potential for bloodshed, although there are some very serious issues, nonetheless. Before starting to understand separatism it is necessary to understand just what the UK is.

'UK' stands for the United Kingdom of Great Britain and Northern Ireland. There were four main stages in the evolution of the UK:

■ England has existed as a unified entity since the 10th century; the union between England and Wales, begun in 1284, was formalised in 1536 with an Act of Union.

■ In another Act of Union in 1707, England and Scotland agreed to permanently join to form Great Britain.

■ The union of Great Britain and Ireland was implemented in 1801, with the adoption of the name the United Kingdom of Great Britain and Ireland.

■ The Anglo-Irish treaty of 1921 formalised a partition of Ireland; six northern Irish counties remained part of the United Kingdom as Northern Ireland and the current name of the country, the United Kingdom of Great Britain and Northern Ireland, was adopted in 1927.

The alliance has never been an equal one. Population numbers make it inevitable that, in a democracy, more power will lie with England than with any of the other constituent parts. England makes up about 84 per cent of the total population, Wales around 5 per cent, Scotland roughly 8.5 per cent, and Northern Ireland less than 3 per cent.

Table 6.3

	Population (mid-2006)	Area (km²)
England	50,762,900	129,355
Northern Ireland	1,741,600	14,121
Scotland	5,116,900	78,772
Wales	2,965,900	20,768
United Kingdom	**60,587,300**	**243,016**

The present constitutional situations of the four countries, and the pressures towards greater separatism within them, are very different.

The situation in Scotland

England and Scotland have shared a monarch since 1603 and a parliament since 1707, but in May 1999, Scotland elected its own parliament for the first time in three centuries. The new Scottish legislature was, in part, the result of British Prime Minister Blair's promise to permit **devolution**, the transfer of local powers from London to Edinburgh. However, this promise was made as a result of a growing movement for more self-rule from Scotland itself.

In a referendum in September 1997, 74 per cent of Scots voted in favour of their own parliament, which controls most domestic affairs, including health, education and transportation, and has powers to legislate and raise taxes. Queen Elizabeth opened the new parliament on 2 July 1999.

Labour won the largest number of seats in the first election for the new parliament, but in May 2007 the Scottish National Party (SNP) became the biggest party, with 47 out of 129 seats. The Labour Party won 46 seats. In that election the SNP had promised to hold a referendum on independence at some time before 2012.

Those people who want independence for Scotland have an economic argument, an accountability argument and a cultural argument.

The economic argument used to be that Scotland should own the oil from the wells off its shores and should enjoy the profits from its 'own' resources. However, the profits that might come to an independent Scotland from oil revenues would be more or less balanced by the loss of money that flows into the country from the UK to pay for general services. Now the main economic argument is that, within the EU, Scotland could thrive by specialising in providing goods and services for the whole EU, developing those niche markets that they could fill more efficiently than any other country. Scottish Nationalists compare the economic growth that has been achieved by Ireland, a country of similar size, within the EU. They also compare Scotland with Norway, which, although it is not in the EU, has many features in common with Scotland but, as an independent, oil-producing country, has grown very rapidly over the last 30 years or so.

The new economic argument is based on changes that have happened in the world economy over the last 30 years. This can be attributed to:

- communications becoming so much faster and more efficient
- the global economy becoming more integrated
- the service economy becoming dominant in most developed countries
- the economic arguments in favour of countries needing a population of over 50 million to survive becoming less strong.

> ### Key terms
>
> **Devolution:** the statutory granting of powers from a central government to government at sub-national level, such as a region or state. The powers devolved might be temporary and ultimately reside in central government, so that the state remains united. Devolution can be mainly financial – i.e. giving areas a budget that was formerly administered by central government. However, the power to make legislation relevant to the area might also be granted.

Fig. 6.16 *One of Scotland's many fine traditions*

In the past, countries had to be big enough for economies of scale to work in large-scale heavy industry. The tariffs in place in most countries meant that home markets had to be big enough to support home industries and employment. But as the economy has become more globalised these pressures for economies of scale have been reduced and replaced, to some extent, with a pressure for increased efficiency and adaptability ... and this has strengthened the argument for separatism in Scotland.

The argument based on greater accountability rests on the extent to which a Scottish government could be closer to the people that it represents, so could respond much more quickly and efficiently to their needs.

The cultural argument is rather less clear, mainly because there are clear cultural splits within the country – between a rural, agricultural tradition in the Highlands and an urban, industrial tradition in the Central Lowlands. However, both traditions would probably claim to have stronger community structures with a more inclusive and supportive outlook than in some other parts of the UK.

Below are some extracts from the manifesto of the Scottish National Party (SNP).

The SNP has clear ambitions for Scotland. We have no doubt Scotland can be more successful.

Healthier ... Wealthier ... Safer ... Fairer

Local taxes can be fairer. The SNP will scrap the Council Tax and introduce a fairer system based on ability to pay. Families and individuals on low and middle incomes will on average be between £260 and £350 a year better off. Nine out of ten pensioners will pay less local tax.

Greener

Scotland can be greener. An SNP government will not give the go-ahead for new nuclear power stations. We will invest instead in developing Scotland's extensive renewable energy potential.

Peace and Prosperity

Together we can build a more prosperous nation, a Scotland that is a force for good, a voice for peace in our world. Free to bring Scottish troops home from Iraq ... Free to remove nuclear weapons from Scotland's shores ... Free to invest our oil wealth in a fund for future generations ...

These are some of the best reasons for independence and why the SNP trusts the people of Scotland to decide on independence in a referendum.

Success for Scotland

Scotland has the people, the talent and potential to become one of the big success stories of the 21st-century. We can match the success of independent Norway – according to the UN the best place in the world to live. We can do as well as independent Ireland, now the fourth most prosperous nation on the planet.

With independence Scotland will be free to flourish and grow. We can give our nation a competitive edge.

A more successful Scotland

The 300-year old Union is no longer fit for purpose. It was never designed for the 21st-century world. It is well past its sell-by date and is holding Scotland back.

The SNP believes Scotland and England should be equal nations – friends and partners – both free to make our own choices ...

Would Scotland be allowed to join the EU? The following is an extract from a discussion that appeared on the Times Online website.

File Edit History Bookmarks Print View Window Help

The United Kingdom is an EU member. If Scotland were to secede from the Union, the UK would still exist. The UK would continue as the Union of England, Wales and Northern Ireland and would retain its EU membership. Scotland, on the other hand, would be a new country and would need to apply for EU membership.

It is possible that the EU members will fast-track Scotland's membership and make it a formality. It is also possible, and perhaps likely, that other countries with restive regions, particularly Spain, will not want to create a precedent. Scotland may not be allowed into the EU, or at least not without huge bribes to Spain.

The situation in Wales

In recent years, a resurgence of the Welsh language and culture has demonstrated a stronger national identity among the Welsh, and politically the country has moved towards greater self-government (devolution).

Until 1999, Wales was ruled solely by the UK government and a secretary of state. In the referendum of September 1997, Welsh citizens voted to establish a national assembly. Wales remains part of the UK, and the Secretary of State for Wales and members of parliament from Welsh constituencies continue to have seats in the British Parliament. Unlike Scotland, the Welsh National Assembly is not able to legislate and raise taxes, but the Assembly controls most of Wales's local affairs. This is the closest approach to self-government for Wales for more than 600 years.

Links

The full article and discussion can be read at: www.timesonline.co.uk/

Did you know?

The SNP is not inward-looking. They try to appeal to all sections of the community. As well as being published in English and Gaelic, their manifesto can also be obtained in Urdu and Polish versions.

Links

The SNP manifesto can be read in full at: www.snp.org

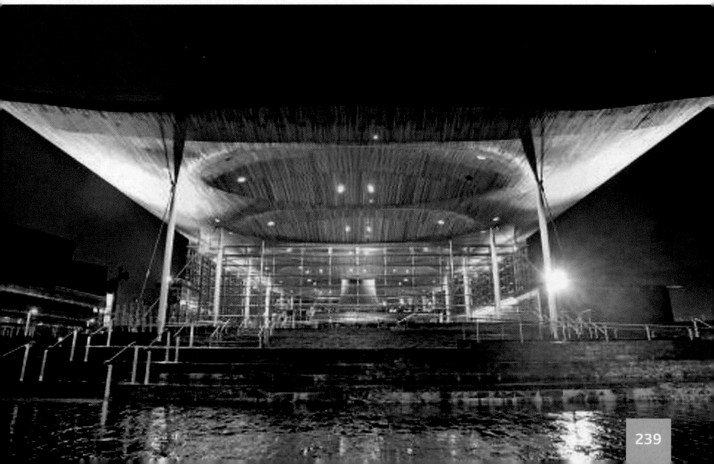

Fig. 6.17 *The Welsh Assembly building*

The population of Wales is little more than half the size of Scotland's and it also lacks any resource base like the oil and gas off the coast of Scotland. Wales also has far less tradition of self-government than there is in Scotland. Like Scotland, though, the separatist pressures come from two quite different communities. In much of north Wales there is still a rural, agricultural community where Welsh is spoken quite widely, as a first language by some. Many people in north Wales support a greater cultural independence for Wales, but there is some fear that any move towards greater independence might see the north dominated by the south of Wales, with its much greater population. Therefore, pressure here is mainly for greater control of local affairs rather than for separation from the UK.

The Welsh language is undergoing some sort of a resurgence in south Wales too, with quite a large number of schools using it as the main language for teaching. However, south Wales has a much more urban, industrial background than the north; and the area has suffered great industrial decline since the peak years of mining and heavy industry in the mid-20th century. This decline has led to frustration with central government in London and a desire for greater local control.

No political party in Wales has, as yet, developed a case for independence as the SNP has done in Scotland. Perhaps this is because Wales is so much smaller than Scotland; perhaps it is because Wales lacks the resources that Scotland has; perhaps it is because the most populated parts of Wales are much closer to the most populated parts of England than is the case in Scotland, and so are more closely integrated; and perhaps it is because there is much less tradition of self-government than in Scotland.

Fig. 6.18 *The two Northern Irish communities used to mark territories with 'gable end' paintings often showing their paramilitaries. This is a more recent, more hopeful effort*

The situation in Northern Ireland

Northern Ireland is an integral part of the UK, but under the terms of the Government of Ireland Act in 1920, it had a semi-autonomous government under a parliament. In 1972, however, after three years of sectarian violence between Protestants and Catholics that resulted in more than 400 dead and thousands injured, Britain suspended the Northern Ireland parliament. The six counties of Northern Ireland were governed directly from London after an unsuccessful attempt to return certain powers to an elected assembly in Belfast.

As a result of the Good Friday Agreement of 1998, a new coalition government was formed in December 1999, with the British government formally transferring governing power to the Northern Irish parliament. The government had to be suspended four times because the UK government insisted that the parliament had to develop a power-sharing agreement between the two different communities.

The historic deal was put into place in May 2007, when Reverend Ian Paisley (of the Democratic Unionist Party, which mainly represents Protestants and supports the union with the UK) and Martin McGuinness (of Sinn Fein – the republican party that mainly represents Catholics and supports moves towards a United Ireland) were sworn in as leader and deputy leader, respectively, of the Northern Ireland Executive Government, thus ending direct rule from London.

Northern Ireland is still a divided society and separatism is one of the issues that exemplifies that division. The 2001 census showed that 43.76 per cent of the population was Catholic and 53.13 per cent was Protestant. Many of the Catholics want Northern Ireland to be separated from the UK and to join with the rest of Ireland, but this would be unthinkable for most of the Protestants. The Protestants describe themselves as 'unionists' precisely because they want to maintain the union with the UK. At present the unionists will go to great lengths to fight any moves towards separatism.

If the Irish Republic continues to prosper within the EU, and as the two economies – North and South – move closer within the EU, and if power sharing starts to build more trust between the two communities, and if Scotland moves towards greater independence, no one knows what the future might hold for Ireland.

The position of England

England has always dominated the UK, but devolution for the other three countries has put it in a strange position. All four countries send MPs to the UK parliament at Westminster. There they can all vote on all matters which affect the UK as a whole: taxation, defence, foreign affairs, etc. They can also vote on the domestic affairs of England: education, health, local government, etc. However, English MPs cannot vote on Scottish and Irish domestic affairs, as those things are decided by the parliaments in Edinburgh and Belfast. (The Welsh Assembly has less power and most of the decisions about their affairs are also taken by the full Westminster parliament.)

At present there is no serious move towards separatism within England, but there have been discussions about a greater degree of regional government within the different regions. Any further moves towards independence from the other countries in the UK might cause moves towards a greater degree of regional self-government to be taken more seriously.

Activities

3 Study Fig. 6.19. It came from a poll carried out for the BBC's *Newsnight* programme. People were asked how long they thought the Union that makes up the UK would last. The results were tabulated separately for people living in England, Scotland and Wales.

Briefly describe the results of the poll shown in the graph.

4 a Make a list of possible advantages for each of the four countries if the UK broke up into four separate countries.

b Make a list of possible disadvantages.

c Which of the four countries would have most to gain from a break-up of the Union? Which has most to lose? Explain your answer.

d How do you predict that the Union will evolve over the next 20 years or so? Justify your answer.

e Suggest why Spain might be opposed to Scotland breaking away from the UK and being allowed to remain in the EU. Refer to separatist pressures from the Basque region and Catalonia in Spain.

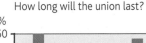

How long will the union last?

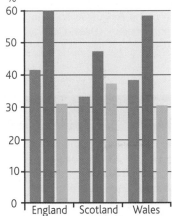

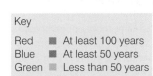

Key

Red ■ At least 100 years
Blue ■ At least 50 years
Green ■ Less than 50 years

Fig. 6.19 *'Separatism' poll results*

Links

You can see the full results of the BBC *Newsnight* poll at: news. bbc.co.uk/1/shared/bsp/hi/ pdfs/16_01_07_union.pdf

The challenge of global poverty

In this section you will learn:

- about the process of development, with reference to the United Nations Millennium Development Goals and to the work of DfID and charitable organisations based in the UK.

Links

Study the global distribution of poverty as shown in the maps at the start of Chapter 5, pp170–71.

Other measures of world poverty are provided in *AQA AS Geography*, pp201–4.

For a case study of difficult climate and soil causing poverty, see the study of the Vungut Gwitchen in Yukon, Canada – *AQA AS Geography*, pp70–6.

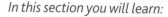 Examiner's tip

In your answers on your exam papers at A2 you have to show 'synopticity'. This means that you have to show awareness of how the different parts of geography are interlinked. This section of the Contemporary Challenge paper seems to offer more opportunities for synopticity than almost any other part of the course. That is why there are so many cross-references to other parts of the course in here. Although it may seem time-consuming to have to keep making these cross-references, you must be aware that it is building up your synoptic understanding, and that is essential for gaining the top marks at A2.

In this section of the specification you are asked to study 'The global distribution of poverty'.

In the option Development and Globalisation there is a section where students must study 'Development – economic … changes associated with development; the development continuum'.

In this book, as part of that option, there is a series of maps in Chapter 5 showing levels of development. The text accompanying those maps discusses ways of classifying development. These maps include measures of gross domestic product (GDP). Low GDP is one of the clearest measures of poverty that there is, so you should refer to that map now, as part of this option. That section also contains a world map showing the Human Development Index. That is a more complicated measurement of development but is equally useful as an indicator of poverty.

Refer back to the maps at the maps at the start of Chapter 5 and complete the activities provided.

What are the causes of poverty?

Many different factors can be given to help explain why poverty occurs in particular places. No single explanation can explain all causes of poverty. Indeed, in almost every example of poverty there are several interlinked causes. Some causes are outlined below but, in any case study of a place that claims to illustrate one of the causes of poverty, there will almost certainly be other causes that also contribute to the problem.

Here, as in many other places in the study of geography, it is useful to classify factors causing poverty into:

- environmental factors
- economic factors
- social and political factors.

Environmental factors causing poverty

Environmental factors that can contribute to the poverty experienced in a region include the following:

- There is a lack of access to fertile land, fresh water, minerals and other natural resources.

- Climate limits what crops and farm animals can be used even when the land is fertile.

- Eroded soil and desertification can often be caused by poor farming, leading to a vicious cycle of exhaustion of soil fertility and decline of agricultural yields and, hence, increased poverty in areas like the Sahel in Africa. Approximately 40 per cent of the world's agricultural land is seriously degraded. In Africa, if current trends of soil degradation continue, the continent might be able to feed just 25 per cent of its population by 2025, according to the UN's Ghana-based Institute for Natural Resources in Africa.

- Deforestation is exemplified by the widespread rural poverty in China that began in the early 20th century and is attributed to non-sustainable tree harvesting.

■ Climate change is already having a huge effect in increasing poverty in many developing countries in Africa and southern Asia. For instance, drought and rainfall unreliability are causing severe problems in many parts of East Africa. Rising sea level and increased river flooding are making poverty worse in the Ganges Delta and on the chars of Bangladesh.

■ Drought and water crisis are causing poverty in many parts of the world. The soil erosion problems in the Sahel, referred to above, are obviously linked to a limited supply of water. So, too, are many of the problems of poverty in Palestine and the limited potential for agricultural development in Israel that were referred to in an earlier section of this chapter.

■ Natural disasters such as earthquakes and tropical storms.

Economic factors causing poverty

Economic factors that contribute to poverty include the following:

■ As of August 2008, increased farming of crops for use in biofuels, along with rising world oil prices, have pushed up the price of grain. Food riots have recently taken place in many countries across the world.

■ Weak formal systems of title to private property are a limit to economic growth and therefore a cause of poverty. When farmers cannot be secure in their rights to the land they are using, they have little incentive to improve it, so yields stay low and poverty increases.

■ Unequal distribution of land is another problem linked to the one above. In many poor countries landownership is concentrated in the hands of the rich, with many of the poor having no land of their own and having to rely on casual employment from the big landowners.

■ Unfair terms of trade, in particular the very high subsidies to, and protective tariffs for, agriculture in the developed world. These increase the prices for the consumers in the developed world; decrease competition and efficiency; prevent exports by more competitive agricultural and other sectors in the developed world; and undermine the very type of industry in which the developing countries do have comparative advantages.

Social and political factors causing poverty

Social and political factors that can cause poverty include the following:

■ Poor access to affordable health care makes individuals less resilient to economic hardship and more vulnerable to poverty.

■ Inadequate nutrition in childhood, itself an effect of poverty, undermines the ability of individuals to develop their full human capabilities and thus makes them more vulnerable to poverty. Lack of essential minerals, such as iodine and iron, can impair brain development. In developing countries it is estimated that 40 per cent of children aged four years and under suffer from anaemia because of insufficient iron in their diets.

■ Some diseases such as HIV/Aids and TB overwhelmingly afflict developing nations, and this perpetuates poverty by diverting individual, community and national health and economic resources from investment and productivity. Further, many tropical nations are affected by parasitic diseases such as malaria that are not present in temperate climates.

AQA Examiner's tip

The second line of this section of the specification states simply 'Causes of poverty'. As the section heading has already referred to 'global poverty' it is safe to assume that this refers to the causes of poverty on a regional or national scale, and not an individual or household scale. Still, to study the causes of poverty on a regional or national scale is a potentially huge task. Here we assume that candidates in the exam can only be expected to know and understand **some** of the causes of poverty – and questions in the exam must be phrased so that any reasonable causes can be given in answers. But note that the specification refers to causes in the plural, so you might be expected to write about more than one – at least two!

Links

For a case study of soil erosion and desertification causing poverty see the study of the Sahel – *AQA AS Geography*, pp145–54. Note that this runs on to a study of how poverty in this area is being addressed.

The possible effects of global warming are discussed on pp39–47 of this book.

The problems of water supply in Palestine and Israel were referred to on pp215–22 in this book.

The effect of earthquakes in causing poverty can be seen on p24 of this book. The effect of tropical storms can be seen on pp60–2.

The issues of land rights in southern India were discussed in *AQA AS Geography*, pp216–8.

The issues of unequal distribution of land were discussed in relation to the Green Revolution in *AQA AS Geography*, pp210–3.

Aspects of world trade in agricultural products were discussed in in *AQA AS Geography*, pp206–9.

There are references to this topic in many places in the chapter on Health issues in *AQA AS Geography*, but in particular see the objectives of the World Health Organisation on p261.

■ Links

HIV/Aids is discussed in detail in *AQA AS Geography*, pp264–9 and p272.

General 'diseases of poverty' are discussed in *AQA AS Geography*, pp279–80.

The links between birth rate and development are discussed in detail in *AQA AS Geography*, pp160–81.

■ Links

The United Nations MDG website is an essential source for the Millennium Development Goals (MDGs). It can be found at: www.un.org

Click on any one of the eight MDGs to go to the page for that goal.

From there you can navigate to the MDG Monitors (to check on progress) or to the Factsheets (which give details about some successful projects and about things that still need to be done.

From the Monitor pages you can go to the interactive maps, which show progress towards achieving some of the targets.

You can also click on any of the targets on the Monitor pages and you will be directed to the relevant part of the latest UN MDG Report. This is a very well-produced document with good statistics and case studies.

■ Key terms

G7: the group of seven richest industrial nations, including the US, Canada, Japan and the biggest EU countries. Russia is included in some of their meetings, forming the G8.

■ A lack of democracy in poor countries seems to make the problems of poverty worse. A paper from the Institute of Social Analysis in Canada stated:

> poor democracies typically enjoy life expectancies that are nine years longer than poor autocracies. Opportunities of finishing secondary school are 40 per cent higher and infant mortality rates are 25 per cent lower. Agricultural yields are about 25 per cent higher, on average, in poor democracies than in poor autocracies – an important fact, given that 70 per cent of the population in poor countries is often rural-based … poor democracies don't spend any more on their health and education sectors as a percentage of GDP than do poor autocracies, nor do they get higher levels of foreign assistance. They simply manage the resources that they have more effectively.

■ Weak rule of law can discourage investment and thus perpetuate poverty.

■ Poor management of resource revenues can mean that, rather than lifting countries out of poverty, revenues from such activities as oil production or gold mining can actually lead to a widening gap between rich and poor and no real advances for the poor.

■ Poor access to affordable education traps individuals and countries in cycles of poverty.

■ Overpopulation and lack of access to birth control methods can slow development.

■ Historical factors, for example, imperialism, colonialism and post-communism have had a big influence on poverty in many parts of the world.

■ War, including civil war, is a major cause of poverty.

■ Addressing poverty on a global scale

In 2000 the UN signed the Millennium Declaration. This contained eight goals (with 21 targets contained within the goals) to be achieved by 2015.

1 Eradicate **extreme poverty** and hunger

2 Achieve **universal primary education**

3 Promote **gender equality** and empower women

4 Reduce **child mortality**

5 Improve **maternal health**

6 Combat HIV/Aids, malaria, and other **diseases**

7 Ensure **environmental sustainability**

8 Develop a **global partnership for development**.

Progress towards reaching the goals has been uneven. Some countries have achieved many of the goals while others are not on track to realise any.

To accelerate progress towards the MDGs, the richest nations met as the **G7** in 2005 and agreed to provide enough funds to cancel an additional US$40–55 billion in debt owed by the poorest nations. This would allow impoverished countries to rechannel the resources saved from the forgiven debt to improving health and education and alleviating poverty.

Any country with annual per capita income of US$380 or less qualifies for immediate debt cancellation, as long as certain conditions are met as to the way the resources saved should be spent on the MDGs.

Although much progress has been made in reducing the debts of the poorest countries, it is quite clear that the richest nations have not all kept to their pledges made at the Gleneagles G7 summit in 2005. The UK government has been at the forefront of attempts to make sure that the commitments are met, but the global financial crisis of 2008 has made the achievement of the MDG targets even more difficult.

■ Other development initiatives

As well as the work of the United Nations and the G7, there are many other initiatives to help the development of the poorest countries. These include **multinational aid** and **bilateral aid** projects, as well as projects funded and managed by non-governmental organisations (NGOs) such as Oxfam and ActionAid.

Several development initiatives have been described in other parts of this and AS book. These include the following:

- An example of multinational development work is International Health Partnerships (IHP), in which a group of developed countries and NGOs has joined with a group of poor countries to make health aid work more efficiently. It aims to coordinate the initiatives of the donor countries and help the receiver countries plan their healthcare delivery systems better.

- Bilateral aid from the UK to Bangladesh is one of DfID's most important development priorities. The UK expects to spend £114 million on aid to Bangladesh in 2008/9. The UK's long-term goal is for Bangladesh to be a stable, prosperous and moderate Muslim majority democracy, playing a positive role in the global community.

- ActionAid is one of the leading development charities in the UK. They do not employ many European workers in the countries that they help. Rather, they try to work through partner agencies in those countries. They feel that local people know best what is needed, and that they can usually communicate better with the people who are being helped to help themselves. So you will see that the study referred to here concentrates on the work of ActionAid India and on small-scale, self-help schemes in Bangladesh.

■ Conclusion

One of the biggest issues in all development work can be summed up as being: 'No development without security and no security without development.' At the completion of the work on the campaign against global poverty it might be useful to examine this phrase and consider how important it is.

Development is about more than making poor countries richer. As the MDGs show, it is also about distributing wealth among all members of the population so that the quality of life of everyone in the society improves.

This means that education and health, particularly infant health, are improved, and one of the surest ways of improving education and health is by involving women in the development process. Also, development has to be sustainable. It is a waste of money and effort to improve conditions for people today if those improvements are at the expense of the environment that will need to support them in the years to come.

Key terms

Multinational aid: development funding that is sent from several countries, usually to a group of poor countries. It is usually channelled through an organisation such as the UN or the World Bank.

Bilateral aid: money sent from the government of one rich country directly to another poorer country. Most of the UK's bilateral aid is sent through the Department for International Development (DfID).

Links

The IHP is described in *AQA AS Geography*, p282.

DfID's work in Bangladesh, and Bangladesh's own efforts at development are described in this book, in Chapter 5, on Development and globalisation, pp195–9.

Action Aid schemes are described in *AQA AS Geography*, pp216–9.

Security might be taken as meaning the kind of security provided by the law and by a stable, well-governed and well-policed society. That kind of security is essential before people can be able and willing to invest in building for future prosperity. There must be security from war and from general lawlessness if people are to develop for the future. If that kind of security is not available then people are too concerned with day-to-day protection of themselves, their families and their homes to think about long-term development.

But **security** also means food security (see *AQA AS Geography*, pp206–7), security in the knowledge that time and money invested in education will lead to improved life chances later on, and security in the knowledge that health care will be available.

For instance, it is a well-known fact that one sign of the start of the development process is a fall in the birth rate (see *AQA AS Geography*, pp160–64). It seems as though people go on having large numbers of children as long as they are insecure and cannot be sure that all their babies are likely to survive. They have to have large numbers to try to ensure some kind of security in their old age. Then, once the development process gets under way, people feel secure that fewer births will lead to an improved lifestyle for the whole family.

However, if development cannot come without people feeling secure, it is equally true that real security cannot come without development.

There cannot be any long-term security for people who do not own any land and who cannot be sure that they will be able to grow enough crops or earn enough money to see them through the year; or for people who live in constant fear of losing everything in a natural disaster; or for people who cannot rely on having their children inoculated against common childhood killer diseases; or for people who do not think that it is worth sending their children to school because they cannot be sure that the school will be able to provide teachers or other resources.

In this chapter you will have learnt:

- about the geographical basis of some conflicts and about the way that geographers can think about ways of resolving those conflicts

- about conflicts over local resources and about the role of planning in resolving or managing such conflicts

- how geographical factors lie at the basis of many international conflicts, and how those geographical factors need to be considered in any attempts to resolve those conflicts

- that the UK is a multicultural society, about how and why that society developed, and about some of the challenges presented by the presence of people from different ethnic groups living in close proximity

- about the growth of separatism in certain parts of the world, and about some consequences and potential consequences of separatist pressures

- about the challenge of global poverty and about attempts by the UN, DfID and other organisations to address the challenge of poverty.

Activity

1 Produce a concept diagram, with the key phrase 'No development without security and no security without development' at its centre. Then add links to show how that concept is linked to all the other ideas and case studies in this section of the chapter, and to many other ideas from your full A Level course.

7 Paper 4A: Geography fieldwork investigation

In this section you will learn:

- techniques that can be used in carrying out your own fieldwork enquiry, including:
  - *planning the enquiry*
  - *collecting data*
  - *presenting data*
  - *analysing data*
- how some of the techniques used in enquiry might be tested in the second part of the Paper 4A exam
- that some of these techniques could be used in other parts of the course and in parts of Paper 4B of the exam.

There are two parts to the 4A examination:

- **Section A** involves questions about a fieldwork-based investigation that you have carried out during your A Level Geography course. You will have to write about a situation that is familiar to you and for which you have prepared carefully.

- **Section B** involves questions that assess your skills by asking you to apply those skills in unfamiliar contexts. For instance, you might be asked to perform tasks involving presentation and/or analysis of data presented to you in the exam paper.

The first part of this chapter suggests some of the ways that you can approach your fieldwork investigation, although it does not try to guide you through all the different stages of specific enquiries. Rather, it suggests some general principles that you might follow and puts forward some alternative approaches. However, there is such a huge variety of potential enquiries that we have to leave it up to you, the student, working closely with your teacher, to choose your topic and to plan your investigation in the way that best suits your circumstances.

The second part tries to guide you through a variety of techniques that you could use in your investigations but that might also be tested in Section B of the exam paper.

Candidates who enter for Paper 4A must be aware that, in the second part of the exam, they could be tested on any of the techniques listed on p16 of the specification and described in this chapter.

Candidates who enter for Paper 4B might also be asked to use one or more of the techniques described here. They will normally be asked to apply the techniques to data provided in the Advance Information Booklet.

Carrying out your own fieldwork investigation

Planning

There might well be questions on the exam paper that ask you to show a detailed understanding of the whole process of planning the investigation. Some students might choose to carry out an individual investigation which they plan on their own with only a minimum of advice from the teacher. Others, probably the majority, will carry out an investigation where the data are collected as a group and then the write-up is completed individually.

The investigations that involve group collection of data are likely to have a much higher degree of teacher input into the planning process, but it is **essential** that all students have an input into the planning process and are fully aware of all the stages of the process.

The planning for an A2 fieldwork investigation should move on some way beyond what was done at AS, and especially beyond what was done at GCSE.

In particular, you need to make sure that your investigation is closely linked to and arises out of the ideas and concepts that you have been studying in class. You need to know how you are going to test those ideas, to extend them, to apply them in new and unfamiliar situations and to try to increase your understanding of them. You must not regard your investigation as an end in itself, but as a way of deepening your understanding of ideas from your course.

Investigations must have a clear aim linked to an aspect of the course. They should focus closely on one of:

- discussion of an argument about a topic in the specification
- examination of a problem in an area
- testing of a **hypothesis** or an assertion
- analysis of a geographical issue.

Many students who followed the old AQA specifications completed very successful investigations that were based on hypothesis testing. They tested ideas such as the following:

- As you move from a town centre towards the edge of town, on a still evening, the temperature falls.
- The density of vegetation increases as you move inland from the coast across an area of sand dunes.
- The quality of housing in 'Town A' improves as you move away from the town centre towards the suburbs.
- People who live in 'Town B' are concerned about the issue of the development of a new shopping centre, but it worries older people more than younger people.

Each of these hypotheses has produced interesting accounts of fieldwork. Each has allowed students to describe techniques for collecting data, presenting them and then analysing them; and each has allowed some basic conclusions to be drawn. However, many students have then found it rather difficult to explain how their work added to their geographical understanding.

Key terms

Hypothesis: a tentative conjecture explaining an observation, phenomenon or scientific problem that can be tested by further observation, investigation and/or experimentation.

It has often seemed that they have tested something that the textbook says is true, and then found out that yes, the textbook is correct – or more or less correct. So when students are asked what they have learned from the experience, they have only been able to repeat or paraphrase ideas from the textbook. Testing such rather obvious hypotheses sometimes leaves the students without any real 'ownership' of the results. They tested obvious ideas and came up with obvious results.

At this point it is worth quoting a sentence from the Introduction to the course, on page 5 of the specification. This states:

> The subject content follows an issues and impacts approach throughout.

If this is one of the most important aspects of the course, it follows that many good investigations are likely to consider this same approach. When planning an investigation students and teachers should, wherever possible, use an issue in geography as a starting point. Then, at the conclusion of the investigation, they should be quite clear what the investigation shows about the geographical causes of the issue, the impacts of the issue on the people and/or the environment in the area that has been studied and, possibly, of ways that the issue could be better managed in future.

Note, though, that some good investigations do not start from an issue. There is nothing in the specification that says issues are the only starting point for investigations. However, examination of an issue does often leave a candidate able to write very interesting final parts to their studies – and to gain good marks for doing so. Some successful issue-based investigations are outlined below.

■ Examples of issue-based investigations

1 The fog patch

A group of students was studying Chapter 2: Weather and climate and associated hazards. They were aware that one road in their district suffered from patches of fog forming in hollows on some mornings, particularly in autumn and early winter. This became an issue because people who had to travel into college along that route often arrived late on those foggy days.

They decided to test the hypothesis that fog patches were more likely to form during periods when the area was affected by anticyclonic weather conditions. They knew that they could follow this up by trying to suggest why the fog formed along *that* stretch of road, during *those* weather conditions. Once they realised what the nature of the problem was, they realised that they could do little to manage it but they could try to predict when the foggy conditions were likely to occur and to plan their journeys to take account of the predicted conditions.

The students realised that, throughout their investigation, they would be able to link observations/geographical theory/specific place conditions/an issue in their own lives.

2 The abandoned tennis court

In the grounds of a school, there was an area of old tennis courts. One court had been abandoned about 10 years earlier and the geography and science departments had kept data on the way that vegetation recolonised the old surface of the court. Now a second court was about to be abandoned and there were proposals to turn both old courts into a garden area with seating for sixth-form students.

The students put forward a counter-proposal to continue the study of the original area and to extend it to include the newly abandoned court. They wanted to compare the biodiversity on the two old courts and to compare it with the biodiversity on an area of managed garden nearby.

The study involved collection of data on present conditions and comparison with the data collected over the past 10 years. They hoped that their results could be used to help guide the final decision on how the area should be managed in future.

The students realised that throughout their investigation they would be linking their work to their knowledge and understanding of different aspects of the 'Ecosystem issues on a local scale' topic.

3 The new retail development

A new retail centre had been built in the catchment area of a school. The new area was to contain shops and services including PC World, Comet, TK Maxx, Matalan, Mcdonald's and JJB Sports. The students had the initial idea of studying how the new centre affected the traditional high street nearby. However, on discussing the matter further they realised that they had not collected data before the new development opened, so they would have no way of working out how the high street had changed once the new development opened, and this limited anything they could do about change to the high street.

Instead, they developed their idea to look at the impact of the new development on the local population. They carried out surveys of shoppers in the new centre to find out where they came from and how often they visited the new centre and the old one. Then they carried out a separate survey, calling at homes within a 2-km radius of the new centre to find out what proportion of local people had been affected. Students could then draw maps that showed the extent of the new centre's influence and the intensity of its influence on the local area.

Finally the students carried out targeted interviews with shopkeepers on the old high street to assess the extent to which they perceived their business had been affected by the new centre.

The study tied in with the section of the specification that stated students should study 'the development of urban centres – impacts and responses ...' They felt they were well able to measure the impact of the centre on the people and they were able to assess some aspects of its impact on the local shops. The centre had not been there long enough to assess what the responses were, but the students were able to make some sensible suggestions about what responses might be in future, basing this on what had happened in other areas where new retail centres had developed.

4 The one-way scheme in the area around the primary school

One group of students based their investigation on the issue raised by a group of parents with children at a local primary school. These parents were concerned with the issues around the safety of their children as they arrived at and left the school. The space around the school was severely limited and a conflict had arisen over how this space could best be managed. The parents had proposed that a one-way system should be put in place in the streets near the school. This would reduce incidents of traffic blockages as parents delivered their children, tried to park and both obstructed and were obstructed by other cars on the road. The frequent obstructions led to safety issues for both cyclists and pedestrians, as well as wasting motorists' time.

Some local people objected to a road scheme that would inconvenience them for 24 hours a day and might reduce a problem that affected parents and children for two periods of about 30 minutes per day and only during term time.

The students carried out measurements of traffic flow at different times of the day. They also developed a way of measuring delays that occurred, and counted the number of 'incidents of danger and potential danger' during the periods when children were arriving and leaving. They also carried out questionnaires and interviews with a variety of interested parties.

Later they observed the meeting called by the ward councillors to discuss the issue and submitted the data that they had collected as evidence for the council. This meant that, as well as studying the issue, they could study and participate in the process that operated to resolve the conflict.

Once you have chosen an issue, research question or hypothesis that forms the basis of the enquiry, you need to plan how you will carry out your research. Bear in mind **three** key concerns at this planning stage:

1 Your study must be coherent and complete. It must move smoothly through data collection, data processing and presentation, data analysis to final conclusions. It should provide you with a geography learning experience leading to increased knowledge and understanding.

2 You should experience a variety of techniques during your study, but you must ensure that it provides you with at least one quite clear example of each of:

- a data collection technique

- a data presentation technique

- a data analysis technique

that you know and understand well enough and in sufficient detail to write up in the exam in a clear and logical fashion. These techniques should be neither so simple that they leave you little to say, nor so complex that you lose the point or cannot finish your answers in the time allowed. Think of them as your 'bankers' that you know you can write about well in the exam.

3 When you have used your techniques to collect, present and analyse the data, you must be able to use your skills of interpretation, drawing conclusions and evaluating both your conclusions and your enquiry process as a whole.

AQA Examiner's tip

All students must also remember to be involved in planning for health and safety while carrying out their fieldwork. In addition to the obvious reasons for this, you should also remember that there might be questions on this topic in the exam. These are unlikely to be high-mark questions, but it is important to be prepared even for the 2- or 4-mark questions that might come up.

Collecting data

The outcome of any enquiry depends on the quality of the data collected, so it is essential that you collect data that are as accurate and as complete as possible. The data must also be relevant for the enquiry that is being undertaken, so it is very important to be focused and not to collect data just for the sake of it. It is also important to be aware of data that have been collected already and are available for use. If such secondary data are available and of good quality, it is not good practice to try to collect the same data again. You should always be prepared to use secondary data in your enquiries, as well as collecting your own primary data.

All data collection operates within a number of constraints, particularly:

- the area that has been selected for study
- the time that is available for data collection.

Given these constraints it is almost always necessary to sample data in order to make an enquiry manageable. The essence of sampling lies in the idea that there is a whole mass of information available on any topic, and this is known as the **parent population**. It ought to be possible to **sample** this population to select a **statistical population** which represents the characteristics of the parent population. This sample, if well chosen, should allow generalisations to be made which apply to the whole parent population.

Sampling methods

The three main types of sampling are called:

- random sampling
- systematic sampling
- stratified sampling.

Each of these is outlined below. Another kind of sampling is 'opportunity sampling', which often plays quite a big part in the selection of a sample.

Random sampling

In a random sample each item in the parent population must have an equal chance of being selected for the sample. This means avoiding bias in the selection.

A random sample can be selected by allocating a number to each member of the parent population and then selecting the statistical sample by using numbers from a random number table or from a computer program that generates random numbers. (If you do not have access to either of these, you can use a telephone directory and use the **last two** numbers of each phone number on a page chosen at random.)

Then the random numbers can be used to choose a sample:

- from a list, such as the electoral roll from which names can be chosen for interview
- by point sampling from a map, such as selecting grid references from an OS map
- by line sampling – drawing a line across a map, between coordinates chosen at random, and then selecting points along that line, again using random numbers

- by area sampling – dividing the whole area (the parent population) into sections – such as grid squares – and then choosing some grid squares by using random numbers.

Systematic sampling

A systematic sample is a way of saving time when compared with a completely random sample. Rather than choosing each individual or point to be sampled, a regular pattern is used. For instance, every fourth house in the street could be chosen, or the pebble directly under the sampler's toe as she walks along the beach, or every grid intersection on an OS map.

When used sensibly, a systematic sample can be just as effective as a random sample and it is quicker, easier and more convenient to carry out. In fact, it can be more accurate than a random sample, because it avoids the remote possibility that the random sample selects too many examples from one part of the distribution. Be careful, though. Imagine a systematic line sample across part of New York City. It could just be drawn along the gridiron road pattern so that all the points selected are covered in tarmac and the sample suggests that there are no homes, shops, services or industry.

Stratified sampling

Stratified sampling can be used when there are significant groups of known size within the parent population. The sample is then selected to make sure that each group is fairly represented. That fair representation **ought** to happen with a random or systematic sample. The stratified sample ensures that it does.

For instance, you might know that 50 per cent of the land in an area is under wheat and 50 per cent is under grass. If the enquiry is to discover how slope, geology and soil type influence choice of land use, you might decide that half the points selected should be under wheat and half should be under grass. A random sample ought to produce this result or at least come very close to it; a stratified sample can ensure that it does.

Students sometimes claim that they are using a stratified sample when this is not true. For example, someone interviewing passers-by might say that they have interviewed an equal number of men and women and equal numbers of young, middle-aged and old people. This is not a stratified sample unless the student knew that the size of the groups in the sample was in the same proportion as the representation of those groups in the population as a whole.

■ Opportunity sampling

All students carrying out fieldwork should, ideally, choose their sample by using one or other of the rational ways of selection that have been described above. Unfortunately, students on A Level geography courses are often more or less forced to choose particular sections of the parent population to sample because they are the only ones available.

For instance, students carrying out a river survey might be well aware that they ought to carry out measurements of the river at intervals of, say, 1 km along the length from source to mouth, i.e. a systematic sample. However, they also have to take into account:

- ease of access
- safety in gaining access to the sample site, as well as safety while carrying out measurements
- legal aspects, including rights of way.

Did you know?

Bias can be introduced into selecting people for interview. For instance:

- the interviewer might approach only friendly-looking people who look as though they will be helpful
- the interviewer might stand outside a fitness centre and so get a sample biased towards the young and active who have enough money to pay the gym membership fees
- some people will refuse to answer because they are in a hurry, selecting out a particular type of person
- the interviewer might be particularly attractive to members of the opposite sex and unwittingly draw those people to be interviewed.

Within these constraints and limitations, samples should still be chosen with as little bias as possible. For instance, having been forced to a particular stretch of stream that is accessible, safe and manageable, it should still be possible to use some element of random or systematic sampling into the choice of the actual measuring site.

■ Size of sample

The size of a sample should always be big enough to be:

■ as reliable as possible

■ suitable for the presentation and analysis techniques that you intend to use later

■ small enough to be manageable in the time that is available for both collection and analysis.

For a simple questionnaire survey, say into shopping habits in a town, a sample of 20 people would generally be considered too small; 50 would be quite acceptable; 100 would be very satisfactory; more than that would probably not be necessary.

For a study of a river, to try to prove a relationship between speed of flow and channel cross-sectional area, the data might well be analysed using the **Spearman Rank Correlation Test**. This technique is generally not thought to be reliable with fewer than seven pairs of data (although some textbooks suggest that more pairs are needed). So at least seven locations need to be studied, with at least 12 being preferable – if that is practical within the constraints of time, safety, etc.

Some more advanced textbooks describe how the statistical significance of a sample can be calculated. You are not likely to be expected to do that for your AQA A2 exam.

■ Data collection techniques

This book is too short to present a full list of the collection techniques that might be used in enquiries for the specification. These are dealt with in many other books elsewhere. However, two aspects of data collection that have proved very useful in work produced for enquiries presented for previous specifications are outlined and discussed here. The lessons that these examples illustrate might well be useful in a wider range of studies.

The pre-test

Drawing up the questions for a questionnaire survey is a difficult task. Questioners have to be aware of avoiding bias, avoiding leading the subject to give particular answers, ensuring that the questions are clear enough so that they are not misunderstood, and so on. They must also consider how they want the answers to be given. Do they ask 'open' questions that can be answered at length, which will give lots of information but which might lead to difficulties in recording and processing that information? Or do they ask 'closed' questions, possibly choosing one of several optional answers, which will limit the interviewees' scope for answering but which will make recording, standardising and processing the results much easier and possibly more accurate?

Although this is difficult, it is important that you draw up your own questionnaires and do not rely on one produced by your teacher. This will give you much greater ownership of the work and will increase your understanding of the whole process, and so it should improve your exam answers.

But can you be expected to get your questionnaires right first time? Maybe you will, but maybe you won't! So this is where the pre-test comes in useful. In this full process:

1 Students discuss what information they need to collect.

2 They discuss the most efficient way of obtaining this information from interviewees.

3 The questions are drawn up, discussed and revised if necessary.

4 The draft questionnaire is taken out and used in a small number of interviews, with clear notes being taken of which questions were clearly understood and which, if any, were not. This pre-test should be carried out in conditions as close to the real test as possible.

5 Results are analysed to check whether the answers are producing the necessary data in a form that is easily manageable.

6 The questionnaire is modified, where necessary, to make it easier for interviewees to answer and easier for students to use the final data.

7 The full test is carried out.

Using two methods to collect the same data

Some students have access to lots of very sophisticated equipment to carry out their data collection. Others have to improvise. Which are the lucky ones?

Many examiners think that the best answers come from those students who have used two different techniques and then compared the two sets of results to check the accuracy of the methods.

For instance, many students carry out river surveys. Some have flow meters to measure the speed of the river's flow; others have to resort to measuring the time taken for a float to travel 10m and then work out the river's speed from this. Both methods produce results that are suitable to analyse, especially if the students ensure that the measurements are carried out in the same way at each measuring station downstream.

However, there might well be a question in the exam that asks students to describe one method used to collect data, and to explain the measures taken to ensure that an accurate method was used and fair data were produced. Again, either method could be used to answer the question, although the student who used the more time-consuming 'float' method might be able to write in more detail about the method.

Some of the best answers to this type of question come from students who have been able to try out both methods. They have used them both, at the same time, to measure the speed of one stretch of river. Then they have compared the results from the two methods and:

■ if they have produced very similar results, it can be assumed that both techniques are fairly reliable

■ if the results differ, but one method consistently produces figures that show a faster (or slower) flow, then an attempt can be made to adjust the figures to improve consistency

■ if the results differ but without showing any consistent pattern, this casts real doubt on the accuracy of one or both methods.

Exam answers that are able to discuss the accuracy of the techniques by reference to two comparable sets of data are usually good and often score very high marks.

AQA Examiner's tip

Do not be upset if your draft questionnaire does not work perfectly. In fact you should be quite pleased, because this means that you can make changes to improve it – doing this will give you something more to discuss in your exam answers, especially if you are asked about how you ensured that your data collection was as accurate and useful as possible.

AQA Examiner's tip

Discussions about accuracy that can be based on comparing data sets, as suggested here, are more interesting to a geography examiner than discussions about the reasons why either dog biscuits, balls of aluminium foil or small oranges make the best floats for timing the speed of a river's flow.

Presenting data

Examiner's tip

Examiners set questions on three distinct sets of fieldwork enquiry skills. These are:

- data collection
- data presentation
- data analysis.

Every year a significant proportion of exam candidates get mixed up and write about collection when asked about presentation, about presentation when asked about analysis, and so on.

This happens to top-level candidates and borderline candidates alike. Exam nerves and stress affect all types of candidate in odd and unexpected ways. However, **you** must be absolutely clear in your mind about the differences between the three types of question; then you must check very carefully what you are being asked to do and stick to that task. No one is satisfied when marks are lost because of simple misreading or misunderstanding of the question.

Data that have been collected through fieldwork, or from secondary sources, must be presented well for two reasons:

- to allow the data to be seen and read clearly
- to prepare the data for analysis.

Analysis flows directly from the presentation and is linked very closely to it, but it is essential that you are very clear in your understanding of the distinctions between presentation and analysis.

Data presentation can be divided into two sections:

- cartographic skills (presenting data on maps)
- graphical skills (presenting data in graphs and diagrams).

On p16 of the specification there are lists of the presentational skills that you need to be able to use. When you are doing your own enquiries in preparation for the exam you will probably choose to use some of the skills listed, but you will not be expected to use all of them. However, in Section B of the exam, where candidates are asked to use their skills in unfamiliar situations, you could be asked about any of the skills listed here, so you need to be familiar with most of them. Note that although candidates might be asked about them, some of the skills on the list are only ever likely to be used in presenting fieldwork enquiries – such as using base maps, sketch maps and detailed town-centre plans. In addition, weather maps have been included in the list because they are essential for one of the A2 option choices. Students who have not studied that option are not likely to be expected to have studied weather maps.

The main skills that you need to be able to complete are described below. There is a discussion of some of the occasions when each skill is likely to be used. There is more detail of how they might be tested in Section B of the exam in the later part of this chapter – pp276–84.

Cartographic skills

Maps with located symbols

These maps might be used for showing the size of the biggest towns in a region. Bars, circles, etc. are drawn to a scale that shows the comparative sizes of the towns. Then the symbols are placed on the map to show the positions of those towns.

Located symbol maps are used to show a limited number of points or areas. They should not be used for showing the spread of distribution of a particular phenomenon throughout an area. For this a choropleth, isoline or dot map would be used (see below).

Proportional bars are easier to draw and read than proportional circles, but if there is a large range in size between the largest and smallest totals to be shown, proportional circles are a more efficient and neater way of showing the range.

Activity

1 Use the data for the world's biggest cities on p184 of *AQA AS Geography*.

  a Mark the locations of those cities on an outline map of the world. (For this exercise you could limit yourself to the top 10, or to those with over 10 million people.)

  b Draw either proportional bars or proportional circles to represent those cities. Place each symbol as close to the city's location as possible.

  c Add a scale and key to your map.

Links

There are instructions on how to draw pie charts on p224 of *AQA AS Geography*.

Sometimes located symbols can be used to show more complex data sets. For instance, proportional divided circles can be drawn in position on a map. The map below shows the proportions of the workforce engaged in primary, secondary and tertiary jobs in selected countries of the world.

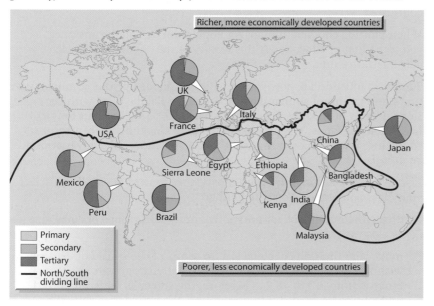

Fig. 7.1

The best way to produce such a map is to draw the pie charts on separate sheets of paper and then to cut them out and put them on the map. Move them around to make sure that they are in the best, clearest positions before you stick any of them in place.

Maps showing movement

These maps show movement by using **flow lines**, or **desire lines** or **trip lines**.

A flow line map shows the movement of people, vehicles, etc. along certain routes. The size of the flow at points along the routes is shown by the thickness of the lines used. As more traffic joins the route the flow line gets thicker. As traffic leaves the route the flow line gets thinner.

The ideal situation in which to use such a map would be when a class has counted traffic moving into a town centre along a number of different routes over a period of, say, 5 or 15 minutes.

A desire line map shows the strength of desire to move from particular areas to a point (or points) on the map. The number of movements from the area to the destination is shown by lines of proportional thickness. However, they differ from flow maps in that they do not show movement along particular routes. They generalise the movement, showing the number of people travelling from each part of the catchment area of a central point.

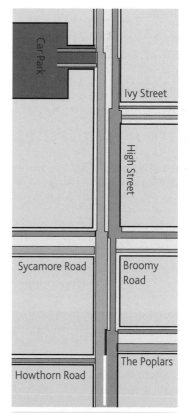

Vehicles passing during 5 min count
1mm = 5 vehicles
Pink and brown lines show opposite flows of traffic

Fig. 7.2 *Flow map of traffic on the High Street from 0850 to 0855 hours*

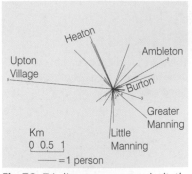

Fig. 7.3 *Trip line map: my party invitations*

Activity

2 Divide this set of administrative units into five groups. Use each of the methods suggested opposite.

Discuss the advantages and disadvantages of each method.

HIGHEST DENSITY	
	48.2 persons/ha
	45.1
	36.7
	35.0
	34.9
	33.2
	23.5
	18.5
	16.3
	12.8
	6.3
	5.4
	4.7
	4.3
	4.1
	3.6
LOWEST DENSITY	3.3 persons/ha

AQA Examiner's tip

While this is a very useful technique, the choropleth map can be misleading because:

■ the choice of divisions is somewhat arbitrary;

■ the whole of each area is shaded in the same way and this might be seen as implying that the population density is identical throughout that area and that the density then changes abruptly at the border of the region.

Trip line maps are the simplest of this group of maps. In a trip line map each journey has to be marked from a starting point to a central point. They are typically used to show the catchment areas of shops or schools. Fig. 7.3 shows the trip line map a student drew to show the homes of the people who were coming to his 18th birthday party.

Maps showing distributions

Distributions can be shown by using choropleth maps, isoline maps or dot maps.

Choropleth maps show spatial distributions, using shadings of different densities to represent different densities of population or different percentages of land under a particular crop, etc.

Choropleth maps do not show total values of the distribution that they are representing; they do show which areas have similar densities and which have very different densities; they allow areas to be compared and contrasted.

When plotting choropleth maps, of population density for instance, you must first of all work out the density of the population in each administrative unit.

Then you must decide how you are going to divide up your administrative units into groups of similar density, which will all be filled with the same density of shading. It is usually desirable to show about four to five different groups. With more groups than this the map can become confusing. With fewer the map does not really show enough variation to be useful.

List all your values in order from most dense to least dense. Then select your class boundaries. You could either:

■ divide the number of administrative units into groups of equal size (or as close as possible)

■ make your divisions of equal size in terms of the spread of densities within the group. (For instance, in the Activity opposite the total range is from 3.3 to 48.2. Therefore, the spread is 44.9. So, if the units are to be divided into five groups, the boundaries should be drawn so that each group includes a range of about 9 persons/ha)

■ draw the divisions at places in the list where there seems to be an obvious break between administrative units.

When you shade a choropleth map you should indicate high and low densities by your choice of the shading system. Common systems are:

■ using line shading, with thicker lines or lines closer together to indicate higher densities, and thinner lines or lines further apart to indicate low densities

■ using dots, with a denser coverage for high-density populations and sparser density of dots for low population densities

■ using colours, with dark shades (e.g. dark brown) for high densities and light shades (e.g. yellow) for low densities.

It is also considered good practice to avoid leaving any areas unshaded – unless they actually have no population at all.

Isoline maps. An isoline is a line that joins places with an equal value for the chosen variable. The isoline map that geography students are most familiar with is the contour map. The contour lines are a particular type of isoline. They join together places at the same height.

Other less familiar isolines include:

- isobars, which join places of equal pressure

- isotherms, which join places of equal temperature

- isohyets, which join places of equal rainfall.

Isolines could also be used to join the parts of a town that have equal flows of pedestrians or equal values of land, to join the areas of an ice cap which have equal thicknesses of ice, and so on.

Usually, when isolines are drawn, the cartographer does not have data for every point on the map. Rather, data have been collected from a sample of points within the area of the map. Unfortunately, the data that are collected are often in an inconvenient form. Suppose someone was mapping the rainfall in an area during a storm. Data were available from a number of recording stations, and when the raw data were plotted on a map they gave the results shown in Fig. 7.4.

The cartographer might decide to draw lines to represent 5, 10, 15, 20 and 25 mm of rainfall during the 24-hour period.

In some places the lines can be drawn straight through places at that value. In other places they have to be 'interpolated', or drawn between two known points to represent the probable point where the line being plotted might be assumed to occur.

Note that isolines can never cross each other. Each point on the map can only have one value and if two isolines cross that implies that the point where they cross has two values.

Also note that when isolines are drawn close together they represent a steep gradient in the values that are being plotted; when they are drawn far apart they represent a gentle gradient.

Dot maps represent spatial distributions by using dots of equal size. Each dot can be used to represent one example of the phenomenon being mapped, or it can represent a number of examples. For example, a dot map showing the catchment area of a school class could indicate each individual's home with a single dot. A dot map to show the distribution of the whole school's population might be too crowded if every individual was represented with a dot, so each dot could represent something like 5 or 10 students, depending on the scale chosen.

One problem with drawing a dot map is knowing where to put the dots within an area. For instance, imagine that a cartographer was drawing a dot map to represent the number of sheep in the different parts of a county. Figures are available for 10 different administrative units:

Area	Total sheep
1	523
2	895
3	97
4	1,234
5	2,583
6	3,428
7	1,243
8	987
9	325
10	83

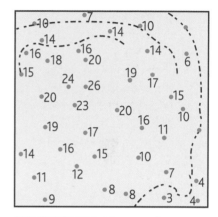

Key

•12   Rainfall recording stations with figures (in mm) for rainfull during the storm

- - -   Isohyets (to be completed by the student)

Fig. 7.4 *Isohyet map*

The cartographer decides that one dot will represent 100 sheep; so the first task is to round the number of sheep up or down, so Area 1's flock will be represented by five dots, Area 2's by nine dots, and so on.

Then these dots have to be placed within the borders of that area on the map. The cartographer can:

1 try to distribute the dots to represent the actual distribution of sheep, but this is only possible if there is sufficient information to make this method valid; ideally this method should be used because it is more realistic and does not imply abrupt changes in density at borders that might have nothing to do with the distribution of sheep on the ground

2 distribute the dots in a random way, but this might be misleading, suggesting concentrations in areas where none exist, and vice versa

3 distribute the dots evenly throughout each area; this is less satisfactory than method 1, but if there is not enough information available it has less potential to mislead than method 2.

Note that if method 1 can be used, the dot map shows a more realistic distribution than a choropleth map, without the abrupt changes at the borders that can confuse the users of choropleth maps. However, method 3 suffers from the same problems as choropleth maps.

Dot maps do have the advantage that they show actual numbers (allowing for some rounding up or down) and so the actual totals represented can be worked out by adding up the dots. This cannot be done with a choropleth map as it represents densities rather than totals.

■ Graphical skills

Bar graphs and line graphs

All geographers are familiar with climate graphs. Two examples are shown in Fig. 7.5.

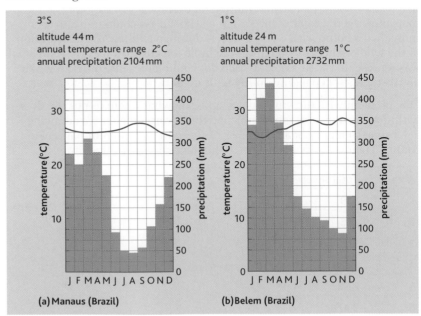

Fig. 7.5 *Two examples of bar and line graphs*

Temperature is shown as a simple line graph at the top of each diagram. The temperature scale is shown down the left side of the graph.

Precipitation is shown as a bar graph at the bottom of each diagram. The precipitation scale is shown down the right side of the graph. Note that the precipitation scale always starts at 0 mm and goes as high as is needed.

The bar graph has been used to show precipitation because rainfall data is measured over a certain period and needs to be shown as a total; so the total for each month is shown as a separate, self-contained bar.

The line graph has been used for temperature because temperature is usually measured at a point in the day and then averaged out over the month. The average for Saskatoon in April is 4 °C and the average in May is 10 °C. These points are marked in the middle of each month and then joined with a line, and this line suggests that the average temperature changes steadily between those two months. From this it can be assumed that the average temperature on 30 April/1 May is 7 °C, as shown on the graph.

There are several different types of line graphs that can be used in geographical enquiries.

Simple line graphs are drawn to show a single series of data, like the rainfall graphs in Fig. 7.5.

Comparative line graphs show two or more sets of data on the same graph. The lines are drawn using the same scales on the x-axis and the y-axis. (See Fig. 7.6(a).)

Compound line graphs are drawn with several different components as in Figure 7.6(b). There, the first line was drawn to show the contribution of coal to the UK's energy mix during 1971–2005. The second line shows the contribution of oil added to that for coal. The total for oil (shaded yellow) can be calculated by subtracting coal (shaded grey) from coal + oil.

In 2005:   coal = 45 mtoe

coal + oil = 120 mtoe

oil = 120 – 45 = 75 mtoe

The whole graph shows that over the period the total energy used has stayed fairly stable, rising very gradually since 1984. However, there has been a big fall in coal's contribution, a big rise in gas's contribution and smaller changes in the other forms of energy.

Activity

3 Would you use a bar graph or a line graph to show:

- the total population in a country on 1 January each year, for 10 years?

- the number of pebbles in a sample that had been divided into categories by diameter (<10 mm, 10–19, 20–29, etc.)?

- total oil production in each of 10 countries during a period of a year?

- oil production for one country, when data are available for average monthly production over an 18-month period?

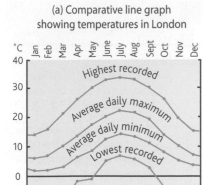

(a) Comparative line graph showing temperatures in London

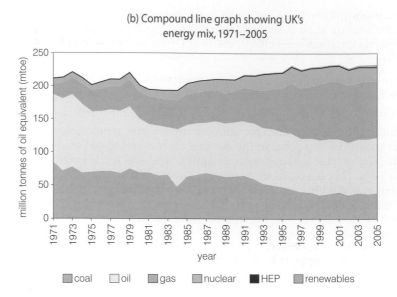

(b) Compound line graph showing UK's energy mix, 1971–2005

■ coal   □ oil   ▨ gas   ▨ nuclear   ■ HEP   ▨ renewables

Fig. 7.6

Divergent line graphs are used when one set of data is provided for part of the period under consideration and then this data set is split into separate components for another part of the period.

There is a similar variety of bar graphs that can be used in geographical enquiries.

Simple bar graphs show a single series of data like the temperature graphs in Fig. 7.5.

Comparative bar graphs show two or more sets of data. The columns for each division along the x-axis are drawn side by side.

Compound bar graphs show how the total in any one bar is divided up between a number of subtotals (see Fig. 7.7).

Divergent bar graphs might start as simple bar graphs but then become compound bar graphs when subtotals become available.

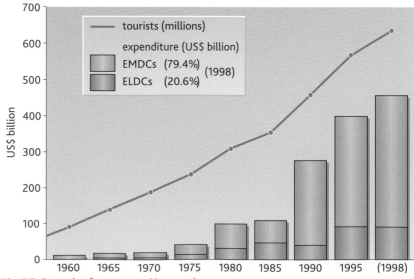

Fig. 7.7 *Example of a compound bar graph*

Scatter graphs

Scatter graphs show the nature of the relationship, if any exists, between two sets of variables. They are designed to show:

■ positive relationships, where as one variable increases so does the other one

■ negative relationships, where as one variable increases the other one decreases

■ no relationship, where there is no pattern and the points seem to be distributed more or less at random.

If a relationship is shown by the graph, it is also possible to see whether the relationship is a strong or a weak one. This can be demonstrated by drawing a line of best fit through the centre of the distribution of the points. If most of the points on the graph are close to the line, the relationship is strong; if they are not, the relationship is weak. These judgements are subjective, so if a relationship is suspected it is often useful to carry out a Spearman rank correlation test on the same data, as this can give a more precise expression of the strength and reliability of any relationship (see p270).

Note that a scatter graph is a way of presenting information, but it is also a way of analysing data. Of course, all graphs can be used for analysis, by visual examination of the information that is presented, but as soon as a best-fit line is drawn on a scatter graph, the graph is allowing analysis on which conclusions can be based.

Pie charts and proportional circles

Pie charts are used for showing how a total is divided up into separate components, just like a pie divided up into separate slices. Each sector of the circle represents one of the components, and the size of each sector shows what proportion that component contributes to the whole.

Proportional circles are used when the size of two totals is being compared. Then the area of the circle represents the total, with bigger circles representing bigger totals.

Proportional circles can also be divided into pie charts.

In the diagrams in Fig. 7.8, the sizes of the circles are drawn to represent the total energy supply in the UK, the amounts produced in the UK and the amounts imported, respectively. The area of the first circle is approximately equal to the sum of the areas of the other two circles. (It is not exact because some energy was imported and stored rather than used.)

Each circle has been divided into sectors to show the proportion of the total made up by each different energy source. Normally, pie charts begin with the largest category and work through to the smallest. In Fig 7.8 (a) and (b), the order represents use of energy resources clockwise through time in the UK.

Links

Full instructions for drawing scatter graphs can be found in *AQA AS Geography*, pp159–60.

AQA Examiner's tip

A scatter graph may be an analytical technique, but if you are asked to 'describe one analytical technique' this might not be the best one to use. There is more to say about a Spearman test, so reasonably well-prepared exam candidates will probably be able to access more marks if they describe Spearman rather than describing scatter graphs.

Links

More detail about Fig. 7.8 can be found in *AQA AS Geography*, p232 (Fig. 7.1).

Full details of how to draw pie charts are given in *AQA AS Geography*, p224.

Examples of compound pie charts are shown in *AQA AS Geography*, p202.

AQA Examiner's tip

Proportional circles and pie charts can be drawn by hand or can be produced using a computer package. If you are producing a coursework enquiry it is usually sensible to use the computer package. However, in an exam you might be asked how you would produce a pie chart. If you plan to write about the use of that package you **must** be able to write about it in enough detail to gain all the marks available.
'I entered the data into package X and then pressed a key and it printed it out', will not score a good mark.

In fact, it might be safer to know how to draw the diagram yourself, just so that you have plenty to write about if such a question comes up in the exam.

(a) Primary energy supply

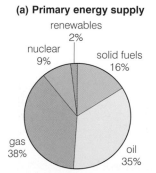

renewables 2%
nuclear 9%
solid fuels 16%
gas 38%
oil 35%

(b) Domestic production

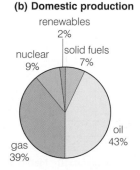

renewables 2%
nuclear 9%
solid fuels 7%
gas 39%
oil 43%

(c) Net imports

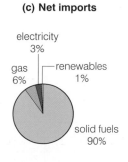

electricity 3%
gas 6%
renewables 1%
solid fuels 90%

Fig. 7.8 *UK energy, 2004*

Triangular graphs

A triangular graph is really a scatter graph that shows three sets of variables and allows the user to see how those variables are interrelated.

It can be used for plotting any data from a fieldwork study where total figures for several different places have been collected, along with the percentage contributions to those totals of three different variables.

They are often used for plotting:

■ employment structures, when employment is divided into primary, secondary and tertiary sectors;

■ soil structure when the percentages of sand, silt and clay particles are given.

A worked example of a triangular graph is shown on p281.

Kite diagrams

Kite diagrams are usually plotted to describe the distribution of different species along a transect line. In geography they are most often used to show the different species across a dune transect. It is common to draw them along with a transect showing the height and gradient of the surface.

The 'kites' represent the presence or absence of individual species along the line of transect, measured using a quadrat. The thickness of the kite shows the number or percentage of each species at each survey point. Each kite is drawn along a central line, with the thickness of the kite balanced equally above and below the line. They can be drawn to represent:

■ the number of each species, as in Fig. 7.9(a)

■ the percentage surface cover of each species, as in Fig. 7.9(b)

■ using the ACFOR scale, as a simplified way of showing the estimated percentage surface cover of species where:

    – A = abundant (≥ to 30 per cent)

    – C = common (20–29 per cent)

    – F = frequent (10–19 per cent)

    – O = occasional (5–9 per cent)

    – R = rare (1–4 per cent)

These types of plots – the kite and the cross section – can be interpreted together to reveal relationships between the organisms and the physical character of the surface. The dune system can be divided into its different zones and the characteristic species for each zone can then be identified. Explanations can then be attempted for any interrelationships between the species or between the species and the surface characteristics.

(a)

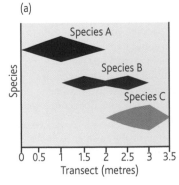

Fig. 7.9 *Ground cover of three species (in %) across a dune transect*

(b)

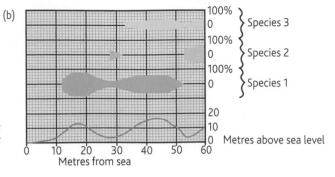

Radial diagrams

Radial diagrams use 'polar coordinate' graph paper, an example of which is shown in Fig. 7.10.

They can be used to show:

■ **orientations** as given by the points on a compass; diagrams like this are often used for showing the orientation of particles in glacial deposits, so that the direction of ice flow can be worked out (see Link opposite); they are also used in glaciation studies to show the orientation of corries.

■ **continuous cycles**, such as daily or annual progressions (see Fig. 7.10).

Logarithmic scale graphs

Logarithmic graphs have been described in some detail in *AQA AS Geography*, pp167–68.

They are used in two main sets of circumstances:

■ when a very large range of data must be shown and when those data would make an arithmetic graph difficult to draw and unclear to read

■ when an arithmetic graph would result in a parabolic relationship but when a log graph would show a much clearer straight-line relationship.

In Fig. 7.11(a), semi-logarithmic graph paper had been used to show the changes in the size of the populations of various continents. Had the data been shown as an arithmetic graph they would have looked like Fig. 7.11(b). What is most interesting about the semi-logarithmic graph is that it shows that the *rate* of increase of population in most continents is declining, although

Links

The use of polar coordinate graph paper to show the orientation of particles of rock in a deposit of glacial till is shown in *AQA AS Geography*, pp60–1.

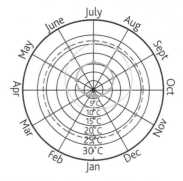

Fig. 7.10 *A circular graph illustrating temperature regimes*

Links

You can obtain free, print-your-own, polar graph paper at: www.printfreegraphpaper.com/ and www.waterproof-paper.com/graph-paper/polar-graph-paper.pdf

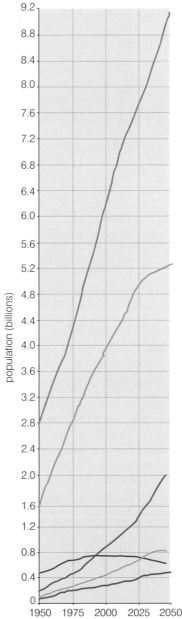

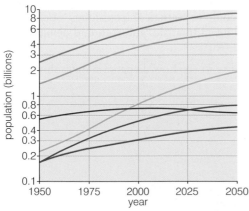

Fig. 7.11(a) *A semi-logarithmic graph*

Fig. 7.11(b) *An arithmetic graph*

Key
World — Europe
Asia — Latin America and the Caribbean
Africa — North America

the total is still increasing. This declining rate is not as apparent on the arithmetic graph.

Fully logarithmic graph paper or log-log paper, with logarithmic scales on both axes is often used to show the relationship between the area of a drainage basin and the length of the stream in that basin. It is also used for showing how the rank-size rule applies when studying the number and size of cities in a country or region. Again, this has the effect of transforming a parabolic curve on an arithmetic graph into a straight line on the log-log graph. It helps to make the relationship between rank and size clearer, as shown in Fig. 7.12.

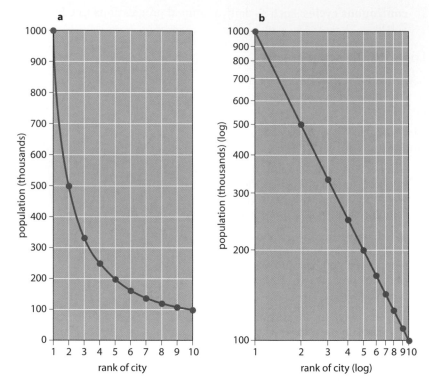

Fig. 7.12

Dispersion diagrams

Dispersion diagrams are sometimes called 'box and whisker plots'. They are used to show the spread of a number of values around the mean value. They enable a comparison of the spread and/or bunching of data. They are often used as a prelude to statistical techniques, such as calculation of median, upper and lower quartile, and standard deviation, which are all explained on pp268–75.

Work through the following exercise to see how dispersion diagrams are drawn and used.

Activity

4 The table below shows data for average monthly rainfall for a station in the tropics, over two periods of 15 months each. The data were collected to see whether rainfall variability was affecting agricultural yields.

	1981/2	2001/2
Jan	3	9
Feb	7	14
Mar	13	26
Apr	38	45
May	107	93
Jun	132	118
Jul	75	87
Aug	25	43
Sep	65	48
Oct	78	70
Nov	23	30
Dec	12	21
Jan	8	12
Feb	7	14
Mar	4	10

a The mean for 1981/2 has been calculated as (the sum of all the values) divided by (the total number of values), or:
$597 \div 15 = 39.8$
Calculate the mean value for 2001/2.

b The figures for 1981/2 have been plotted on a dispersion diagram (Fig. 7.13). Make a copy of this diagram and plot the figures for 2001/2 in the adjacent spaces.

c The median value for 1981/2 has been calculated by working out which value is equidistant between the top and the bottom values. Calculate the median value for 2001/2.

d The range for 1981/2 has been calculated by subtracting the lowest value from the highest value, or: $132 - 3 = 129$. Calculate the range for 2001/2.

e The interquartile range is a more useful measure of dispersion. It has been calculated for 1981/2 by:

Upper quartile (UQ) = $\frac{n = 15}{4}$ th position
= 4th position
= 75

Lower quartile (LQ) = $\frac{3(n + 1)}{4}$ th position
= 12th position
= 7

Interquartile range (IQR) = UQ − LQ = 75 − 7 = 68

f The positions of the median, UQ and LQ have been plotted on the dispersion diagram. Complete this for 2001/2.

g Compare the distribution of rainfall for the two periods, 1981/2 and 2001/2.

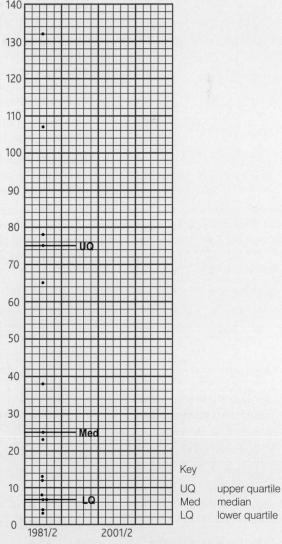

Key
UQ   upper quartile
Med median
LQ   lower quartile

Fig. 7.13

Statistical skills

Measures of central tendency

One of the most useful ways of analysing any set of geographical data is to calculate the 'average'. Ideally this should be calculated from all the data that are available within the range. It should also be 'typical' of the data and represent something near the midpoint of the data. This is important because it will probably be used to compare against the average of other sets of data. There are three types of average that are commonly used by geographers. These are the mean, the median and the mode.

The **mean** is probably the most useful measure. In fact, it is often referred to as 'the average' in everyday usage.

The mean (often written as x̄) is calculated by adding together the sum total of all the values (Σx) and dividing this by the total number of values, or the frequency (n). The formula is written as $\bar{x} = \frac{\Sigma x}{n}$.

The median is the middle value of a set of values when that set is arranged in order of size. To calculate the median find the $\frac{n+1}{2}$ th value of the set. If there is an odd number of values in the set it is obvious which is the middle value. If there is an even number of values the median will work out as a fraction, ending in .5. Therefore, it will lie midway between the values above that value and below it.

The **mode** is the most common value in the set. It can be thought of as the most popular or fashionable value.

If a set of values has a normal distribution (or a symmetrical distribution), as shown in Fig. 7.14a, the mean, median and mode will be at the same place.

If the distribution is skewed, as in Fig. 7.14b, the mode will still be at the point of the highest frequency. However, the median and mean will lie to the right of the mode on this graph. This is because more values have been added to the distribution and these are of a value higher than the mode.

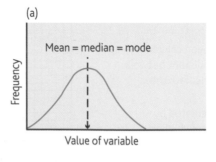
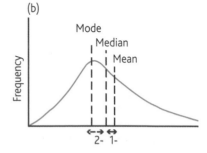

Fig. 7.14 *Normal distributions: (a) symmetrical; (b) skewed*

Activity

1 Calculate the median values in these three sets of numbers.

a 1 2 2 2 3 5 7 7 8 9

b 2 2 2 3 6 7 7 8 9

c 1 2 2 5 6 6 8 9 9 9

2 Calculate the modal values for each of the three sets of data in Activity 5.

Note: the answers to the calculations of the medians and the modes are printed on p269.

Measures of dispersion – interquartile range and standard deviation

The calculation of interquartile range has been explained above, in the section on dispersion diagrams (p267). However, it is often useful to take this procedure one stage further and to calculate the standard deviation. This actually describes the average amount by which the values in a data set vary from the mean for that set. It indicates the amount of clustering around the mean. Showing how much the values are clustered allows the analysis of data to be taken much further than simply measuring the central tendency.

In a normal distribution:

- 68% of the values lie within $\pm$ 1 standard deviation (1SD) of the mean
- 95% of the values lie within 2SD of the mean
- 99% of the values lie within 3SD of the mean.

The calculation appears complex. However, it is not difficult if simple rules are followed carefully and methodically.

1 Calculate the mean ($\bar{x}$) for the set of data. (See column **1** below.)

2 Subtract the mean from each value in turn ($x - \bar{x}$). The minus signs must be recorded here, although the process of squaring at the next stage will eliminate the minus values. (See column **2** below.)

3 Square the result $(x - \bar{x})^2$. (See column **3** below.)

4 Calculate the sum of the $(x - \bar{x})^2$, given as $\sum(x - \bar{x})^2$

5 Divide that number by the number of variables (n) =, given as $\dfrac{\sum(x - \bar{x})^2}{n}$.

6 Calculate the square root of that figure. $\sqrt{\dfrac{\sum(x - \bar{x})^2}{n}}$.

A low SD indicates a **more** clustered distribution. A higher SD indicates a more spread-out or dispersed distribution.

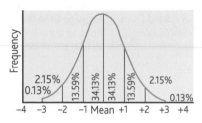

Fig. 7.15 *Standard deviations within a normal distribution*

Answers

1 **a** It is the 5.5th number, so midway between 3 and 5, so equal to 4, even though 4 does not occur in the list.

b It is 6, because this is the middle number in the sequence.

c It is 6. The calculation gives a value midway between the 5th and 6th numbers in the sequence, but as these are both equal to 6, the answer must also be 6.

2 The modal values are:
a 2   b 2   c 9

Activity

3 In the following tables the figures from Activity 4 on p267 have been used.

In the first table the SD for rainfall from 1981/2 has been calculated.

Use the data in the second table to calculate the SD for the data from 2001/2.

For 1981/2:

$\sum x = 597$

$\bar{x} = 39.8$

$\sum(x - \bar{x})^2 = 24\,144.4$

$\dfrac{\sum(x - \bar{x})^2}{n} = 1609.6267$

$\sqrt{\dfrac{\sum(x - \bar{x})^2}{n}} = 40.12$

Using the information from these calculations, is it possible to add anything to the conclusions that you drew from the dispersion diagrams drawn in the earlier exercise?

	1981/2	$x - \bar{x}$	$(x - \bar{x})^2$	2001/2	$x - \bar{x}$	$(x - \bar{x})^2$
Jan	3	−36.8	1354.24	9		
Feb	7	−32.8	1075.84	14		
Mar	13	−26.8	718.24	26		
Apr	38	−1.8	3.24	45		
May	107	67.2	4515.84	93		
Jun	132	92.2	8500.84	118		
Jul	75	35.2	1239.04	87		
Aug	25	−14.8	219.04	43		
Sep	65	25.2	635.04	48		
Oct	78	38.2	1459.24	70		
Nov	23	−16.8	282.24	30		
Dec	12	−27.8	772.84	21		
Jan	8	−31.8	1011.24	12		
Feb	7	−32.8	1075.84	14		
Mar	4	−35.8	1281.64	10		

Distance from source (km)	Average time for float to travel 10 m (s)
1.2	18.8
1.7	15.2
2.2	14.4
2.8	15.2
3.5	13.0
4.0	13.6
4.7	12.0
5.6	6.2
6.7	9.2

■ Key terms

Null hypothesis (Ho): a statistician's term that states that there is no relationship between two variables.

Alternative hypothesis: the statistician's term given to the geographical idea that you are hoping to find is correct. It is possible to accept the alternative hypothesis when the null hypothesis has been disproved.

Examiner's tip

In the null hypothesis it is always best to start with 'There is no relationship …' Sometimes exam candidates make the mistake of stating a null hypothesis that is the opposite of the alternative hypothesis, but, 'As distance from the source increases, the river slows down' would be **wrong**!

■ Links

An interesting explanation of the null hypothesis may be found at: www.null-hypothesis.co.uk/science//item/what_is_a_null_hypothesis

■ Spearman's rank correlation test

The Spearman's rank correlation test involves comparing two sets of data to see whether and how they are related. It is used to compare the ranks rather than the actual values of the data. In geography coursework it is often used after the data have been displayed on a scatter graph. If the scatter graph suggests that there is a correlation, the Spearman test can be carried out to test the strength of that relationship. The test also shows whether the relationship is statistically significant or if it is quite likely that the correlation has just occurred by chance. For instance, the technique might be used to test whether there is a significant relationship between:

■ distance downstream and the speed of flow of a river

■ slope of land and depth of soil

■ distance from the centre of the CBD and number of pedestrians passing

■ GNP of countries and their birth rates, etc.

For instance, a group of students was planning a study of a stream. They thought that the flow rate of the stream would increase with increased distance from the source. They collected data from nine points along the course of the stream. To do this they timed how long it took for a float to travel a distance of 10 m. They measured the time of the float three times and worked out an average at each point. Their results are given in the table on the left.

Setting the hypothesis and null hypothesis

The hypothesis that the students were trying to prove was: 'As the distance from the source of the stream increases, the speed of the river's flow will also increase.'

However, when doing statistical tests such as Spearman, it is important to state a **null hypothesis**. Statistically it is more reliable to disprove a null hypothesis than to prove the **alternative hypothesis**.

So, in this case, the null hypothesis would be: 'There is no relationship between distance from the source and the time of the float of the stream.'

Ranking the values

In the Spearman test it is ranked values that are compared, not the actual figures that were collected. So the first task is to put the figures in a table and rank both sets of variables. The two sets of ranks are known as R1 and R2.

Distance from source (km)	R1	Average time for float to travel 10m (s)	R2*	R1 – R2 (D)	D²
1.2	1	18.8	1	0	0
1.7	2	15.2	2.5**	–0.5	0.25
2.2	3	14.4	4	–1	1
2.8	4	15.2	2.5	1.5	2.25
3.5	5	13.0	6	–1	1
4.0	6	13.6	5	1	1
4.7	7	12.0	7	0	0
5.6	8	6.2	9	–1	1
6.7	9	9.2	8	1	1
					$\sum D^2 = 7.5$

Note that the high values were ranked at the top because these are the slowest speeds.

**There are two tied values at 15.2 seconds. In a ranking table these would occupy the 2nd and 3rd positions so these positions are averaged out to give 2.5. (Note that if there had been three values all tied they would have occupied 2nd, 3rd and 4th positions and this would have averaged out to give 3.)*

Finding the difference, squaring the differences and summing the squares

Now you need to find the differences between the two ranks by subtracting R2 from R1 to give D. The minus signs must be recorded in the D column, although the process of squaring the differences will eliminate the minus values.

Square the differences, making sure that the results are tabulated in clear columns with tens under tens, units under units and decimal points under decimal points.

Sum the D² values. The symbol $\sum D^2$ means 'sum of the D² values'.

Substituting in the formula

The formula for calculating the Spearman coefficient is

$$1 - \frac{6(\sum D)^2}{n^3 - n}$$

(where n is the number of pairs of data).

So in this example the substitution gives

$$1 - \frac{6 \times 7.5}{9^3 - 9} = 1 - \frac{6 \times 7.5}{729 - 9}$$
$$= 1 - \frac{45}{720}$$
$$= 1 - 0.0625$$
$$Rs = \mathbf{0.938}$$

Interpreting Rs

It is possible to tell several things from the Rs value that has been reached:

1   There is a positive correlation between the distance from the source of the stream and the speed of flow. As one increases so does the other.

If the result had been negative you could have concluded the opposite – that as one value increased the other decreased. For a fuller explanation of this see the references to interpreting a scatter graph on p263.

The rank correlation coefficient

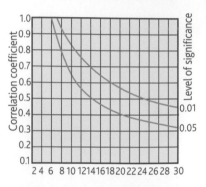

Fig. 7.16 *Graph of the rank correlation coefficient*

AQA Examiner's tip

Spearman works well when there are at least seven pairs of variables and it works better when there are more. However, with more than about 15–20 pairs of variables the calculations become very unwieldy. You should select a sample of data pairs if more than 20 have been collected.

Level of deprivation	GPs practising in wards
1 (least deprived)	44
2	39
3	42
4	35
5 (most deprived)	30

2 The correlation is strong. The Rs figure should always lie somewhere between 1 and −1. (If it lies outside this range something must have gone wrong with the working of the sum.) As this figure is very close to 1, the relationship is strong.

3 The statistical significance of Rs can be checked to see how likely it is that this relationship could have been due to chance. If the likelihood of it occurring by chance is low, the null hypothesis can be rejected and the alternative hypothesis can be accepted.

To check significance the result must be checked against a table of significance or a graph showing critical values.

Read off the number of pairs of variables used along the x-axis of the graph. In this case there were 9.

Read off the Rs result along the y-axis. In this case it is 0.938.

If the point of intersection comes above the 0.05 level of significance line, it is 95 per cent certain that the correlation was not a result of chance, so there is a significant relationship between the two variables.

If it comes above the 0.01 level of significance line, it is 99 per cent certain that there is a relationship that did not occur by chance.

As long as there is a 95 per cent certainty that the relationship was significant, it is safe to reject the null hypothesis and accept the alternative.

However, even a very strong relationship does not mean that changes in one variable have **caused** the changes in the other variable, although it is **possible** that this has happened. It is also possible that the variations in both factors have been due to changes in a third variable.

Chi-squared test

The chi-squared (often written as x^2 test is used to examine spatial distributions. As a geographer you must assume that the distribution is not random. The chi-squared test compares the data that have been collected against a theoretical random distribution of those data.

The collected data are known as the **observed** distribution.

The theoretical, random distribution is known as the **expected** distribution.

The null hypothesis states that: 'There is no significant difference between the observed distribution and the expected distribution.'

In the example below, students were trying to discover whether the provision of GP services in a city was evenly spread, or if provision was more concentrated in wards with a higher average income. They collected data on income from the National Census website, which divided the wards in the city into five groups based on levels of deprivation. These five groups of wards have population totals that are approximately equal in size. They collected data on GP services from the NHS Choices website.

The null hypothesis

In this case the expectation was that there would be fewer GPs in the more deprived areas. The null hypothesis stated:

> There is no relationship between the number of GPs in a ward and the level of deprivation.

Completing the calculation

First, the expected distribution of GPs must be calculated. There are 190 GPs altogether. If they are distributed at random it would be expected that there would be $190 \div 5 = 38$ in each type of ward. These data are entered on the second row of the table below, with the observed data on the third row.

The two sets of data are subtracted on the fourth row and the result is squared on the fifth row.

This result in each column is divided by E on the final row. These results are then totalled to give the x^2 value for these data. Here it is 3.32.

Deprivation level	1	2	3	4	5	Total
Expected data (E)	38	38	38	38	38	190
Observed data (O)	44	39	42	35	30	190
E – O	–6	–1	–4	3	8	
$(E - O)^2$	36	1	16	9	64	
$(E - O)^2/E$	0.95	0.03	0.42	0.24	1.68	$x^2 = 3.32$

Testing for significance

The raw data showed that more GPs are found in the least deprived areas and fewer in the most deprived areas. This suggested that there might be a correlation. However, the result has to be tested to check its significance. The graph in Fig. 7.17 can be used.

To work out the degrees of freedom, take the number of sets of data (in this case, 5 types of ward) and subtract 1 from that number ($n - 1$). In this case that gives 4. Find this number on the x-axis.

Find the calculated value for x^2 on the y-axis. In this case it is 3.32.

The intersection of the two lines lies below the 0.05 significance line (and obviously also below the 0.01 significance line). To be 95 per cent sure that any relationship has not occurred by chance the intersection must fall above the 0.05 line, and to be 99 per cent sure of a significant relationship it must fall above the 0.01 line.

In this case we cannot be sure that any relationship did not occur by chance. We cannot reject the null hypothesis, nor can we accept the alternative hypothesis. At first glance it appeared as though there was a relationship, but this is obviously too small to be statistically significant. The possibility that it might have arisen by chance is too strong.

Maybe collecting more data from a larger area would show that there is a significant relationship. Or, possibly, refining the data and dividing up the wards into more groups based on levels of deprivation would produce a significant relationship.

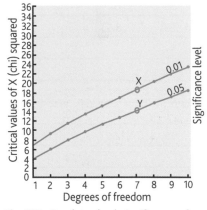

Fig. 7.17 *Graph to check significance of critical values of x^2*

■ Mann-Whitney U test

This is a straightforward test, designed to see whether two sets of data come from the same population or from two different populations. It assumes that if they are from the same population they will show the same pattern of distribution; if they are from different populations their distributions will be significantly different.

In this example, the number of acacia trees growing in 1 km² survey squares in two neighbouring parts of Tanzania was calculated. Area 1 had been used for seasonal grazing by herdsmen, while Area 2 had been part of a national park for the last 20 years.

	Number of acacia trees per survey square							
Area 1	70	18	31	55	14	53	15	31
Area 2	85	55	73	102	98	55	59	55

The Mann-Whitney U test was used because it is not clear if these are samples taken from the same set of data. If they are, they will appear to be part of a continuous sequence. If they are not both taken from the same set of data they will show distinct differences in their pattern of distribution.

Set up the hypothesis

In this case the null hypothesis states:

There is no difference between the density of acacia trees in the two areas.

The alternative hypothesis states:

There is a difference between the density of acacia trees in two areas with different histories of human occupancy.

Complete the calculation

If the two sets of data are of different sizes, call the smaller data set 'n1' and the larger set 'n2'. Here, they are both the same size so it does not matter which is which, n1 = 8 and n2 = 8.

1 Rank all the values for both samples from the smallest (= 1) to the largest. Complete a table as shown opposite.

2 Total the ranks in each column.

3 Calculate the U values for both samples using the following formula:

$$U1 = n1 \times n2 + \frac{n1(n1 + 1)}{2} - R1$$

$$U2 = n1 \times n2 + \frac{n2(n2 + 1)}{2} - R2$$

$$U1 = (8 \times 8) + \frac{8 \times 9}{2} - 41.5 = \textbf{58.5}$$

$$U2 = (8 \times 8) + \frac{8 \times 9}{2} - 94.5 = \textbf{5.5}$$

4 Find the critical value for the U statistic at a chosen significance level. You can find a critical values table at the website given in the Link on the next page. With a sample size of 8 for both n1 and n2 at 0.05 significance level the critical value is 13.

Area 1	Rank 1	Area 2	Rank 2
14	1		
15	2		
18	3		
31	4.5		
31	4.5		
53	6		
55	8.5		
		55	8.5
		55	8.5
		55	8.5
		59	11
70	12		
		73	13
		85	14
		98	15
		102	16
R1 =	41.5	R2 =	94.5

Where the values are the same and share the same rank, the average of the rank values is taken. There were four areas that each had an average of 5.5 trees per km². These came after number 6 in the ranking, so occupied positions 7, 8, 9 and 10 in the ranking.
(7 + 8 + 9 + 10)/4 = 34/4 = 8.5

If the lowest statistic for **U** is less than the critical value (or U_{crit}) the null hypothesis can be rejected and the alternative hypothesis can be accepted. In this case the lower value (that for U2) is 5.5. This is less than U_{crit} so the alternative hypothesis can be accepted. So, 'there is a difference between the density of acacia trees in two areas with different histories of human occupancy'.

(Note that this critical value applies in this case because the test was used to test a 'non-directional' alternative hypothesis. The Mann-Whitney test can be used in other circumstances, but there is not enough space here to describe them. Reference should be made to a specialised book on statistics in geography.)

5 It is important that the statistical result should now be used to aid the geographical explanation of the distributions mapped. It seems clear that there are more acacia trees in the areas that have been managed by the National Park authorities than there are in the areas that have been used for grazing. The low number of acacia trees in the grazed areas might be due to cattle destroying the trees, especially when they are very young. On the other hand, it might be due to the pastoralists burning off the dead vegetation at the end of the dry season to encourage new growth.

(Note that the result of the test tells us that there is a significant difference between the two types of area. It cannot be used to **explain why** that difference exists. That must be left to the geographical knowledge and understanding of the person using the test.)

Links

A table of critical values can be found at: www.saburchill.com/IBbiology/stats/003.html

Using techniques in Section B of the examination

The previous section has explained how various techniques might be used on data that have been collected through either primary research or secondary study. Of course, many of these techniques could be used in the second part of the 4A examination. In this section of the chapter it is assumed that you have learnt how to carry out the techniques. Here, some of these techniques have been used to form the basis of examination-style questions.

However, it should be noted that in the AQA AS and A2 examinations the questions that are set are unlikely to require candidates to carry out all the stages of the presentation or analysis techniques that have been shown here. They are more likely to give most of the working and leave the exam candidates to complete part of the technique.

The full procedures have been given here as it is important to help students to understand the full process of each technique so that it could be used elsewhere, even though the full process is unlikely to be needed in the examination.

■ Questions on map skills – isoline map

Draw an isoline map to illustrate the results of the pedestrian count. Use Fig. 7.18 as your base map. Use an interval of 10, beginning at 10.

A group of students carried out a pedestrian count in the town centre. Their results are shown in Fig. 7.18.

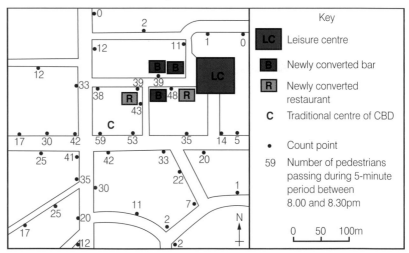

Fig. 7.18 *Isoline map*

Advice on completion

1 The commands include, 'Use an interval of 10, beginning at 10'. Check which points are less than 10. They must all lie outside the 10-isoline.

2 Always start drawing lines with a pencil. Exercises like these can be tricky and it is always sensible to allow for alterations to be made.

3 Are there any points showing exactly 10? If there were, the 10-isoline would go through them. As there are none it must be drawn close to the points showing 11 and 12, making sure that they stay on the inside of the line. Estimate where the line would best go between the other points.

4 Can the line be completed running right round the map, or will it have to go to the edge of the map and stop?

5 Counts of 20 were recorded at two of the points. The 20-isoline will run through them. On the western edge of the map it will run closer to the 17 point than to the 30 point and slightly closer to the 12 point than to the 38 and 39 points. Then estimates will be needed as the line is drawn round by the leisure centre back to the eastern 20 point.

6 There are two count points marked 30. The rest of the 30-isoline has to be estimated, following the same principles as with the 20-isoline.

7 If the first three isolines have been plotted well, plotting the 40- and 50-isolines should be fairly straightforward.

8 The question does not ask for the key to be completed – but good maps should always have complete keys.

9 Label each isoline by writing the relevant number in a gap in the line, as shown on Fig. 7.19.

10 The question asks for an isoline map. It does not ask for it to be shaded, so shading would be a waste of precious exam time, and it might obscure details.

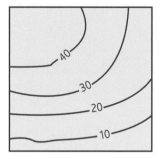

Fig. 7.19 *Labelling isolines*

■ Questions on map skills – choropleth map

A group of students undertook a fieldwork enquiry into the proposal to build a new warehouse and distribution centre in their town. The table shows some data obtained by the students about the workforce in the warehouse. Fig. 7.20 is a map of the town showing the wards referred to in the table.

a Present the data for the number of employees/km2 of each ward in 2006 in the form of a choropleth map, using four classes of data.

   i Give the class boundaries that you will use.

   ii Complete the map, Fig. 7.20, using the classes that you gave in **(ai)**.

Ward	Residents of ward employed at warehouse (2006 total)	Number of employees/ km² of ward in 2006
1	16	5.1
2	2	0.5
3	1	0.5
4	91	15.8
5	37	6.4
6	49	21.8
7	106	77.1
8	32	18.3
9	15	15
10	9	9
11	127	53.5
12	27	14.4
13	18	11.1
14	12	5.1
15	5	1.5
16	3	0.6
Total	550	

Fig. 7.20

Key
● Existing warehouse
⊕ Proposed new, larger warehouse

0 ½ 1 km

77.1
53.5
21.8
18.3
15.8
15
14.4
11.1
9
6.4
5.1
5.1
1.5
0.6
0.5
0.5

Advice on completion

1 Note that the figures have been presented in terms of density/km². This means that they are suitable for plotting on a choropleth map.

2 The 16 density values in the margin should be arranged in order from highest to lowest, probably using a piece of scrap paper. This will help in making rational decisions in (ai).

3 Decide whether to use:

 a four groups of 4 with a relatively equal spread of densities (0–19, 20–39, 40–59 and 60–80)

 b four groups of 4 with an equal number of wards in each (0–3.9, 4–7.9, 8–16.9 and 17–80) or

 c four unequal groups divided where big gaps make logical break points (somewhere between 1.5 and 5.1, between 11.1 and 14.4 and between 21.8 and 53.5). Note: there is also a big gap between 53.5 and 77.1, but making two groups with only one ward in each would not be sensible.

4 Choose the types of shading to use. To avoid confusion mark these in the key before starting to shade the map. The highest value should have the densest shading and the lowest value should have the lightest. The highest value should be placed in the top box of the key, with the lowest in the bottom box.

5 Shading must be clear and consistent. Line shading should be done using a ruler and the gaps between the lines should be as consistent as possible, in the time allowed. It is not advisable to leave the least dense wards blank, nor to shade the most dense wards solid black.

AQA Examiner's tip

Suggestion (a) would produce very uneven group sizes. It is not advisable. Suggestions (b) and (c) both have advantages and disadvantages. Either would be acceptable. In this particular question the choice of boundaries does not have to be justified, but on other occasions candidates might be asked to justify their choices.

Questions on graphical skills – pie charts

A pie chart question could also have been set as a follow-up to the choropleth map question.

A group of students obtained data showing changes in the size and gender balance of the workforce.

	Gender of workforce 1986		Gender of workforce 2006	
	Total	%	Total	%
Male	1257	84	309	56
Female	238	16	241	44

The students decided to draw proportional pie charts to represent the data. Complete Fig. 7.21 by drawing another pie chart, using the data for 2006. Use the formula to calculate the radius of the pie chart

$$r = \sqrt{\frac{A}{\pi}}$$

where:
r = the radius of the circle in mm
A = the area of the circle, in which $1\,mm^2 = 1$ worker.

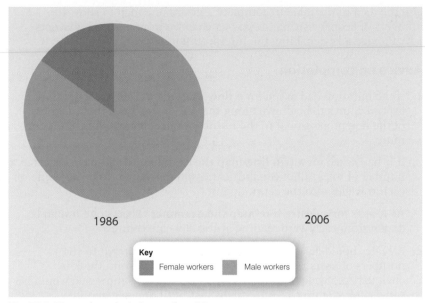

1986   2006

Key
Female workers   Male workers

Fig. 7.21 *Size and gender balance of workforce*

Advice on completion

1 You must be prepared for questions like this. Essential equipment here includes compasses, protractor and calculator as well as the usual pencil, rubber and ruler.

2 Show all your working on the paper. Credit will be given for correct stages in the working even if the final outcome is wrong.

3 The pie chart should be drawn in the space provided. Follow the same scheme for shading and labelling as used in the 'model' that has been provided.

4 When drawing the slices of the pie, it is the convention to start at '12 o'clock' and to work round clockwise, drawing the biggest sector first.

■ Questions on map skills – desire line maps

A group of students was studying the area served by a day-care centre for the elderly. The students obtained information about the postcodes of 115 people who used the centre.

Their results are shown in the table.

Postcode district	Number of users	Distance*
1	18	1.0
2	7	2
3	8	1.5
4	17	0.5
5	8	3
6	23	3
7	18	1.5
8	10	3.0
9	6	3.5

Approximate distance, in km, from centre of district to the day-care centre

Use the data in the table to complete a desire line map to show the numbers of people visiting the day-care centre from postcode districts 1–9. Provide a key enabling the interpretation of your map.

Advice on completion

1 If the question had asked for a **flow map** the examiner would have expected lines to be drawn along the routeways, with the thickness of the line proportional to the number of people travelling along that route.

If it had asked for a **trip line map** the examiner would have expected a number of lines, all of equal thickness, to be drawn from the home of each traveller into the central point.

As it asks for a **desire line map** the examiner expects one line to be drawn from each ward, ending at the day-care centre.

2 A scale should be chosen that allows lines to be drawn to show numbers of users ranging from 6 to 23. A line 23 mm thick is obviously too wide. Lines ranging from 1 mm to 4 mm wide would be satisfactory; 2 mm to 8 mm might just fit, if drawn carefully.

3 The lines from the nearby wards should be drawn first. The lines from more distant wards can then be fitted in round these. It is more difficult to do the task the other way round.

4 As such a map nears completion it is likely to look crowded towards the centre. This is inevitable and, unless it is extreme, not really a problem; the map is meant to show converging flows of people.

5 The scale must be shown in the key.

■ Questions on graphical skills – triangular graphs

This table shows the areas covered by three main land use types in the standard statistical regions of England (2002).

Standard region	Perm. grass	Rough grass	Arable	Total	Perm. grass	Rough grass	Arable
North-east (NE)	2860	150	20	3030	91	5	4
North-west (NW)	206	187	69	462	45	40	15
Yorks & Humberside (YH)	464	144	373	981	47	15	38
East Midlands (EM)	259	36	495	790	33	5	62
West Midlands (WM)	359	21	248	628	57	3	39
Eastern (E)	146	28	706	880	17	3	80
London (L)	19	4	15	38	50	11	39
South-east (SE)	321	33	366	720	45	5	51
South-west (SW)	812	99	336	1247	65	8	27

(Figures in thousands of hectares)   *(Figures in percentages)*

a **i** Use the data in table on p280 to complete a suitably labelled triangular graph showing the three types of land use in the regions of England.

ii Describe the pattern shown on your graph. Comment on the extent to which groups of regions can be identified.

Advice on completion

1 The axes must be labelled, with figures for the percentage of each land use running along each of the axes. The 0 per cent line has already been labelled for the rough grass up the left side of the graph. This axis should be completed by labelling in 10s up to 100 per cent. The little line next to the 0 per cent shows the direction in which these figures should be read.

2 The permanent grass axis should then be labelled from 0 per cent on the right to 100 per cent on the left; and the arable axis should be labelled from 0 per cent at the top to 100 per cent at the bottom.

3 A point should be plotted for each region in turn. For instance:

■ NE has 91 per cent permanent grass. Find the 90 per cent line reading across the bottom axis. 91 per cent then comes between the 91 per cent and the 92 per cent line. Follow this imaginary line upwards and to the left.

■ Then find the imaginary line representing 5 per cent rough grass, which runs horizontally across the graph. Follow it until it intersects the previous line. Mark this point with a dot or cross. It represents the NE region.

■ Just to check that your point is correct, find the 4 per cent line for arable. Follow it down and to the left and it ought to come to the intersection marked previously. If it does not, start again, checking more carefully.

4 All nine regions need to be plotted, using the same technique.

5 Study the graph carefully to find whether any points seem to lie close together. The points in each group must have similar combinations of land-use types and this allows geographical conclusions to be drawn.

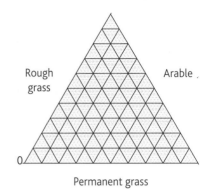

Fig 7.22 *Incomplete triangular graph*

■ Questions on graphical/statistical skills – dispersion

The table shows the figures for total annual rainfall for two recording stations over a 15-year period.

Year	Annual rainfall total for a station in south-east England (mm)	Annual rainfall total for a station in north Nigeria (mm)
1	781	490
2	618	986
3	563	832
4	586	1037
5	545	594
6	884	855
7	600	376
8	793	350
9	580	479
10	699	761
11	842	688
12	737	1143
13	824	356
14	695	470
15	530	635
Total	10 277	10 052

a   Calculate the mean annual rainfall at each station, to two decimal places:

   i   south-east England

   ii   north Nigeria.

b   i   Fig. 7.23 shows the rainfall statistics for south-east England on a dispersion diagram. Complete Fig 7.23 using the rainfall figures for north Nigeria.

   ii   Identify the upper quartile and lower quartile for each set of rainfall figures by drawing lines on the dispersion diagram.

   iii Calculate the interquartile range for each recording station.

Advice on completion

1   In (a) to calculate the mean, all the values for a station should be added up and the sum should be divided by the number of values (15 in this case). This again points up the need for a calculator in the exam.

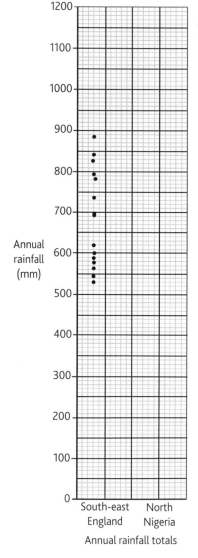

Annual rainfall (mm)

South-east England   North Nigeria

Annual rainfall totals

Fig 7.23

2 In (b) the dispersion diagram should be drawn to resemble the model diagram as closely as possible. All the dots should be of the same size, or as close to that as possible.

3 When doing the calculation, working should be shown as marks are available for correct working, even if the final answer is wrong.

4 The interquartile range is the difference between UQ and LQ.

5 The skills part of this question would probably be followed by a question asking candidates to compare the rainfall and rainfall reliability at the two stations. They would be expected to comment on all the pieces of information that they had been given and that they had calculated.

■ Questions on statistical skills – Spearman rank correlation

A student was doing a coursework enquiry into the hazard of malaria in Africa. He collected the data in the table.

Country	% of children with malaria who received drug treatment	Rank 1 (R1)	GNP per capita (US$)	Rank 2 (2)	Difference (R1 – R2) (d)	d²
Central African Republic	69	1	1100	5.5	–4.5	
Cameroon	68	2	1900	3	–1	
Angola	63	3	2100	2	1	
Benin	61	4	1200	4	0	
Tanzania	54	5	700			
Zambia	51	6	900			
Equatorial Guinea	50	7	2700	1	6	
Congo	46	8	800			
Nigeria	36	9	1000			
Burundi	33	10	600			
Malawi	29	11	600			
Kenya	28	12	1100	5.5	6.5	
Somalia	18	13	600			
						$\Sigma d^2 =$

a Carry out a Spearman rank correlation test on the statistics in the table, to test the hypothesis that the percentage of children with malaria who received drug treatment in African countries is directly related to GNP.

  i Complete the table.

  ii Substitute the formula below (where n = the number of pairs of variables) and complete the calculation.

$$Rs = 1 - \frac{6(\Sigma d)^2}{n^3 - n}$$

  Rs=

Advice on completion

1 Exam questions on statistical techniques often ask candidates to **complete** a calculation rather than carrying out the whole of the calculation. It is important though that candidates work through the remaining steps in the correct, logical order.

2 In column 5 it is important that the equal ranks are calculated correctly. Malawi, Kenya and Somalia occupy the 11th, 12th and 13th places in the ranking, i.e. $\frac{(11 + 12 + 13)}{3} = 12$.

3 In column 6 it is important to put the minus signs in when necessary, even though they will disappear when the values are squared.

4 A calculator might well be needed to complete column 7. Every candidate should take one into the exam.

5 All stages of the working should be shown in part (ii), even though a calculator will probably be used.

6 Check your results for significance. Use Fig. 7.16 on p272. A 0.05 level of significance means that it is 95 per cent certain that the relationship between the variables has not arisen by chance. A 0.01 level of significance means that it is 99 per cent certain. However, this does **not** necessarily mean that one variable has caused the other.

Note that when a question like this was used in a real exam it was followed up by two further parts which asked:

■ Suggest what type of graph would be the best way to present these data. Justify your choice of graph.

■ Suggest a suitable presentation technique that could be used to see if there was a spatial pattern to the data on the percentage of children with malaria who received drug treatment. Justify your choice of technique.

The expected answers were:

■ Scatter graph, mainly because it is designed to show relationships between two sets of variables.

■ Proportional symbols – bars or circles – could be used. They would show the data in a form that preserved the original detail. They could show groupings and spatial patterns if a clear scale was chosen. A choropleth map could also show if groupings existed, but it would lose some of the detail by putting all the data into groups.

In this chapter you will h ave learnt:

- the skills needed to complete a fieldwork enquiry
- how those skills can also be used to complete Section B of Paper 4A
- some skills that might also be relevant to candidates entered for Paper 4B.

AQA Examiner's tip

Both these questions ask candidates to justify a choice. It obviously means that the positive reasons for choosing one technique should be given. However, a choice also often involves rejecting less suitable alternatives. Credit will usually be given if other possible choices are considered and then reasons are given for their rejection.

Paper 4b: The Issue Evaluation Exercise

What is an issue in geography?

In geography there are facts. These include:

■ Rivers have flood plains and, under certain circumstances, these can be inundated.

■ Burning fossil fuel produces carbon dioxide.

■ There are deposits of oil and gas beneath the surface of Alaska.

■ The birth rate in the UK fell during the last quarter of the 20th century and then rose again in the early years of the 21st century.

Facts can be seen, measured and recorded. They are not open to discussion.

However, facts can lead on to a consideration of other linked possibilities. There are issues that arise from the facts listed and they are not so clear-cut: they are open to discussion. For instance:

■ Rivers have flood plains and, under certain circumstances, these can be inundated … and human activity has made flooding more likely … so building of houses on flood plains should not be allowed.

■ Burning fossil fuel produces carbon dioxide … and this is leading to global warming … so we should all cut our use of fossil fuels by 50 per cent.

■ There are deposits of oil and gas beneath the surface of Alaska … and these are so important that exploration for oil should be allowed in the Arctic Wildlife Refuge … but they should not be exploited or we will destroy one of the few remaining wildernesses in the world.

■ The birth rate in the UK fell during the last quarter of the 20th century and then rose again in the early years of the 21st century … which means that we will need to be more concerned with providing schools for the future than with providing more care homes for the elderly … so we risk becoming overpopulated.

The clear facts can all lead into discussion points. In each of the above cases, an issue (or often several issues) can be seen to be arising. Some people say that an issue in geography can always be fitted into the following sentence:

'People are concerned about … W … because of … X … and it has arisen because of … Y … but it might be resolved if … Z ….'

where:

W = the issue

X = the possible consequences of the issue

Y = the geographical causes of the issue

Z = possible solutions from better management of the issue.

■ What is an Issue Evaluation Exercise?

In the AQA Geography Specification the Issue Evaluation Exercise is an exam with a two-month preparation period and a 90-minute writing period. The exam may be taken in either January or June.

The Advance Information Booklet (AIB) will be issued to schools and colleges on 1 November or 1 April preceding the examination session. Teachers will decide when and how to issue it to candidates.

The copy of the AIB provided for candidates must be taken into the exam in an unmarked state. Candidates may not take any other research material into the exam with them. Most centres actually make copies of the AIB so that all their students can work on the booklets and add notes, highlight key points, work out sums, complete maps and so on. Then they take the unmarked original into the exam.

The exam will consist of a series of questions on the topic which has been introduced in the AIB. The exam will test some parts of the Issue Evaluation process. The whole process can involve:

- presenting and analysing data presented in the AIB
- interpreting and drawing conclusions from these data
- researching additional information on the issue(s) presented in the AIB
- considering how fieldwork could be used to research the issue
- relating this issue to the body of geographical knowledge and understanding that you have developed during your course
- defining the issue(s) in the AIB
- considering the issue(s) from different points of view
- recognising the strengths and weaknesses of the data in the AIB
- establishing criteria for the evaluation of the issue(s)
- evaluating a range of possible options concerning the management of the issue(s)
- identifying and analysing possible causes of conflict between parties affected by the issue(s)
- considering ways of resolving those conflicts
- recommending a way (or ways) of managing the issue(s)
- considering possible impacts of those management recommendations
- suggesting how the issue(s) might develop in future
- reviewing the process of issue evaluation.

Of course that list is far too long for all aspects to be considered in a 90-minute exam. However, the AIB will contain many clues – and some very clear guidance – on the type of questions that will probably be set in the exam.

So, how do you prepare for the exam?

The best way to prepare for the Issue Evaluation Exercise is to do it!

Many schools use some, or all, of past Issue Evaluation Exercises in their teaching of topics at AS and, more particularly, at A2 level. For instance, the exercise on the group of African immigrants in Bolton, which was provided as a Specimen Paper for this specification, could be used as part of the teaching course in the AS core module on Population change or in A2 modules on Contemporary urbanisation, or in Development and globalisation, or in The challenge of multicultural societies in the UK.

Similarly, the Polish question which is discussed later in this chapter could be used in many human geography modules – particularly in the A2 option on Globalisation.

During your course it is very useful to practise at least one full Issue Evaluation Exercise from start to finish. The rest of this chapter will guide you through one such exercise: the Polish question. This has been adapted from an examination set on the old AQA Specification B in June 2008. The AIB material has been adapted to fit the pattern that might be found in AIBs produced for the present AQA specification.

In this chapter, the AIB is presented on pp288–306. The AIB is actually printed on the left page of each double-page spread with an examiner's commentary and tips on the opposite page. This makes suggestions as to how you could use the booklet during your two-month preparation period.

Then some specimen exam questions are presented on pp310–17, again with the questions on the left page and a commentary opposite.

The intention is that you will be able to work through this alone, or as a group, and then apply similar skills and processes to your own Issue Evaluation Exercise when the time comes.

STUDY ALL THE INFORMATION IN THIS BOOKLET

The information in this booklet comprises the following:

Item 1   **General geographical and economic background to Poland**

Item 2   **Article from *The Warsaw Voice* – a Polish government-sponsored website**

Item 3   **Measures of regional economic development**

Item 4   **So far, migrant workers have been just the job (*Observer*, 27 August 2006)**

Item 5   **Further research – Pay in the private sector for selected EU countries: February 2006**

AQA Examiner's tip

Top Issue Evaluation advice

You could use the rest of the space on this page to add your own references for further research.

These references could include mention of your own class notes, handouts that you have received, relevant pages in this and other textbooks, web addresses, videos/DVDs in the geography department collection and so on.

The table of contents is quite important.

It might give you some ideas about the nature of the task that you are being set. For instance, it tells you:

◼ the case study area is Poland

◼ topics that are to be covered will include regional development (Item 3) and migration (Item 4)

◼ there seems to be some sort of link to the EU with a comparison of wage rates in Germany and Poland, and various references to migration within the EU.

It might give you some idea about the strength and reliability of the different items in the AIB. For instance, in this case it tells you:

◼ Item 2 is from a Polish government-sponsored website. Should that make you question its objectivity? You certainly need to read it carefully. It might be purely factual – and the Polish government is well placed to know the facts about the country. On the other hand, it might be trying to make a political or economic point, in which case it needs to be considered with some caution.

◼ Item 3 is described purely as '*Measures* of development'. No source is given. However, it is unlikely that the examiners would have provided you with data that were not the best obtainable.

◼ Item 4 is from the *Observer*. This is a respected, serious national weekly newspaper. It might be best described as holding a 'centre-left' political viewpoint.

◼ Note that the article is dated August 2006. The exam paper from which this was taken was set in June 2008. The setting, checking and printing process for any exam will always take about two years so, at best, sources will be at least two years old. The Issue Evaluation Exercise will usually deal with issues that are as current as the examiners can make them and circumstances might have changed between the writing of the paper and your sitting of the exam. Therefore, you might well be able to find more up-to-date facts and opinions. You will be given credit for doing this where appropriate.

◼ The further research section will be new to schools and colleges that used to do the old AQA Specification B. It offers some suggestions for internet research and for thinking about fieldwork. You can be fairly sure that these areas will be tested in the examination, although the fieldwork is unlikely to form a major question, but will probably be the basis of a shorter question in the more structured part of the paper.

AQA Examiner's tip

Top Issue Evaluation advice

Make yourself well aware of the source of each item in the AIB, of its reliability and of the aims of its writer.

Item 1   General geographical and economic background to Poland

Poland, officially the Republic of Poland, is a country of just over 38 million people, located in central Europe.

In the north, the landscape consists almost entirely of the lowlands of the North European Plain, at the average height of 173 m (568 feet). Several large rivers cross the plains; for instance, the Vistula and the Oder. Poland also contains over 9,300 lakes, mostly in the north of the country.

Fig. 8.1 *Map of Poland*

Item 1 Background

The title calls this 'Background'. Treat it as such. You will probably not be asked very detailed questions on this item of the AIB, but you need to read it and understand it before you go much further into the case study.

The first two paragraphs are, as the title said, just background. However, an inquisitive geographer might just wonder how and why Poland came to have 9,300 lakes.

In fact, many of those on the northern plains are a result of glacial activity. Ice from northern Europe spread across this area and then left deposits of till which impeded the drainage, producing the lakes and the marshes.

However, don't worry about this. There is no reference to glaciation in the booklet so you will not be asked questions about it, but if you could bring in some background knowledge like that you would be given credit for it … *as long as it was relevant to the question that was asked*.

The map presents a number of issues for consideration.

- There is a scale and a north point but no key. Does that matter? It is obvious that the shades of brown represent higher land, but how high is it? Look carefully and you should see some heights marked in the Sudeten and Carpathian mountains. Of course, as good geographers you will be used to having an atlas available to check on points like that. Even without the key the picture should be fairly clear: a division between northern plain, central plateau and southern hills (at 1,725 m the Carpathian mountains are much higher than any peaks in the UK).

- The borders of Poland are shown quite clearly. 'Ch Republic' obviously means the Czech Republic and 'Russian Fed' shows Russia to the north but how far does Russia go? Does it continue beyond that border marking the east of Poland? At this point you really do need to consult an atlas …

- … and were you surprised when you did? Were you aware that a small area of Russia, around Kaliningrad, was detached from the rest of the country? Lithuania, Belarus and Ukraine actually border Poland to the east.

- The red lines are major roads, and the double red lines are motorways. The major roads show a fairly well-developed network; the motorway network is only starting to develop.

AQA Examiner's tip

Top Issue Evaluation advice

Your Issue Evaluation Exercise will almost certainly be based on a real place. Make sure you know where it is. Use an atlas, Google Earth, www.ordnancesurvey.co.uk or similar to find out about the area.

To the south of the country, the Polish uplands form a belt varying in width from 90 to 200 kilometres, made up of the gently sloping foothills of the Sudeten and Carpathian mountain ranges and upland ranges in south central Poland. The Silesia-Kraków area contains rich coal deposits.

Poland has a temperate climate, with cloudy, moderately severe winters and mild summers with frequent showers and thunderstorms.

The Polish state was formed more than 1,000 years ago and reached its golden age near the end of the 16th century, when Poland was one of the largest, wealthiest and most powerful countries in Europe. In 1791, the Polish-Lithuanian parliament adopted the constitution of 3 May, Europe's first modern codified constitution, and the second in the world after the United States. Soon after that the country ceased to exist after being partitioned by its neighbours Russia, Austria and Prussia. It regained independence in 1918, after the First World War, as the Second Polish Republic. After the Second World War, it became a communist satellite state of the USSR known as the People's Republic of Poland. In 1989, the first partially free elections in Poland's post-war history concluded the Solidarity movement's struggle for freedom and resulted in the defeat of Poland's communist rulers. The current Third Polish Republic was established, followed a few years later by the drafting of a new constitution in 1997.

In 1999, Poland joined Nato and in 2004 it joined the EU. The reasons were to support democracy, to provide security against any territorial ambitions that Russia might have in the future, to encourage the growth of a market economy, to strengthen the country's infrastructure through subsidies, to allow migration and to give access to new technology. Membership allows access to the whole EU market area for any TNCs that locate in Poland. They will not have to pay tariffs on any goods produced in Poland and exported to other EU countries.

Table 8.1

	Urban area	Inhabitants (Estimated, 2005)
1	Katowice	3,487,000
2	Warsaw	2,679,000
3	Kraków	1,400,000
4	Łódź	1,300,000
5	Gdańsk	1,100,000
6	Poznań	1,000,000

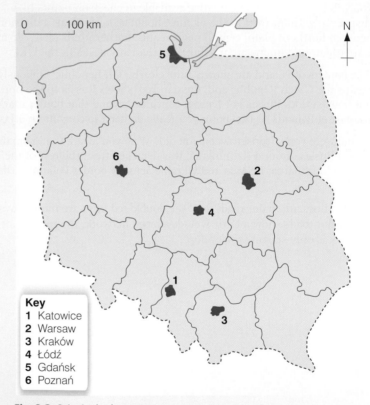

Key
1 Katowice
2 Warsaw
3 Kraków
4 Łódź
5 Gdańsk
6 Poznań

Fig. 8.2 *Principal urban areas*

The text really is just background. You will not be asked questions on Polish history, although you need to read this all carefully!

There are references in the last paragraph to the development of the EU.

The specification (p12) states that the Development and globalisation option includes: 'Reasons for the social and economic groupings of nations, with particular reference to the European Union.'

The specification (p15) also states that: 'Where the context [of the Issue Evaluation Exercise] is drawn from areas … which are optional, material will be provided in the AIB in such a way as to enable all candidates to be assessed to A Level standard.'

So you might be expected to make some reference to knowledge of the EU, but only in the context provided in the AIB.

The table shows that just under one-third of Poland's population lives in the six major cities. It is also interesting that almost half of these people live in Katowice and Kraków – the two cities in Silesia which contain the coal deposits.

Note that Warsaw, the capital, is not the biggest city, although information later in the booklet will show that it is of very great economic importance.

This is the first time we have really encountered the Polish alphabet, which is rather different from the English alphabet. (Note that Łódź is pronounced more like 'Wudj'.) Don't worry too much about this. If you use the names of places, do try to copy them correctly – but you will not lose marks if you miss off accents, just as long as the names are recognisable.

By the end of 2002, Poland's largest trading partners were in the EU, with the country exporting nearly 70 per cent of goods to the EU-15 (the 15 members of the EU before enlargement in 2004). Poland's imports from these countries were a little over 60 per cent, with Germany being the single largest partner. The largest foreign investor in Poland is France, followed by the US and then Germany, with the Netherlands fourth. Most investment has been in the sectors of manufacturing and financial services.

A major problem is unemployment, which is hovering around 18 per cent (3.2 million people). There are enormous differences between the development in Poland's core regions, with low unemployment and higher wages found in the urban areas around Warsaw and Szczecin, and the south-east and north-eastern peripheral regions where there are considerable hurdles to overcome. The demand for highly qualified, senior professionals and the lack of supply have led to salary packages which are similar to certain EU-15 levels, though the wage rates for manufacturing industry and in the state sectors are very low.

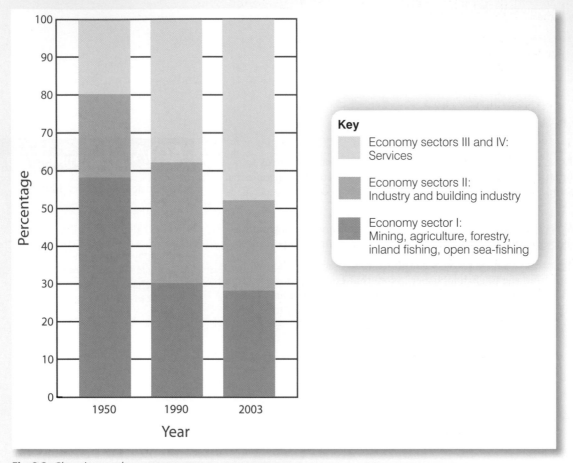

Fig. 8.3 *Changing employment structure*

The food-processing industry constitutes one of the most important sectors of the Polish economy in terms of the volume of production sold (over 20 per cent of the total sales value of Polish industry), the number of industrial establishments (about 30,000) and employment (8.4 per cent of the total national employment or about 16 per cent of the total employment in industry). This sector's share of the total industrial production is about 24 per cent, while in the EU its average share is around 15 per cent. The sector generates about 6 per cent of the GDP.

The first paragraph contains more detail about Poland joining the EU. This is clearly of major importance in understanding the country's economic development in recent years.

It is interesting to note that most investment has been in 'manufacturing and financial services'. These are two very different parts of the economy. Consider why foreign investors might be interested in each of them.

- Manufacturing investment might be for either the Polish market or for the wider European market.

- When you look at the graph (Fig. 8.3) it is clear that percentage share employment in the manufacturing sector increased during the period of communist rule – when manufacturing was actually shrinking in the UK and many other more developed economies. Then the sector shrank in the post-communist period.

- During the communist period heavy industry was developed, particularly coal-based industry. The economies of eastern Europe were very integrated and a lot of the industrial production was for export to these countries.

- If Poland prospers in the EU there is likely to be an increased demand for consumer goods.

- Foreign investors might also want to use cheap Polish labour to produce goods for export to western Europe.

- The investment in financial services will probably involve banking, insurance, etc. – the infrastructure that is needed to develop a market-based economy.

The second paragraph contains a reference to Poland's 'core' and to 'peripheral regions'. Myrdal's core–periphery model of economic development tries to show how, in many countries, economic development was originally concentrated in a core region which drained resources and labour from the peripheral regions. Then, as the country develops, secondary cores develop and investment and wealth eventually spread out into the more peripheral regions. It would be useful to consider this model during your preparation period. See how well it fits with the Polish situation.

Compare the graph with similar statistics for the UK and other countries in western Europe.

Be aware that:

- in 1950 Poland was just starting to recover from a devastating war in which the country had suffered massive loss of life and economic infrastructure

- in 1990 the Communists had just been voted out of power

- in 2003 Poland was preparing to join the EU.

The last paragraph introduces the food-processing industry.

- How can it manage to be so important in a country where employment in the primary sector of the economy is shrinking so quickly?

- Does it suggest that farming is being modernised as the labour force shrinks?

- How might EU membership have affected, and continue to affect, employment in agriculture?

- How might this be affecting the core–periphery relationship?

AQA Examiner's tip

Top Issue Evaluation advice

Make sure that you know what every word in the AIB means. Perhaps you and the class could work with your teacher to produce a glossary.

During the last 10 years, the Polish food industry has been restructured and privatised to a large extent. Large multinational corporations were active from the very beginning of the privatisation process in Poland, e.g. Coca-Cola, Nestlé, Gervais Danone and Cadbury Schweppes. Eighty per cent of the production of confectionery, over 50 per cent of the sugar market, most beer and tobacco manufacturing companies, the largest meat-processing plants, beverage bottling plants, and fruit and vegetable processing are currently in foreign ownership. Apart from the leading manufacturers, the sector consists of many small and medium-sized companies, which serve mostly local markets.

The Polish telecommunications market is one of the most dynamically growing markets of the central and east European (CEE) countries. The ICT market in Poland is the biggest of all the CEE countries (40 percent of the total regional ICT spending). Production of audio-video and telecommunications equipment amounts to nearly 90 per cent of the value of production in Poland's ICT sector.

Foreign production and service companies play a leading role. By 2006, only 2 per cent of all ICT companies were in state or co-operative ownership. There were 250 foreign-owned companies (e.g. Siemens, France Telecom and Tele Denmark). In 2004, the Polish telecommunications market increased by 13 per cent. It will continue to grow in 2005–7, thanks to the rapid expansion of mobile telephony, data transmission and broadband internet access.

Poland experiences large disparities in regional distribution of ICT production. The ICT sector is concentrated in and around large cities in Poland (Warsaw, with the majority of ICT companies, and Poznań) and along the so-called 'highway cluster' (cities in southern Poland linked by the A4 motorway), between Kraków, Katowice and Wrocław and adjacent areas.

One problem facing western companies investing in the EU new CEE states is the uncertainty about how long the cost advantages over the older EU-15 states will last. There is already a move within the EU administration to achieve greater harmonisation of corporate taxation rates, which could threaten low-tax regimes. But how quickly will labour cost differentials disappear? Cost elements such as social security are a matter for governments to decide, but wage costs, which make up the bulk of labour costs, can be projected more readily.

If Germany and Poland are taken as points of comparison, and it is assumed that gross (pre-tax) pay levels rise at an average annual rate of 10 per cent in Poland and 1 per cent in Germany, then gross pay levels in Poland would not catch up with those in Germany until the year 2027. This means that a significant cost advantage would exist for at least 15–20 years, long enough to justify a financial return on most investments in plant and equipment.

Table 8.2 *Pay in the private sector for selected EU countries: February 2006*

Country	Gross hourly pay (%)*	Real net spending power (%)**
Denmark	100	100
Luxembourg	67	106
Germany	63	83
Netherlands	58	92
Finland	53	68
Ireland	53	77
UK	48	77
France	47	69
Portugal	18	46
Poland	13	32
Hungary	12	29
Slovak Republic	10	29

* *Shows average gross hourly pay as a percentage of that in Denmark*

** *Shows average real net spending power of the hourly wage as a percentage of that in Denmark*

This is a very important page. It shows how two sectors of Poland's industry are modernising and attracting foreign direct investment (FDI). It also makes some very interesting points about the concentration of certain industrial activities in the core and about the nature of some industry in the periphery. Finally, it considers some aspects of the country's future development potential.

In agricultural processing there is a clear divide between large, foreign-based transnational corporations (TNCs) and small and medium-sized local industry.

How do you think the spatial distribution of these two will differ from each other?

Will one locate largely in core regions and the other in the periphery, or not?

Is the structure likely to continue into the future or is the foreign-owned sector likely to expand at the expense of local companies?

The ICT sector is very different, with a very high proportion in foreign ownership. There appears to be an equally marked spatial concentration in the core regions.

What might the markets be for this industry? There are four main possibilities:

- a growing demand for ICT from the growing and modernising economy, including both hardware and the infrastructure such as cable networks

- a growing demand from private individuals, as prosperity increases, for communications and entertainment hardware

- exports to the old EU countries which will welcome cheaper prices which result from the cheaper labour force

- exports to the rest of eastern Europe for which Poland is well placed on account of its position, its well-trained labour force and its head start in the industry compared to less developed neighbours such as Slovakia and Romania in the EU and Belarus and Ukraine beyond.

The core–periphery model suggests that, over time, development might spread from the core into sub-cores and finally into the peripheral regions of the country. Do you think that this will apply to the ICT industry? At the development stage there are certainly advantages in companies clustering together to gain benefit from the close personal contacts needed by the creative people in the industry. However, production can be much more dispersed and can move towards the cheaper labour and land in more peripheral regions in Poland; or it can move to even cheaper locations outside Poland.

The final section discusses one aspect of the long-term future for investment in Poland. It compares Poland and Germany, and this comparison suggests that Poland will continue to offer a cost advantage to TNCs for another 15–20 years. However, this section does not compare wage rates in Poland with those in south Asia, or even those in new EU entrants such as Romania and Bulgaria.

AQA Examiner's tip

Top Issue Evaluation advice

Keep asking yourself: 'How does this relate to the case studies I have done in class?' and 'Could I use those case studies in the exam to compare with this area?'

Item 2 Article from *The Warsaw Voice* – a Polish government-sponsored website

Poland is once again becoming attractive to foreign capital. Foreigners' level of satisfaction with the possibility of making investments in Poland is also growing. A recent survey of 706 companies with foreign capital, commissioned by the Polish Information and Foreign Investment Agency (PAIiIZ), showed that the main factors influencing foreign investors' decisions to start a business in Poland include the size of the Polish market and the economic development prospects.

The survey results also show the positive impact of Poland's EU accession on the operations of companies with foreign capital. Almost 75 per cent of investors say that Poland being included in European structures has improved the conditions for their companies' operations. Investors consider harmonisation of Polish law with EU regulations as the greatest benefit of Poland joining the EU.

According to PAIiIZ estimates, the value of foreign direct investment in Poland in 2005 will be comparable to that achieved in 2004, when it was US$7.86 billion. This was the highest value since 2000. In 2004, foreign investors created almost 15,000 new jobs. In 2005, this figure may have grown to as much as 20,000.

Table 8.3 *Investment attractiveness ranking list – consulting firm*

Question	Answer
Which country in the world is most attractive for new investment?	Poland was rated 4th in the world. This was the highest in Europe and above the UK, Germany and France.
What particularly attracts you about Poland?	Availability of land; land prices; labour costs.
Rank countries in terms of labour productivity.	Poland was ranked 2nd highest in Europe behind the UK, but above Germany, the Czech Republic and Spain.

Before enlargement, the problem of opening up labour markets caused a lot of controversy. Many countries of the 'old' EU feared that citizens of the new countries would destabilise their labour markets, and therefore introduced transition periods. These fears turned out to be groundless. A European Commission report published at the start of February 2006 shows that the movement of workers from the new CEE EU member states to the 'old EU' mostly had positive effects. Workers from the new EU-10, which joined in 2004, helped to satisfy the needs of the labour markets and contributed to better economic results in Europe.

This report shows that the countries which did not introduce restrictions as of May 2004 (the UK, Ireland and Sweden) reported high economic growth, a drop in unemployment and increased employment.

Item 2

In the Issue Evaluation Exercise candidates should always consider the sources of documents that they are presented with in the AIB. You should try to work out how reliable each document might be and think about why the writer of the document produced it.

This item is taken from a website published by the Polish government. How much can it be trusted?

- Everything that it says appears to put Poland in a favourable light, but that is to be expected. The information might have been carefully selected but that does not make it wrong.

- Two sources are quoted: one is a survey that sounds as though it was carried out by a **quango** funded by the government to attract FDI into Poland.

- The other is a report from the European Commission which can probably be relied on for its accuracy.

- The survey by PAIiIZ looked at 706 companies. This provides a very substantial database and suggests thoroughness and attention to detail.

- Nothing in the item contradicts anything elsewhere in the AIB. In fact, some of the points about FDI are supported elsewhere, especially in Item 1.

So, unless you know better and can quote other sources of information in support of what you think, you ought to accept this as a valid document.

Treat it with caution. You may be justified in thinking that the website is trying to paint a good picture of the country, but you cannot dismiss it.

The table lists a number of attractions of Poland for foreign investors. If you read the text above the table carefully you can find more. And even then you might be able to think of at least one more. No mention is made of the advantages of being inside the EU's tariff boundaries.

With regard to that last point you should always try to think of other case studies that you have done which might be useful comparisons with this study. Many of you at GCSE or A Level will have studied one or more examples of investment in the UK by TNCs. The Nissan car plant in Sunderland is one well-known example of a Japanese TNC investing here in order to access the whole EU market.

The last part of the item introduces migration from Poland to the other EU countries. Note that this topic is dealt with more fully in Item 4. However, some issues are introduced here.

Key terms

Quango: Quasi-autonomous, non-governmental organisation. This usually means an organisation that is funded by the government but which is more or less independent and not completely controlled by the government.

AQA Examiner's tip

Top Issue Evaluation advice

If an item in the AIB refers to a website you should think about visiting that site to see how it has been updated. Don't spend too long on this though. Sites can contain a lot of irrelevant material. They are usually not aimed specifically at helping A Level geography students!

Item 3 Measures of regional economic development

Table 8.4 *Employment and wage rates*

Voivodship (see map below)	Unemployment as percentage of the registered workforce (2005)	Average monthly wage/ salary (zloty) (5.52 zloty = £1) (Jan–Mar 2006)	Total registered workforce (thousands) (31 December 2005)
1. Łódzkie	18.1	2,349	888
2. Mazowieckie	13.1	3,480	2,025
3. Małopolskie	13.9	2,523	1,012
4. Śląskie	14.6	2,755	1,491
5. Lubelskie	17.5	2,361	725
6. Podkarpackie	18.6	2,241	636
7. Podlaskie	15.7	2,420	389
8. Świętokrzyskie	20.7	2,346	430
9. Lubuskie	20.8	2,345	282
10. Wielkopolskie	14.7	2,445	1,210
11. Zachodniopomorskie	25.5	2,518	476
12. Dolnośląskie	20.6	2,604	876
13. Opolskie	18.9	2,494	291
14. Kujawsko-Pomorskie	22.6	2,370	640
15. Pomorskie	19.4	2,715	656
16. Warmińsko-Mazurskie	27.6	2,299	387

Note: *a voivodship is an administrative area similar to a county in the UK*

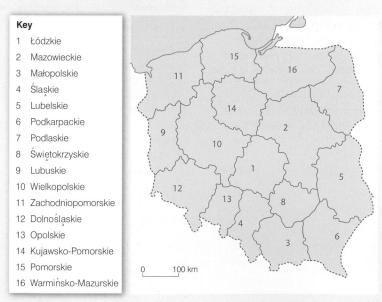

Key

1 Łódzkie
2 Mazowieckie
3 Małopolskie
4 Śląskie
5 Lubelskie
6 Podkarpackie
7 Podlaskie
8 Świętokrzyskie
9 Lubuskie
10 Wielkopolskie
11 Zachodniopomorskie
12 Dolnośląskie
13 Opolskie
14 Kujawsko-Pomorskie
15 Pomorskie
16 Warmińsko-Mazurskie

Fig. 8.4

The names are a problem! But each voivodship is also given a number. You will not lose any marks for using those numbers rather than the names, and you could save yourself a lot of time. You might even gain some gratitude from your examiner as not many geography examiners are fluent in Polish.

It is essential to spend a lot of time and thought on data like these. Regional economic development is one of the key topics in any geography course. The data show a great deal of information about the Polish regions and you need to get to know it thoroughly.

The first, and probably most obvious, way to process the data is by mapping them. You have been provided with a base map. Make three copies of it, at least, and present the three sets of information on those maps. (Alternatively, you could use tracing paper to make a series of overlays to go with the map.)

One map interpretation is presented below.

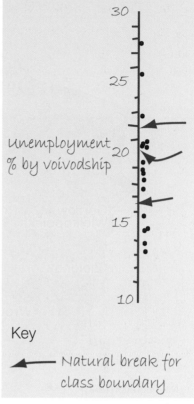

Fig. 8.6 *Student-drawn dispersion diagram to show average monthly wages in Poland in 00 zlotys, by voivodship*

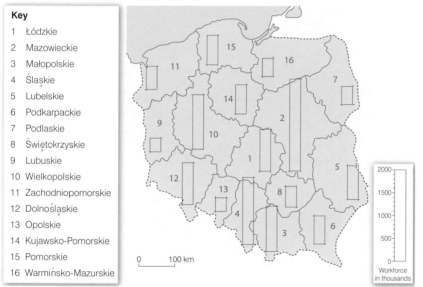

Fig. 8.5 *Student-drawn map to show total workforce of Poland by voivodship*

A dispersion diagram has also been drawn to try to see how a map of wage rates could be drawn. Unfortunately, once this had been completed it showed a lot of bunching of values with very few obvious groupings that could be used as classes on a choropleth map. Moreover, when attemps were made to draw a choropleth map it showed very little geographical pattern. In fact, the only real pattern that emerged was the striking difference between Mazowieckie and 'the rest'.

AQA Examiner's tip

Top Issue Evaluation advice

You **must** be prepared to work with the data in the AIB. Manipulate it; select from it; map it; graph it; use statistical techniques on it; draw conclusions from it; and then be prepared to refer back to that work in your exam.

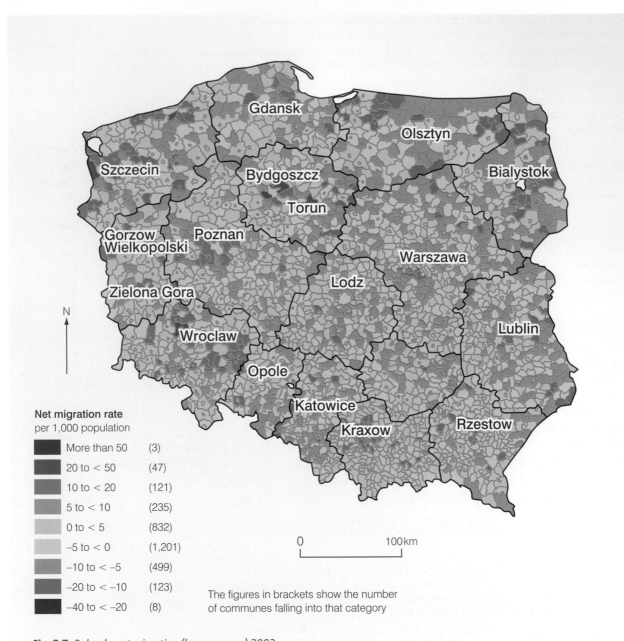

Net migration rate
per 1,000 population

	More than 50	(3)
	20 to < 50	(47)
	10 to < 20	(121)
	5 to < 10	(235)
	0 to < 5	(832)
	−5 to < 0	(1,201)
	−10 to < −5	(499)
	−20 to < −10	(123)
	−40 to < −20	(8)

The figures in brackets show the number
of communes falling into that category

Fig. 8.7 *Poland – net migration (by commune) 2002*

This is an extraordinarily detailed map. It is also extraordinarily interesting to geographers!

■ 1,238 communes gained population in 2002.

■ 1,831 communes lost population.

■ 2,033 communes only gained or lost less than 0.5 per cent of their population, which is fairly insignificant.

■ 171 communes gained more than 1 per cent of their population in a year.

■ 131 lost more than 1 per cent in a year.

There is obviously a big movement of people affecting all parts of the country. This was two years before Poland joined the EU and Poles were allowed to migrate freely to Sweden, Ireland and the UK and, less freely, to the other EU countries.

Most of the communes along the eastern borders are losing population, many at a rapid rate.

All the communes along the north-east coast are losing population at a rapid rate.

Many of the communes in rural Pomorskie (15), west of Gdansk and Zachodniopomorskie (11) are losing population rapidly.

Several inner-city areas, particularly Łódź, Poznań and Katowice are losing population.

Other areas of population loss are found round the edges of voivodships, in rural areas away from the major cities. This is particularly true in Mazowieckie, away from Warsaw; in Lodzkie, away from Łódź; and in Wielkopolskie away from Poznań.

All the big cities are gaining population, generally in suburban rings.

There are small population gains in several parts of the Sudeten and Carpathian mountains along the southern border.

It appears that the map indicates several movements of population:

■ rural depopulation

■ urbanisation

■ suburbanisation

■ movement away from the eastern border regions

■ possibly also a north–south movement.

It also helps to define:

■ a national core and periphery

■ urban cores and rural peripheries in many of the voivodships.

This latter point might make you wonder just what variations are hidden by the presentation of the data in Table 8.4 based on voivodships. Mazowieckie might have the lowest unemployment rates, the highest wage rates and the largest working population of all the voivodships, but it also has some peripheral areas in the north and east that are losing population rapidly. It might be assumed that people are leaving these areas because of high unemployment and/or low wage rates, and this is in the voivodship that comes out top on each of the measures used in Table 8.4.

Item 4 So far, migrant workers have been just the job
(*Observer*, 27 August 2006)

Since the European Union surged eastward two years ago, embracing 10 additional countries, more than 400,000 citizens from new members have arrived to work in the UK, sparking a fierce debate about the benefits they bring. With Bulgaria and Romania waiting to join in January 2007, many on both sides of the political spectrum are saying it is time to raise the drawbridge.

Imaginary Polish plumbers who struck fear into the hearts of British workers before the eight accession countries from eastern Europe joined the EU in 2004 have given way to a much more vibrant, complex reality. According to the Home Office, the most common occupation for the new arrivals is not plumbing or bricklaying, but 'administration, business and management'. The newcomers, mostly young and without dependants, have spread across the country, transforming communities which have rarely experienced migration on this scale. Weighing up the costs and benefits these arrivals have brought has become urgent, as Bulgaria and Romania, with GDP per capita less than half that of Poland, queue to join the EU next year.

Britain was one of only three countries, with Ireland (whose fast-growing economy has absorbed proportionally far more accession country migrants than the UK) and Sweden, to extend full working rights to citizens of the new European countries in 2004. Now it must decide whether to do the same for the new members.

For those with secure, well-paying jobs and a mortgage, Czech waiters, Slovakian fruit-pickers and the rest have been a boon. A pool of tax-paying workers, by most accounts diligent, keen to work and willing to take on jobs for which they are over-qualified, has helped to keep the lid on wages and prices.

As well as hiring the accession country workers, many businesses have seen lucrative opportunities in their arrival. One explanation offered for the strength of the buy-to-let property market has been the demand for accommodation from east European workers, while Polish delicatessens, internet cafés and money-transfer agencies have sprung up to cater for new needs.

But for lower-skilled workers – and, as former Labour minister Frank Field pointed out, for students seeking holiday jobs in pubs and restaurants – the influx of keen eastern Europeans looks very different. The government's labour market figures have not shown unemployment rising for more than a year, at the same time as employment is also going up. That shows jobs are still being created, but suggests that some of them are being soaked up by new workers instead of going to the home-grown unemployed.

That may be because the arrivals have skills local workers can't offer, but it may also be for other reasons. There is anecdotal evidence from employers that in some cases they prefer to take on a young Pole or Slovak who has the gumption to leave home and travel hundreds of miles in search of a job, than a bumptious UK school-leaver with few skills and little enthusiasm.

Finally, when assessing the impact of accession-country migration, as with most things, the past is not always a reliable guide. Workers have been sucked into the UK by the rapid rate of job creation in the economy; harder times could lead them to look elsewhere.

Immigration has also been artificially boosted by the barriers other EU members have kept around their labour markets. Migrant workers considering Britain as a destination will soon have other options. Free movement of labour is a fundamental pillar of the single market, and all EU members are expected to open their doors by 2011, when the 'transitional arrangements' blocking workers from entering Germany, Austria, Italy and other countries are due to expire. France has already said it will phase out restrictions in the next three years.

Looking at Britain's economy as a whole, with high growth, low unemployment and low interest rates, the arrival of Poles, Czechs and the rest seems an unequivocal bonus, helping to fill skills shortages, boosting productivity and creating new taxpayers. For almost a million workers who remain unemployed while eastern Europeans win new jobs, the analysis may look rather different. But closing the doors to Bulgarians and Romanians won't help – while better training and education might.

This is taken from a newspaper article. As you saw with the website, it is important to try to evaluate the degree of objectivity of any such article. Ask yourself the following questions:

- Is the article factual news or comment on the facts, or does it contain both?

- Are any facts quoted from reliable sources?

- Is the newspaper from which the article was taken generally considered to be a serious paper of news and comment, or an entertaining tabloid?

- Where does the paper fit on the general left-to-right spread of political opinion?

- As this article is about migration does it appear to be broadly supportive of migration or broadly against?

- Does the article appear to be fairly balanced or is it sensationalising the issue?

The article was written in 2006. It relates to a topic that has been discussed, in great detail, in the press since then. There have been many attempts to update the statistics.

It is very important to try to find information that is as up to date as possible on this topic.

What are the issues that might be discussed in this article?

What different points of view might be considered?

Note that the article deals mainly with the issues involved with migration into the UK, but the rest of the AIB has been mainly about Poland, so you must also consider the issue of migration from a Polish point of view.

There are benefits and problems caused by migration, in both the source country and the destination. You could consider drawing up a matrix to summarise these.

	Benefits of migration	Problems caused by migration
In the UK		
In Poland		

You could consider the issues under the geographers' three classic headings:

- social issues

- economic issues

- environmental issues.

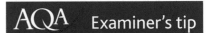

AQA Examiner's tip

Top Issue Evaluation advice

When dealing with issues, remember that they are always open to different interpretations. That is what makes them 'issues'! Try to see issues from different points of view, and try to discuss them in detail rather than simplifying them.

Item 5 Further research

1. Internet study

The Polish Investment Agency, PAIiIZ, which was mentioned in Item 2, has a very good website. It can be found at www.paiz.gov.pl

You can visit this site to update your information on Poland's population and economy.

The site also has detailed information about the economy of the different voivodships. You should try to look at the information about at least one prosperous voivodship in the centre of the country and at least one voivodship in a difficult, peripheral area.

2. Fieldwork ideas

The issues surrounding migration of workers from eastern Europe into the UK since the expansion of the EU have caused a lot of discussion in the British media in recent years. Unfortunately, these issues have often become confused with the issues linked to asylum seekers, illegal immigration, trafficking of people and other economic issues.

During your period of preparation for the exam **think about** how A Level geography students could carry out fieldwork to discover the attitudes of people towards migration of eastern European workers into the UK.

How could they draw up a questionnaire that collected relevant and useful data?

How could they select a sample of the population?

What problems might A Level students face in carrying out such research?

(**Note**: You are not expected to carry out such research as part of your preparation.)

Note that there is no commentary on this page of the AIB on the page opposite. However, if you turn to p312 headed Questions on fieldwork, you will see how the examiner might interpret the Fieldwork ideas paragraph above.

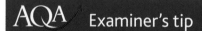

Examiner's tip

Top Issue Evaluation advicea

Keep these fieldwork ideas in proportion. You are likely to be asked questions on them in the exam, but they are not likely to be the long questions with 15 marks attached to them. You are more likely to get a 5- 8-mark question on fieldwork. So think about the topic clearly. Try to arrange for a lesson to discuss it with your teacher. Try to link the topic back to work that you have already done as part of your course. Remember that you are certainly not being advised to carry out a fieldwork enquiry of your own on this topic.

▪ Summary map

Three main themes appear to have come out from the study of the AIB. These are:

▪ the issue of spatial patterns of development in Poland

▪ the issue of FDI in Poland

▪ issues connected with migration, as these affect both Poland and the UK.

The map below shows an attempt to summarise a lot of the main ideas connected with these themes – particularly with the first theme – the spatial patterns. The references to 'core' and 'peripheral' Poland are based on a synthesis, or pulling together, of ideas from the four main sets of spatial data – unemployment rates, wage rates, workforce numbers and migration patterns.

The map is divided into main core and periphery areas and then the arrows attempt to show the strongest parts of the core (red arrows) and the weakest parts of the periphery (green arrows).

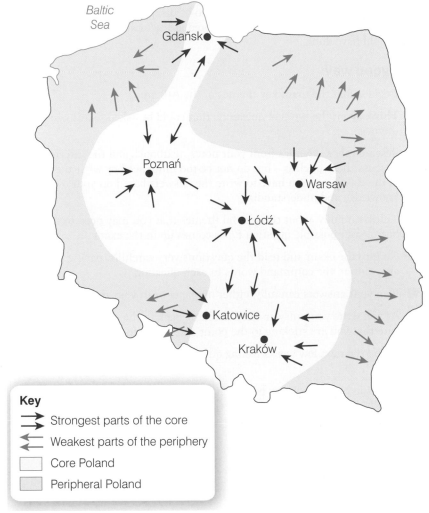

Key
⇒ Strongest parts of the core
⇐ Weakest parts of the periphery
☐ Core Poland
☐ Peripheral Poland

Fig. 8.8 *Student-drawn map to summarise the core–periphery relationship in Poland*

Thinking about possible questions

When you are preparing with the AIB you will inevitably start to think about the type of questions that might come up on the paper. You will also try to think about how you might answer those questions if they do come up. There are two possible ways of doing this – the 'good way' and the 'bad way'.

The bad way:

- Using all your skill, expertise and knowledge of how examiners think, work out the questions that must inevitably appear on the paper.

- Discuss these in class, research them in the AIB and in your class notes. Search the internet for relevant material.

- Write model answers to the questions that are going to be set.

- Learn these answers.

- Go into the exam and write out your learnt answers. Do not worry too much about the actual questions that have been set … because you know best.

- Spend the next few weeks preparing to be disappointed when the results are published. You have probably scored at least two grades lower than you should have done.

The good way:

- Decide what the main key themes of the AIB are.

- Think about the types of questions that could be asked relating to these themes.

- Research those themes from your notes, textbooks and the internet. Discuss them in class – but do not be too influenced by what the rest of the class says. You have to write the answers based on your own knowledge and understanding.

- Think carefully about the general themes that you may need to develop if one of your possible question types comes up in the exam.

- Go into the exam and read the questions very carefully, paying particular attention to the command words in each question.

- Plan your answers carefully, either on paper or in your mind.

- As you write your answer, keep checking back to the question to make sure that you are sticking to the point and not drifting.

- Spend the next few weeks feeling quietly confident that you have done well.

This section of the book has been written by the person who used the Polish case study as the basis of a paper for the old Geography specification. On the next page are suggestions as to how the case study could be used to write a paper on the new specification.

■ Comparing questions on the specimen

Note: Your teacher probably has a copy of the specimen questions. If not, hard copies can be obtained from AQA or copies can be downloaded from the AQA website.

The specimen paper that was published with the new specification was divided into:

1	(a)		State a hypothesis …	(2 marks)
	(b)		Use the data (to complete a Spearman correlation) …	(6 marks)
	(c)	(i)	Interpret the significance of your calculation …	(2 marks)
		(ii)	What conclusions can you draw …?	(3 marks)
2	(a)		Suggest what factors …	(5 marks)
	(b)		Evaluate the factors …	(8 marks)
3			Using the map and data compare …	(10 marks)
4			Outline one fieldwork technique that you could use …	(9 marks)
5			Suggest which solution and justify your suggestion …	(15 marks)

The Specimen Paper illustrates the type of question that could be asked on the paper. On any paper there is likely to be:

■ some data presentation and/or analysis

■ some reference to fieldwork

■ at least one question that looks at aspects of the main issues involved

■ at least one question that comes to some sort of conclusion. This question might involve decision-making. It will almost certainly involve a major element of justification or evaluation of the views that you present.

Questions on the data

The data presentation and/or analysis questions could include examples like the following:

1   You have been asked to present the data from Table 8.4 for the total registered workforce in each voivodship on the copy of the map below.

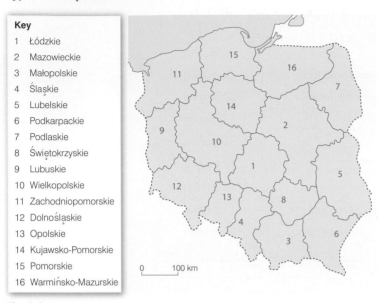

Key

1 Łódzkie
2 Mazowieckie
3 Małopolskie
4 Śląskie
5 Lubelskie
6 Podkarpackie
7 Podlaskie
8 Świętokrzyskie
9 Lubuskie
10 Wielkopolskie
11 Zachodniopomorskie
12 Dolnośląskie
13 Opolskie
14 Kujawsko-Pomorskie
15 Pomorskie
16 Warmińsko-Mazurskie

0   100 km

Fig. 8.4

(a) Name and briefly describe the technique that you would use.   *(5 marks)*

(b) Show the total registered workforce for Mazowieckie, Podlaskie and Warmińsko-Mazurskie on the map, using the technique named in (a).   *(3 marks)*

(c) Complete the key that you need to show the values for all the voivodships using your chosen technique.   *(2 marks)*

Or:

2   You have been asked to complete a choropleth map to show the percentage unemployment data from Table 8.4.

(a) To help you to decide the class intervals to use on your map, complete a dispersion diagram on graph paper, showing the percentage unemployment data for each of the voivodships.   *(4 marks)*

(b) Mark lines on the dispersion diagram to show the class intervals you would use to draw the choropleth map.   *(2 marks)*

(c) Draw a key in the space below to show how you would shade the map.   *(4 marks)*

In your answer to Question 1 you should choose a map that shows distribution of the total numbers of the workforce in each voivodship. Therefore, you should use a located proportional symbol in each area of the map.

Use symbols because you are trying to show a total, which applies to the whole of the area and which is influenced by the size of the area. You should not use choropleth shading because that is used to show a density of distribution. You could only do that with the figures for total workforce if you knew the area of each voivodship and could work out the density of workforce throughout the voivodships.

You could use any of these symbols:

■ squares – where the area of each square is proportional to the size of the workforce

■ circles – where the area of each circle is proportional

■ bars – where the length of each bar is proportional.

Squares or circles would be useful if you had to show a very big range of totals. Here the range is from 282 to 2025. That would be quite easy to fit on bars. The biggest bar would not be too long and the smallest bar would still be clearly visible if you chose a sensible scale. It would also be easier and quicker to draw in the exam.

Draw your symbol for Mazowieckie so that its base line is clearly in the area of the voivodship. The whole length of the bar should lie within Mazowieckie – but if it spreads beyond the border it should not spread far and should not clash with any of the other bars still to be drawn.

Your key should show clearly the scale that you have chosen to use. You should draw a scale line against which each of the bars on your map could be measured.

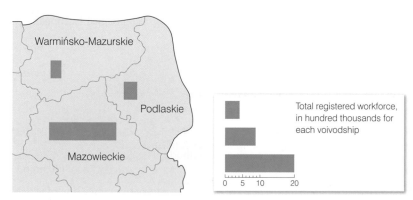

Fig. 8.9 *Voivodships*

In Question 2 you are asked to think about drawing a choropleth map because the figures are expressed as percentages and these do not depend on the size of the voivodship. Shading a large area in one tint would not be misleading. It would if you tried to show totals, which is why a choropleth map would not have been suitable for the data in Question 1.

When you choose your class boundaries you have 16 voivodships to consider. You need enough different classes to make an interesting pattern, but not so many that your map becomes confusing. Three, four or five classes would seem to be a sensible number.

Look at your dispersion diagram. There might be some clear breaks in the sequence which would form sensible class boundaries. But you do not want to have some very big groups and some very small groups.

Fig. 8.10 *Dispersion diagram showing unemployment by voivodship – basis for class divisions for choropleth map*

The boundaries could come at the points marked. It would give four groups of 5, 5, 3 and 3, which would be reasonably balanced. Alternatively, the voivodships could have been divided into four groups with 4 in each, but then the class boundaries would have separated a value of 18.6 from another of 18.9 and a value of 20.7 from one of 20.8. This would have produced a misleading map.

When choosing the shades for the map, make sure that high numbers are represented by denser shading and lower numbers by lighter shading. Do not leave any areas blank because that could look as if there was no unemployment, and do not shade anywhere in solid black because that could give the impression everyone was unemployed!

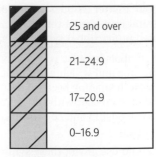

Fig. 8.11 *Unemployment %*

Try to be consistent by using four different densities of diagonal line. Avoid mixing line shading and dot shading because that might be interpreted as showing two quite different types of area when the areas being shaded are actually part of a continuum.

Finally, make sure that the values do not overlap or leave gaps. That is why the key to the map ends one class at 24.9 and starts the next higher class at 25.0.

Questions on fieldwork

The questions that refer to fieldwork must be quite predictable. On p306 the section of the AIB referring to fieldwork stated:

> How could they draw up a questionnaire that collected relevant and useful data?
>
> How could they select a sample of the population?
>
> What problems might A Level students face in carrying out such research?

So questions on the paper could be taken from the following:

You have been asked to carry out a fieldwork survey of the attitudes, in a local area, towards migration of east European workers into the UK.

(a) Outline the principles that would guide you when you were drawing up the questions to ask. Explain why these principles are important. *(10 marks)*

(b) If you decided to use the survey with 100 respondents, suggest **two** ways of selecting your sample so that you gained a representative cross section of the local population.

Explain a method you would use to collect your sample. *(10 marks)*

(c) Outline some of the practical problems of carrying out a survey by the chosen method. Suggest how you could try to overcome those problems. *(10 marks)*

Note that these three questions would not all be asked on a single paper. They are offered as alternatives, only one of which is likely to be asked.

AQA Examiner's tip

Top Issue Evaluation advice

If you use a questionnaire you must keep the aims of the data collection in mind at all times – when drawing up your questions, when selecting your sample, when asking the questions and when presenting and analysing the results.

In order to answer (**a**) you would need to know exactly what you are aiming to find out.

- What is your hypothesis or research question?

- How do you hope to present and analyse your data?

- How long can you spend with each respondent? And how long do you think repondents will be willing to spend with you?

- Do you need background information such as age, sex and employment status?

- Do you want open-ended or closed questions?

- Are you interested in what people **know** about immigration, about what they **feel** about immigration or about a **combination** of knowledge and feelings?

You need to consider these points and then explain why they are important. You might mention some of the types of question that you will ask, but always explain the underlying reason for asking each question. All of this illustrates another principle of answering questions in this exam and in most other exams too:

> Read the whole of a multi-part question, and start to plan all your answers, before you begin to answer any part of it.

In your answer to (**b**) you should write about two of the following:

- random sampling

- systematic sampling

- stratified sampling.

Then decide whether you are going to choose your sample:

- opportunistically, from passers-by on the street

- in a planned way by targeting people selected from an electoral roll or other such list

- in a planned way by targeting particular areas and selecting houses.

You could combine principles from these two lists so that, for example:

- random selection from the electoral roll, where you pick out names at random with the help of random numbers from a computer program

- stratified selection from an electoral roll, where you worked out what percentage of the local electors lived on each street in the area and then chose a number of people from each street to represent those percentages.

In answering (**c**) you need to be aware that this is a very sensitive topic and you might find difficulty getting people to answer your questionnaire; even if they are willing to answer, they might give answers that are difficult to deal with. Discuss such problems in your answer.

However, you should also be prepared to deal with more general problems with carrying out questionnaires, such as:

- If you do a random street survey, what will you do if a very high proportion of your interviewees are old people because it is pension day at the post office?

- If you select house numbers, what do you do if people are not in?

- How do you deal with the situation where a person you select to interview looks or speaks like a non-British person who appears to be an immigrant herself?

- If you carry out the survey as a group exercise, how do you ensure that each member of the group asks questions in the same way so as not to prejudice the results?

Questions on the issues

This is where the biggest proportion of the marks will be available, so it is the part of the paper on which you should spend most time. It has been stated that:

> Three main themes appear to have come out from the study of the AIB. These are:
>
> ■ the issue of spatial patterns of development in Poland
> ■ the issue of FDI in Poland
> ■ issues connected with migration, as these affect both Poland and the UK.

Questions that could be asked on these themes might include the following (although note that not all of these would be included on one paper):

1   Discuss how internal migration is affecting the distribution of population within Poland.   *(15 marks)*

2   Suggest how the patterns of migration in Poland might change over the next 20 years or so. Refer to internal migration within Poland and to migration into/out of Poland.   *(10 marks)*

3   Why is Poland seen as attractive for inward investment by foreign companies?   *(10 marks)*

4   Discuss how the attitude of foreign investors to investing in Poland might change over the next 20 years or so.   *(10 marks)*

5   Discuss issues associated with continuing migration from Poland and other east European countries into the United Kingdom.   *(15 marks)*

6   Discuss how some of the factors affecting the migration of east Europeans into the United Kingdom might change over the next few years.

What might be the consequences of such changes?   *(15 marks)*

1 Key points here include:

■ Which areas are losing population?

■ Do these areas have anything in common? Is there a pattern to the areas of population loss?

■ Which areas are gaining population?

■ Do **these** areas have anything in common? Is there a pattern?

■ Is there evidence to show that any of the following processes are taking place: rural depopulation, urbanisation, suburbanisation, counter-urbanisation, move towards the centre from the border regions, east-to-west movement, north-to-south movement, etc.?

2 Key points here include:

■ Will FDI continue to come into Poland?

■ If it does, will it continue to go to the core, urban areas or might it be attracted to the peripheral, rural areas?

■ Will this FDI be mainly to produce cheap goods for the whole EU market or will it be directed towards a growing market for consumer goods in Poland?

■ If the location of such investment within Poland changes, how will that affect population and migration?

■ Will EU agricultural support policies affect the core–periphery relationship?

■ How will EU structural support for building infrastructure and developing the labour force affect different areas?

■ Will investment in agriculture increase the demand for rural labour, or might it lead to mechanisation and reduced demand for labour?

■ How will the answers to the question above affect migration?

■ What might happen to external migration? Will emigration from Poland to the EU core areas continue or will there be a 'backwash effect', with former migrants coming home bringing new skills and perhaps accumulated capital? Where might these returning migrants settle, in the cities or in the villages?

3 Many points to help you answer this question can be found in the AIB. You are perfectly at liberty to quote as much as you want from the AIB, but remember that:

■ Answers that just string together useful quotes can get good Level 1 marks but they cannot progress to Level 2.

■ The examiners know the AIB even better than most of you. They can tell when you are copying ideas without adding much of your own thought. So do not try to pretend that what you are writing is original when it is not. Acknowledge quotations by using inverted commas or speech marks.

■ This is a good opportunity for you to refer to your own research. However, you should acknowledge your sources here too. First of all, it is the honest thing to do, but also it may well gain you credit for extra, relevant information.

4 An easy answer here is to say, 'There will be more of the same', and that is a fine thing to say if you can support it with facts. However, you could also consider the effect of:

■ continued expansion of the EU – recently Romania and Bulgaria, possibly Turkey, possibly Ukraine …

■ possible moves from export-led investment to investment to meet the needs of the changing Polish market

■ increasing wage rates and land prices in Poland

■ economic recession

■ continued development of industry in China, India, Bangladesh … and what about southern Africa?

5 and 6   Three tips here:

a   The question asks about issues connected with migration. That gives you a lot of scope. Write about the effects of migration in the UK and in eastern Europe; about short-term and long-term effects; about the way it might affect different areas; about how it affects different groups of people.

Be prepared to show off the breadth of your geographical understanding.

b   You are given some data here, but not a lot of hard evidence. Also you know that this evidence is not the most recent available. But you cannot dismiss it unless you can quote something more recent and equally reliable.

If possible, present up-to-date evidence that you have researched but describe its source. Evidence from the Home Office is generally more reliable than a headline from the *Daily Express*. Evidence from your local authority is generally more reliable than what a man said to you at the bus stop last week.

Be sensible and take an academic approach to this topic.

c   These can be dangerous questions!

They can be dangerous because they can attract a lot of poorly supported, general, ungeographical waffling. Avoid both 'right-wing, anti-immigrant, tabloid-style ranting' and 'woolly-minded, bleeding-heart, pro-immigrant waffling'. Neither type of answer gains much credit.

On the other hand, candidates who draw definite conclusions that are either clearly pro- or clearly anti-immigration, and whose views are backed up with well-sourced facts and logical argument will gain good marks. There are no obvious 'right' or 'wrong' answers to these questions, but you are expected to discuss the topics as real geographers. You must relate what you write to the whole body of geographical facts, ideas, theories, case studies and concepts that you have spent your A Level course developing.

Geography teachers get very frustrated when an exam ends and the invigilator scoffs, 'That was easy. It was just common sense. Any intelligent sixth-former could have answered that.'

The geography teachers know that any intelligent sixth-former could have produced a load of half-baked ideas and generalised waffle, just like anyone in the local pub could do on a Friday night. But only a well-prepared geographer could produce a high-quality, geographical answer and gain good marks.

Make sure that your answers are those of a well-prepared geographer.

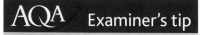

Examiner's tip

Top Issue Evaluation advice

The examiners will give you credit for presenting your own opinions, but only if these are argued clearly and supported with reliable evidence.

In this chapter you will have learnt:

- about the nature of the Issue Evaluation Exercise
- how to prepare for using the AIB
- how to answer questions on this exam paper
- about issues linked to the development of Poland within the EU
- about issues of foreign direct investment by TNCs
- about the patterns of development and migration in Poland
- about some of the issues involved in the migration of workers within the EU
- about some techniques of data collection, presentation and analysis and their practical applications
- how to draw conclusions in Issue Evaluation Exercises.

AQA Unit 3 questions

You have to answer three questions from this paper:

- one from Section A – a physical, structured question
- one from Section B – a human, structured question
- one from Section C – an essay question that could be either physical or human.

Your essay question must not be taken from the same topic area that you took one of your structured questions from.

So, for instance, if you had studied Topics 1 (Tectonics), 2 (Weather) and 4 (Cities):

- You would have to do the Cities structured question from Section B.
- Then you would have to choose which essay to do from Section C. Would you choose Tectonics or Weather?
- Then you would use the other physical topic to do your structured question from Section A.

On the other hand, some people might study four topics and choose which three to answer when they are in the exam. Even these people must be very careful when choosing their questions, and they have a more complicated choice to make.

If in doubt about your question choice, remember:

- the essay question is worth 40 marks
- each structured question is only worth 25 marks.

Therefore, it is particularly important that you choose the essay question that best suits you.

SECTION A

Answer **one** question from this section.

You must not answer the question number that you will answer in Section C.

1   **Plate tectonics and associated hazards**   **Total for this question: 25 marks**

(a) Study Fig. 1, which was taken during the eruption of Mount Pinatubo.

Fig. 1

Comment on the probable short-term and long-term consequences of this eruption
for the lives of the people living in this area.   *(7 marks)*

(b) Explain what hot spots are and explain why they are often associated with lines
of volcanoes.   *(8 marks)*

(c) Referring to examples that you have studied, discuss how people in different
parts of the world can plan to reduce the dangers that are associated with seismic
activity.   *(10 marks)*

2 **Weather and climate and associated hazards** **Total for this question: 25 marks**

(a) Study Fig. 2 which shows the number of extreme storm events in the UK between 1960 and 2005.

Number of extreme storms around the UK 1960–2003
(a) Jan–Mar

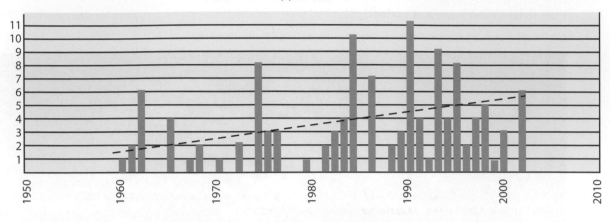

(b) Oct–Dec

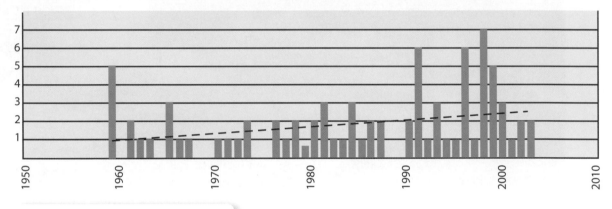

Key

 Running mean–storm/month

Fig. 2

Comment on the pattern shown and suggest any possible causes of changes in the pattern over this period. *(7 marks)*

(b) Explain how urban temperatures can differ from the temperatures of surrounding rural areas, and why these differences occur. *(8 marks)*

(c) With reference to two examples that you have studied, assess how the authorities in different areas prepare for and react after revolving tropical storms strike areas of dense population. *(10 marks)*

3   **Ecosystems: change and challenge**   **Total for this question: 25 marks**

(a) Study Fig. 3 which shows an extract from a website:

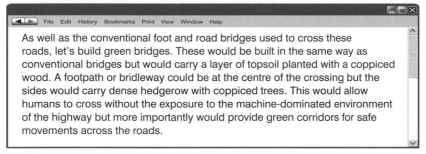

As well as the conventional foot and road bridges used to cross these roads, let's build green bridges. These would be built in the same way as conventional bridges but would carry a layer of topsoil planted with a coppiced wood. A footpath or bridleway could be at the centre of the crossing but the sides would carry dense hedgerow with coppiced trees. This would allow humans to cross without the exposure to the machine-dominated environment of the highway but more importantly would provide green corridors for safe movements across the roads.

Fig. 3   *www.globalideasbank.org/site/bank/idea.php?ideaId=4538*

Comment on how the ideas contained in this extract might affect the ecosystems or areas alongside main roads and motorways, if they were put into practice.   (*7 marks*)

(b) Describe the main characteristics of the vegetation in one tropical biome that you have studied, and explain how these characteristics are adapted to the area's climate.   (*8 marks*)

(c) With reference to two contrasting case studies, evaluate attempts that have been made to manage and conserve fragile ecosystems.   (*10 marks*)

SECTION B

Answer **one** question from this section.

You must not answer the question number that you will answer in Section C.

4 **World cities** **Total for this question: 25 marks**

   (a) Study Fig. 4 which shows the bus system of Curitiba in Brazil. Map 4(a) shows the express lines and Map 4(b) superimposes a map of the local lines on top of the express lines.

        Curitiba (population: 1.8 million) is often described as having one of the most integrated and sustainable urban transport networks in any of the world's millionaire cities. To what extent does the information on the map support that description? *(7 marks)*

   (b) Illustrating your answer with references to one or more cities that you have studied, explain the meaning of the word 're-urbanisation'. *(8 marks)*

   (c) To what extent do you agree with the statement that 'urbanisation is an essential condition in allowing economic development of countries in the modern, globalised economy'? *(10 marks)*

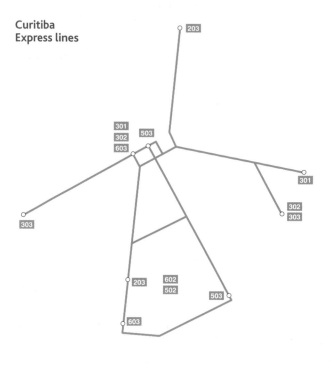

Curitiba Express lines

Fig. 4(a)

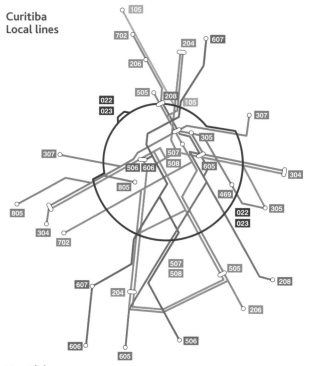

Curitiba Local lines

Fig. 4(b)

5 **Development and globalisation**

(a) Study Fig. 5 which shows the growth of the area of the EU, and its possible future growth.

Fig. 5

Croatia and Turkey started accession talks on 3 October 2005. Turkey could complete them in 15 years, Croatia in five.

The other Balkan countries have been told they can join the EU one day, if they meet the criteria. These include democracy, the rule of law, a market economy and adherence to the EU's goals of political and economic union.

Comment on the growth of the EU since 1995 and suggest reasons why other countries of south-east Europe are applying to join now. *(7 marks)*

(b) Explain how the globalisation of the world's service economy has helped the economic growth of some countries, such as India, that used to be classed as 'less developed countries'. *(8 marks)*

(c) With reference to one or more case studies, discuss the role that aid can play in the development of the economies of poor countries. *(10 marks)*

6   **Contemporary challenges and conflicts**   **Total for this question: 25 marks**

(**a**)   Study Fig. 6 which shows the global distribution of GDP per capita.

Key

- 30,000+
- 20,000–29,999
- 15,000–19,999
- 10,000–14,999
- 5,000–9,999
- 3,000–4,999
- 1,000–2,999
- 0–999
- No data

Fig. 6

        Comment on the world distribution of poverty as shown by this map.   (*7 marks*)

(**b**)   With reference to one area in the UK where a multicultural society has developed, explain why the area became multicultural and discuss one or more of the issues that have arisen in the area as a consequence of the multiculturalism.   (*8 marks*)

(**c**)   With reference to one major international conflict that has occurred within the last 30 years, evaluate the social, economic and environmental issues that have been associated with it.   (*10 marks*)

Section C

Answer **one** question from this section.

You must not answer the question number answered in either Section A or Section B.

Note to candidate:

You should bear in mind that the essay questions below are synoptic in nature. In your response to these questions you are required to show your knowledge and understanding of different aspects of geography, the connections between these different aspects and, where relevant, of human perspectives on geographical themes and issues.

1   'The world distribution of population is as important as the world distribution of areas of tectonic activity in predicting the hazards of volcanic activity' Discuss this statement.   *(40 marks)*

2   Evaluate the extent to which knowledge of the origins and nature of air masses is necessary for an understanding of the way that weather patterns affect life in the UK.   *(40 marks)*

3   Some ecological conservation areas are designed to stop seral progression towards a climatic climax vegetation. With reference to one (or more) examples explain how and why this is done and discuss whether this approach to the environment can be justified.   *(40 marks)*

4   'The development of world cities and megacities has only been possible because of developments in transport, but now transport problems threaten to limit further growth of the biggest cities.' To what extent do you agree with this view?   *(40 marks)*

5   'Globalisation has allowed the economies of some poor countries to develop, but such development has often led to increasing gaps between the rich and the poor in those countries.' Discuss this statement with reference to contrasting countries that you have studied.   *(40 marks)*

6   'Immigration is making the UK an increasingly multicultural society; and the only way that immigration can be controlled in the long term is by making increased efforts to address poverty on a global scale.' Discuss this statement.   *(40 marks)*

Glossary

A

Abiotic environment: the non-living things in the environment – water, light, warmth, humidity, carbon dioxide, rocks and minerals, soil, etc.

Air mass: a large body of air with relatively similar temperature and humidity characteristics.

Albedo: the reflectivity of the Earth's surface.

Alternative hypothesis: the statistician's term given to the geographical idea that you are hoping to find is correct. It is possible to accept the alternative hypothesis when the null hypothesis has been disproved.

Anticyclone: a high-pressure system.

Aquifer: a porous layer of rock that carries water that falls in one area, below the ground surface, so that it becomes available elsewhere, either by flowing to the surface under its own pressure or by being pumped out.

Asylum seeker: someone who has fled his or her home country to find a safe place elsewhere. Under the 1951 Convention on Refugees, an asylum applicant must be able to demonstrate a well-founded fear of persecution in his or her country of origin for reasons of political opinion, religion, ethnicity, race/nationality, or membership of a particular social group.

Atmosphere: the mixture of gases, predominantly nitrogen, oxygen, argon, carbon dioxide and water vapour, that surrounds the Earth.

Autotroph: plant that is capable of producing its own food through photosynthesis.

B

Bilateral aid: money sent from the government of one rich country directly to another poorer country. Most of the UK's bilateral aid is sent through the Department for International Development (DfID).

Biome: a major, world-scale ecosystem. It is the climatic climax vegetation across an area of continental size, with one dominant vegetation type.

Biotic environment: living things – plants, animals, bacteria, fungi, etc. and people.

C

Carnivore or **secondary consumer:** meat-eater.

Carr woodland: forms when shallow water or fen is left unmanaged and small shrubs and trees start to grow, leading to the natural creation of carr woodland.

Climatic climax vegetation: the vegetation that is thought to evolve in a climate region if the seral progression is not interrupted by human activity, tectonic processes, impeded drainage, etc.

Comparison goods: goods that are bought less often than everyday 'convenience goods'. They include things such as clothes, shoes, electrical and household goods for which people make special shopping trips so that they can compare prices, styles, etc.

Conflict: a state of opposition, disagreement or incompatibility between two or more people or groups of people, which is sometimes characterised by physical violence. The disagreements are based on incompatible goals, needs, desires, values, beliefs, and/or attitudes.

Coriolis force: an effect that causes any body that moves freely with respect to the rotating Earth to veer to the right in the northern hemisphere and to the left in the southern hemisphere.

Counter-urbanisation: the process in which the population of cities actually falls as people move out beyond the rural-urban fringe into areas that are truly rural.

Cyclone: an atmospheric low-pressure system that gives rise to roughly circular inward-spiralling wind motion, called vorticity.

D

Decomposer: organism that takes the remains of dead plants and animals, as well as their excreted waste, and converts them back into carbon dioxide and nutrients. This releases raw nutrients in a chemical form usable to plants and algae, which incorporate the chemicals into their own cells.

Development gap: the difference in the level of economic development between richer and poorer countries.

Devolution: the statutory granting of powers from a central government to government at sub-national level, such as a region or state. The powers devolved might be temporary and might ultimately reside in central government, so that the state remains united. Devolution can be mainly financial – i.e. giving areas a budget that was formerly administered by central government. However, the power to make legislation relevant to the area might also be granted.

Dominant plant: the largest and tallest species present in a community.

E

Ecological niche: the place of each species within an ecosystem. This includes the space that it occupies and also the role it carries out within the community and its relationship with the other species living around it.

Ecology: the study of communities of living organisms and the relationships among the members of those communities and between them and the physical and chemical constituents of their surroundings.

Eco-quarter: bids will be invited from local authorities for £15 million to 'retrofit' existing homes with energy-saving measures. Carbon-neutral shops, offices, etc. will be built alongside these houses to make a section of a town very energy-efficient.

Ecosystem: system in which organisms interact with each other and with their environment. There are two parts: the entire complex of organisms, or biome, living in harmony, and the habitat in which the biome exists.

Environment: everything that surrounds us, including ourselves.

Environmental lapse rate (ELR): the normal decline of temperature with altitude, usually about 6.4 °C per 1,000 m.

Ethnic group: a group that is distinct from the rest of society and identified on the basis of religion, colour, cultural practices and/or national origin.

Evapotranspiration: the combined losses of moisture through transpiration and evaporation.

Extrusive rock: igneous rock formed by the crystallisation of magma above the surface of the Earth.

Eyewall: tropical storms will typically have an eye approximately 30–65 km across, usually situated in the geometric centre of the storm. With some storms, particularly when wind speeds exceed 185 km/ph, the diameter of the eye narrows to less than 20km and a cycle of eyewall replacement may begin. Outer rain bands intensify into a ring of thunderstorms to become an outer eyewall, which steadily rob the original eyewall and eventually leave a larger, more stable eye. The temporary weakening of the storm during eyewall replacement is followed by a gradual strengthening once replacement is complete.

F

Food chain: the transferral of energy through an ecosystem with each link in the chain feeding on and obtaining energy from the link that precedes it. In turn it provides energy for the following link.

Food web: more complex than a food chain, but more common as simple food chains are rare. In a food web there are a variety of different sources of food at each trophic level and most animals in the web have more than one source of food, and/or provide food for more than one consumer in the level above.

Front: a boundary between a warm air mass and a cold air mass, resulting in frontal rainfall.

G

G7: the group of seven richest industrial nations, including the US, Canada, Japan and the biggest EU countries. Russia is included in some of their meetings, forming the G8.

GDP per capita (that is, it is given as an average for each person in the country): Total GDP is divided by the number of people in the country. The figures are further adjusted to take account of the purchasing power of money in each country rather than simply using exchange rates to convert local currency into $US. Figures converted like this are called GDP PPP per capita.

Globalisation: at AS Level globalisation was defined as a set of processes leading to the integration of economic, cultural, political and social systems across geographical boundaries. It refers to increasing economic integration of countries, especially in terms of trade and the movement of capital.

Grameen Bank: a micro-finance organisation and community development bank started in Bangladesh that makes small loans to the impoverished without requiring collateral. The system of this bank is based on the idea that the poor have skills that are underutilised. A group-based credit approach relies on peer pressure within the group to ensure the borrowers conduct their financial affairs with strict discipline, ensuring repayment eventually and allowing the borrowers to develop good credit standing. A distinctive feature of the bank's credit programme is that a significant majority of its borrowers are women. The bank was founded in 1976. The organisation and its founder, Muhammad Yunus, were jointly awarded the Nobel Peace Prize in 2006.

Gross Domestic Product (GDP): a measure of the value of all the goods and services produced in a country during a year, in $US.

H

Herbivores or **primary consumers:** animals and occasionally plants that obtain their energy by eating green plants.

Housing association: independent non-profit-making organisation for managing, building and renovating housing. Funded by central government through the Housing Corporation, they can also receive funds from local authorities.

Human Development Index (HDI): a comparative measure of life expectancy, literacy, education and standards of living. It is a standardised way to compare well-being, especially child welfare, in different countries. It can be used to measure the impact of economic policies on the quality of life of people in the country.

Humidity: a measure of the amount of moisture in the air. Absolute humidity tells us how much moisture is in the air (g/m^3). Relative humidity expresses this amount as a percentage of the maximum that air of a certain temperature could hold.

Hurricane: a tropical cyclonic storm having winds that exceed 120 km/hr.

Hypothesis: a tentative conjecture explaining an observation, phenomenon or scientific problem that can be tested by further observation, investigation and/or experimentation.

I

Informationalisation: the increasing importance of the information-based sector of the economy which relies on electronic data transfer.

Instability: unstable atmospheric conditions leading to rising air frequently associated with cloud formation and precipitation.

Inter-tropical convergence zone (ITCZ): a result of the heating of part of the Earth's surface, caused by the concentrated insolation from the overhead sun. This leads to heating of the air lying on that surface. The heated air becomes less dense and rises. This draws in cooler air that flows across the surface to replace the rising air. Air streams are drawn in from both north and south of the equator and they meet in the area from which the air is rising.

Intrusive rock: igneous rock formed by the crystallisation of magma below the surface of the Earth.

Isostatic lift: uplift of a land mass resulting from tectonic processes.

J

Jet stream: an intense thermal wind in the upper troposphere.

L

Leaching: occurs when rain water, which is slightly acidic, drains through the soil, dissolving basic minerals and carrying them away. They may be deposited lower down in the soil or washed away to the rivers and lost to the ecosystem.

M

Megacity: metropolitan area with a total population in excess of 10 million people. They usually have a population density over 2,000 persons/square km. A megacity can be a single metropolitan area or two or more metropolitan areas that converge upon one another.

Millionaire city: a city with over a million inhabitants.

Multinational aid: development funding that is sent from several countries usually to a group of poor countries. It is usually channelled through an organisation such as the UN or the World Bank.

N

Null hypothesis (Ho): a statistician's term that states that there is no relationship between two variables.

O

Offshore outsourcing: the practice of hiring an external organisation to perform some business functions in a country other than the one where the products or services are actually developed or manufactured.

Omnivore: organism that eats both plants and animals.

P

Photosynthesis: the process in green plants and certain other organisms by which carbohydrates are synthesised from carbon dioxide and water using light as an energy source, usually releasing oxygen as a by-product. The carbohydrates produced by photosynthesis are then used as food by the organism.

Precipitation: the conversion and transfer of moisture in the atmosphere to the land and sea. It includes all forms of rain, snow, frost, hail and dew.

Q

Quango: Quasi-autonomous, non-governmental organisation. This usually means an organisation that is funded by the government but which is more or less independent and not completely controlled by the government.

R

Rainfall regime: the distribution of rainfall throughout the year at a particular place.

Refugee: someone who flees for refuge or safety, usually to a foreign country, at a time of political upheaval, economic hardship, war, natural disaster, etc.

Retrofit: make changes to improve the structure of buildings to incorporate technological advances that were not available when the buildings were originally constructed.

Re-urbanisation: the movement of people back to live in old city centres which have been redeveloped.

S

Separatism: a move, by a minority group or a region within a country, towards greater independence or 'separation' from the country that governs them.

Seral progression: the move from one sere to another.

Sere: a stage in the development of the vegetation of an area over a period of time.

Service sector: provision is defined as an economic activity that does not result in ownership. It is a process that creates benefits by facilitating a change in customers, a change in their physical possessions, or a change in their intangible assets.

Shared equity: when the residents of a property buy a part share, usually with the help of a mortgage, but the housing association also keeps part-ownership and charges the resident rent. This arrangement allows people who cannot afford the full cost of buying to get at least a share of the home ownership – and to profit from any rise in the value of the property.

Soil moisture budget: the seasonal pattern of water availability for plant growth.

Stability: balanced pressure conditions; air is unable to rise above a low level, associated with dry conditions and little cloud cover.

Subduction: occurs when two tectonic plates move towards one another and one plate slides underneath the other, moving down into the mantle. This usually involves oceanic crust sliding beneath continental crust.

Substrate: the surface on which a soil forms. This is usually rock but it can also be a deposit such as river sediments, glacial till or builder's rubble.

Suburb: a residential area outside a city's central area but within, or just outside, the city.

Suburbanisation: the process of population movement from the central areas of cities towards the suburbs on the outskirts or the rural–urban fringe.

Synergy: a term originally used in biology to describe the way that two organisms or two systems work together to produce a better result or output than they could alone. The term is now applied in economics when two or more companies, groups or individuals achieve mutual benefits by working closely together.

T

Total diversion rate: the amount of material (in kg/household/yr) that is recycled and/or composted instead of going to landfill.

Transnational corporation or **multinational corporation (TNC/MNC):** at its simplest level, this is a corporation that has production establishments or delivers services in at least two countries. However, some TNCs have grown so large that they have budgets that exceed those of many countries in which they operate.

Trophic level: an organism's position in the food chain. Level 1 is formed of autotrophs (plants), which produce their own food. Level 2 is formed of primary consumers that feed on the Level 1 plants. Level 3 feeds on Level 2, and so on.

Troposphere: one of the four thermal layers of the atmosphere, extending from the surface to a maximum of 16 km.

U

Urbanisation: the growth in the proportion of a country's population that lives in urban as opposed to rural areas. The word is also used, less accurately, to describe the actual process of moving from a rural to an urban area.

W

World city: a city that acts as a major centre for finance, trade business, politics, culture, science, information gathering and diffusion, publishing and mass media, and all the associated activities – serving not just a country or a region but the whole world. New York, London and Tokyo are the three pre-eminent world cities, although there are some others that could be considered 'important multinational cities'.

Index